RETHINKING THE PACIFIC

RETHINKING THE PACIFIC

GERALD SEGAL

CLARENDON PRESS · OXFORD
1990

Oxford University Press, Walton Street, Oxford OX2 6DP
Oxford New York Toronto
Delhi Bombay Calcutta Madras Karachi
Petaling Jaya Singapore Hong Kong Tokyo
Nairobi Dar es Salaam Cape Town
Melbourne Auckland
and associated companies in
Berlin Ibadan

Oxford is a trade mark of Oxford University Press

Published in the United States
by Oxford University Press, New York

British Library Cataloguing in Publication Data
Segal, Gerald 1953–
Rethinking the pacific.
1. Pacific region. Social conditions
I. Title
909'.09823
ISBN 0–19–827345–2

Library of Congress Cataloging in Publication Data
Segal, Gerald, 1953–
Rethinking the Pacific / Gerald Segal.
p. cm.
1. Pacific Area—Foreign relations. I. Title.
DU29.S43 1990   327.99–dc19   89–16258
ISBN 0–19–827345–2

Typeset by Colset Private Limited, Singapore
Printed and bound in Great Britain by
Courier International Ltd,
Tiptree, Essex

For Rachel Jessie

Acknowledgements

Peculiar as it may seem, there is a long tradition of thinking Pacific from Britain and especially from Bristol. John Cabot set out from the city in 1497 to find China but instead found his passage blocked by North America. In fact, when Cabot sailed across the Atlantic the Pacific was still unexplored, and it was not until other Europeans sailed across it more than 20 years later that the extent of the Pacific was first understood. Thus, from the very start, it was Europeans who brought the Pacific into the world-wide pattern of international relations, linking the Atlantic and Pacific worlds. In fact, the central theme that has emerged from this book is that thinking of the Pacific as a separate region has never made much sense and will make increasingly less sense, despite all the talk of the coming Pacific Century. The main reason for thinking about the Pacific is that large parts of the area have become increasingly important for *global* patterns of ideology, security, and trade. John Cabot had the right idea.

The global approach to Pacific politics is also rooted in my own background as a Canadian/American living in Britain. As my North American and British families have made clear, the concept of 'mid-Atlanticism' is foremost a question of ideology and culture. An awareness of these common ideological roots of the Atlantic community, and the lack of them in the Pacific world, is at the heart of the scepticism about a Pacific community.

While undertaking the essentially impossible task of doing justice to all the complexities of Pacific politics, I incurred great debts to those who helped me through the wide range of analytical problems. I am especially grateful to a number of people for reading all, or parts, of earlier drafts. Brian Bridges, Barry Buzan, Michael Lee, Edwina Moreton, and Bob O'Neill paid full fare for the trip around the Pacific rim. I am also grateful to the anonymous (although I can guess) advisers for OUP, and the library staff of the Royal Institute of International Affairs.

G. S.
Bristol and London,
December 1988

Contents

List of Figures

Introduction to the Pacific

Does it make much sense to 'think Pacific'? Is the Pacific anything more than 'a geographical expression'?[1] Although it has been fashionable to speak of 'Pacific shift' and the 'Pacific Century', are these more slogans than useful concepts? Considering just how much has been written about the importance of the Pacific, especially in the past decade, there have been remarkably few attempts to assess the trends in the international politics of the region as a whole.[2]

To be sure, there are fine studies of international economic[3] and military issues,[4] and thorough analyses of the domestic or foreign policies of individual states in the region. There are also a few edited, collective efforts that try to integrate some of these issues, but at best these represent the disparate, albeit stimulating, thoughts of the individual contributors.[5]

Broad-ranging analyses have been attempted earlier in the post-war period, but all have focused on 'the Far East' or 'Asia'.[6] What has been conspicuously absent is a broad, strategic analysis of the trends in the international relations of the Pacific. If the discussion about the Pacific Century replacing the age of the Atlantic is to be taken further, it needs to deal with these issues in the same breadth and depth as the assessments of Atlantic and European politics. There is a need for a strategic assessment of the Pacific that integrates the narrower aspects of culture, ideology, economics, and military affairs into a wider appreciation of the patterns in the international politics of the region.

Of course, undertaking such a broad analysis is always risky. Emmanuel Le Roy Ladurie warns that, while 'truffle hunters' miss a great deal, so do the

1 The derisive dismissal was Metternich's view of Italy in 1849.

2 One of the first books to publicize the subject took what remains a typical approach—the focus was on individual states' successes with only passing reference to the region as a whole. Roy Hofheinz and Kent Calder, *The Eastasia Edge* (New York: Basic Books, 1982).

3 For example, Steffan Linder, *Pacific Century* (Stanford: Stanford University Press, 1986); Willy Kraus and Wilfred Lutkenhorst, *The Economic Development of the Pacific Basin* (London: C. Hurst, 1986); Harry Oshima, *Economic Growth in Monsoon Asia* (Tokyo: University of Tokyo Press, 1987).

4 For example, Douglas Stuart (ed.), *Security Within the Pacific Rim* (London: Gower, 1987).

5 James Morely (ed.), 'The Pacific Basin' in *Proceedings of the Academy of Political Sciences* (1986). For a sample of the stimulating but one-off articles in recent years see Nathaniel Thayer, 'The Emerging East Asian Order' in *SAIS Review*, 4/1 (1984), which also carried other articles on the subject.

6 Nathaniel Peffer, *The Far East* (Ann Arbor: University of Michigan Press, 1968); Wayne Wilcox, Leo Rose, and Gavin Boyd (eds.), *Asia and the International System* (Cambridge: Winthrop, 1972).

'parachutists' floating at a great height. One might take solace in Aquinas' remark that shedding some light on large topics is better than analysing trivial ones *ad infinitum*. Inevitably, complex details need to be simplified, but 'a little knowledge' is not always a dangerous thing.[7] Given the vastness of the Pacific region, this study must necessarily be interpretive, integrative, and eclectic. Indeed, some scholars have had the confidence to attempt even larger mega-analysis.[8] This book is an attempt to integrate already existing analyses of more specific issues and patterns by focusing on the 'big issues' in the Pacific. While it cannot do justice to the intricacies of all the components of Pacific politics, it is intended to help place the parts in a larger perspective. Just as military strategy is incompletely understood without reference to the ties of culture and ideology, so economic relationships in the Pacific need to be assessed in the context of regional military security.

The breadth of the subject makes it sensible to stick to a few fundamental themes. The first theme is whether it makes sense at all to think of the Pacific as a coherent region. The clear conclusion is that the Pacific never has been, and does not look like becoming, such a coherent region. The point may be laboured at too great a length for some, but stress is necessary because of the steady stream of efforts designed to raise consciousness of the Pacific, and to shape the region. In fact, the original idea behind this book was to assess the main characteristics of the Pacific as a region, and only while undertaking the research did it emerge that it was not helpful to see the Pacific as a coherent area. It is argued here that the idea of thinking about a Pacific community might have once made some sort of sense, but now is clearly out of date.

It is out of date because the most powerful trends in the Pacific are pulling the area apart in two distinct ways. The first way, and indeed the second theme of this analysis, is the globalization of aspects of Pacific politics. Key connections and interdependencies are being established in economics, politics, and culture on a global scale with societies that share certain very specific needs and/or characteristics. The third theme is the opposite and sometimes simultaneous trend of entrenchment of divisions between certain parts of the Pacific, again on cultural/ideological as well as military and economic lines.

---

[7] Lawrence Stone, *The Past and Present Revisited* (London: Routledge & Kegan Paul, 1987) 20.

[8] Fernand Braudel, *The Mediterranean and the Mediterranean World in the Age of Philip II* (London: Fontana, 1975); Paul Kennedy, *The Rise and Fall of Great Powers*, (New York: Random House, 1987); William McNeill, *The Pursuit of Power* (Oxford: Basil Blackwell, 1982); J. M. Roberts, *The Pelican History of the World* (London: Pelican, 1980); Geoffrey Barraclough, *An Introduction to the History of the World* (London: Pelican, 1967).

The fourth theme is that, even though it makes little sense to 'think Pacific' if it means thinking of a coherent region, it is increasingly important to understand some of the more specific, complex developments taking place in the region. It is precisely the potent mix of regional diversity, and inter-connections with the global patterns of international politics, that makes it vital to appreciate the Pacific's new political issues. The decline of the superpowers, the rise of new trading states and international economic powers, the development of new ideologies of modernization, and the fading out of the concept of the Third World, are all emerging in the Pacific. These changes suggest the pattern of international politics is undergoing fundamental change and an understanding of Pacific politics is vital to analysing the implications of the new trends.[9]

METHODOLOGY

These large issues in a vast region raise a host of methodological problems. Most such difficulties are tackled in individual chapters, but some comment must be made here about the term 'coherence' or 'community'. This study is strongly influenced by the European experience of both creating a 'community' in western Europe and shaping a broader mid-Atlantic (mostly north mid-Atlantic) community. While the E C has opted more for the closer links of amalgamation and the north-Atlantic community remains more pluralist, it is still necessary to identify at least some criteria for judging the relative coherence of a community. Of course, this task can be undertaken without falling victim to the ethnocentrism of seeing other people's politics through a European lens.

The literature on the subject of 'community building' is vast and, of course, controversial.[10] Suffice it to say that a community is judged in terms of the commonality of values, expectations, communications, level of transaction, predictability of behaviour, and capabilities.[11] All of these components of community or coherence are relative and thus the comparison

---

[9] Related themes are taken up in the broader international relations literature, e.g. Robert Keohane, *After Hegemony* (Princeton: Princeton University Press, 1984); Robert Gilpin, *The Political Economy of International Relations* (Princeton: Princeton University Press, 1987).

[10] For example, Ernst Haas, *Beyond the Nation-State* (Stanford: Stanford University Press, 1964); Amitai Etzioni, *Political Unification* (London: Holt Reinhart & Winston, 1965); various articles in Paul Tharp (ed.), *Regional International Organisations* (London: Macmillan, 1971); Barry Buzan and Gowher Rizvi (eds.), *South Asian Insecurity and the Great Powers* (London: Macmillan, 1986).

[11] Karl Deutsch *et al.*, *Political Community and the North Atlantic Area* (Princeton: Princeton University Press, 1957).

of regional communities must also be relative. At the least formal end of the spectrum is the 'interdependence' that comes from trade or co-operation in security affairs. While interdependence may be tighter on different levels, it need not depend on regional linkages, especially for modern developed economies.[12] When shaping a more ambitious sense of community, there is no need for a complete surrender of sovereignty. But the parts of sovereignty that are surrendered or changed are useful indications of the new basic patterns of international politics.[13] The old French adage that 'Africa begins at the Pyrenees' has clearly changed, just as notions of sovereignty in the E C have changed.

In order to highlight the different levels at which there is relative coherence in the Pacific, three main levels of analysis have been identified: culture/ideology, military affairs, and economics. But before assessing these three themes in their post-1945 details, it is essential to understand the history of the idea of the Pacific. A great deal of the 'Pacific-chic' of our own era is put into perspective by appreciating the complex evolution of the region and previous attempts to shape it ideologically, militarily, and economically.

Most thinking about the Pacific has focused on the military and economic levels, while in the Atlantic world there has always been great emphasis on the cultural and ideological ties that bind. At each level, the emphasis is placed on patterns of conflict, communication, and co-operation. The Pacific construct has many parts and straddles a great ocean. Its ground floor and outside walls are shaped by the geographic realities—the relatively unchanging foundation. The first floor of culture and ideology is split up into rooms of different sizes, with numerous doors, some of which are blockaded in anger. Similarly, the second floor of military relations and the third floor of economic relations have their own different layouts.

Given the very different nature of each of these levels of analysis, it is only natural that there will be a wide variation in the types of evidence available. In fact, it has been an unavoidable necessity of such a broad analysis of such a large topic that a wide range of sometimes unconventional sources be exploited. But as other analysts of unconventional subjects have made plain, it can be fruitful to break down such rigid analytical barriers as, for

---

[12] Robert Keohane and Joseph Nye, *Power and Interdependence* (Boston: Little Brown, 1977).

[13] Bruce Russett, *International Regions and the International System* (Chicago: University of Chicago Press, 1967); Murray Forsyth, *Union of States* (Leicester: Leicester University Press, 1981).

example, those dividing area studies from security studies or international economics.[14] The first, historical section relies on the large body of historical studies of specific states in the region and international trends broader than the Pacific. The detailed focus on the Pacific requires a synthesis of the two types of history. The second section, on culture and ideology, is perhaps the most unusual for orthodox students of international relations. The evidence used is inevitably patchy and impressionistic. It is drawn in part from academic analysis, but primarily from reports of the local media and cross-national statistics where they are available. The third section on military affairs relies on more detailed analysis of past conflict, as well as a more orthodox use of official statements, press reports, and statistics to assess current military issues. Similar tools are used in the final section covering economic issues.

Finally, it should be clear by now that what follows is an admittedly experimental attempt to think Pacific and to explain the basic features of this important part of international relations. It is true that, until recently, little analysis of international relations in the Pacific has been undertaken in Europe. But in recent years, a new, more confident European perspective on international relations has begun to emerge. With the adaptation to a post-colonial world, most West Europeans have now come to welcome the challenge of thinking about their own success and the need to compete in a global political and economic system.

When applied to discussions of the Pacific Century, and undertaken against the background of epithets about 'Eurosclerosis', the European tendency is to temper the Pacific-optimism with a dose of European scepticism.[15] In the new age of greater global interdependence there is much that the European perspective can contribute, hence the stress on the obsolescence of the idea of Pacific community and the stress on the 'new globalism'. After centuries of appreciation of what it means to be 'European', or more recently 'mid-Atlantic', Europeans will tend not to be bowled over by the concept of a Pacific community. If analysts, and indeed the people of the Pacific, are looking towards the idea of a regional community, they are looking backwards. We would all be better served by looking forward to the Pacific as an arena where new ideas and politics are born, but

---

[14] For example, Maxime Rodinson, *Europe and the Mystique of Islam* (London: I. B. Tauris, 1988).

[15] For example, *The Proceedings of the London Conference: The Future of the Asia–Pacific Region* (Tokyo: NIRA, 1986), especially William Wallace, 'The Far, Far East' and John Roper, 'Out of Sight, Out of Mind'. Also Jens Biermeier, 'Atlantic–Pacific: The New Trends in the USA' in *Aussen Politik*, 38/1 (1987). The publication of the *Pacific Review* from Britain beginning in 1988 is part of the new Pacific-awareness in Europe.

with a recognition of the diversity of the region and the increasing inter-
connections with other parts of the world.

PACIFIC GEOGRAPHY

The politics, economics, and strategy of any area are played out in a
distinctive environment. While individuals may pass swiftly from the scene,
and institutions may last decades, they all need to respond to the far more
slowly changing geographic environment. The politics of the Pacific basin
can be understood only if the geographic realities are appreciated.[16] To be
sure, new technologies have effectively altered the impact of geography on
politics, especially since 1945 and the advent of mass travel and rapid
communication. Nevertheless, at least three relatively unchanging realities
of the Pacific basin continue to shape the politics of the area. The first
geographic factor is the immense size of the Pacific area.

The Dimensions of the Pacific

The Pacific itself is by far the largest ocean: at 165 384 000 km^2 it is more
than twice the size of the Atlantic. With a shoreline of over 80 000 km it
stretches north from the Bering Sea (at 65 degrees north), to Antarctica (at
65 degrees south). In the midst of its expanse, the Pacific straddles the international date-line. In the west it runs into the South China Sea
(2 318 000 km^2). The greater Pacific basin can be said to end at the tip of
Sumatra, 95 degrees east of Greenwich. In the east the Pacific basin touches
the tip of Tierra del Fuego at 65 degrees west of Greenwich. The total 200
degrees of longitude is nearly two-thirds of the earth's surface. Curiously
enough, the Pacific is shrinking, as ever so slowly the floor of the Ocean is
dragging California and parts of the eastern rim to the north-west.[17]

These dimensions of the Pacific are not merely of academic interest. They
remain the basis for an essential Pacific basin reality—vast distance. A
traveller from Beijing to Sydney, Australia (8949 km) can, in fact, reach the
very non-Pacific London (8138 km) a little more quickly. The trip across
the Pacific from Hong Kong to Mexico City (14 122 km) is almost twice the
distance from Hong Kong to Moscow (7144 km). The business traveller
from Tokyo to Singapore (5321 km) has to travel almost four times as long

---

[16] These concepts are adapted from Braudel, *Mediterranean and the Mediterranean World*,
especially the first part on geographic factors.

[17] The movement along the San Andreas fault is part of a number of shifts around the rim.

as his competitor in Europe jetting from London to Rome (1431 km). An American travelling from Los Angeles finds London (8758 km nearly twice as close as Singapore (14 123 km). When it is 8 a.m. and breakfast-time in Los Angeles, Singapore is going to bed at 11 p.m. and London is having tea at 4 p.m. Thus the Americas have a Pacific coast, but it is still far quicker to get to Europe than to Asia.

These vast distances in the Pacific basin have certainly helped make it difficult to create a sense of regional cohesion. Thus the Pacific has developed many faces. Like other basins, for example the Mediterranean, historically the Pacific was closed to outside influence from the sea. Most contact came overland, whether across Eurasia to China and down to South-east Asia, or across the Americas. But unlike the Mediterranean, the waters were too vast for any interchange across the Ocean until the sixteenth century. If only because of its expanse, the Pacific remains more of a rim than an arena of exchange.

The rim is forbiddingly marked for much of its distance by the mountain peaks stretching up from South America, across the Bering Strait, and down to the ridges of Japan and Korea. The so-called volcanic 'ring of fire' skirts the basin, as do attendant earthquake zones. On average, there are one million recognizable earthquakes every year around the Pacific rim. The great boom of Krakatoa's volcanic explosion in 1883 was reportedly heard 2500 km away in Australia.[18] Only in the heartland of central East Asia is the land largely open and suitable for intensive agriculture and population growth. Here the bulk of today's billion Chinese developed the most dominant of the ancient East Asian civilizations. Geography helped shape the basic patterns of civilization and politics.

The Pacific waters themselves are characterized by vast expanses and, unlike other oceans, the Pacific is dotted with more than 5000 islands (more than those scattered about the rest of the world combined). The sea-bed holds huge reserves of minerals but it is so vast, and still relatively uncharted, that we know more about the face of the moon than the bottom of our largest ocean. While the western portion of the Ocean has more and larger islands, there are vast emptinesses of water, especially north of Japan and east across to North America and down the eastern side of the Pacific. Lonely Easter Island lies furthest to the east, but still some 4000 km from landfall at Los Angeles. These islands vary in size from tiny atolls that rise from the ocean depths and disappear whence they came, to the huge expanse of Australia. Thus the gap between central and eastern Pacific people is accentuated. In contrast to microscopic atolls, Australia is easily the largest

18 William Thomas Jr., 'Introduction' in Herman Friis (ed.), *The Pacific Basin* (New York: American Geographical Society, 1967), 4.

island, some 7 682 300 km², and can be more properly considered a continent. New Guinea at 808 510 km², Borneo at 757 050 km², and Sumatra at 524 100 km² are the next largest. The main Japanese island of Honshu at 230 455 km² is just a bit larger than Great Britain, the largest of the heavily inhabited Atlantic islands. Thus the huge scale of the Pacific brings us the second dimension—diversity of the basin.

The Diversity of the Pacific

The Pacific basin can be said to have at least six relatively distinct zones, each of which in turn has its own important subdivisions. The variations from north to south are stark, ranging from polar permafrost to tropical rain forests. As a result, differences in rhythm of life are apparent between island and continent, north and south, all of which are reflected in the different impact of seasons, life-styles, food, culture, and even ideology. It is hard to escape the conclusion that there is no single Pacific in anything but the nautical sense.

The first of the six zones is that in the south and centre—'Island Pacific'. The territory includes islands ranging from atolls to Australia, but all these islands are notable for their dependence on the sea and, more recently, the air for contact with the outside world. The islands fall into three broad groups, but these subdivisions are based on human rather than physical geography. The Melanesian people occupy the larger islands in the southwest Pacific. The Polynesians live on islands from Hawaii to Easter Island in the south-east and to New Zealand in the south-west. Micronesia lies to the north and west of Melanesia in the central and western Pacific and is spread out over a larger area than the continental United States. With the exception of the more southern territories, the climate is mostly tropical, the islands are tiny, and their populations are negligible. In modern political terms these states are said to comprise the South Pacific and many have only recently obtained their independence.

Eight independent states can be identified. Australia is obviously the largest, comprising 91 per cent of the zone's land and 68 per cent of its population. Papua New Guinea, on the eastern side of New Guinea island, has 5 per cent of the region's land and 14 per cent of its population. New Zealand has the same percentage of population and only 3 per cent of the region's land. The other states are Fiji, Kiribati, the Solomon Islands, Tonga, and Tuvalu. Additional, equally tiny but non-independent territories include American Samoa, French Polynesia, Guam, New Caledonia, Caroline Islands, Marshall Islands, Pitcairn Island, and the various Antarctic territories. All these islands share a deep concern with the sea, although continental Australia is obviously less preoccupied in this respect. But Australia does have one of the world's longest coastlines, weaving its way round 25 760 km. Even much smaller New Zealand has a coastline of 15 134 km and the Solomon Islands and Papua New Guinea both have more than 5000 km of ocean coast themselves.

The second major Pacific area has, since the 1940s, been loosely called South-east Asia. Its nine modern states are geographically divided between the continental territories of Vietnam, Laos, Kampuchea and Thailand, and the mainly island areas of Malaysia, Indonesia, Brunei, Singapore, and the Philippines. All of the states have been heavily influenced by the sea, although the more continental ones less so, and consequently have been more inward-looking.[19] Indonesia has the world's second-longest coastline (54 716 km) and the Philippines ranks sixth (22 540 km). Malaysia, Vietnam, and Thailand all have coastlines between 3000 and 5000 km long.

Sitting as it does between the great civilizations of India and China, South-east Asia was both a barrier between and a target of competing cultures.[20] The area clearly marks the western gate of the Pacific, and even in modern times its vital straits retain their importance for naval strategists as choke points. Unlike the vast zone of Island Pacific, South-east Asia is a more coherent area. Almost all the states of the region have tropical climates and the islands especially are strongly affected by the course of prevailing winds and their seasonal variations. Distances between the individual states are not great, especially by Pacific standards. As a result, the people and states of the area developed some of the closest interrelationships. The pattern here is much more akin to that of the European states who share the same continent than to the rest of the widely divided Pacific basin.

In modern times, the nine states do not vary as widely in size as do the components of Island Pacific. Of course, tiny Singapore and Brunei do contrast in size with Indonesia, which has 50 per cent of the region's territory and some 46 per cent of its people. But bunched in the middle is a range of states from Kampuchea with 5 per cent of the territory to Thailand with 13 per cent. The divergence in size of population is wider, with Laos, Kampuchea, and Malaysia all having less than 4 per cent each. Thailand, Vietnam, and the Philippines each have about 15 per cent of South-east Asia's people.

The third part of the Pacific comprises the dominant land-mass powers of China and the eastern portion of the Soviet Union. Together they take up the

[19] Charles Fisher, 'Southeast Asia' in W. Gordon East, O. H. K. Spate, and Charles Fisher (eds.), *The Changing Map of Asia* (London: Methuen, 1971), 221.

[20] Paul Wheatley, *The Golden Khersonese* (Kuala Lumpur: University of Malaya Press, 1971).

vast majority of continental East Asia's Pacific coastline, with the Soviet Union's 26 720 km (China has 18 000 km) the second longest of any continental Pacific state. China is of course the dominant civilization in East Asia, and was for millenniums the only power in the Pacific. Today, with its 1.1 billion people, it has nearly a quarter of the entire world population and more than half the population of the Pacific basin. Yet despite China's dominating presence in the Pacific and its population concentrated in eastern seaboard provinces, it has remained almost entirely a continental power. However, simply by virtue of its place and size (9.5 million km²), historically China's Pacific neighbours have been forced to consider China as a potential maritime power and therefore a looming Pacific power.

By contrast, the Soviet Union is a more recent Pacific power. By history and weight of population it remains a European power. But for the purposes of this tour around the Pacific rim and its hinterland, some 6.2 million km² of territory can be identified as the Soviet far east. This area comprises one-quarter of Soviet territory and includes Kamchatka district, Magadan, Amur, Sakhalin, Maritime Territory, Khabarovsk, and the sprawling Yakutia ASSR.[21] Yet, with a population of 7.6 million in 1986, the Soviet far east accounts for less than 3 per cent of the total Soviet population.

Comparisons of the Soviet and Chinese Pacific territories reveal more contrasts that commonalities. China's huge population contrasts with the tiny Soviet figures. China's climate ranges from the frigid to the tropical while the Soviet Union's Pacific territory is 80 per cent permafrost and dominated by polar ice-caps. One-third of the Soviet territory is forest, where the fearsome Siberian tiger (the region's symbol) roams wild. The coastal zone is dominated by mountain ranges and active volcanoes. To be sure, China also has its wild frontiers, but they are in the west, whereas the area bordering on the Pacific has been home to the cream of Chinese civilization.

The fourth Pacific zone is what might be called 'Fringe East Asia', including Japan, Taiwan, Hong Kong, and the two Koreas. This is clearly a contentious way to group states. But in the modern age they are all political units on the fringe of the continent and relatively isolated either geographically or politically, or both. Of course, properly speaking, Korea is merely a peninsula of Eurasia, but in its role as the gateway to Eurasia, known sometimes as 'the Palestine of East Asia', it has always been distinguished from the continental Chinese empire. The division of Korea into two is merely a creation of post-1945 great-power politics. The status of Hong

---

[21] E. B. Kovrigin, 'The Soviet Far East' in John Stephan and V. P. Chichkanov (eds.), *Soviet–American Horizons on the Pacific* (Honolulu: University of Hawaii Press, 1986), 3 ff.

Kong and Taiwan as independent states is also contested by China and by 1997 Hong Kong is due to revert to Chinese sovereignty.

Thus Japan is the only straightforwardly offshore state. Strung out as it is along the North-east Asian coast, its position is often compared to that of Britain off the mainland of Europe. As a largely rocky but heavily populated set of islands, it has generally been able to escape continental politics and has often looked seaward for new vistas. Its coastline of 12 075 km is the thirteenth longest in the world.

North Korea is roughly half Japan's size but with only some 13 per cent of Japan's population. In fact, South Korea has more than twice the people of North Korea but is some 20 000 km² smaller. Taiwan is a quarter the size of North Korea but with an almost identical-sized population. All the states are dominated by mountains, although Taiwan and Hong Kong have more temperate climates. This is clearly only barely a geographically consistent region, and certainly one in political flux.

The fifth Pacific region begins 5 km from the Soviet maritime provinces across the Bering Strait. North America essentially has four sub-zones belonging to three modern states. The first zone, Alaska, is 1.5 million km² but with a population of fewer than half a million people. It resembles the Soviet far eastern territories in its vastness, emptiness, and relative inhospitality to human life.

The second sub-zone is the Canadian Pacific territory. Also like the Soviet Union, most of Canada and its people are oriented away from the Pacific. With its population strung out along the United States border, most of Canada looks south before it looks west. The eastern portions from Ontario eastward also look further east to the Atlantic and Europe. Pacific Canada includes the permafrost expanse of the Yukon territory and the Rocky Mountain province of British Columbia. In total these territories roughly equal the size of Alaska, although their population is some 2.5 million. Defining the Pacific component of the United States is somewhat controversial.[22] Counting the five Pacific states of Washington, Oregon, California, Hawaii, and Alaska and the Rocky Mountain states of Arizona, Colorado, Idaho, Montana, Nevada, New Mexico, Utah, and Wyoming, roughly half of the United States can be said to lie on the Pacific rim.[23]

Of course, there are important variations in the types of United States territory facing the Pacific. Hawaii sits one-third of the way out in the

[22] William Byers, 'Changing Economy of the American West' in Stephan and Chichkanov (eds.), *Soviet–American Horizons*, 85.

[23] The basis on which states in the Americas are classified as Pacific-oriented is essentially the direction of external trade. Territory on or west of the Rocky/Andes Mountains are considered to have a Pacific orientation.

Pacific, some 4117 km from Los Angeles (and 8160 km from Beijing). The United States also administers various tiny islands in the western Pacific, including American Samoa, Guam, the Caroline Islands and the Marshall Islands. California dominates the economy of the Pacific United States, with some two-thirds of the region's population. The climate of most of the contiguous continental states is temperate, although with notable variations between baking New Mexico and coolish Washington.

The fourth sub-region of North America is the state of Mexico. With 1.9 million km² it is only slightly smaller than the United States Pacific territory. With a population approaching 70 million it is more than twice as heavily populated as the United States Pacific region. Yet with a per-capita GNP of less than one-sixth the United States total, Mexico is clearly in the wealth league of South Korea.

By the time one gets to southern Mexico at longitude 93 degrees west, the Pacific bends sharply eastward and Asia stretches further from the eastern Pacific rim. More than 90 per cent of this southern, Latin American zone lies further east than Boston on the east coast of the United States. Thus the final Pacific region, Central and South America, is in many senses the least Pacific oriented of the six main Pacific regions. To date, few of these states have had a Pacific orientation, but in geographic terms at least six Central and four South American states are clearly on the Pacific rim.

Guatemala, Honduras, Nicaragua, Costa Rica, and Panama are comparable to the Koreas in size and per-capita GNP. In population terms they are much smaller, with the largest, Guatemala (8 million), having merely half the population of North Korea. El Salvador is the size of Fiji, but with a population slightly larger than that of New Zealand. These small Central American states also all face the Gulf of Mexico and the Caribbean Sea as much as the Pacific. Indeed, since the early 1900s the traditional orientation of these states has been towards the United States and to some extent still towards their former colonial masters in southern Europe.

The South American states of Colombia, Ecuador, Peru, and Chile are all much larger. The smallest, Ecuador (461 475 km²), is larger than Japan, and the largest, Peru (1.2 million km²), is more than twice the size of Thailand. The most populous, Colombia (27 million in 1982), has less than half the population of Thailand but is nearly twice its size. At about 60 million the total population of these four states is similar to that of Vietnam, but spread out over ten times the territory. South America is clearly less crowded, at least along the Pacific basin.

None of these states is especially oriented towards the Pacific, except for long and thin Chile, and perhaps Peru. Chile's absurd, but distinctive, geography is both cut off from neighbours by the Andes and forced to look outward by its 6435 km coastline. As a proportion of its overall size, Chile's coastline is seven times longer than that of China.

Thus there are at least six distinct geographic sub-regions of the Pacific. Taken together, the Pacific basin can be said to hold some 40 per cent of the world's population, on some 30 per cent of the world's land surface. But the diversity hidden in these bulky figures is equally important. The Pacific basin ranges by territory from the 9.6 million km^2 of China to the slip of the geographer's pen that is Tuvalu. China's more than one billion souls contrast with the 70 000 of Kiribati. Wealthy North America contrasts with parts of South-east Asia which house some of the world's poorest people. Some of the world's coldest places, in the Soviet and Canadian Arctics, contrast with the baking heat of Australia or tropical Vientiane in Laos.

Each area of the Pacific has distinctive geographic qualities, but each also shares characteristics with other parts of the Pacific basin. There is a geographic argument for transpacific co-operation, but there are obviously more powerful arguments for diversity. Links between north and south in the separate eastern and western parts of the Pacific seem stronger than links across the ocean. Yet in geographic terms, such as climate, there is much that unites the eastern and western portions of the north Pacific, as there is much that unites the respective parts of the central and southern Pacific. On balance, the size of the Pacific remains more a barrier than a binding force for states along its rim.

The Wealth of the Pacific

We now have an appreciation of the vastness and diversity of the Pacific's geography. It remains to be seen whether this geography leaves a legacy of wealth in natural resources. Once again, it appears that the conclusions to be drawn reinforce the theme of diversity. What is more, the natural resources of the Pacific basin have as often been a source of adversity as of advantage.

The Pacific has its fair share of energy resources on a per-capita basis. Some 40 per cent of the world's natural-gas production comes from the Pacific basin.[24] The superpowers and Canada are by far the largest producers in this category. Some 34 per cent of world crude-petroleum production is from the Pacific, with leading roles taken by the superpowers, Canada,

---

[24] These, and indeed most of the figures that follow, are a compilation from such sources as the World Bank's *World Development Report* series and George T. Kurian, *The New Book of World Rankings* (New York: Facts on File, 1984). Figures for Canada, the United States, and the Soviet Union have been adjusted to take into account only those territories delineated above as part of the Pacific basin.

Indonesia, Mexico, and China. The Pacific accounts for some 45 per cent of world coal production, with the superpowers, China, and Australia leading the pack. North Korea and Canada are also significant coal producers. The region also accounts for some 45 per cent of world hydroelectricity production, with the superpowers, Japan, Canada, and China taking a leading role. Finally, the Pacific contains some 70 per cent of world uranium reserves, with the superpowers, Australia, and Canada well ahead of any others.

Thus the production of energy in the Pacific is concentrated in the large states of the region. If energy is an essential requirement for power and wealth, then only the superpowers, Canada, Australia, and China can claim this special status. China is of course a poor country, in large part because, unlike the superpowers, Canada, or Australia, it is densely populated. Indonesia, with its large population and oil wealth, still has a narrow energy base. Some other states in the region are significant producers of specific sources of energy. Mexico and Indonesia are major oil and gas producers and North Korea is a major coal producer. But apart from them, the 30-odd other states of the area are energy deficient. The distribution of energy within the Pacific is not even, though as a whole it has its fair share of the world's energy wealth.

When turning to mineral production, the picture is a little less clear. The Pacific produces 50 per cent and 54 per cent respectively of the two main mineral products, iron ore and copper. Australia, China, and the Soviet Union are major iron-ore producers, with the United States and Canada also producing significant quantities. Chile, the superpowers, and Canada are the leading copper producers in the Pacific, with Peru, the Philippines, Mexico, and Papua New Guinea producing major quantities as well.

When looking at less essential minerals, the figures fluctuate more widely. The Pacific accounts for a tiny proportion of world bauxite production, with only Australia producing significant quantities. Yet some 40 per cent of world aluminium production is in the Pacific, with Australia itself producing over 20 per cent of the world total. Other major producers include the Soviet Union, the United States, China, New Zealand, Japan, and Canada. Some 60 per cent of world nickel is produced in the Pacific, with the Soviet Union, Canada, Australia, and Indonesia way out in front. A similar 60 per cent of world tin is produced in the Pacific, but here the leading producers are Malaysia, with some 20 per cent of the world total, Indonesia, China, the Soviet Union, and Thailand. In contrast, the Pacific states produce merely 20 per cent of world gold, but then six of the top seven gold producers are Pacific states.

Thus mineral wealth is spread more evenly. Yet only the superpowers, China, Canada, and Australia have a range of minerals. The pattern of energy wealth seems to be repeated. Other Pacific states, such as Malaysia or

Chile, are major producers of special minerals, but they lack the diversification once considered necessary for great-power status. Once again, some 30-odd Pacific states are clearly resource-poor. There are 'natural' hewers of wood and drawers of water in the Pacific, but in most cases they also seem to be among the richest states in the region.

Geography also has an influence on that other great necessity for power and wealth—food. Vast tracts of the Pacific rim states are next to useless for food production. The mammoth arc from Canada through Alaska to the Soviet far east is a case in point. Much of the mountain ridge of South America is also inhospitable to food production, as indeed are vast tracts of Australia. The only real bread-basket of the Pacific is the Chinese heartland, but then more than one billion people in China alone need to be supported there. South-east Asia is also a prolific rice-growing area. In fact, 60 per cent of world rice is grown in the Pacific basin states, with China, Indonesia, Thailand, Japan, Vietnam, the Philippines, and Korea leading the way. Rice is clearly the vital food in tropical East Asia.

Wheat is another matter entirely. Merely 20 per cent of world wheat is produced by the states of the Pacific, although Canada and the superpowers do have huge wheat-growing areas outside their Pacific territories. Australia and China are the only major Pacific wheat producers. Wheat is clearly the food of the more extreme northern and southern Pacific, but most of it is not grown in the basin itself.

The only other staple food of the region, fish, is not caught in as great abundance as one might have expected. Some 50 per cent of the world fish catch is taken in the Pacific, a surprisingly low proportion considering the vast coastlines and the huge watery expanse. Yet seven of the top ten fishing nations are situated around the Pacific. Japan leads, followed by the superpowers, China, Peru, South Korea, and Thailand. Chile, North Korea, Indonesia, the Philippines, and Canada are also significant fishers in Pacific waters. Not surprisingly, the sea remains a vital food source for Pacific people, with the major coastal nations taking the leading role. The absence of Australia, Malaysia, and the Pacific micro-islands from this list says more about the origins of their people and the sizes of their populations than anything else.

Apart from basic foods, there is a variety of cash crops made possible by a variety of climates. Less than 20 per cent of the world's sugar is produced in the Pacific region, with China leading the way.[25] Australia and Mexico are also in the top ten of world producers, and the Philippines, Thailand, and Indonesia are not far off. Tropical climates certainly help explain the importance of this crop for some Pacific states.

---

[25] The superpowers are both major sugar producers, but not in the Pacific region.

The Pacific is a far more significant producer of coffee (44 per cent) and palm oil (80 per cent). In the former case, South-east Asian and Central American states lead the pack; in the case of palm oil, Malaysia alone accounts for 50 per cent of total world production. Tropical climates, and colonial policy as we shall see below, help explain this cash crop.

Two other contrasting cases, cotton fibre and rubber, have less to do with climate than with colonialism. A mere 25 per cent of world cotton-fibre production comes from the Pacific basin, with China the world's second-largest producer and Mexico the only other Pacific state in the top ten. Yet over 80 per cent of world rubber is produced in the region, led by tropical Malaysia, Indonesia, Thailand, China, the Philippines, and Vietnam. Neither of these crops is a food, and the amount of food it can buy on the open market is notoriously variable. The Pacific is also responsible for some 25 per cent of world tobacco production, but this time the major regional producers are less tropical, including China, Japan, and the Koreas.

In sum, cash crops, like essential food production and basic minerals, are unequally distributed throughout the Pacific. It is true that specific states do not dominate all categories. Those with more minerals are usually richer, and their food production is often in non-Pacific parts of their territory. Only Australia and China are important in both food and minerals production in the Pacific. Some South-east Asian states have important roles in minerals and energy, but they also tend to produce primarily cash crops rather than basic food. The tropical climate in large part explains this distinctive position.

Thus the Pacific is a huge and diverse place with basic and barely changeable inequalities. There is little in geographic terms that has united the area, compared, for example, to Europe or the Mediterranean, except for the vast ocean. Of course, the pattern of geographic wealth is a poor guide to economic prosperity and in some sense diversity is required before political unity can be achieved. Resource-poor Japan, Taiwan, and Korea have some of the most successful economies in the region and fit nicely with resource-rich North Americans. But the power of the resource-poor must be considered ultimately fragile, for they are vulnerable to blockade and sanction. Geographic diversity may not tell us much about the chances of successful regional integration, but it does say a great deal about the basic strengths and vulnerabilities of states.

The explanation for the way in which this diversity of geography was remoulded into even more complicated political patterns requires a closer analysis of Pacific history. It is to that history, and the evolution of the present pattern of international relations, that we now turn. The essential realities of Pacific politics as set by geography remain relatively unchanged with the passage of time. But the passage of time also brings new social systems, ideologies, institutions, and personalities, all of which do change more regularly. They cannot reshape the geography of the Pacific, but they can reshape how people live out their lives in that geographic environment. An analysis of Pacific politics must properly span the range of factors from geographic time to individual time.

I

THE EVOLUTION OF
PACIFIC POLITICS

The concept of the Pacific Ocean is relatively new. Before the sixteenth century no one even knew its dimensions. The inhabitants of its shores and islands had no idea where they fitted into the pan-Pacific picture. Even the very name 'Pacific' is relatively recent. Clearly it is essential to step back and survey the evolution of Pacific politics. The main purpose is to outline the basic trends in political, military, economic, and cultural relations. What were the main lines of co-operation, conflict, and communication in the region? Inevitably, it is impossible to do justice to anything but the broadest of these strands in such a short survey. The task is, however, essential. Trying to understand modern Pacific politics without reference to its history is like trying to diagnose an illness without knowing the patient's case history. In the case of the Pacific, it is a history of exploration, exploitation, and the evolution of a highly diverse pattern of politics. There may have been times when 'thinking Pacific' might have made more sense, but at most times the Pacific was deeply divided and/or closely tied into different parts of a global political and economic system. The history of the Pacific goes some way to explaining both the failure of attempts to build a Pacific consciousness and the reasons why different portions of the Pacific have looked beyond the region for inspiration, friends, and trade.

1

Spreading Around the Rim

Some 100 000 years ago, the first humans made their way eastwards to the western rim of the Pacific Ocean. They spread south through South-east Asia and across the then relatively shallow waters to Papua New Guinea and Australia. They also spread north through China and by the mid-palaeolithic age had edged north and east to Japan. In the late-palaeolithic age people wandered up to the less hospitable wastes of the Arctic.

During the last great ice-age some 40 000 years ago, enough water was frozen that land bridges linked Japan to Korea in the south and to Manchuria in the north. The continents of Asia and North America were linked by the largest of the northern land bridges, Beringia. The earliest settlers in the Americas may have made their way south as early as 30 000 years ago.[1] But this original unity of the Pacific was not to last long.

The traffic of people, both before the ice-age and for millenniums after, was one-way. There is no serious evidence that the peoples of Asia received return visits from their American brethren. Certainly, as the ice melted and water levels rose, many of the 'land bridges' were flooded. There is evidence that some people drifted across the Pacific to the Americas, riding the prevailing currents from the north-east down the American coast.[2] There is also evidence from pottery that around 3000 BC some drifters from Japan reached modern Ecuador, and that others reached British Columbia in 2000 BC.[3] But apparently no one ever travelled back across the vast waters and against the prevailing currents.

Some minor trade among the inheritors of Mongol traits, the Aleuts and Inuit, apparently did take place across the narrow frozen straits in the north. Part of the trade included the exchange of seal oil for domesticated reindeer. But the main spread of people around the Pacific rim in the Americas was south to warmer climates and more fertile lands. Although no written

[1] 'Were Americas Settled Before the Ice Age?' in *International Herald Tribune* (21–2 June 1986) for new findings.

[2] Alvin M. Josephy jun., *The Indian Heritage of America* (London: Jonathan Cape, 1968), 40.

[3] Ibid.; J. Arthur Lower, *Ocean of Destiny* (Vancouver: University of British Columbia Press, 1978), 7; Katherine Plummer, *The Shogun's Reluctant Ambassadors* (Tokyo: Lotus Press, 1984).

cultures were developed, some, like the Mayans, developed picture symbols and built magnificent civilizations.[4]

These American cultures were eventually to give the world corn, potatoes, peanuts, cacao, cotton, and tobacco, but they never made effective use of metal. Nor were they much inclined to travel. Some minor contacts up and down the Pacific coast did take place. A few, like the more adventurous Kwakiutl Indians of North America, had sea-going canoes to trade, raid, and hunt along the north-west coast. But they never crossed back to Asia. Not surprisingly, independent, but isolated cultures and powers developed.

By far the earliest and most impressive civilizations developed back in Asia. In more southerly climes, people continued their drift eastward. The first occupants of Melanesia arrived in 2000–1000 BC and maritime traders covered vast distances on their way to Polynesia. Hawaii was not to be occupied until AD 400 and the South Cook Islands and New Zealand until AD 850. But the real 'progress' of civilization was made earliest further north in China.

The first Chinese cities emerged after 3500 BC, and by 1600 BC and the Shang dynasty the Chinese bronze age had developed. The rivers became the focus of civilization, and the coming of horses in 2000 BC increased mobility. Chinese civilization was unusual for not developing an elaborate religion as its power grew, but Confucianism did emerge as a system of beliefs for the governing élite.

But unlike other great civilizations of the time, China had no rivals in Asia. This isolation was to breed a sense of superiority and a blasé attitude to much international trade. At home, the development of 'hydraulic cultures' reinforced authoritarian rule. Ideograms as the basis of language emerged to help the élite control an increasing territory and population.[5] The Zhou dynasty of the eleventh century BC extended the territory of China. Under the Chin dynasty, China was united in the third century BC. But the absence of real competition to keep the Chinese empires on their mettle was, in the long term, to make China defenceless when rivals did come to stay. Unlike the Mediterranean or the Atlantic, the Pacific was dominated by a single power—China—for centuries.

To be sure, China did assimilate some things from the outside. Some developments in metallurgy spread to China via India. Regular trading contacts with the Mediterranean and Rome were established by 100 BC. The famed silk route brought little that was essential to China but, along with the sporadic coast-hugging trade south to the islands of South-east Asia, it meant that China became somewhat less isolated.

[4] Josephy, *Indian Heritage*, 11–40.
[5] Hugh Thomas, *An Unfinished History of the World* (London: Pan, 1979).

South-east Asia itself developed more slowly than China. The idea of rice as the agricultural staple came from China and its cultivation helped establish the first civilizations and states to China's south, as well as east in Japan. Population grew more rapidly than in grain-based societies in Europe.[6] The first major 'import' into the Pacific region, apart from its people, came in the form of Buddhism. Theravada Buddhism established itself as far east as Thailand, and the more universalist Mahayana Buddhism took hold even further east. It reached China in the first century AD, Korea in the fourth century and Japan in the sixth century. Much like the spread of Christianity in Europe to the Slavs and Germans, Buddhism was also the medium for cultural exchange.[7]

In sum, the early history of the Pacific is the history of spreading population, but of very few great civilizations. Unlike the more crowded, competitive Mediterranean world, the Pacific was dominated by China. However, few people outside the Sinitic world knew about China or cared about its existence. There were few states, let alone contact between them or their people. It was distinctly an age before international relations existed.

PACIFIC EMPIRES

So long as China had no rivals, there was little incentive for contacts between civilizations. To be sure, trade routes did hug the East Asian coast in the first century AD, but most of the stages of the route were in the hands of various foreigners and subject to piracy, especially in the Malacca Straits.[8] Geography obviously meant that he who controlled the narrow straits established power. Other features of geography framed the nature and place where rival states could emerge. Monsoons and trade winds controlled sea travel. Plateaux and river deltas helped determine where civilization would develop, and as a consequence also helped keep the Pacific region divided.[9]

Not surprisingly, the first great civilizations in South-east Asia emerged in the straits at Sumatra, in the Mekong River delta and around the central lakes of Cambodia.[10] The water highways first brought power to the island kingdom of Srivijaya from the sixth century. By then, the much smaller kingdoms of Indo-China had fallen into decay.[11] Srivijaya's power came from its domination of the trade between India and China. The Chinese

---

6 Thomas, *Unfinished History*.
7 L. S. Stavrianos, *The World Since 1500* (Englewood Cliffs, NJ: Prentice Hall, 1982), 30.
8 Donald Macintyre, *Sea Power in the Pacific* (New York: Crane & Russak, 1972), 9.
9 C. P. Fitzgerald, *A Concise History of East Asia* (London: Penguin, 1966).
10 Milton Osborne, *Southeast Asia* (London: Allen & Unwin, 1985), 9–10.
11 D. G. E. Hall, *A History of South-East Asia* (London: Macmillan, 1968), 24–40.

were not directly involved in the trade, preferring to let the Malays control the contacts with the area China called the Southern Seas. In fact, China remained remarkably unconcerned with managing this trade so long as the Malays paid tribute to China (see below).

Before Srivijaya, but not as grandiose, were the first kingdoms of Indo-China. This aptly named area was the recipient of both Indian and Chinese influence.[12] China dominated the emerging Red River delta kingdom of Vietnam, mainly for political reasons, while India influenced the creation of the other two kingdoms further south. Funan, in the Mekong River delta area, reached its height in the sixth century, while Champa, around Hue, was smaller and less powerful. Indian influence was less long-lasting than that of China, and India's involvement was more for economic and religious reasons. China's purpose was political control.

From the ninth to the fifteenth centuries the Khmer empire succeeded Funan. By dint of superior mastery of waterworks, the Khmer controlled the cultivation of rice and reached its cultural peak in the twelfth century with the monumental architecture at Angkor. Although their empire did not expand much beyond its ethnic base and had little dependence on trading relations, it did have some military and economic contacts with its neighbours.[13] In the fourteenth century, when Mongol rule in China pushed south to challenge the Khmer, the Thai and related Lao kingdoms expanded to pick up the pieces of the Khmer empire.[14] The decline of Indian influence and the regional fragmentation laid the basis of the eventual format of states we see today.[15]

But these trends take us ahead of the unfolding Pacific story. Elsewhere in the Pacific, other people were spreading out to territories previously unoccupied by humans. Settlers in Melanesia had reached Fiji by 1300 BC and by AD 300 had begun island-hopping into Polynesia. By 850 they had spread to all Pacific islands, creating island universes largely unconnected to one another. Some have suggested that these 'Vikings of the Pacific' in fact had a highly sophisticated sense of their place in the world.[16] But little evidence of such complex contacts between islands remains. Much like the spread of people into the Americas, the movement of people to the islands was one-way and created no far-reaching pattern of relations between islands, let alone between states. Most islanders had little contact, even between 'bush' and 'beach' on individual islands. Some had knowledge of

[12] G. Coedes, *The Making of Southeast Asia* (Berkeley, Calif.: University of California Press, 1966), 40–77.

[13] Hall, *A History*, 94–103; Osborne, *Southeast Asia*, 20–30.

[14] Lea Williams, *Southeast Asia: A History* (London: Oxford University Press, 1976), 32.

[15] Coedes, *Southeast Asia*, 88–138.

[16] Peter Bellwood, *The Polynesians* (London: Thames & Hudson, 1978), 43–4.

their immediate neighbours up to about 100 km out. But by and large they were less akin to Vikings than to the 'flotsam and jetsam of wind and wave'.[17]

The spread of people was deeply affected by serendipity and wind currents. The resulting mix of peoples was most marked in Melanesia, but the people of Polynesia were more homogeneous. Yet the Polynesians on different islands were not really aware of each other's presence, and it took the westerners in more recent times to name them (Polynesia meaning 'many islands').[18] These south Pacific islands were the last great area of the world to be settled by humans, and the process apparently was the result of accident.

Micronesia to the north was perhaps the most heterogeneous of the island groups. It was also more common for its inhabitants to trade between islands and this obviously required at least a basic understanding of currents and winds. The Micronesians even had a rudimentary chart of their place in the island universe, although frequently its boundaries did not extend very far. The western Micronesians had a sense of Asia and of their own roots, but in central and eastern Micronesia it was impossible to disentangle myth from real knowledge of place in the Pacific. The slowness of the spread of people is largely accounted for by the huge distances involved. A pattern of international relations was consequently slower in evolving. Nevertheless, it remains true that, while Pacific islanders were navigating huge spaces of open water, Europeans were still paddling around the safe waters of the almost-closed Mediterranean.

It is also true that at this time even China and Japan were largely oblivious to what lay out in the Pacific. While both countries traded and travelled south down the Asian coast, remarkably they did not explore eastward. The Chinese may have been the 'boldest seamen of the Orient', deriving important government profits from trade and deploying huge navies when needed, for example in the thirteenth century. But they did not expand eastward. In the Sung dynasty China had impressive ocean-going ships and the sailors already knew the skills of sailing into the wind. In the twelfth century it took only 40 days to reach Sumatra from China, but still the Chinese apparently never tried to sail the Pacific.[19] Early Chinese lore suggested that beyond their shores stretched 'the boundless place'.[20]

17 These controversies over the extent of islanders' knowledge of their place in the world are well covered by Gordon Lewthwaite, 'Geographical Knowledge of the Pacific Peoples' in Herman Friis (ed.), *The Pacific Basin*, (New York: American Geographical Society, 1967).

18 The name is from the Greek, and first used by the Portuguese explorer, Barros, in the 16th century. For background see Douglas Oliver, *The Pacific Islands* (Honolulu: University of Hawaii Press, 1975), 63–74.

19 Teobaldo Filesi, *China and Africa in the Middle Ages* (London: Frank Cass, 1972), 5–15.

20 Lewthwaite, 'Pacific Peoples', 63; Nobuo Muroga, 'Geographical Exploration by the Japanese' and Chiao-min Hsieh, 'Geographical Exploration by the Chinese' both in Friis (ed.), *The Pacific Basin*.

The Japanese were even less adventurous. In the seventh century they sent a voyage of exploration north, but they reached the Asian mainland and Manchuria, not the arc of land stretching round to North America. The main impetus for Japan's exploration of its northern waters was to come only when the Russian empire swept out from Europe in the seventeenth century.[21] Japan, like China, was well aware of vast expanses of land to the west in Eurasia, and fourteenth-century Japanese maps demonstrate at least a mythological recognition of India and central Asia as the origin of Buddhism. Yet on those same maps, the Pacific itself is shown as blank and empty.[22]

Still further across the Pacific in the Americas, the development of civilization seemed more akin to South-east Asian levels. In AD 300 the Mayan civilization of Central America began to develop and by 600 it had reached its apogee. But unlike the empires of East Asia, there was no contact with the main empire of the Pacific, China.[23] Nor was there any contact with the central Andean empires that coalesced after AD 600 in the Huari and Tiahuanaco empires. The Mayans did, however, spread their knowledge of the cultivation of maize into North America.

The next major Central American empire, that of the Aztecs in Mexico, rose in the fourteenth century, reaching an apogee in the fifteenth. Although the Aztecs had a complex local trading network, they had no significant contacts with the somewhat later developing Inca civilization of Peru.[24] Some minor sea trade was carried out along the Pacific coast, but voyages were never long.[25] A not insignificant reason for the general absence of contact between empires was the already-existing illusion of knowledge—mythology. For example, the Incas conceived of the world as a box-like structure with a ridged roof. The Aztecs conceived of the world as five squares with themselves in the central one.[26]

This tendency on the part of empires to see themselves as the centre of the world when unchallenged by rival empires was understandable. It was also a characteristic of early Pacific international relations that stood in contrast to the more crowded and conflict-ridden pattern of relations around the

---

[21] Muroga, 'Geographical Exploration', 99–105.

[22] Nanba Matsutaro, Nobuo Muroga, and Unno Kazutaka (eds.), *Old Maps in Japan* (Osaka: Sogensha Inc., 1973). See also *Chinese and Japanese Maps* (London: British Library, 1974). I am grateful to Dr Helen Wallis of the British Museum for developing these points.

[23] N. Hammond, *Ancient Maya Civilisation* (Cambridge: Rutgers University Press, 1982).

[24] N. Davies, *The Ancient Kingdoms of Mexico* (London: Penguin, 1982); M. P. Weaver, *The Aztecs, Maya and their Predecessors* (New York: 1981). See generally A. D. Smith, *The Ethnic Origins of Nations* (Oxford: Basil Blackwell, 1988).

[25] O. H. K. Spate, *The Spanish Lake* (London: Croom Helm, 1979), 63. Also see generally G. Bowden and G. W. Conrad, *The Andean Heritage* (Cambridge: Peabody Museum, 1982).

[26] Daniel Boorstin, *The Discoverers* (London: Penguin, 1986).

Mediterranean. But for all the importance of the American and South-east Asian empires, by far the most continuous and developed civilization was China's.

CHINA AND ITS SPHERES

Early maps speak volumes about the world-view of their authors. Therefore it is striking that no Pacific society before 1500 had a map that showed even a vague notion of the Pacific Ocean. To be sure, Marshall Islanders were making stick maps of their nearest islands before the coming of the Euro-peans, and South-east Asian traders mapped their nearest trade routes.[27] But even the great Chinese civilizations had a poor sense of where they were in the world.

The early Chinese did contemplate the shape of the earth, for the fabled emperor Yu in 2000 BC reportedly sent out a man to measure the earth well before the Greeks produced Ptolemy.[28] Other civilizations, in contrast, looked less far afield and their world-views were shaped by the basic features they could observe, such as the place of the rising and setting sun. The very names of Asia and Europe are said to have derived from the Assyrian words for 'sunrise, east' (*Asu*) and 'sunrise, west' (*Ereb*). Originally, Asu referred only to the east coast of the Aegean Sea and, even in the first century, Asia was merely the name of a Roman province.[29] Early European maps placed the east, the so-called Orient, where the sun rose, at the top of maps. Thus the true 'orientation' of the Mediterranean world was towards China.[30] But with the Chinese discovery of the compass and magnetic north, maps were turned round to place north at the top.[31]

Yet despite the compass and probably the world's most sophisticated civilization, the Chinese maps were wholly ignorant of the wider Pacific. While some third-century maps understood India and seventh-century ones had a detailed sense of the South-east Asian islands, the Chinese orient was blank.[32] Eleventh-century Chinese maps knew of Hainan island but not even

[27] John Wilford, *The Mapmakers* (London: Junction Books, 1981), 7; Boorstin, *The Discoverers*, 101–25.

[28] Ibid., 18.

[29] Adrian Room, *Place Names of the World* (London: Angus & Robertson, 1987).

[30] And also apparently because of the early Christian belief that it was the location of paradise.

[31] Certainly in maps after the famed Greek map-maker Ptolemy, the Orient was placed to the right. See Wilford, *Mapmakers*, 7–52 for details. According to Boorstin, *The Discoverers*, 220 for a time the Chinese compass pointed south.

[32] For the following details consult Joseph Needham, *Science and Civilisation in China* (Cambridge: Cambridge University Press, 1959, 1961, 1971), i, iii, iv.

of Taiwan. Fourteenth-century maps knew the coast of Africa but not Australia. In part because of extensive trade with the Arabs, even the Mediterranean world and the so-called Western Ocean appeared on Chinese maps, while the waters east of South-east Asia were labelled the Southern Seas or the Eastern Ocean. The Chinese knew the earth was spherical, but never set out on eastward voyages of discovery.

It seems probable that some Chinese did stray across the waters, never to return. At various times they did understand at least basic facts about the north Pacific current. But they never set out to find new lands. Chinese fables spoke of the abyss that lay in eastern waters and some even believed that a Kingdom of Women lay in the Eastern Ocean. In AD 285 a Chinese writer noted that 'the Eastern Ocean is yet more vast, and we know of no one who has crossed it'. The Chinese reported that beyond their shores stretched 'the boundless place'. The only brief bit of counter-evidence is that, in the Ch'in dynasty, it was believed that drug plants giving immortality lay in the Eastern Ocean and during the third century sea captains were sent out in vain searches.[33]

This passivity on the part of Chinese explorers goes a long way to explaining why the Pacific was not understood until the coming of the Europeans. Yet this great Chinese civilization was more advanced than that of the Europeans, having bigger ships, more advanced cartography, the compass, and greater resources. During the Ming dynasty, before the arrival of the Portuguese, the Chinese were to travel further west and in greater numbers than the Portuguese travelled east to South-east Asia.[34]

What held China back were social and political factors. From the Chinese perspective of superior civilization, what reason was there to travel or to 'discover Europe' if China was 'already there', that is, already a self-satisfied culture? With a view of itself as the centre of the earth, and without rivals in civilization, there was little to be obtained from travel and trade. As Braudel explains, as far as it was concerned, China was already a 'world economy'.[35]

The Chinese empire was big enough to satisfy most emperors and if expansion was undertaken it was easier, and more natural, for human beings to try it on land rather than at sea. Certainly the conservative agrarian culture of continental China had little interest in exploring the seemingly empty waters beyond China. Because of a self-sufficiency in basic foods, there was little need to take to the sea to trade for basic necessities.

Of course, China did trade with the outside world, even with far-off Rome along the silk route, or by hugging the Eurasian coast in sea-trade

---

33 Details ibid., iv.
34 Filesi, *China and Africa*, chs. 5–10.
35 Fernand Braudel, *The Perspective of the World* (London; Fontana, 1985).

through middlemen. But while Chinese exports were coveted in the Mediter-ranean world, China only collected in return such curiosities as jugglers, acrobats, and giraffes.[36] Many have suggested that such Sinocentrism was unusual and derives from an especially Chinese approach to international relations.[37] But it is remarkable the extent to which any empire that dominates its own living space develops an equivalent ethnocentrism.[38] Unlike the Mediterranean or European world where rival political units constantly vied for advantage, China had no real rivals or reason to change.

The absence of rivals to China helped develop a Chinese approach to its neighbours that was disdainful when it could afford to be and cautious when it needed to appease external threats. In the inner, Sinitic zone, was 'core China'. In the next zone out was inner Asia, usually including Tibet and Korea. In the outer zone there was Japan and South-east Asia, all states that were supposed to pay tribute to dominant China.[39]

The anti-egalitarian system held for as long as China was strong. When China was weak, or invaded, for example by the Mongols, the reality was a submissive and adaptable China. Even at times of strength, tribute in the outer zone merely meant recognition of the greatness of Chinese civilization. Certainly in financial terms China paid out far more than it received. Non-Chinese refused to accept this Sinocentric world-view and were able to carry on free from any serious Chinese attempt to make the theory of tribute match the reality.

Despite their delusions of grandeur, the Chinese did recognize other great, albeit distant, civilizations. In times of weakness they certainly recognized close neighbours as equal adversaries.[40] Thus China did have real experience of more equal interstate relations, whether it was due to strong neighbours or internal Chinese rivalries. China recognized the notion of alliances, boundary disputes, and buffer states, all of which are essentials to the evolution of a more egalitarian international state system. China accepted all this when it had to, or else fell silent in order to not face the harsh reality. It may have been disdainful, but in 1397 it did call Srivijaya 'this petty little country'.[41]

[36] Ibid., vol. 1.

[37] Hedley Bull and Adam Watson (eds.), *The Expansion of International Society* (Oxford: Clarendon Press, 1984); John K. Fairbank (ed.), *The Chinese World Order* (Cambridge, Mass.: Harvard University Press, 1968).

[38] See Braudel, *Perspective* for discussions of such 'world economies'. See also L. S. Stavrianos, *The World Since 1500* (Englewood Cliffs, NJ: Prentice Hall, 1982), chs. 2, 3.

[39] This theory is discussed critically in Gerald Segal, *Defending China* (Oxford: Oxford University Press, 1985), ch. 2.

[40] Lien-sheng Yang, 'Historical Notes on the Chinese World Order' in Fairbank, *Chinese Order*, 20–2.

[41] Gungwu Wang, 'Early Ming Relations with Southeast Asia' in Fairbank, *Chinese Order*, 52.

Nowhere was the gap between illusion and reality greater than in trade relations. China engaged in what the rest of the world called trade, although it regularly described it as tribute. To be sure, little of this trade was vital for China, especially when compared to the role it assumed among the South-east Asians who built their power on controlling trade routes.[42]

Neither was China shy about military conquest when the niceties of tribute were not acceptable, for example in the attack on Java in the thirteenth century or the absorption of peoples in the inner-Asian zone. China's relations with South-east Asia in the Ming dynasty are fine examples of alliances and balance-of-power politics, all carried out under the cloak of what China saw as the tribute system. In reality it was 'different self-centred views of superiority existing side by side'.[43]

Thus the Chinese world-view in theory may have been special, but the practice was no different from that of any other great power, such as Egypt or India.[44] Rarely facing serious or durable rivals, however, the Chinese empire was able to sustain both the illusion and sometimes the reality of great-power status and self-sufficiency. Thus it was that the Chinese ethnocentric world-view kept the Pacific largely unknown to the greatest Pacific power.

THE PACIFIC ON THE EVE OF THE EUROPEANS

Although the absence of equal states in the Pacific did not encourage exploration and development as in Europe, by the fifteenth century the societies of the Pacific were becoming more adventurous. The leading example is, of course, the magnificent Ming dynasty voyages of Cheng Ho as far as the coast of Africa. In seven expeditions between 1405 and 1433, Cheng Ho travelled further than the Portuguese would do when they came to Malacca in 1509. Up to 37 000 men set out on one voyage, in ships five times the size of those used by the Portuguese. While the Europeans were to come to conquer, the Chinese came for friendly port calls. The venture was a demonstration of Ming power; trade was incidental.[45] But China never exploited its achievements. The Confucian élite saw the trips as a challenge to their power at court and renewed threats from northern nomads pulled China back to its land-based obsessions.

It is curious that this Chinese naval triumph was westward rather than out

[42] Braudel, *Perspective*, 486–7.
[43] Wang, 'Early Ming', 60.
[44] Benjamin Schwartz, 'The Chinese Perception of World Order, Past and Present' in Fairbank, *Chinese Order*, 276–8. See also Braudel, *Perspective*.
[45] Needham, *Science and Civilisation*, iv. 486–517.

to the Pacific. But it is perhaps less surprising if one considers that the intention was probably not conquest or discovery, but rather 'showing the flag'. The westward routes were also well understood because of extensive trade networks developed by Arab traders in the Indian Ocean. Since the seventh century, the Arabs had come east in search of drugs and spices.[46] Indeed it was the Arabs who provided most of the detail for early maps of this middle zone between the Pacific and Atlantic worlds.[47]

The Arabs sat astride this middle ground, calling all Europeans 'Franks' and focusing on South-east Asia as the main Pacific post. But Arabs did travel up the Pacific coast to China, and by the ninth century they had even established trading posts.[48] They sacked Canton in 758, but the real growth in Arab power came in the twelfth century when the trading post of Gujarat in India came under Muslim influence. Arab dominance of the trade routes brought the remarkably swift spread of Islam to South-east Asia and a further mix to the long-established cultural patterns.[49]

While Arab influence spread swiftly from the west, new island traders came into contact with South-east Asia from the north. Japan was slow in moving outside its waters, but by the fifteenth century it was an active trader throughout the region.[50] Japan's past isolation was largely the result of geography. Although Japan is often compared to Britain, sitting off the coast of Europe, the Straits of Tsushima separating Japan from Eurasia are, at some 185 km, five times the width of the Straits of Dover. Like Britain, Japan is shaped by the sea, but with an even stronger sense of isolation.[51] Until 1945 it was one of the few countries never to have been invaded. When Japan did become interested in mainland Eurasia, its interest naturally turned first to Korea as the 'land bridge' to Chinese civilization.

Japan had certainly been conscious of Chinese power for centuries. China was the origin of many aspects of Japanese culture, including proper names, but cuisine and clothes, to name but two, had developed in different ways.[52] Although Japan was a borrower, therefore, by virtue of its geography it was selective, and could more easily identify what it borrowed and from where.

Japan became integrated into the evolving pattern of East Asian

[46] Wheatley, *The Golden Khersonese*, pt. 4.

[47] Hiroshi Nakamura, *East Asia in Old Maps* (Tokyo: Centre for East Asian Cultural Studies, 1962), 1; William McNeill, *The Pursuit of Power* (Oxford: Basil Blackwell, 1983), ch. 2.

[48] Hall, *A History*, 205–6.

[49] Williams, *Southeast Asia*, 35–43.

[50] Charles Fisher, 'The Maritime Fringe of East Asia' in W. Gordon East, O. H. K. Spate, and Charles Fisher (eds.), *The Changing Map of Asia* (London: Methuen, 1971), 461.

[51] J. M. Roberts, *The Pelican History of the World* (London: Penguin, 1980), 445.

[52] Edwin Reischauer and J. K. Fairbank, *East Asia: The Great Tradition* (London: Allen & Unwin, 1960), 394–7.

international relations after the eighth century. In the previous century, Tang China had evolved the name Jih-pen ('source of the sun') for its offshore neighbour, thus giving us our modern name for Japan. As some trade flowed around China's coasts, by the eleventh century the Japanese gradually became involved. In the thirteenth century Japan was particularly active, but with a strong tendency towards piracy. In part as a result, Mongol China gave Japan its only serious threat of invasion. In 1404 Japan agreed to what China called a tributary relationship, but Japan merely saw this as a way to ensure regular profits from trade.[53] Japan obtained copper coins and silk in return for mineral copper, sulphur, and wood.

Thus Japan was a relative latecomer to the game of Pacific politics but, by virtue of its position, it was more willing to make use of the sea as a route for contacts. Although Japan, like all other Pacific states, did not look across the wide Ocean, it did not share their obsessions with land power. More like the South-east Asians, it had a flexible, trade-oriented perspective on the Pacific.

On the other hand, Korea was very much fixed in the Chinese, land-based mind-set. Korea became organized by the seventh century into a distinct political unit. Although under regular pressure from China from the land and Japan from the water, Korea survived by adopting a close tributary relationship with dominant China.[54] But much like Palestine, Korea remained a crossroads and one that would naturally be an active participant, however unwillingly, in East Asian and Pacific international relations.

However, the real focus of flourishing international relations in the Pacific was clearly in South-east Asia. Geography made these narrow trade routes the obvious hub of interstate relations. As China and Japan expanded their interests in what they called the Southern Seas, the straits of South-east Asia assumed even greater importance.

By the fifteenth century, all this activity was beginning to reshape the political balance in South-east Asia. The trading city of Malacca, supported by Mongol China, emerged as a powerful new trading empire. Sitting astride vital waterways, Malacca controlled the spice trade. China's influence was important in supporting an independent Malacca against local rivals, but China was unconcerned with the swift conversion of Malacca to the Muslim faith.[55] Nor was China greatly troubled that its switch of allies ended the empire of Srivijaya.

Meanwhile, in the distant and relatively underdeveloped Mediterranean, events were unfolding that would revolutionize the affairs of the Pacific

[53] Ibid., 452, 539–61.
[54] Ibid., 411–47.
[55] Hall, *A History*, 209–13; Osborne, *Southeast Asia*, 30.

world. In the age of the Renaissance, a new spirit of enquiry and invention and the extension of commerce stimulated Europeans to look further afield. They desired spices from the Orient because without them the meat that they slaughtered and salted in November each year was unappetizing. But Muslim rulers barred the trade routes overland so the Europeans looked to the sea for spices.[56]

In 1488 the Portuguese sailed round the tip of Africa and in 1497 the Portuguese explorer Vasco Da Gama carried on round to India and opened the route east. He was in search of the great prize—the spice trade—where one cargo of cloves could turn a profit of 2500 per cent.[57] When he arrived, he found an already highly developed pattern of trade and thus the incentive for the Portuguese to take control was heightened by the increased value of the prize.[58]

In 1492 Christopher Columbus had tried to find the same place by travelling west. Much to his surprise, he found another continent in the way. The knowledge of the existence of the east coast of the Pacific Ocean was still to come, but man was making huge strides in discovering the size of the planet on which he lived. In 1509 Portuguese warships sailed into Malacca, bringing in their wake the influence of a vibrant and expanding European world.

The coming of these 'Franks', as the Arabs and Asians called them, was perhaps as important an event in Pacific history as any, although the 'Franks' found already well-developed patterns of domestic and international politics. In fact, it was precisely because of the superiority of China and the East Asian trade that the Europeans were so anxious to come. There was one great civilization, China, far more developed than anything Europe had yet known. There was another area, South-east Asia, where trade flourished and which, like the Mediterranean world, was strongly affected by outside factors. The international games of balances of power, alliances, and wars were already well developed in South-east Asia. The Portuguese brought superior determination and fire-power, but they had nothing to teach in the game of international relations.

Elsewhere in the Pacific the picture was more fragmented. Scattered communities lived in North America, Oceania, and north of Korea as far as the Arctic. More developed societies, but still less powerful than the empires of China and Malacca, existed in South-east Asia, Japan, Korea, and Central and South America. The Pacific was fragmented but, unlike Europe, the components were far from equal in power. It was the very rivalry of

[56] Eric Wolf, *Europe and the People Without History* (Berkeley, Calif.: University of California Press, 1982), ch. 2.
[57] Macintyre, *Sea Power*, 24.
[58] Braudel, *Perspective*, 217.

roughly equal European states that sparked competition, exploration, and expansion. The Pacific was dominated by a China too complacent in its superiority.

Therefore the pattern of international politics in the Pacific, although sharing the essentials of balances of power, alliances, wars, and a system of states, was different from the Atlantic and Mediterranean world. The Pacific states were unequal in power and still dominated by one empire. Many Pacific states were ripe for a new order that would destroy Chinese power, and China was too self-satisfied to care until it was too late. Some Pacific states well understood sea power, but, like China, saw little need to expand by conquest. It was ironic that the Europeans who were to have such a major impact on Pacific politics were less developed than the Pacific people they had come to control. But at least the Europeans could show the Pacific peoples where they were on the globe.

2

1500–1850: Discovery and Rivalry

The European impact on the Pacific was slow to develop. Like a less virulent cancer, it struck out gradually from its initial penetration in South-east Asia in 1509. In two years the Portuguese spread east to the Moluccas and by 1514 they had reached the coast of China near Canton. Yet while the Portuguese were undoubtedly a new force on the scene, they prospered more by taking over existing trade routes than by creating new ones.[1] Thus, for much of the sixteenth century, most people of the Pacific were oblivious to the coming of the Europeans, apart from the South-east Asians, who had their trade empires smashed. European influence was otherwise contained within coastal enclaves and periodic visits by ships.

International relations in East Asia continued in their old pattern. A vibrant Ming dynasty in China was still relatively secure, especially as Japan was riven by civil war and the threat of pirates to coastal trade was therefore reduced. Only in the late sixteenth century did Ming rule begin to disintegrate. A resurgent Japan under Hideyoshi repeatedly attacked Korea in the 1590s and China had to expend huge amounts of money and men to shore up its tribute state. While the Europeans were extending their trading power, hot wars and balance-of-power politics were taking place in traditional North-east Asian fashion.

Meanwhile, the Pacific was also being approached from the other side. In 1494 the Spanish–Portuguese pact, the *Tordesillas Capitulación*, arranged by Pope Alexander VI, had the temerity to divide the world into two spheres of influence at a line 370 leagues west of the Cape Verde Islands. Spain was allocated the western portion and Portugal the eastern. However, such high-handed geopolitics did not last long in an age of discovery. The North European nations were merely provoked to contest the carve-up.

The search was on to find a route to the Orient. Some set out to find a passage through the north-west, such as John Cabot, who sailed from Bristol in 1497. In those days the Americas were initially seen more as a barrier than of intrinsic value or as part of the Pacific.[2] Canada is littered with names of explorers who, like Cabot, died in the great search for the

---

[1] L. S. Stavrianos, *The World Since 1500* (Englewood Cliffs, NJ: Prentice Hall, 1982), 94.

[2] John Wilford, *The Mapmakers* (London: Junction Books, 1981), 140.

North-west Passage.[3] In the 1520s Verazanno tried going through the middle of North America as Cartier led the French hopes up the St Lawrence. But the discovery of a route to the east was to come from further south.

Columbus's voyage of 1502–4 in search of Asia took him to Honduras and Nicaragua.[4] When he found the north coast of Cuba, he thought he had reached Japan.[5] In 1519 voyages by Pineda in the Gulf of Mexico also failed to find a strait leading through to the Pacific. But such exploration added key elements to European explorers' sense of their planet. The shape of the Pacific was still not understood, but by now it was only a matter of time.

In 1513 Núñez de Balboa struggled through the Honduran jungles on the Central American isthmus and beheld the great mass of seemingly endless water which he called the South Seas. He waded into the water and claimed it and its shores for Spain. Neither the Spanish nor the Portuguese knew just how wide the water was, but for the first time western explorers had seen the Pacific from its eastern shore. Most explorers believed firmly that the Pacific was small, no doubt for reasons of ethnocentrism and as self-encouragement to carry on exploring.

The name 'South Seas' was to stick for some 200 years until northern Pacific powers began to assert themselves. The name 'Pacific Ocean' derives from the optimism of the commander of the most heroic voyage of all times—Magellan.[6] In 1519 Magellan set out from Europe with five ships and rounded the tip of South America into the Pacific on 28 November 1520. Despite the defection of several ships, and such severe starvation that the remaining sailors were reduced to eating rats and the leather on the sails, Magellan gave thanks for the peaceful waters beyond the straits by naming them the 'Pacific'. He sailed for three months before sighting land at Guam on 2 March 1521, thereby establishing the first contact with Pacific islanders and their outrigger seamen. Magellan then sailed on to the Philippines, but there he was murdered by local inhabitants. His last remaining ship eventually sailed on west to Spain in 1521, thus circumnavigating the globe for the first time and proving that the earth was round.[7] Magellan also proved that the Pacific was vast.

---

[3] The first true passage of the north-west was made only in 1969, when the reinforced tanker *Manhattan* crashed through the ice. In 1958 the nuclear-power *Nautilus* submarine 'cheated' and travelled underwater.

[4] On the voyages of discovery see Samuel Eliot Morison, *The Great Explorers* (Oxford: Oxford University Press, 1978).

[5] George Pendle, *History of Latin America* (London: Penguin, 1976), 34.

[6] Morison, *Great Explorers*.

[7] Ernest Dodge, *Islands and Empires* (Oxford: Oxford University Press, 1976), 3–4; O. H. K. Spate, *The Spanish Lake* (London: Croom Helm, 1979); Wilford, *Mapmakers*, 70–1.

While most of the people of the Pacific continued to live in ignorance of the European invaders, the Portuguese carried on up the East Asian coast, reaching Japan in 1542. Spain was far more adventurous: despite relinquishing the Moluccas to Portugal in 1529 by the Treaty of Saragossa, it rapidly consolidated its control of most of South America.

In the 1530s various expeditions worked their way up the eastern shore of the Pacific to California. In 1519 Hernando Cortés had set out from Spain for Mexico, defeating the already decaying Aztec empire under Montezuma. In 1532 Francisco Pizarro, a member of Balboa's party that 'found' the Pacific, set out on his conquest of the already divided and fading Inca empire. In 1541 Pedro de Valdivia began a 12-year struggle to control Chile for Spain.[8] Up to 80 per cent of the local inhabitants quickly died, most from the 'microbiotic shock' of the new European diseases.[9] The Spanish came for the twin great causes of their time, gold and God, and in a matter of decades had transformed the eastern face of the Pacific.

The Spanish *conquistadores* had established their first permanent settlement by 1493 and in contrast to North America, where the first settlement was established only in 1607, they created separate centres of power. The English colonists in the north settled close by each other, and only gradually spread out to the Pacific. In the south, the separate centres were scattered along the Pacific, thereby encouraging a sense of division in Latin America. In contrast to North America, where a relatively unified continent and Pacific perspective would emerge, in the south the natural tendencies of local geography towards separateness were magnified by Spain's settlement policy.[10]

For most of the sixteenth century, the Pacific was a Spanish lake. Trade routes swept from Seville to Acapulco to Manila and on to Macao, carrying American silver in exchange for silks and spices. In 1565 Urdaneta discovered the favourable winds from west to east and the great galleons could now link the shores of the 'lake' by travelling eastward across it. The island of Guam was a convenient base on the route, thus becoming a Spanish colony before any other island. The voyages were still agonizingly long, taking about three months on the westward voyage. The galleons themselves were often built in Manila using imported Chinese labour, and for much of the time only sailed once a year in each direction. Spain was not pleased that trade in Chinese silk would undermine its own exports from Europe to the colonists in the Americas. Remarkable as it may seem, the orientation of Latin America remained overwhelmingly to the Atlantic, even for Pacific colonies in

---

[8] Pendle, *Latin America*, 36–47.

[9] Alfred Crosby, *Ecological Imperialism* (Cambridge: Cambridge University Press, 1986). See also William McNeill, *Plagues and People* (London: Penguin, 1979).

[10] Pendle, *Latin America*, 51.

Mexico, Peru, and Chile.[11] The pattern of Latin American states ignoring the Pacific was set in colonial times.

Although Spain can be said to have discovered the Pacific, the Spaniards certainly did not introduce trade to the region. Their arrival, as with Portugal's from the east, was encouraged by, and made swift use of, existing lucrative trade connections. As one observer has noted, South-east Asia was already a long-established 'geopolitical fracture zone', where local traders found the most convenient fissures to make their profits.[12] The difference was that for China, the great empire of Asia-Pacific, trade was peripheral. For Spain, it was vital to the *raison d'être* of the colonies and its presence in the Pacific.

Spanish control of the 'lake' was completed in the late sixteenth century following its annexation of Portugal. But with the Reformation in Europe and the rise of Holland and Elizabethan England as naval and trading powers, the days of the Spanish age of the Pacific were numbered. Francis Drake circumnavigated the globe in 1577–80, raiding Spanish treasure, claiming territory such as New Albion (California) for Elizabeth and seeking a western entrance for the north-west passage.[13]

Both Portugal and Spain had squandered resources on religious wars with Protestants and Turks, not to mention their own dynastic squabbles. Perhaps more importantly, the great economic engines of capitalism developed first in northern Europe as Spain was generally more dismissive of traders and petty commerce. Spain thus lacked the shipping to exploit its colonies.[14] Spain's fade-out from the Pacific was less sharp than it was in Europe, but the trend was clear.

NEW RIVALRY IN THE SEVENTEENTH CENTURY

The Europeans came to the Pacific in human waves. The initial waves were shallow, barely lapping the coasts of already-formidable empires, and established societies along the Pacific rim. This was the early stage in the Pacific of a process taking place around the world, the mixing of races. Until 1500 the world was basically divided into distinct racial groups, but global travel brought one of the most evil scourges of the modern world, racism. More positively, with the exchange of people came an exchange of cultures and hence a more sophisticated world.

11 Ibid., 63.
12 Ibid., 144–5.
13 Morison, *Great Explorers*.
14 Stavrianos, *The World*, 94–104.

In the seventeenth century, new waves of Dutch and then British influence made it clear that the Europeans would not be leaving the area. While the newcomers began to make their influence felt, Spain still lingered on as an important power. The key to Spain's Pacific perspective was the Philippines, named after Philip II. Spain came in search of spices and souls, and found both in plenty. The Philippine archipelago became the base for the triangular trade with Spain's Latin American holdings and the motherland. In fact, so much Mexican silver was traded across the Pacific for silk and spices that the Mexican dollar became the standard currency for trade along the coast of China.[15] According to some accounts, some 15 per cent of Spanish silver was spent in the Pacific trade.[16]

The trade itself was not novel, but the fact that it traversed the Pacific was. In fact, trade from Mexico and Peru across the Pacific has never been as important since to these Latin American states as it was during the period of Spanish colonialism. Both colonies soon found themselves in fierce rivalry for the Philippine trade, eventually forcing up prices in Manila and causing serious problems for Spain's exchequer.[17]

The influence of Spain also helped integrate the Philippines into Pacific politics. Previously, the archipelago had not been organized into a coherent unit and, unlike the rest of South-east Asia, it had virtually escaped the spread of Buddhism. The Muslim influence reached the Philippines just before Spain did, but was contained by Catholic Spain's strong desire to convert as many souls as possible. In contrast to most other states in Asia-Pacific, the Philippines had not been organized into a political unit before Spain came.[18]

But while Spain continued to prosper in the Pacific in the seventeenth century, Portuguese influence virtually disappeared. The Portuguese were replaced by Holland, yet another small, but dynamic, seafaring people. At the start of its Golden Century in 1602 the Dutch East India Company was given its charter.[19] In 1619 the Dutch took Jakarta and in 1641 they grabbed control of Malacca and began exploring the area. Most importantly, Dutch sailors discovered the 'roaring forties', the Indian Ocean's westerly winds that allowed them more regular passage to and from Java. The Dutch then became relatively independent of the once-dominant seasonal monsoons for contacts with their new holdings.[20] As a result, they also focused on the trade potential of Java and the area south of the old main empires in Malacca.

15 Lea Williams, *Southeast Asia* (Oxford: Oxford University Press, 1976), 64–5.
16 Spate, *Spanish Lake*, 201.
17 Ibid., 215–18.
18 C. P. Fitzgerald, *A Concise History of East Asia* (London: Penguin, 1966).
19 'East India' was the general term at the time for areas east of India, i.e. South-east Asia.
20 Donald Macintyre, *Sea Power in the Pacific* (New York: Crane & Russak, 1972), 31–3.

Dutch discoverers sailed further, even reaching Tonga. But their largest and most unexploited discovery was Australia. Abel Tasman approached from the west in 1642 but never got close enough to see anything but inhospitable desert and scrub. 'New Holland' was noted, but ignored because little trade potential was perceived. Holland concentrated on the spice and silk trade with China, and further up the coast with Japan.

By the late seventeenth century, Holland was able to control much of the exchange of Chinese silk and porcelain for Japanese silver. But its main emphasis was in Java and the spice trade. At first, the Dutch were content to control local trade and merely maintain coastal ports. But later in the seventeenth century Holland set out to raise spice prices by forcing cuts in production and in the planting of rice. When the rice crop failed, the Javanese were forced to buy expensive rice from Holland. This allowed the Dutch to extend their control further inland.[21] This adaptation of 'mono-agriculture' was debilitating to the local economy, although it had also been a feature of the pre-European phase of local history.[22] A new phase of colonialism was being born.

The Dutch contribution to the new order in international affairs was also apparent in the gradual adoption of the ideas of Hugo Grotius. His early notions of international legal rules, and especially the doctrine of the 'freedom of the seas', served the interests of the trading states.[23] But such freedoms as existed were not applied evenly, especially to the peoples of East Asia, who were coming under increasing subjugation by European colonial powers. The supposed rules of international affairs that the Europeans 'invented' were always politically inspired and often represented little more than a convenient justification for imperialism.

Further to the north, yet another European challenger made its appearance—Russia. Although the Mongols in the thirteenth century had seized control of south-east Siberia, the Golden Horde disintegrated in the late thirteenth century and independent khanates were established, including Sibir (a name derived from the Mongolian word meaning 'marshy wilderness').[24] For much of the sixteenth century Sibir continued to pay tribute to Moscow but by later in the century the system began to break down. By the late sixteenth century, Russian explorers were making their way across Siberia—most notably, the Russian 'Cortez', Yermak.[25] As early as 1639

[21] Ibid., 37–43.

[22] Fernand Braudel, *The Perspective of the West* (London: Fontana, 1985), 218.

[23] G. V. Scammell, *The World Encompassed* (London: Methuen, 1981).

[24] W. Gordon East, 'Asiatic USSR and the MPR' in W. Gordon East, O. H. K. Spate, and Charles Fisher, *The Changing Map of Asia* (London: Methuen, 1971), 563.

[25] Alan Wood, 'From Conquest to Revolution' in Alan Wood (ed.), *Siberia* (London: Croom Helm, 1987).

Ivan Moskvitin extended tsarist rule to Pacific waters and the Sea of Okhotsk. Russia's first Pacific port, at Okhotsk, was established in 1647. In 1648 a Cossack traveller called Dezhnev reached the Pacific at the north-east tip of Siberia and showed that Eurasia was divided from America.[26] Later in the seventeenth century, Russian explorers survived the forbidding wastes of Kamchatka and moved down towards Japan from the Kuriles. Under Peter the Great, Russia became obsessed with sea power and the need to establish a Pacific as well as a European naval presence. To an important extent, Russia inherited the Mongol empire and, driven by a quest for fur and other minerals, including salt, a military system for control was set up at an extraordinary speed considering the vast distances involved.

The serious vulnerability of Russia to the local rivals in the Pacific was a key factor dictating the speed of conquest and control. Russia's expansion took advantage of rivers and open country to reach the Pacific 250 years before it explored Central Asia. While Russians were gazing at Pacific waters, British settlers in North America were struggling to cross the Allegheny Mountains. In North America France founded Montreal in the decade that Russia founded Okhotsk across the Pacific. Although Russia was to be the first new land power in Asia, the British were not far behind in pushing their settlers across North America. This 'race' to the north Pacific was clearly won by Russia, but the very competition itself was to focus the attention of Pacific politics to the north, rather than the south where it had all begun. Only by the end of the seventeenth century, with this new north Pacific trend under way, did the name 'Pacific' replace 'South Seas' as the usual title for the huge waters between the Americas and Asia.[27]

But for much of the seventeenth century, it was Russian expansion that was most notable. By the late seventeenth century, up to one-third of total Russian state revenue came from the Far East fur trade.[28] Not surprisingly, this expanding, confident Russian empire came into contact with China. For the first time, China had a rival in the Pacific region that was large, confident, land-based and therefore likely to stay. Russia–China relations can be said to have begun properly with the Russian exploration of the Amur river basin by Khabarov in the 1640s. In 1651 Khabarov established his first fort on the Amur and a year later he reached the banks of the Ussuri River. China could no longer ignore the threat.

At the Treaty of Nerchinsk in 1689, the Russians were excluded from the

---

[26] B. N. Slavinskii, 'Russia and the Pacific to 1917' in John Stephan and V. P. Chichkanov (eds.), *Soviet–American Horizons on the Pacific* (Honolulu: University of Hawaii Press, 1986), 32; Terence Armstrong, *Russian Settlement in the North* (Cambridge: Cambridge University Press, 1965), 24.

[27] O. H. K. Spate, 'South Sea to Pacific Ocean' in *Journal of Pacific History*, 12 (1977).

[28] Ibid., 33.

Amur area. Russia had to step back from initial confrontation with China in part because it had failed to establish a grain base in the Amur region and therefore could not support full-scale colonization.[29] But while Peter the Great was stalled, in the meantime he had plenty of new territory to consolidate before pushing Russia deeper into Pacific political waters.

Russia's early gains in the seventeenth century were made possible by the transition in China from the Ming to the Qing dynasty. By 1652 most of China had been subdued by these Mongol invaders, thus creating a vacuum in the north which Russia exploited. By the 1660s, Chinese unity was consolidated, to the extent that rule was extended to Taiwan in 1662. Taiwan had been held for 20 years by the Dutch, but had never previously been under Chinese rule.

Thus the international politics of Europe and of the Pacific were beginning to come into direct contact. China was certainly able to take on all comers, so long as the ruling dynasty was strong and while the Europeans were in their initial stages of testing Pacific waters. But in the longer term, it is possible with hindsight to identify a number of underlying weaknesses in the Chinese approach.

Chinese society consistently put less emphasis on trade and commerce, limiting merchants' profits and thereby preventing the emergence of a vibrant entrepreneurial class.[30] China clearly had the technology and power to expand, but it was its very success at home that stifled its spirit of exploration. This disdainful and isolationist approach meant that new inventions remained curiosities rather than tools of new power. It was those very successes that attracted Europeans to the east, but which also helped ensure that China was vulnerable, in the long term, to foreign pressure.

The other great Confucian state, Japan, reacted in a similar fashion to China, but not for as long. Japan had been reunified under Hideyoshi in the late sixteenth century and missionaries from Europe were banished. But trade relations with China continued and Japan took an active part in the rejuvenated seventeenth-century trade with South-east Asia. Economic changes began in Japan as such items as tobacco, potatoes, guns, and improved castle-building techniques were imported from the Europeans. But by the 1630s social dislocation was growing and so much Japanese silver was being expended on such goods as Chinese silk that the shogun, Tokugawa Iemitsu, banned Japanese from sailing abroad and building ocean-going ships.[31] This self-imposed isolation was not complete until the

---

29 East, 'Asiatic USSR', 574–6.

30 See generally Hugh Thomas, *An Unfinished History of the World* (London: Pan, 1979); J. M. Roberts, *The Pelican History of the World* (London: Penguin, 1983).

31 Edwin Reischauer and J. K. Fairbank, *East Asia: The Great Tradition* (London: Allen & Unwin, 1960), 583–99.

eighteenth century, but the trend was already apparent as the seventeenth century drew to its close.

Thus by the turn of the century, important aspects of Pacific international politics had been changed by the coming of the Europeans. The traditional South-east Asian empires were destroyed and trade was now controlled by Europeans. Russia reached the Pacific and challenged Chinese dominance. Spain linked its empire across the Pacific and integrated parts of Latin America into Pacific trade patterns. European culture, in the form of religion, was brought to all parts of the Pacific rim.

But the Europeans did not bring 'modern' international relations to the Pacific.[32] The Treaty of Westphalia in 1648 is supposed to have marked the dawning of the new age of equal states, recognizing a system of states based on sovereignty and diplomatic convention. In fact, equality persisted in Europe only as a result of force of arms. Conquest and subjugation was still the aim. Nowhere was this more obvious than in the Europeans' treatment of the Pacific peoples. Imperialism did not recognize equality for non-whites, even if they had more highly developed civilizations.

What is more, parts of the Pacific were already well versed in international relations before the Europeans came on the scene. Trade and wars helped create states, alliances, balances of power, and regular contacts between states. The move from dynasticism to nationalism had already been well under way in the Pacific states much before the coming of the Europeans. Until Magellan, the Chinese knew more about their place in the world than any European power. South-east Asians had a more sophisticated trade pattern at longer distances than any European power. What the Europeans brought to the Pacific were new faces, new techniques of war, and a sense of the water as a means of communication with other parts rather than a barrier. But they had little to teach the people of the Pacific about international relations.

1700–1850: EMPIRES OLD AND NEW

Exploration of the Pacific was an essential precursor to the development of Pacific international politics. It not only defined the extent of the basin, but also made the often-treacherous waters safer for business. In the 150 years

---

[32] See for example the Eurocentric introduction in Hedley Bull and Adam Watson (eds.), *The Expansion of International Society* (Oxford: Clarendon Press, 1984). It is true that diplomatic conventions were more regularized under the Europeans, but this is largely a matter of degree, and was not a new concept to many inhabitants of the Pacific, especially those involved in regular trade.

from the dawn of the eighteenth century to the 'opening' of Japan, nearly the full extent of the Pacific and its people was mapped out. In the north, Vitus Bering, a Dane in the service of the tsar, sailed from Kamchatka between 1725 and 1743 to discover that a strait separated the Americas from Eurasia. The northern tip of the Pacific had been properly marked.

In the centre and south, the legendary James Cook undertook the most meticulous series of voyages of discovery and charting.[33] In 1768–71 he visited Tahiti, New Zealand, and Australia, and ascertained that these southern territories were indeed very suitable for settlement. In 1772–5 Cook sailed further south to map the South Pole, discovering much ice but no great land mass as cartographers had surmised. Jonathan Swift had located Lilliput and Brobdingnag of *Gulliver's Travels* (1726) in the Pacific and many early cartographers were convinced that a huge continent lay in the direction of the South Pole. But the first sighting of Antarctica was only in 1820 (the first major survey was not until 1946). Daniel Defoe's *Robinson Crusoe* (1719) was the first great Pacific novel of the age and it said much about the spirit of individualism and attitude towards labour that the European explorers brought to the Pacific.

In 1776 Cook turned his attention northwards, to Hawaii and then to Oregon and up the North American coast towards the straits discovered by Bering. His voyages were a mixture of the spirit of adventurism, the thrill of discovery, and the pursuit of science. Imperialism was, at least then, a lesser motive.[34] Tragically, Cook was killed by Hawaiian islanders in 1779, but he left as his epitaph a magnificent modern map of the Pacific that was missing only a few Pacific islands. As a contemporary noted, 'he left his successors with little to do but admire'.[35] In 1792–5 George Vancouver carried on Cook's legacy and charted in detail the west coast of North America, leaving his name for the premier city of Canada's west. By the early nineteenth century most expeditions were concentrating on the intensive, dreary work of hydrography and meteorology. Most charting had been done and it was accomplished almost entirely by Europeans or Americans sailing from Atlantic waters.[36]

These eighteenth-century voyages mapped one-third of the globe and were critical in changing man's view of his place on the planet. Charles Darwin's Pacific studies, especially at the Galápagos Islands in 1835,

---

[33] Morison, *Great Explorers*.

[34] Dodge, *Islands and Empires*, 52–3.

[35] Peter H. Buck, *Explorers of the Pacific* (Honolulu: The Museum, 1953); Wilford, *Mapmakers*, 143–52; Douglas Oliver, *The Pacific Islands* (Honolulu: University of Hawaii Press, 1975), 93–5.

[36] Earnest Dodge, *Beyond the Capes* (Boston: Little Brown, 1971), ch. 9. More American voyages departed from Salem than from anywhere else: ibid., ch. 18.

resulted in his important study on the origin of the species. The voyages marked the end of discovery of the essential, populated parts of the planet, and shattered the myth of Europe as the centre of culture and civilization. Regrettably, this great spirit of adventure that brought the Europeans to the Pacific also brought conquest and exploitation.

Although the Europeans may have refined their principles of diplomacy, international conferences, and international law in the eighteenth century, few of these fine words were applied to the Pacific. The so-called 'system of states'[37] was little more than the rivalry of empires for the shards of shattered Pacific politics. Although this new system of international relations was supposed to be 'non-hegemonial', it was certainly every bit as hegemonial as anything the Pacific had known before. What is worse, instead of hegemony being exercised by a dominant Pacific state, like China, it was exercised by distant, yet powerful, European empires.

The most dominant of the empires was Britain. In the eighteenth century the decline of the Dutch empire, due to the breaking of its spice monopoly and European setbacks, left space for Britain to expand. Britain had concentrated on building a superior fleet and was less concerned with the details of continental European politics than Holland. The enclosure movement at home produced huge numbers of dissatisfied people ready to sail out to populate new colonies. British influence and culture spread in a far more basic way than merely periodically sailing ships into harbours. The conclusion of the Seven Years War in 1763 marked the end of France as a major rival and left Britain free to stamp a firm presence on Pacific culture and politics.[38] Britain's role later increased with the need to confront Napoleon and the related desire to exercise firmer control of the seas.[39] Britannia ruling the waves was hardly the 'non-hegemonial' action of just another equal sovereign state.

Britain was deeply concerned with trade with China and controlling the routes that made it possible. As a result, after the defeat of Napoleon Britain consolidated control of Malaya and dominated South-east Asian trade and power. In 1824 Britain and Holland formally agreed to divide their imperial interests, with the Dutch concentrating on what was to become Indonesia.

As part of the booming industrial revolution in Europe, the Europeans required raw materials from their colonial holdings. Britain shipped in hundreds of thousands of Chinese and Indians to work the plantations of

[37] The notion of the European system is developed in Adam Watson, 'European Society and its Expansion' in Bull and Watson, *The Expansion*, 24–31. For a more critical analysis see David Gillard, 'British and Russian Relations with Asian Governments in the Nineteenth Century' in the same volume.

[38] Stavrianos, *The World*, 115–18.

[39] Fitzgerald, *Concise History*, 296–9.

Malaya, thereby fundamentally altering the ethnic balance and local economy of the area. Local economies were also oriented towards the European
priorities of cash crops and exports. New boundaries were drawn for
administrative purposes, and 'white rajahs' such as James Brooke in
Sarawak took control of vast areas.[40] The most famous example is Sir
Stamford Raffles, who in 1819 took control of Singapore for the British East
India Company and set up an entrepôt and base so that Britain could
control the 'free trade' in the Pacific.[41]

More positively, Britain developed road and rail systems and created cities
where none had previously existed. The standard of living for at least some
'natives' did improve, but at a huge cost. The most important limit on
further expansion of colonialism was geography, and the problems of
taming the jungles of South-east Asia.[42]

A different and longer-lasting colonial system was practised in North
America, Australia, and New Zealand. In these cases, where the local
population was sparse, the huge influx of European immigrants could
spread out, virtually unopposed. In North America, Britain overcame
France to push its empire westward. While Canada remained loyal to the
British crown, the United States revolted in 1776 and pushed to the Pacific
coast with its own priorities. Before independence there was only minor
trade between the American east-coast colonies and Asia, often through
British intermediaries.[43] The first United States ship to sail around the world
set out from the north-east in 1789, in search of fur.[44]

Australia and New Zealand, like Canada, remained within the British
fold. But because of their geographic location, commanding the southern
Pacific, the history of these two territories was more closely related to the
development of the Pacific. Australia was first a base for naval supplies, flax
for sails and pine for masts. In 1787 the first convict ship sailed from Britain
with colonists for Australia, but needless to say it was not easy to make
farmers out of pickpockets. The first free settlers did not arrive until 1792
and prisoners were transported until 1868. In the nineteenth century
Australia developed trade in wheat, wool, and beef, thereby establishing
itself as the most important 'island' in Oceania. Both Australia and New
Zealand were prime beneficiaries of the spread of new crops that came with
the expansion of foreign races and cultures. Sydney emerged as the effective

---

[40] Milton Osborne, *Southeast Asia* (London: Allen & Unwin, 1985), 76–8.
[41] Macintyre, *Sea Power*, 74.
[42] Williams, *Southeast Asia*, 88–113.
[43] H. F. MacNair and Donald Lasch, *Modern Far Eastern International Relations* (London:
D. Van Nostrand, 1950), 84.
[44] William Goetzmann, *New Lands, New Men* (New York: Viking, 1986), 237–40.

capital of trade.[45] New Zealand was slower to develop, in large part because of its more hostile natives and more forbidding geography. It did not become a British colony until 1841. But none of these territories could develop independent trade with the rest of the Pacific, and certainly until the 1830s most trade was strictly controlled by the British East India Company.

Elsewhere in Oceania the pattern of British supremacy was far less clear. The independent monarchies of Fiji, Tonga, Tahiti, and New Caledonia were quickly subdued by a mixture of French and British imperialism. Tonga had perhaps the most extensive independent influence, including at one time much of western Polynesia. But it was no match for the iron and gunpowder of industrial Europe.[46]

Spain had initially been interested in Melanesia but found neither gold nor converts, so sailed on.[47] The islands were first seen as bases for a revival of the whaling industry, stimulated by Britain and a generous bounty system.[48] Sperm whale were hunted first off the coasts of Chile and Peru, then off New Zealand and Australia, and by 1819 the hunting grounds had shifted to near Japan and the Kodiak islands. The islands of Oceania became essential for 'wooding and watering' of the whalers. By the nineteenth century Russia and the new United States were matching the British lead in whaling, thereby increasing the importance of bases in Hawaii and the Marquesas. The whaling trade was not a European invention, but its European scale was certainly unprecedented in the Pacific.

While the whales were gradually killed off, new trade patterns emerged based on the sea otter. Pelts were much in demand, especially in Russia, and could fetch up to $120 each in China.[49] Trade on the North American coast was notionally controlled in the late eighteenth century by the British East India Company and the British South Sea Company, but in reality there was plenty of scope for freelance operation for everyone except the British. Hawaii emerged as the crucial fur-trade base, providing ship services, such as rope and boats, and men to sail. By the 1790s Hawaii had become the crossroads of the Pacific and a hang-out for deserters. Needless to say, the character of the islands and its people was swiftly changed by this European influx.[50] The Hawaiians had traditionally been excellent sailors, but never venturing such distances. In the early nineteenth century sandalwood was

[45] Oliver, *Pacific Islands*, 159.
[46] Bellwood, *The Polynesians*, 73.
[47] Dodge, *Islands and Empires*, 17.
[48] Oliver, *Pacific Islands*, 100.
[49] Eric Wolf, *Europe and the People Without History*. (Berkeley, Calif.: University of California Press, 1982), ch. 6.
[50] Dodge, *Beyond the Capes*, 143.

traded to China from the Pacific islands, and by 1825 the sea slug was a much sought-after delicacy in China.[51]

As a consequence of such trade, the islands became drawn into inter-locking patterns that had never previously existed. Few white settlers were foisted on the local inhabitants, but the latter's lives were certainly deeply affected by the fresh priorities of the new Pacific powers. They were told to believe in principles of private property, sovereignty of states, and national-ism, all of which had little foundation in their experience of isolated, primitive life.[52] In the case of Oceania, the Europeans truly did bring international relations to the region for the first time.

For much of this period, Britain's hegemonic role was challenged by a number of different and often unconnected states. The most notable zone of conflict was where interstate relations had been established longest—in South-east Asia. While Britain sat astride the vital Strait of Malacca, the declining Dutch empire retreated into Indonesia and turned their attention towards the land. The impact of imperialism on the people widened. As in Malaya, the demands of industrial Europe for rubber, tin, and other raw materials increasingly distorted local economies. Spain did much the same for the Philippines, its last remnant of Pacific empire, where it established a unified state with strong Catholic ties, neither of which had existed before.

Further north on mainland South-east Asia, France established colonies in Cambodia and Vietnam. France had coveted the area as a springboard to trade with China, only to discover that Indo-China was not heavily engaged in trade with its great neighbour to the north. Only Laos and Thailand remained outside this process of overt colonization. Thailand survived largely because it suited both France in Indo-China and Britain in Burma to maintain a buffer zone between them. Laos did not exist as anything but a jumble of remote, tiny kingdoms.[53]

But by far the most dramatic shifts in Pacific politics in this period took place in the northern latitudes. In the north-west it was Russia that now stormed into the region. Peter the Great set the tone in the late seventeenth century and his successors supported various explorers and traders in extending Russian influence. In 1714 Peter sent a mission to establish control in the Sea of Okhotsk. Because contact by land was so arduous, the search was begun for a northern sea route to the Russian far east. The Bering missions were part of that vain effort to navigate through the Arctic icefloes.

After a brief decline in Russian naval strength after Peter's death in 1725, Catherine the Great drove Russian interests into direct confrontation with

---

[51] Dodge, *Islands and Empires*, 56–65.
[52] Ibid., 30.
[53] Osborne, *Southeast Asia*, 71–4.

Spain and Britain in Pacific waters.[54] The main attraction for the rival empires was the trade of fur for gold, silver, and silk in China. Russia had an advantage over other European empires in that it controlled a vast swathe of territory in the Pacific with few unruly natives. While other Europeans were manoeuvring to find suitable coastal trading bases with China, Russia loomed more permanently and menacingly in the north. From 1727 a new system of Sino-Russian trade at Kiakhta was established. By 1760 it accounted for 60 per cent of all Russian trade in the Pacific, and 7 per cent of Russia's total trade.[55]

At the same time as its presence in the Pacific and its land trade were being consolidated, Russia also tried adventures further afield. It set out to grab a share of the lucrative trade in sea otters, the so-called 'soft gold' of Pacific waters. In 1799 a charter was granted to the Russian–American Corporation to hunt for pelts down the American coast into Spanish territory and to establish a series of forts to support that trade. This was the strategy of direct commercial penetration pioneered by the Dutch and the British. However, Russia failed to build the necessary fleet to support such long-distance ventures and the Russians were cautious about antagonizing the British in particular, who were needed as allies in European conflicts. The linkage of European and Pacific securities in Russian policy was a natural problem for a Eurasian power.[56]

Having found the northern sea route blocked by ice, and the land route too slow, Russia looked for other options to reinforce its position in the Pacific. Between 1803 and 1806 Russia's first circumnavigation of the globe under A. J. van Krusenstern set out from Krondstadt. The purpose was to see if Russian Pacific interests could be more easily supplied by sea from Europe. In the course of the voyage, extensive mapping of the still-secluded Japan was accomplished.[57] Russia sent voyages to Polynesia in 1804 and Hawaii in 1809. It even claims to have discovered Antarctica before the United States in 1820.[58] President Jefferson of the new United States declared in 1807 that Russia was its firmest friend because of their common struggle against British and Spanish colonialism. In 1809 the United States and Russia established diplomatic relations.

But Russia was wary and was looking after its own interests. In 1811 it founded Fort Ross, just north of San Francisco, in an attempt to push its

[54] Glynn Barratt, *Russia in Pacific Waters, 1715–1825* (Vancouver: University of British Columbia Press, 1981), 42–74.

[55] Slavinskii, 'Russia and the Pacific', 35–6.

[56] Terence Armstrong, *Russian Settlement in the North* (Cambridge: Cambridge University Press, 1965), 26–30.

[57] Dodge, *Beyond the Capes*, ch. 12.

[58] Slavinskii, 'Russia and the Pacific', 37.

influence down both sides of the northern Pacific. Russia's biggest opportunity came with the collapse of Spanish power in the 1820s. California appeared to be open to Russian influence, but once again Moscow was distracted by events in Europe (particularly those concerning Napoleon) and lacked the fleet to support its aims and to provision its settlers.[59] It was also in competition with US and British interests on the American Pacific coast. Fort Ross was abandoned in 1839 and Russian power retreated to the western Pacific.

Meanwhile, in the eastern Pacific in 1793, Alexander Mackenzie became the first person to cross the North American continent, accomplishing the task for Britain. The 1805 Lewis and Clark expedition was the first to take American explorers out to the Pacific. Also in the first decade of the new century, John Jacob Astor expanded his trading interests in the Pacific. He was one of the first American visionaries about the Pacific, and his complex trade between China, Pacific Russia, the United States, Hawaii, Ecuador, Chile, and Europe was in many senses the first genuinely global commercial operation.

Astor's dream was to break British dominance in the Pacific, and for that he needed an American Pacific port—previous trade was done through Atlantic ports. The founding of Fort Astoria in 1811, and its subsequent conquest by Britain, was both a testament to Astor's vision and an example of the sharpness of great-power rivalry in the Pacific.[60] Astor, like the United States government at the time, saw Russia as a tacit ally in dislodging Britain from its dominance of trade and its spreading power across British North America. The United States was eventually to establish its presence in the Pacific and pursue regular cross-Pacific contacts, although Astor was clearly ahead of his time. Only with the rise of the United States was there the real counter-pressure that was to limit Russian, and indeed British and Spanish, influence. The eighteenth century had clearly been dominated by British power and the few contacts from the United States with the Pacific were carried out from New England and by sea around the tip of South America.[61]

The earliest contacts with California were by sea from the Pacific, making it a separate world from the colonization on the Atlantic coast of North America.[62] Initial rivalry between Britain and Spain in the region had even

59 John Stephan, 'Russian–American Economic Relations in the Pacific' in Stephan and Chichkanov, *Soviet–American Horizons*, 63.

60 Washington Irving, *Astoria: Adventure in the Pacific Northwest* (London: Kegan Paul International, 1987, a reprint of the 1839 original).

61 Ibid., 63; Franklin C. L. Ng 'American Economic Interests in the Pacific to 1945' in Stephan and Chichkanov, *Soviet–American Horizons*, 52.

62 Richard Batman, *The Outer Coast* (New York: Harcourt Brace Jovanovich, 1985).

led to rivalry and the threat of war in Europe in the 1780s. But Spain was soon in retreat and by 1830 the United States and Britain dominated Pacific navigation, sending 500 ships on voyages in that year alone.[63]

The first United States ship engaging in casual trade with Australia arrived in 1792, but it was not until 1813 that the monopoly of the British East India Company was shattered.[64] Initial United States interests were in the fur and whaling trade, and sovereignty and control of territory was not the main objective. By 1820 some three million seals had been killed in the south Pacific alone. The Americans were key players in the slaughter of animals for their pelts, and in the related great-power rivalry. Americans, pioneered by John Jacob Astor, specialized in supplying food to Russian fur traders in exchange for furs which were then sold in China. The new United States became increasingly entangled in Pacific island politics in its search for sandalwood, pearl shells, and sea slugs to trade with China.[65] But as we have seen from other expanding empires in the Pacific, the needs of trade led to the search for bases, which in turn required the control of local people. Beginning in the 1820s, the United States maintained a regular naval squadron in the Pacific.[66]

In the case of the United States, as with that of Russia, the move to the Pacific was both on land and at sea, but it was the land base that was eventually to provide the firmer footing for international interest in the Pacific. In 1803 the United States purchased the Louisiana territory from France, in 1844 it obtained the Oregon territory along the Pacific, in 1845 Texas was annexed, and in 1848 Mexico was forced to give up the vast swathe of land in the Rockies and the California coast. It was of course the 1848 gold-rush in California that gave the sharpest pull to United States interests in the Pacific, laying the foundation for a much more broadly based economy in the area.[67]

To a large extent, the spread of American power was made possible only by the distractions and defeats suffered by key European powers in their wars back in Europe. The Napoleonic Wars in Europe, and above all the invasion of Spain by Napoleon in 1808, had shattered the Latin American world. Encouraged by the spread of liberal ideas from revolutionary France and the United States, the Spanish colonies rebelled against European control. Between 1810 and 1825 nearly the entire Spanish empire was shattered by revolution. Mexico led the way in 1821 and by 1830 Latin

---

63 Dodge, *Beyond the Capes*, 315.
64 C. Hartley Grattan, *The United States and the Southwest Pacific* (Cambridge, Mass.: Harvard University Press, 1961), 71–80.
65 Oliver, *Pacific Islands*, 101.
66 Goetzmann, *New Lands*, 247.
67 Batman, *Outer Coast*.

America had virtually assumed its present political shape except for the five Central American states that were notionally still united until 1838.

The decay of Spain as an American and Pacific power led the United States President Monroe to declare to Congress in December 1823 that European 'systems' should be kept out of the American continent. This Monroe Doctrine was as much focused on those parts of Latin America facing the Atlantic as it was on the international politics of the Pacific. But it was also part of a United States belief in its 'manifest destiny' in the Americas. In 1822 Mexico annexed California but the United States then saw its opportunity to pick up the pieces of the Spanish empire and assert its 'destiny' to dominate the American Pacific. The 1848 war with Mexico cut the Mexican state in half and the United States picked up California for $15 million.

Further north, the British in North America were not giving up their interest in the Pacific, but they were less hasty in their rush to get there. Alexander Mackenzie was the first to cross North America in 1793, but few settlers followed until the United States developed its own Pacific territory. The United States also formalized its position of dominance with British North America in the 1840s. The Washington Treaty of 1846 set the boundary at 49 degrees west of the Rockies and in 1849 Britain declared Vancouver Island a colony and formally took power from the Hudson Bay Company that had ruled Britain's sprawling trading empire. But perhaps the United States' greatest weapon in controlling the Pacific was its ideology of revolution and its opposition to European colonialism. The result was the end of the Spanish empire and the creation of smaller South American states that could be dominated by the United States. To the north, a docile, vulnerable Canada was to emerge as Britain also came to recognize that its days as a Pacific power were ending.

The focus of the Pacific had clearly shifted north, and into the hands of the two newest Pacific empires, the United States and Russia. But unlike previous 'white' intruders, these empires were land based and there to stay. While Russia was arguably an old empire, at least as a Pacific power it was new. The United States was undoubtedly a new power, in fact it was one of only two great powers (Japan being the other) that were to be born after 1500.

Australia and Canada, both set on their course of independence from Britain, also had an influence on the international politics of the Pacific. Latin American states beat them to independence, but remained too fragmented and weak to make a strong contribution to Pacific politics. The older powers of the Pacific were in a state of disarray, unable to meet these vibrant new challenges. Japan was in the isolation of the Tokugawa period refusing to face the new music. South-east Asia was fragmented and dominated by rapacious European empires. China was the saddest case of all. This once proud empire also refused to accept the changing situation in the Pacific. China declined to open up to outside contact, for as the emperor told an envoy from George III of England in 1793, 'our celestial empire possesses all things in prolific abundance and lacks no products within our borders. There was, therefore, no need to import the manufactures of outside barbarians in exchange for our produce.'[68]

Regrettably, that sense of superiority was no longer justified. China was falling behind in most technological spheres as the European world leapt ahead, powered by the industrial revolution. The original explorers of East Asia had been no richer than the 'discovered' and as late as the early nineteenth century the per-capita GNPs of China, Russia, and western Europe were roughly equal.[69] But by the 1850s the development gap was yawning in front of the states of East Asia. When the Chinese were informed of the existence of new lands across the Pacific, the only slight adjustment they made to their maps was to add a few scattered tiny islands across the Pacific to represent the Americas.[70]

China's trade had always been far more valuable than the acquisition of parrots and ostrich eggs as the emperor suggested.[71] But in the nineteenth century China was challenged as never before to open its doors or have them violently prised open by avaricious Europeans. When China refused to open its market to British goods, the result was the Opium War of 1839–42. The resulting Treaty of Nanking forced faltering China to cede Hong Kong to Britain and open five treaty ports to foreigners, free of Chinese jurisdiction. The rape of China had begun.

The arrogant phase of western imperialism in the region was far from the idealistic notion of competition among equal sovereign states. But the Asian-Pacific people were gradually coming to learn that they would have to play by western rules of modernization if they were to stand proudly. By the nineteenth century international trade had become so important and extensive that the 'white' intruders were clearly not going to go quietly. The growing international division of labour was reshaping international relations and the gap between developed and underdeveloped states began to yawn much wider.

Because Asia in general and China in particular had such powerful cultures, they were able to hold off the European influence longer than most

---

[68] Quoted in Braudel, *Perspective*, 145.
[69] Braudel, *Perspective*, 534.
[70] *Chinese and Japanese Maps* (London: British Library, 1974).
[71] G. B. Sansom, *The Western World and Japan* (Tokyo: Charles Tuttle, 1977), 13–18.

other parts of the globe. But by the nineteenth century even Asians had to adapt. The great strength of that cultural tradition was eventually to produce a more robust, multicultural pattern after 1945. But in the meantime there was a century of trauma to be endured. The next phase of Pacific international politics was the story of how China failed the test of modernization, while Japan succeeded with flying colours. The outcome was yet another revolution in the pattern of Pacific politics.

3

1850–1920: The Rise of Japan

On 8 July 1853 Commodore Perry sailed his squadron of 'black ships' into Yedo Bay to force Japan to open its doors to foreigners.[1] The United States had taken the leading role, because it sought base facilities for its expanding whaling interests. But more generally, by the mid-nineteenth century the United States had arguably become the most economically and politically dynamic Pacific power.[2] On 31 March 1854, in the Treaty of Kanagawa signed at Yokohama, Japan agreed to open its ports to the United States, and similar treaties with the envious British, Russians, and Dutch followed within the next two years. The Japanese door had been prised open, but what emerged from behind it was a dynamic people, ready to assert their place as a new great power in the Pacific.

NEW JAPAN AND OLD CHINA

Just as the emergence of the United States and Russia had shifted the locus of Pacific power northward and out of the hands of the West Europeans, so the emergence of Japan reinforced that trend and gave it an Asian dimension. Moreover, Japan was the only 'non-white' power to emerge. In a sense it was the inheritor of the Confucian tradition of dominating East Asia, especially as China was so obviously incapable of the task of leadership in the Pacific.

The reasons for the Japanese success and the Chinese failure in meeting the challenge of modernization are hotly debated.[3] The most important explanation seems to be that China's very strength and superiority over millenniums made its old structure more robust than that of Japan. Like a building with firmer foundations, it was tougher to knock down when making way for a new development. What is more, Japan was more keenly aware of how much of its past came from the outside, especially from China. Thus it was less hostile to outside ideas than Sinocentric China.

---

[1] Curiously for such an important Pacific venture, Perry sailed from Norfolk and went *east* to Japan. The Pacific had yet to obtain a 'natural' American presence.

[2] G. B. Sansom, *The Western World and Japan* (Tokyo: Charles Tuttle, 1977), 276.

[3] Edwin Reischauer and J. K. Fairbank, *East Asia: The Great Tradition* (London: Allen & Unwin, 1960), 601–74.

Furthermore, the very size of China helped keep foreigners on the coasts and away from most of the population for longer than in the islands of Japan. The Chinese political system was also more centralized, thereby preventing foreigners from prospering by 'divide and rule', as they did in the early days of expansion in Japan. Korea shared China's system but lacked its size as a means of protection, so that, when Japan decided to break into Korea, its collapse was swift.

Finally, Japan's essentially feudal structure in the mid-nineteenth century was more like that of the Europeans on the eve of expansion. Thus the role of trade, expansion, and entrepreneurs was more easily adapted to than in the more developed, but equally more ossified, Chinese political system. In combination, all these factors helped ensure that Japan rose to the challenge of modernization, while China sunk into the abyss of internal rebellion and external manipulation.

The modernization of Japan after the Meiji Restoration is arguably the most rapid rise of any great power, matched only by Bismarck's Germany. By 1888 Japan negotiated its first treaty with a western country, Mexico, on the basis of equality and in 1911 the western-imposed extraterritoriality was abolished. Not surprisingly as Japan grew strong and independent, it also emulated western ways in its foreign policy. The obvious targets for Japanese imperialism were neighbouring Korea and China, neither of which was meeting the modernization challenge.

In 1871 Japan signed the Tientsin Treaty with China, thereby gaining similar commercial rights to those held by westerners in China. In 1876 a similar treaty was signed with Korea. But Japan was hardly satisfied with such gestures. It stirred up events in Korea in order to break the Chinese grip and enhance Japan's international standing. Korea traditionally had 'familial' relations with China, while it maintained 'contractual' relations with Japan.[4] In the late nineteenth century China had pushed Korea into more contact with the West, hoping to stave off first Russian pressure and then Japanese imperialism.

Japan was to prove unstoppable. A combination of Japanese mystique about ancient rights in Korea, supported by modernization and western arms, encouraged Japan to seize Korea in 1894 and attack Chinese forces at sea and in Manchuria. The April 1895 Treaty of Shimonoseki declared Korea independent, but in reality it was now under Japanese control. The Liaodong peninsula was ceded to Japan, as was Formosa and the Pescadores.

---

[4] Key-Hiuk Kim, *The Last Phase of the East Asian World Order* (Berkeley, Calif.: University of California Press, 1980), 30.

Japan also expanded the number of its treaty ports in China and, in one fell swoop, became the leading imperial power in China.[5]

The balance of power in Asia and the Pacific was suddenly shifting. European powers, and especially Russia, were alarmed at the new rival's temerity, and forced Japan to give back the Liaodong peninsula in exchange for an even greater indemnity from China. The 'muscular Confucian' foreign policy had brought a new era to Pacific international politics. A new power had arrived. A more intense scramble for the pieces of faltering China had begun and Japan was in the forefront, sending the largest contingent to put down the Boxer Rebellion. The creation of a legation quarter in the heart of Beijing led many to believe, especially in Japan, that the break up of China was imminent. It was an opportunity that Japan could not afford to miss, and was best placed to seize.

But Japan's first experience of regional great-power politics was not without its unhappy lessons. Japan had learned to use military power, but it was slow to learn the finer points of diplomacy, except as a preliminary to the use of force. Japan had been concerned with keeping Russia at bay and picking over the Chinese bones, but it failed to build proper alliances with Britain.[6]

THE RETREAT OF RUSSIA

The main challenge to Japan was not from China, nor even from the European empires, but rather from that hybrid power, Russia, with an old boot in Europe but a new, very restless foot in Pacific waters. In 1855 Russia and Japan had established diplomatic and trading relations but, as Japan grew stronger, Russia recognized that this upstart was more likely to be a rival than an ally in the Pacific.

The last half of the nineteenth century was a period of retreat for Russian power in the Pacific. In 1867 Alaska was sold to the United States for $7.2 million. Russia was unable to afford its far-flung Pacific pretensions, and the United States was seen as a lesser threat than Britain.[7] Russia strengthened

[5] H. F. MacNair and Donald Lasch, *Modern Far Eastern International Relations* (London: D. Van Nostrand, 1950), 54–5. See generally Ian Nish, *Japanese Foreign Policy, 1869–1942* (London: Routledge & Kegan Paul, 1977).

[6] Richard Storry, *Japan and the Decline of the West in Asia 1894–1943* (London: Macmillan, 1979), 27–32.

[7] B. N. Slavinskii, 'Russia and the Pacific to 1917' in John Stephan and V. P. Chichkanov (eds.), *Soviet–American Horizons on the Pacific* (Honolulu: University of Hawaii Press, 1986), 40–2.

its base in Sakhalin, but gave up claims to the central and northern Kuriles to Japan.[8] Russian trade with Japan remained at around 1 per cent of Japan's total, while Britain and the United States led the way in integrating the new Asian power into Pacific economic relations. Russia's premier Pacific port, Vladivostok, founded in 1860, was not living up to its name of 'ruler of the East'.

The retreat of Russian sea power was not, however, a sign that Russia was giving up on Asia. It was merely consolidating its position, leaving the eastern Pacific to the United States and later leaving Pacific waters to Japan. What interested Russia most was the scramble for lucrative bits of decaying China—the 'sick man of Asia'. In treaties in 1858 and 1860 Russia gained territory from China in the Amur basin and access to Vladivostok was eased. With the defeat of China by Japan, Russia wisely calculated that it shared a common interest with China in containing Japan. In a secret treaty in 1896, the two parties agreed to help each other against what was an increasingly confident Japan. Russia was allowed to build railways to the Pacific through Manchuria, thereby increasing the strategic importance of Harbin and Manchuria. Russia saw the railways as a vital 'civilizing' force in Asia, and of fundamental strategic importance for its Pacific position.[9] With completion of the rail lines in 1904, the fastest route from Europe to East Asia was along the trans-Siberian railway.

While the competition to slice up China was a major attraction for both Japan and Russia in the north-east Pacific, their competition was more deeply rooted in the inevitable confrontation of expanding empires. With all the confidence of youth, Japan was determined to make up for the lost time of Tokugawa isolation. But unlike in the Sino-Japanese War, this time Japan prepared its position by forming an alliance with Britain in 1902. While Britain was weakened by the Boer War and concerned about Russian threats to India, Japan wanted greater freedom in Korea and coveted Soviet advantages in Manchuria.[10] Not surprisingly, Japan became known as the 'Britain of the East'. It certainly developed a sense of equality and power with other great empires in the Pacific. The result was the 1904–5 Russia–Japan War.

As a result of the 1905 Treaty of Portsmouth arranged under United States mediation, Russia lost Liaodong, Port Arthur, and the southern railways in China and South Sakhalin. Clearly all the existing powers of the Pacific, except Russia and China, connived in Japan's emergence as a power 'of the junior first rank'.[11] China had been treated harshly by European

[8] John Stephan, *Sakhalin: A History* (Oxford: Oxford University Press, 1971).
[9] Ian Nish, *The Origins of the Russo-Japanese War* (London: Longman, 1985), 2–17.
[10] Storry, *Decline of the West*, 44–51.
[11] Ibid., 73–87; Nish, *The Origins*.

powers, but Japan was showing itself to be every bit as rapacious. With the disdain and arrogance of a successful brother for his failed sibling, Japan despised the faded glory of China. The result was a strong desire to show the world that Asian, Confucian powers could be more independent.

THE UNITED STATES' RESTRAINED POWER

The short-sightedness of Japan's rivals at this time of uncertainty in Pacific great-power politics meant that Japan went virtually unchallenged for the next 30 years. Yet it was already clear to that other dynamic Pacific power, the United States, that Japan was running out of control. Japanese–United States problems were already emerging over restrictions on Japanese immigration in the late nineteenth century. Many villages of Japan's inland sea became emptied like parts of Ireland and Scotland, after large numbers of relatives settled in the United States.[12]

By the time Japan had routed its North-east Asian rivals, the United States had been a major actor in the Pacific for close to a century. It was not by chance that the United States was the first to force open the Japanese door. But in the last half of the nineteenth century the United States seemed more concerned with the islands of the Pacific than with its Asian rim. The chief architect of this new policy was undoubtedly Secretary of State William Seward.[13] His argument in favour of the Alaska purchase was merely part of a broader strategy that coveted Canada and sought to turn the north Pacific into an American lake.[14]

In 1869, after the debilitating and distracting civil war, the United States' rail lines were extended to the Pacific shores, built mostly with imported Chinese labour. In 1871 the trans-Pacific steamship began a regular service, albeit with a subsidy. In 1898 the United States defeated Spain in a brief war and as part of the spoils picked up the Philippines and Guam. The war made plain the close linkage of events in the Atlantic and Pacific theatres for the growing global power of the United States.

The United States' seizure of the Philippines was hardly undertaken for economic reasons, especially in the light of a shortage of capital for domestic development.[15] Its concern was overwhelmingly strategic, eventually tying this acquisition into a string of bases from the United States Pacific coast and

[12] Storry, *Decline of the West*, 100.

[13] MacNair and Lasch, *International Relations*, 104.

[14] William Goetzmann, *New Lands, New Men* (New York: Viking, 1986), 413.

[15] Alfred McCoy, 'The Philippines' in Robin Jeffrey (ed.), *The Winning of Independence* (London: Macmillan, 1981), 43.

Panama out to the East Asian rim. In 1889 United States control over Hawaii was formalized and in 1899 it took partial control of Samoa. With the expansion of naval power and the United States' reliance on steamships, such coaling stations as Midway assumed new strategic importance. In 1890 Alfred Mahan's thesis of the United States as a power with naval priorities was well received by those urging a more powerful United States presence in Pacific waters. In 1904 the first trans-Pacific cable was laid by the United States. With the establishment of United States rail links to the Pacific, its trade there tripled in a few years, setting the stage for new horizons and priorities in its international economic policy.[16] The creation of new ports at Portland and Los Angeles followed the boom in trade.

The United States also developed extensive contact with Asia, but in some senses it was Japan's growing role that supplanted China in United States perceptions.[17] Tens of thousands of Chinese had been imported into the United States during the gold-rush and to build rail lines. This near-to-slave trade meant at one stage that 10 per cent of the population of California was Chinese.[18] But immigration controls, racism, and riots soon put a strict limit on the 'friendship' of the Chinese and American people. The United States remained aloof from the series of bloody wars that accompanied Japan's rise to power. Although the United States had demanded an 'open door' for trade with China, this was not supported by concerted action and certainly was little more than an attempt to ensure its own imperial rights of access in China. There was little genuine support for the independence of China.

The United States was clearly becoming a world power and, much like Russia's rise, this required power in both the Atlantic and the Pacific. But for the time being, the United States and Russia were distant enough to make common cause against other imperial powers. United States–Russian relations were set on solid footing after the Alaska sale, Russian support for the north in the United States Civil War, and United States investment in Siberia in the 1890s. Yet the total United States–Russia trade across the Pacific at this time was still merely 10 per cent of their Atlantic trade.[19]

---

[16] Details from J. Arthur Lower, *Ocean of Destiny* (Vancouver: University of British Columbia Press, 1978), 82–126.

[17] This was certainly true in trade terms. See Franklin C. L. Ng, 'American Economic Interests in the Pacific to 1945' in Stephan and Chichkanov (eds.), *Soviet–American Horizons*, 54.

[18] 200 000 went to California between 1852 and 1875, another 42 000 had gone to Australia by 1859, and 80 000 went to Peru between 1849 and 1957. Eric Wolf, *Europe and the People Without History* (Berkeley, Calif.: University of California Press, 1982), ch. 12.

[19] John Stephan, 'Russian–American Economic Relations in the Pacific' in Stephan and Chichkanov (eds.), *Soviet–American Horizons*, 61–74.

NEW PATTERNS IN LATIN AMERICA

Perhaps the most striking sign of the United States' emergence as a Pacific naval power was the construction of the Panama Canal. With the defeat of Spain, and the need for quicker access to new bases in the Pacific such as the Philippines, the United States set about satisfying its own economic and strategic needs. In 1903 the United States decided on the building of a canal through Panama, and thereby supported a revolt by locals against their Colombian rulers. The canal was completed by August 1914 and the sea route to Yokohama from New York was made 5400 km shorter.[20]

In 1904 President Roosevelt added a 'corollary' to the Monroe Doctrine, declaring that the United States would also intervene in Latin America to keep order and 'civilization'. In 1912 their marines landed in Nicaragua to keep order the United States way and to support the *caudillos* who favoured US interests.

This dominating United States influence in Latin America and down the east coast of the Pacific was still fairly new. Only after the 1890s, when the exploration of North America was complete and enough domestic capital had been accumulated, did the United States turn its gaze south.[21] But unlike in the rest of the Pacific, and especially the more vital north-east, the United States had no great-power rivals in Latin America. In the age of the *caudillos*, there was little to worry the United States.

The only major conflict, apart from the triumph over Spain, was the Nitrate War of 1879–83 between Chile, Bolivia, and Peru. The Chile–Bolivia frontier had never been clearly defined, so Chile used its superior military power to grab the small Bolivian stretch of Pacific coast with its nitrate deposits. Peru, which supported Bolivia, lost territory further up the coast as far as Arica. But this so-called 'War of the Pacific' was badly misnamed. In an age of great-power rivalry in the north-west Pacific waters, this Latin American squabble was largely inconsequential.

CANADA AND OTHER 'COLONIES'

Elsewhere in the Pacific, other signs emerged of the decay of European power and the rise of independent states. The first steps came from Canada where independence was granted by Britain in 1867. On the Pacific coast, British Columbia was merged into the Vancouver Island colony in 1866 and

[20] George Pendle, *A History of Latin America* (London: Penguin, 1976), 176.
[21] Ibid. 128–45.

preoccupied with Bismarck back in Europe, Britain was anxious to relinquish responsibility in north-western Pacific waters. In 1873 a definite border in the west of Canada was set with the United States, but the fear of US encroachment drove British Columbia to join the Canadian Dominion as the sixth province in 1871. Nevertheless, the telegraph lines linking British Columbia to the eastern part of Canada first travelled south to the United States' transcontinental lines.[22] The Canadian Pacific railway was not completed until 1895, while the United States by then had five lines across the same continent.

By the turn of the century, Canada was beginning to stake out its own priorities, all the while firmly under the careful gaze of an interventionist United States. The abolition of the monopoly of the Hudson Bay Company in British Columbia liberalized trade and encouraged links to other British territories across the Pacific. Canada demonstrated its serious intent to join in the politics of the Pacific, albeit a little late, by completing a trans-Pacific cable to Australia and New Zealand in 1903. But in most foreign policy matters, Canada remained guided by Britain's lead well into the twentieth century. For example, Canada was less able than the United States to impose curbs on Japanese immigration because of close Britain–Japan relations.

Elsewhere in the Pacific, the decline of European, and especially British, colonial power was beginning to have more bloody consequences. New Zealand was the only Pacific island territory that had a large enough indigenous population to offer violent and prolonged resistance to British colonialism.[23] Britain began gradually to disengage from the 'cannibal isles', but for strategic reasons the islands could not be abandoned. They were needed as coaling stations, telegraph posts, and simply to keep them out of the hands of such interested parties as Germany.[24]

Thus new reasons were found for staying in the middle of the Pacific, including the availability sugar, coffee, cocoa, fruit, and rubber. New trading companies and eventually settlers followed. France took the lead, with its settlement of Tahiti and New Caledonia in 1853, and soon all the islands except Tonga were under the control of some external power.[25] What followed was the inevitable integration of the islands into the growing world economy and the disregarding of the interests of local people. The colonies of the Europeans in the Pacific ran a large trade deficit with their colonial masters, but managed to balance their trade by running a surplus

[22] Lower, *Ocean of Destiny*.

[23] V. G. Kiernan, *European Empires from Conquest to Collapse, 1815–1960* (London: Fontana, 1982), ch. 7.

[24] Douglas Oliver, *The Pacific Islands* (Honolulu: University of Hawaii Press, 1975), 117–20.

[25] Earnest Dodge, *Islands and Empires* (Oxford: Oxford University Press, 1976), 164–83.

with the United States.[26] Such global trade connections also laid the basis for American influence in the international economics of the Pacific. Although in most cases the population of the islands was altered by European colonists, in no case was the transformation as complete as it was in British America or Australia and New Zealand.

With the fading of Spain from the Pacific, the United States and Germany picked up the spoils, and even Chile joined in by grabbing the Easter Islands. Few local inhabitants could resist the tide. But it was in South-east Asia that western civilization was seen at its most brittle. Superiority in the technology of war and in food, drink, health, and professionalism had ensured control of native colonies for centuries. The opening of the Suez Canal in 1869 certainly eased the communication and control of unruly locals in the Pacific. But unlike the white commonwealth, South-east Asians did not share British and European values and culture. In the long sweep of Pacific history, revolt and independence were inevitable.[27]

In the period from 1853 to 1920, however, the decay of European power was still not always apparent. By 1900 all of South-east Asia was subjugated except for Thailand, which survived as a buffer zone between French and British colonies, and only partially as a result of the skill of its enlightened ruler.[28] The Thais were still forced to surrender such territories as Laos to a self-confident French authority. The local ruling élites in South-east Asia began to be educated in European values of freedom and the 'cancer' of nationalist ideology began to spread. However, fragmentation of the local populations, a natural phenomenon in Indonesia but exacerbated by the colonial power in Malaya, helped ensure relatively smooth colonial government until the 1920s.[29]

The opening of the Suez Canal and full-scale industrialization in Europe combined to help change the trading pattern in South-east Asia. The shift from small, high-value items such as spices to bulk trade in tin, rubber, oil, rice, and sugar helped integrate local economies into global patterns of trade.[30] It was not surprising that these ancient trading peoples should be so closely integrated into the new pattern of global trade. But for the local people, it meant they lay at the mercy of wild international price fluctuations, suffering the frustrations of being under someone else's thumb while having little control over their own resources. Faced with a potent mix of the

---

[26] Michael Schaller, *The American Occupation of Japan* (Oxford: Oxford University Press, 1985).

[27] Ibid., ch. 9.

[28] G. Coedes, *The Making of Southeast Asia* (Berkeley, Calif.: University of California Press, 1966), 169–70.

[29] See various chapters in Jeffrey (ed.), *Winning of Independence*.

[30] Lea Williams, *Southeast Asia: A History* (Oxford: Oxford University Press, 1976), 114–77.

colonists' racism, jingoism, social Darwinism, and economic liberalism, intercommunal tensions, for example in Malaya, not surprisingly grew as a result. The mix was unstable and, although the 1920s was not a decade of revolt, it was already clear that the area was soon to become one of the most unstable in the Pacific.

REVOLUTION IN THE PACIFIC

By the turn of the century, the battering of China had gone on long enough for that country to give up its struggle against modernization. The main push for revolution came from domestic decay, but the incessant hammering on China's doors by Japan, Russia, the United States, and European powers, helped topple the old Chinese order. The republican revolution of 1911 soon faltered, as no coherent alternative emerged to take its place. But at least the first step was taken by China on the road back to great-power status in the Pacific.

While China was split by the effect of revolution, it was given a chance to put its house in order by that other great revolution of the decade, the 1917 Bolshevik uprising in Russia. But unfortunately for China, there remained Japan, anxious to pounce for the spoils of revolution.[31] Its opportunity was made all the greater by the near total distraction of every other rival with the outbreak of the misnamed First World War.

From the standpoint of the Pacific, this was a European civil war that allowed Japan to consolidate its power and further expand its influence. No other power was anxious for Japan to join the war against Germany, but Japan knew it could seize German concessions in China and deal with China before its revolution could take hold. Japan swiftly took the German holdings in Shandong, disregarding China's neutrality in the war. In 1915 Japan presented 21 demands to China, which, had they been accepted, would have reduced China to a Japanese puppet.[32] The upshot of the matter was an even more dominant Japan in the north-west Pacific, even though the 1919 peace conference refused to recognize all Japanese gains in the Pacific. The 21 demands were also a symbol of the anachronism of Japan treating China as a vassal, for Japanese imperialism was expanding just as European imperialism was in retreat.[33]

---

[31] Shinkichi Eto, 'China's International Relations, 1911–1931' in J. K. Fairbank and Albert Feurwerker (eds.), *The Cambridge History of China* (Cambridge: Cambridge University Press, 1986), xiii, pt. 2, 76–92.

[32] MacNair and Lasch, *International Relations*, 184.

[33] Eto, 'China's Relations', 100.

Japan had also led the attack on Russia in 1918, following Lenin's revolution. Japan sent the largest contingent of troops to defeat the Bolsheviks, but was forced to give up its expansionist desires when the allied mission collapsed in disunity over objectives. Japan was the last to withdraw and the most miffed, having stood to gain the most from a carve-up of Russia. By 1922 Japan had withdrawn completely.

But despite Japan's forced retreat in China and Russia, its position by 1920 was incomparably stronger. The European powers were exhausted by the war, and China and Russia were only just recovering from revolutions. Only the United States was able to offer resistance, but its preoccupations were at home, to some extent in Europe, and to an even lesser extent in Pacific waters, rather than on the coast of Asia.

With the rise of Japan and the United States, and the globalization of international trade, the Pacific was becoming a much more integrated area. Some powers had faded, such as Spain and the smaller Europeans, but new states, such as Australia and Canada, were emerging as important actors alongside the stronger powers of Russia, the United States, Britain, and Japan. This was, above all, a period of flux in the Pacific. There was no single system of international order in military, economic, or cultural relations. Not surprisingly, the next 25 years were to be some of the most bloody in Pacific history.

4

1920–1945: The Pacific Revolution

After the First 'World' War, the Pacific basin stood in sharp contrast to Europe. Whereas European powers had been left devastated and exhausted by the unprecedented bloodletting of their 'civil war', the Pacific escaped virtually unscathed. Whereas Europe took revenge on defeated Germany, in the Pacific the war and its aftermath merely enhanced great-power rivalry. In both cases the international scene was unsettled, but in the European case this was because Germany sought a repositioning of the European balance. In the Pacific there was a proliferation of centres of power and therefore nothing that could be rightly called an 'international order'. The rival sovereign states in Europe, which had caused so much disorder and bloodshed, were at least chastened for a while by their recent experience.[1] In the Pacific, the conflagration was still to come, as rival empires sought to shape a new order.

The Pacific between 1920 and 1945 was a zone in flux. At the start of the period, dynamic Japan looked for a new status quo that granted it greater recognition. Confronted by the incoherence of American and other great powers' policies, Japan took the opportunities for expansion.[2] Meanwhile the old empires of Europe tried to play one rival off against another in the age-old tactic of waning powers. Russia, once the most dynamic of the new Pacific powers, spent most of the period engrossed in domestic and European affairs. The United States, the region's premier power, remained in self-imposed isolation. China, the sick man of Asia, was recuperating from abortive revolutions and was a ripe target for Japanese imperialism.

Thus Japan was clearly the empire making the running for most of the period, but only because it was allowed to do so by its dormant or distracted rivals. The First World War had shown just how vulnerable the European powers could be in Asia. Not surprisingly, Japan, as the first modern non-white empire in the Pacific, attempted to reorder Pacific politics in its own image. The result was, of course, failure in the Second World War. But the result was also the undermining of European colonial foundations and the creation of a power vacuum. The great Pacific powers after 1945, the

---

[1] As discussed in Elie Kedourie, 'A New International Disorder' in Hedley Bull and Adam Watson (eds.), *The Expansion of International Society* (Oxford: Clarendon Press, 1984).
[2] Akira Iriye, *The Origins of the Second World War in Asia and the Pacific* (London: Longman, 1987).

United States and the Soviet Union, were then to try their hands at rival schemes for order in international Pacific politics.[3]

TO THE WASHINGTON NAVAL TREATY

It took no special insight to see in 1920 that Japan was the most active challenge to what passed for a status quo in the Pacific. Britain had long recognized, certainly since its 1902 alliance with Japan, that it was best to keep Japan happy if British colonies were to be retained.[4] For a Britain exhausted from the First World War, the concern with Japan was even more strong. But the legacy of the war also left Britain more dependent on the United States. The Naval Conference that opened in Washington in November 1921 was precisely intended to satisfy the mutual American and British desire to control Japanese power, while not having to engage in a costly arms race. Some British allies, such as Canada, concurred, but others, such as Australia, were opposed to this shift to reliance on North American power.[5]

The United States under President Wilson was failing the test of the new Pacific politics, much as it failed in Europe. The United States had the opportunity to undermine Japan's appeal to its fellow non-white Pacific people by genuinely championing a new world order, including, for example, a declaration of racial equality in the covenant of the League of Nations.[6] But pressure from European allies concerned about their colonies, including those in the Pacific, forced Washington to back off.[7]

Japan was therefore increasingly aware of its free hand in the Pacific. Japan had learned modernization, imperialism, and great-power machinations by watching the antics of European empires. As those empires faded, and the remaining potential rivals also failed to challenge Tokyo, it was not surprising that Japan carried on building its empire. It consolidated its control of Korea and picked up German colonies after the war. Its corporations, such as Mitsui and Mitsubishi, spread out in the Pacific.[8] As a result, Japan began to see even greater need to control wider parts of the region, for markets and resources.[9]

[3] C. P. Fitzgerald, *A Concise History of East Asia* (London: Penguin, 1966), 330.

[4] Christopher Thorne, *The Limits of Foreign Policy* (London: Hamish Hamilton, 1972), 25–6.

[5] Richard Storry, *Japan and the Decline of the West in Asia* (London: Macmillan, 1979), 121.

[6] Michael Schaller, *The American Occupation of Japan* (Oxford: Oxford University Press, 1985).

[7] Ibid., 24.

[8] Storry, *Decline of the West*, 100.

[9] James Crowley, *Japan's Quest for Autonomy* (Princeton: Princeton University Press, 1966).

Not surprisingly, Japan's first target was China. But in order to allay the suspicions of other empires about the aims of Japanese imperialism, Tokyo saw the benefit of a formal agreement with Britain and the United States. The result was the 1922 Washington Naval Treaty, the first formal Pacific treaty and the first Pacific arms-control pact at that. According to one observer, this was the first, albeit vain, attempt to formulate a system of security for the Pacific.[10] That it failed said more about the incompatible visions of the powers concerned and the novelty of thinking Pacific. The treaty provided for a ratio of United States, British, and Japanese capital ships of 5–5–3. While Britain and the United States had global tasks for their ships, Japan could concentrate on the Pacific. But more vitally for Japan, no new naval fortifications could be built in the western Pacific, thereby ensuring Japanese hegemony. The United States base at the Philippines was grossly underfortified, as was British-controlled Hong Kong. The agreement also included pledges to recognize existing possessions in the Pacific and, contradictorally, the sovereignty of China.[11]

Although this was the Pacific's first formal treaty, it was next to useless. In reality, the mutual interest in avoiding an arms race and the mutual recognition of Japan's predominance in the western Pacific meant that this treaty merely ratified the status quo. It was not a new form of diplomacy, but rather the addition of the 'diplomacy of confusion' to the already anarchic phase of the 'diplomacy of imperialism'.[12]

Like modern arms control, further treaties were bedevilled by a series of political problems. Most importantly, the great-power rivalry was too uncertain and the definition of threat to security too unstable. What is more, allies had conflicting attitudes and far too much time was spent haggling over minor technical specifications.[13] The treaty was also notable for the exclusion of China and the new Soviet Union from its drafting (neither had significant fleets in the Pacific). Although these two were preoccupied with domestic affairs, it was naïve to believe that an arms-control regime in the Pacific could succeed for any length of time without including these two great powers. In the 1920s, when there were at least five great powers in the region, it was largely a waste of time to shape treaty diplomacy for some but not all regional powers.

Both China and Russia had been invaded by Japanese troops during the war and China in particular felt that the peace treaties had failed to force

---

[10] Iriye, *The Origins*.

[11] Donald Macintyre, *Sea Power in the Pacific* (New York: Crane & Russak, 1972), 183. The region was defined by the line at 110 degrees longitude.

[12] The latter phrase is that of Akira Iriye, *After Imperialism* (Cambridge, Mass.: Harvard University Press, 1965).

[13] Crowley, *Japan's Quest*, 28–48.

Japan to give up the fruits of its imperialism. When Chinese nationalism was to assert itself, it was not surprising that it should be directed in anger against Japan, and with disdain for other empires who had failed to contain Japanese power.

THE UNCHECKED RISE OF JAPAN

So long as Japan had China to pick on, many Japanese imperial instincts were satisfied. But in the last half of the 1920s China was progressively united by Chiang Kai-shek and Beijing fell to his Guomindang in 1927. China then set about undoing the damage of the unequal treaties with a slew of imperial powers, Japan included. While the United States and the Europeans eventually capitulated to Chinese demands to abolish extraterritoriality and China successfully claimed the right to set its own tariffs, Japan dragged its feet.[14] Perhaps more than any other power, Japan saw its role in China as 'civilizing' and vital for the legitimate defence of its interests against plundering Europeans.[15]

Divisions of opinion in Japan on the proper reaction were increasingly apparent. Similar factional politics were also evident in disputes over whether to accept the 1930 London Naval Limitation Agreement. This agreement prolonged the life of the 1922 Washington Treaty and imposed further limits on other types of naval weapon. The more expansionist factions in Japan resented the limits placed on their military power, although in practice they had little to complain about.[16]

Japan's other flank, with the Soviet Union, remained unsettled in the 1920s. With the withdrawal of Japanese forces from Russia in 1922, Communist control stretched across the top of Asia to the Pacific and the Japanese door. Between 1922 and 1938 the far eastern territory of the Soviet Union was given special status and allowed to be somewhat less directly involved in the political campaigns dictated from Moscow. The territory was clearly not seen as a priority in Moscow, but equally Japan was not seen as a pressing military threat.[17] In 1925 Japan recognized the Soviet Union and received coal and oil concessions in exchange for northern Sakhalin. Unlike many western powers, Japan was far less fearful of Communist

---

[14] Akira Iriye, 'Japanese Aggression and China's International Position, 1931–1949' in J. K. Fairbank and Albert Feurwerker (eds.), *The Cambridge History of China*, (Cambridge: Cambridge University Press, 1986), xiii, pt 2, 497.

[15] Thorne, *The Limits*, 33.

[16] H. F. MacNair and Donald Lasch, *Modern Far Eastern International Relations* (London: D. Van Nostrand, 1950), 286–8.

[17] Walter Kolarz, *The People of the Soviet Far East*. (London: George Philip, 1954), 2–12.

ideology.[18] What concerned Japan more was Soviet pressure on China in the late 1920s and the fear that a resurgent Russia would reassert its rights in Manchuria at Japan's expense.

What emerged was a more jumpy Japan, anxious that the new forces in the Pacific were shackling it at every turn. The revolution of rising expectations for foreign policy success based on the experience of previous decades was creating demands that could no longer be met. With the onset of the great depression, the havoc in international trade, and the failure of the United States model for development, more radical voices began to triumph in Japan.[19] Japanese dependence on trade, especially with the United States, was a well-recognized basic flaw in Japanese imperial ambition and a cause of the extreme perceptions of national security.

The predictable flash-point for great-power rivalry and, according to some, the opening shots of the Second World War, was in Manchuria. The territory was coveted by Russia and Japan, although both recognized Chinese sovereignty in this territory north of the Great Wall. Japan eyed the territory as a bulwark against Russia and a source of raw materials and 'living space' for a people crammed into a small island. With Europe distracted by the rise of Germany and Manchuria in turmoil as warlords fought off the centralizing actions of Beijing, Japanese hard-liners saw their chance.

After a stage-managed incident on 18 September 1931, Japanese forces spread out easily across Manchuria, with the larger Chinese forces putting up little that could be dignified with the name 'resistance'. While the League of Nations temporized and then 'investigated' the causes of the invasion, Japan consolidated control. In January 1932 Japan extended its invasion to Shanghai, capitalizing on domestic rivalries in China and the limp-wristed reaction of other world powers. From their ringside seats in still-protected enclaves in Shanghai, western powers watched as Japan levelled the Chinese section of what many called the greatest city in the Pacific. In February 1932 Japan organized the declaration of an 'independent' state in Manchuria—Manchukuo—and declared its own version of the Monroe Doctrine for China. In March 1933 Japan quit the League of Nations.

The pusillanimous response by other powers to Japan's attack on China is largely explained by the particularly complex limits on their foreign policies.[20] Many of these limits were in fact a combination of aspects of their domestic politics. Germany no longer had possessions in China but was an important trading partner with China. France saw China as more of a threat

[18] Storry, *Decline of the West*, 129.

[19] Iriye, *After Imperialism*, 278–80; Thorne, *The Limits*, 38.

[20] The thesis is fully-developed, and the causes of war fully covered, by Thorne, *The Limits*, 39–126.

to its holdings in Indo-China. Holland knew its colonies in South-east Asia were vulnerable and thought Japan could help it hold on. Britain's trade with Japan was increasingly important and, in its appeasing mood, Britain was willing to recognize that Japan had 'special interests' in China and was justifiably aggrieved by the United States' limits on Japanese immigration. The United States was locked in isolation and Russia was distracted by domestic events. Some observers, especially in imperial Europe, looked on Japan's action as a variation on their own imperialism in China. They saw it as a variant of 'internationalism' and viewed Japan as a fellow great power with legitimate great-power aspirations.[21] In the period after 1945 such appeasement was seen for the bogus internationalism that it was. Genuine international security required collective defence against aggression.

Sanctions against Japan could have had a major effect, but both powers with major clout, the United States and Britain, would also have suffered in the short term. The United States had less to lose, even in economic terms, in the Pacific, yet its domestically determined isolationism kept it passive. The limits of other powers' foreign policy left Japan virtually unlimited in its expansion.[22]

The failure of international diplomacy, treaty obligations, or the League of Nations to prevent the dismemberment of China was further evidence of the absence of anything that could be called international order in the Pacific. With Japan now joining the United States and the Soviet Union outside the League of Nations, until 1934, this already marginal body became an irrelevance for Pacific politics.

As Japan stormed out of the League, Hitler assumed control in Germany and firmly focused international attention on Europe. The Pacific world was in disarray, with only the forward push of Japanese imperialism to set the agenda for the local states.[23] From Tokyo's and the extreme nationalists' point of view, there was every reason for Japan to continue its aggressive course.

THE JAPANESE EMPIRE

Japan's acquisition of Manchuria was, of course, an 'informal' addition to its empire. Japan formally controlled Taiwan, Korea, South Sakhalin, Liaodong, and Micronesia in what had been one of the most unusual colonial experiences. Japan was a latecomer to the colonial game and, like

---

21 Developed by Iriye in 'Japanese Aggression'.
22 Ibid., especially 376–419.
23 Akira Iriye, *Power and Culture* (Cambridge: Harvard University Press, 1981), 3–4.

the United States and Russia, took most of its newly acquired territory from its neighbours. But unlike its north Pacific rivals, Japan's new territory was acquired by deliberate decision and by force of arms often in a direct clash with another empire. Furthermore, most of the territories were heavily populated. Although Japan was also unusual in colonizing mostly those who were culturally affiliated to Japan, the subject people were none the less sullen and resentful.[24] Japan's control of Korea was akin to Britain's control of Ireland or German control of Poland.[25]

Because of their proximity to Japan, the pattern of imperialism was different from that of the more distant western powers. Japan tried to integrate the colonies into the Japanese economy and not merely direct their economies towards exports. Such regionalism became more common in the 1920s and 1930s for European colonies, but arguably Japan had set the trend.[26] Tokyo approached the colonies with idealism, as did western powers, but for Japan the ideals began to emerge as an anti-European, pan-Asian co-prosperity sphere. The stress on one race and on Confucianism led Japan to try to wipe out national differences and, at least culturally, to subordinate its colonies to Japanese strategies.[27] Like the Europeans, Japan was quick to see the advantage of resources, trade, and investment that colonies provided.

But on balance, political rather than economic motives were predominant in explaining Japan's colonization.[28] Great-power status was Japan's main objective, although it was far less Kiplingesque than many Europeans about the motive. The absence of significant opposition from other great powers is also a major factor determining the pattern of Japanese colonialism.

The distinctive qualities of Japanese colonialism naturally resulted in a different pattern of control than that exercised by western powers. Japan eventually came to stress economic self-sufficiency, education, central bureaucracies, termination of élite privileges, changes in land tenure, and the placing of the main burden of modernization on the agricultural sector. Students of the Meiji Restoration will recognize the pattern as distinctively Japanese.[29]

By the 1930s, as Japan moved to a war footing, its colonies were

---

[24] This section relies heavily on 'Introduction' in Ramon Myers and Mark Peattie (eds.), *The Japanese Colonial Empire, 1895–1945* (Princeton: Princeton University Press, 1984).

[25] Bruce Cumings, 'The Legacy of Japanese Colonialism in Korea' in Myers and Peattie (eds.), *Japanese Empire*, 486.

[26] Iriye, 'Japanese Aggression', 505.

[27] Mark Peattie, 'Japanese Attitudes Towards Colonialism' in Myers and Peattie (eds.), *Japanese Empire*, 97.

[28] 'Introduction' and Lewis Gann, 'Western and Japanese Imperialism' in Myers and Peattie (eds.), *Japanese Empire*, 499.

[29] 'Introduction' in Myers and Peattie (eds.), *Japanese Empire*, 23–30.

integrated in the effort. Japan appealed to anti-western anti-colonialism by speaking more of pan-Asianism and less of its own colonies.[30] However, the veneer was always transparent. Japan also benefited by taking large proportions of its colonies' food production, but by 1930 the colonies took less than 20 per cent of Japan's industrial exports.[31] This did not mean Japan let its colonies suffer from neglect. On the contrary, Japan's intervention also contributed positively to social mobilization, literacy, urbanization, industry, technology, and centralization.

Yet the frustrated nationalism of the subject people, combined with Japanese authoritarianism and discrimination, left the colonies as rebellious as any western holdings. Japan may have been distinctive in its imperialism, but the end result was similar to the European experience. Japan's period of control was too short to have a deep impact on popular culture and local politics. Certainly the expectation of a natural pan-Asian or pan-Pacific unity against the whites was never near to realization. The Pacific, and even the Japanese Pacific in its widest colonial sense, was never unified in anything but colonial administration. Divisions between cultures, continental and maritime, and types of economy, ensured that, despite its huge power, Japan could not even begin to unify the Pacific. Like Britain and Ireland, such grounds for unity as did exist were present before the colonial stage. Colonialism merely resulted in greater enmity rather than friendship.

COLONIALISM IN SOUTH-EAST ASIA AND ISLAND PACIFIC

Japan's call to the inhabitants of European colonies in the Pacific to rebel may have been self-serving, but it did appeal to incipient nationalism across the southern Pacific. In the period between 1920 and 1945 the rumbling thunder of anti-colonialism grew louder. An only partially intended result of Japan's success in this period was to increase the frequency and intensity of the thunder.

Until anti-colonialism took hold, the Pacific remained dominated by the international relations of empires, not sovereign states. Of course, in the north Pacific the great empires met more directly, with Korea the only major colony. But in the southern Pacific there were no independent states apart from Thailand, Australia, and New Zealand. Anti-colonialism was primarily a struggle in the southern Pacific, and not until it was completed could a genuine system of international relations in the Pacific as a whole begin.

[30] Peattie, 'Japanese Attitudes', 122–4.
[31] 'Introduction' in Myers and Peattie (eds.), *Japanese Empire*, 34.

The weakest links in the imperial system were those held by Holland and France. Some in Holland noted that 'The Indies are the cork which keeps the Netherlands afloat',[32] but the whole imperial construction was fast taking on water. The European population was less than a quarter of a million, or less than 1 per cent of the Indonesian population. With western education and increasing involvement in the local economy, Indonesians began to demand an increasing stake in their own future. To be sure, this anti-colonialism was part of a larger movement, with signs of success most evident in China and India. But in Indonesia, as in other Pacific colonies, the course of anti-colonialism was a distinctive mix of local political culture and imperial practices.

The very name Indonesia ('island India') is a fine example of the peculiar mix of historical factors. 'Indonesia' was coined by a European ethnologist in the late nineteenth century, but adopted by the nationalists in the 1920s.[33] The very notion of unity in this, the largest South-east Asian state was mainly a creation of the centralizing habits of colonial masters. Java, accounting for 40 per cent of the people, had of course been a great independent state with a succession of brilliant kingdoms before 1500. But the potent mix of Islam, animism, and Christianity, on a base of already far-flung islands, was a recipe for disunity. The Dutch organized export-directed industries, such as sugar, rubber, oil, palm oil, and coffee, ruined local economies, and reshaped local politics.[34] With fading Dutch power, the world-wide economic depression, and an emerging local middle-class élite, Indonesia was well on its tortuous way to independence when Japan occupied it between 1942 and 1945. The break in the old colonial order made it impossible to return to the 'good old days' of Dutch colonialism.

France was to hold on to its colonies a bit longer, but the essential causes of the decay of its colonialism were the same. In 1936 there were only 40 000 Europeans in Indo-China, or less than 1 per cent of the local population.[35] The economy was centred on rice and rubber production, directed by the French, managed by the Chinese, but worked by the locals. Even in neighbouring, notionally independent Thailand, a similar economic system prevailed.

But Indo-China was different in that the French had only arrived in the mid-nineteenth century and were less well entrenched. The people it ruled were already split into separate, well-developed political cultures. Vietnam

[32] Cited in Christopher Thorne, *The Issue of War* (London: Hamish Hamilton, 1985), 38.
[33] Anthony Reid, 'Indonesia' in Robin Jeffrey (ed.), *Asia: The Winning of Independence* (London: Macmillan, 1981), 114.
[34] Ibid., 114–21.
[35] John Cady, *The Roots of French Imperialism in Eastern Asia* (Ithaca: Cornell University Press, 1967).

was the toughest nut to crack, largely because its people had long experience in fending off Chinese imperialism. The links to Chinese events also meant that the Chinese Communist struggle for independence and revolution was quickly spread to Indo-China and Vietnam.[36] Like Indonesia, the break in French rule caused by the Japanese occupation was the catalyst for violent anti-colonial revolution.

The strongest European colonizer, Great Britain, was also fading in the 1920–45 period. Its main colony, Malaya, was a potent mix of Chinese, Indians, and Malays, with the economy focused on tin mining and tea and rubber plantations. The Chinese population was emerging as the entrepreneurial class, which created extra problems for those favouring gradual, peaceful decolonization. While the Malays learned about independence from the Indonesians, some Chinese were learning the different example of revolution from China.[37]

Further east in the southern Pacific, the struggle for independence was a study in contrasts. Australia and New Zealand were increasingly independent of Britain, although Australia did not establish an external affairs department with cabinet rank until 1935.[38] But despite their obvious success and wealth, Australia and New Zealand were still operating economies based on the export of agricultural and mineral products to Europe, a pattern not very different from the South-east Asian colonies.[39] Only the phosphate trade, so critical for agriculture, suggested a growing pattern of intra-Pacific trade.

The smaller islands were, by contrast, much more firmly under the control of a number of European, Japanese, and American imperial authorities. Minor trade in palm oil, coconuts or tuna was hardly a reason for holding these islands. Some crops, such as sugar-cane, were harvested by imported Chinese labour, thus complicating the ethnic mix in such places as Hawaii and Fiji.[40] As a result, in both places, as well as in New Caledonia and the Marianas, the local inhabitants were outnumbered by settlers of various types.

---

[36] David Marr, 'Vietnam' in Jeffrey (ed.), *Winning of Independence*, 165–74.

[37] Lee Kam Hung, 'Malaya' in Jeffrey (ed.), *Winning of Independence*, 216–23.

[38] C. Hartley Grattan, *The US and the Southwest Pacific* (Cambridge, Mass.: Harvard University Press, 1961), 147.

[39] Douglas Oliver, *The Pacific Islands* (Honolulu: University of Hawaii Press, 1975), 314. Canada, although in the northern Pacific, was just slightly ahead of Australia in the independence race. The 1931 Statute of Westminster all but gave Canada full sovereignty. In 1905 Britain had turned over its naval bases to Canada and in 1910 Ottawa organized its own navy. Yet in the First World War, Japan provided naval protection for Canadian waters. In the inter-war period the United States clearly took on the dominant military role on the North American coast. See J. Arthur Lower, *Ocean of Destiny* (Vancouver: University of British Columbia Press, 1978), 123–7.

[40] Ernest Dodge, *Islands and Empires* (Oxford: Oxford University Press, 1976), 191.

The only clear trend in the scattered Pacific islands was the tendency to view the area in strategic more than economic terms. Of course, the islands could provide few soldiers for war.[41] But with Japan's new control of former German island colonies in the Marianas and the Caroline and Marshall Islands, it was increasingly important for 'white' empires to consolidate their own bases.

New Guinea was seen as a protective shield for Australia, and Fanning Island was crucial for the Empire Cable linking Canada to Australia. In 1928 the first transpacific flight was made from California to Australia, and the United States began to think about the meaning of air power for future Pacific wars. The importance of securing airbases was obviously the first lesson. Tiny Johnston Island was important only for that reason.[42] Much as the needs of whaling or coaling stations helped determine nineteenth-century strategy, so air power was transforming the geography and politics of the Pacific in the early twentieth century. Tiny atolls became useful merely as landing strips, and by the 1940s air traffic across the Pacific became a regular feature. The 'geographic' time, much like historical and economic time, was rapidly changing.

These 'coconut strategists' began to mould the concept of the Pacific as a unit, at least in military terms. Economic relations were not creating ties between the northern and southern Pacific, although some important east–west ties had been formed. On the contrary, it was the needs of war, or at least the perceptions of strategists, that were making the most immediately important contribution to the concept of the Pacific.

Nevertheless, the perception of the Pacific as a united area was an illusion. As decolonization made clear, what was emerging was a multicultural arena for international politics.[43] In both northern and southern Pacific waters, few states could have even the vaguest hopes of controlling the process of change. That Japan would fail in its attempt to do so was predicted at the time. It may have been clear that colonialism was collapsing under the pressures of new ideologies, new economic relationships, and new technology, but there was little that was coherent to replace it.

The domestic politics of most Pacific states developed in distinctive and often diverging directions.[44] But this very development also created more 'socially brittle' states, subject to the uncontrollable upheavals of modernization. Even the successful case of Japan showed that the rapid urbanization and stress on factory workers as part of a more integrated international

---

[41] Yet some Hawaiian and Maori battalions fought in the First World War.

[42] Oliver, *The Pacific*, 332.

[43] Thorne, *Issue of War*, 47.

[44] Developed ibid., ch. 3; Ernest Gellner, *Nations and Nationalism* (Oxford: Basil Blackwell, 1983).

economy created new political challenges. The economic depression helped deepen the dislocation as well as the rural poverty in South-east Asia. The struggle to modernize was also a struggle to adapt distinct cultural patterns to the new needs of economic change.[45] Some societies, such as China's, had a political culture unable to adapt to anything but the slowest change.[46] For them, revolution was virtually inevitable. For others, such as Malaya, the local culture had been so strongly reshaped that longer-lasting unrest and racial tension was more likely. Whatever the case, the Pacific, and especially its southern part, was in the throes of 'cultural despair' or a 'struggle for the soul of society'. Any expectation that such an atmosphere of international relations could be anything but unstable was likely to be disappointed.

JAPAN'S ROAD TO WAR

The precise causes of the first War of the Pacific cannot be clearly identified. The seeds of unrest, as already seen, were sown decades earlier. The more immediate causes of Japan's aggression were also complex, involving domestic politics, the absence of powerful regional rivals, and the economic and political attractions of imperialism.

In January 1936 Japan walked out of the latest naval arms-control conference, firing the starting-gun for a race in naval and air-force equipment, as well as military fortifications across the Pacific. Military strategists in various parts of the Pacific emphasized the northern Pacific as a theatre of operations, but they also considered allies in the south. From 1935 Britain had turned its back on the Pacific to concentrate on the gathering clouds of war in Europe.

The United States was able to confront Japan more directly, but was unwilling to shed its isolation. President Roosevelt had other priorities in Europe, and the United States was unwilling to take on Japan by itself. The American calculation was that China was the key to stopping Japan, but China seemed incapable of an effective response.[47] The Soviet Union was consolidating its control of Mongolia and was increasingly concerned with Japan's alliance in November 1936 with anti-Soviet Germany. Sporadic border clashes with Japan continued from 1935. Russia then consolidated its relations with China, taking advantage of the new 'official' unity between the Communists and Chiang Kai-shek.

---

[45] Thorne, Issue of War, 56–70.

[46] Lloyd Eastman, The Abortive Revolution (Cambridge, Mass.: Harvard University Press, 1974).

[47] Dorothy Borg, The US and the Far Eastern Crisis of 1933–1938 (Cambridge, Mass.: Harvard University Press, 1964), 522–8.

But Japan was pleased to see that, even though rhetorical concern with its power was growing, in practice the response was timid. China remained the obvious place to expand its influence, while coveting the resources of oil, bauxite, and rubber in South-east Asia. Japan's call for East Asian Co-prosperity was not being answered, but it was an indication of the direction of Japan's unchecked desires.

Japan's decision to concentrate its pressure on China in part reduced the chance of an early conflict with the United States. Japan's continental strategy bought it time, although not peace. The meeting of two imperialisms, those of the United States and Japan, was bound to take place,[48] thus creating the first genuinely Pacific-wide war. But the first stage of the war was a purely East Asian affair. China had developed an ambiguous attitude to the Japanese, despising them as 'East Ocean pygmies' and yet respecting their achievements in modernization. Japan looked on China as a drug-addicted, ailing older brother. The war that followed was not so much 'two tigers fighting' as a wounded, elderly tiger savaged by a young, vicious one.[49]

On 8 July 1937 Japan created yet another 'incident', this time at the Marco Polo Bridge (near Tianjin), and launched a massive attack on China. Chiang Kai-shek was driven to the fringes of Han China, and Japan seized most of China's great cities and nearly all its coastline. It was as if Britain had invaded the rest of Europe and controlled everything as far east as Prague. The conquest gave Japan's new order for Asia its greatest symbol. The Pacific part of the Second World War was begun two years before the war in Europe, and Japan grabbed more territory than Germany was to hold before it foolishly took on Russia.[50]

The Pacific war was, at least until the outbreak of war in Europe, a separate conflict. To be sure there were some interconnections. For example, Japan's enmity with Russia was linked to Russo-German conflict. But the causes of the Pacific war are largely to be found in the long-standing rivalries of Pacific powers, the decay of European colonialism, and the varied domestic politics of local states. In many senses, it was the politics of the Pacific that set the example for the Europeans to follow.

THE COURSE OF THE PACIFIC WAR

The expansion of Japan's war effort in the Pacific would probably have come, albeit more gradually, even if the war in Europe had not begun in

---

[48] Akira Iriye, *Pacific Estrangement* (Cambridge, Mass.: Harvard University Press, 1972).
[49] The reference is of course to Dick Wilson, *When Tigers Fight* (London: Penguin, 1982).
[50] Storry, *Decline of the West*, 147–55.

September 1939 with Germany's attack on Poland. But with Europe and the North Americans distracted by war in Europe, and eventually by the invasion of France and Holland, it was not surprising that Japan accelerated its own invasion plans.

The causes of Japanese expansion, including the vital domestic component, have already been outlined. Japan was also in need of the minerals and fuels that lay invitingly within reach and vulnerable in South-east Asia. In 1939 the United States finally abrogated the Treaty of Commerce and forced Japan to look elsewhere for oil, rubber, and tin. Trade restrictions were tightened further in 1940.[51] The two great imponderables for Japan were the reactions of the Soviet Union and the United States. By securing a non-aggression treaty with Russia in April 1941, Japan felt free to move south. Relations with the United States were clearly deteriorating, but once on the course of war it was difficult to know where to stop.

Part of the Japanese calculation was that the United States, if it found itself standing alone in the Pacific while preoccupied with the German victories in Europe, might tolerate Japan's rise to prominence. But with the Japanese attack on Indo-China in July 1941, the United States froze Japanese assets and revoked Japan's permit to buy American oil. Japan had less than two years' supply of oil left and as a trading nation was fundamentally vulnerable in the case of protracted, large-scale war. War with the United States could not be avoided, and Japan calculated that it was best to strike a pre-emptive blow before the United States could organize its defence.[52] Hence the strike at Pearl Harbor on 7 December 1941. Japan's star was to burn fiercely, but was doomed to fail. It was not that Japan did not know its limits, rather that it manoeuvred itself into having no choice but to face those limits in the most devastating fashion.[53]

Until Pearl Harbor, the Pacific war was really an East Asian war. Although Europeans were involved in the first phase by virtue of having their colonies invaded, the wider war reached the doors of Australia and out to Hawaii. The conflict itself was determined primarily by the ability of the United States economy to support a protracted naval strategy at long distance.[54] This Pacific war was the first to be fought across the expanse of the Pacific, and in a bloody struggle for scattered islands on the way to Japan. The United States was finally to live up to Henry Luce's description of the twentieth century as 'The American Century'.[55]

[51] Macintyre, *Sea Power*, 193–4.
[52] Akira Iriye, *Power and Culture* (Cambridge, Mass.: Harvard University Press, 1981), 4–34.
[53] Storry, *Decline of the West*, 155–9.
[54] Macintyre, *Sea Power*, 196.
[55] Cited in Thorne, *Issue of War*, 25.

Yet the Pacific war remained a side-show for most great powers except China and Japan. Britain lost 30 000 soldiers in the Pacific as compared to 235 000 in Europe. The United States had a somewhat more ambiguous experience. Only 20 per cent of United States casualties were suffered in the Pacific, and as late as September 1942, 40 per cent of the United States public did not know 'what this war was all about'.[56] But at least according to some analysts, until early 1943 the United States viewed the Pacific war as the main conflict and by the end of the year there were 1.8 million Americans fighting there, as opposed to 1.7 million in Europe.[57] The Soviet Union, that other power with divided perspectives, was even less concerned with the Pacific theatre, that is until 1945.

Yet there was a special tone to the way in which the United States waged its war in the Pacific. The shrill rhetoric and racism were much more extreme than in the Atlantic theatre.[58] The mutually shared Japanese–United States image of treachery and biological differences left little room for the image of the 'good Japanese' as there was one of the 'good German' throughout the war. The internment of Japanese in North America was matched in Japan by the mythologizing of its own purity and the ban on all western influences, down to Coty perfumes.

This difference between the two main theatres of war helped encourage the view in the Pacific that this war was not actually part of the Second World War. Japan, with its louder emphasis on East Asian Co-prosperity, certainly stressed the separation from Europe. In November 1943 it organized a conference in Tokyo to discuss co-operation in Great East Asia. But in practice this was little more than the rhetoric of war. Similarly the United States and Britain agreed in August 1941 to the principles of the Atlantic Charter which, despite its name, suggested that the world of racism and colonialism might well change in the Pacific.[59] But all such appeals to grand principles made in wartime were not taken as a firm promise of post-war policy.

Pacific people had heard promises of the end of colonialism before. What was more impressive was the real sacrifice made by Americans slogging their way across the Pacific after the June 1942 Battle of Midway.[60] Japanese control of former European colonies failed to live up to the expectations raised by Tokyo and independence was not granted.[61]

As compared to the European war, the conduct of the anti-Japanese war

---

56 Ibid., 103–22.
57 Christopher Thorne, *Allies of a Kind* (Oxford: Oxford University Press, 1979), 156, 219.
58 John Dower, *War Without Mercy* (New York: Pantheon, 1986).
59 Thorne, *Issue of War*, 114–16.
60 Ibid., 161.
61 Iriye, *Power and Culture* 54–64.

was overwhelmingly directed by the United States. In March 1942 Churchill and Roosevelt agreed that the United States should run the Pacific war while the British ran what combat there was in the Indian Ocean to Singapore. China was placed in the United States sphere and South-east Asia (as it became known at the time) was a 'no man's land'.[62] The United States came to scorn Britain's Asian efforts and, as it pushed towards Japan from the sea, it paid decreasing attention to British and Chinese efforts to attack Japan from Eurasia. The only significant contribution of the land war was to come from the Soviet Union in 1945, but by then the war in the Pacific was all but over.[63]

Until 1945 the only significant co-operation between the United States and the Soviet Union was the provision of Lend-Lease aid to Russia via the Pacific. Convoys to Vladivostok began in 1942 and carried 75 per cent of the tonnage of United States aid. In order to avoid the problem of the Russo-Japanese neutrality treaty, ships built in the United States were used, under Soviet registry and with Soviet crews. Some 15 000 Russian sailors were trained in Alaska and American airmen in the air war over Japan made discreet emergency landings in Russian territory.[64] The 2500 km highway linking Alaska and Canada was completed in 1943, which allowed the easier flow of aid and the closer integration of the north Pacific.[65]

Apart from promoting the rise of the United States as the first genuine Pacific power, the war also gathered those thunder-clouds of nationalism in European colonies into still more menacing patterns. Japan's easy victory over the Europeans demonstrated the weakness of the white man. Cohabitation with Vichy French authorities in Indo-China for a number of years suggested that the Europeans did know how to share power. Britain's arming of Chinese guerrillas in Malaya taught the locals how to fight against a more powerful enemy, skills that would soon be turned on the Europeans.[66] In general, the South-east Asians were politicized by the Japanese occupation in a way that the mere defeat of Japan could not undo.[67]

The colonies never really took to Japanese occupation. The Philippines was already well on the way to independence before the United States was forced out, and most felt the Americans would soon return, as MacArthur promised. Japan was also unlikely to take the Philippines' key sugar exports.

---

[62] Thorne, *Allies*, 135.
[63] Ibid., 296, 407, 526.
[64] John Stepham, 'Russian–American Economic Relations in the Pacific' in John Stephan and V. P. Chichkanov (eds.), *Soviet–American Horizons on the Pacific* (Honolulu: University of Hawaii Press, 1986), 75–80.
[65] Lower, *Ocean of Destiny*, 145.
[66] Milton Osborne, *Southeast Asia* (London: Allen & Unwin, 1985), 118–56.
[67] Lee, 'Malaya', 224.

The war left Manila the most devastated major city after Warsaw, but 'consecrated' United States–Philippines friendship.[68] In Indo-China, Vichy forces were not deposed until March 1945 and so the colonial link was maintained longer there than anywhere else in South-east Asia. But Ho Chi Minh's forces did take over in August 1945 until the French returned, and thereby gained valuable experience and higher expectations.[69]

Thus the Pacific war, unlike any previous conflict or event, touched nearly every part of the region. Only Latin America was able to escape in splendid isolation from the blood-letting across both oceans.[70] From mid-1942 it was becoming clear that the United States would replace Japan as the major power in the Pacific and that the Europeans were bound to withdraw from the area. But the role of Asia's other two great empires, China and Russia, was less certain.

By virtue of its European contribution and its Pacific geography, the Soviet Union earned a place in the consideration of how to defeat Japan. The United States had become the arbiter of the China theatre, but Russia would benefit by the post-1945 rise of the partly Soviet-supported Communist Party of China. Another uncertainty was what Russia would do in the Pacific after Hitler was defeated in Europe. The United States knew that the Soviet Union could take what it wanted in mainland North-east Asia and so it was best to involve Moscow in wartime planning. The United States recognized the importance of land power in Asia, suggesting that Mackinder rather than Mahan was right about the basics of Pacific power. Thus the United States was forced to reconsider its relative neglect of the fate of China.[71]

The United States also feared a bloody fight for every inch of Japan's home islands and so wanted Soviet help in the Pacific war.[72] At Yalta in February 1945, it was agreed that Russia would join the war and in return get southern Sakhalin, the Kuriles, the lease of Port Arthur and its rail interests in Manchuria. The United States was clearly not very keen to protect Chinese interests and was prepared to tolerate a variation on Europe-like spheres of influence.[73] The idea was that a balance of Russian and Chinese power would allow the United States to dominate the Pacific. But 'the loss of China' to Russia would ruin that neat model. At Potsdam in August 1945, Russia also agreed to enter Korea.

The dropping of the atom bomb and the sudden ending of the war in the

68 Alfred McCoy, 'The Philippines' in Jeffrey (ed.), *Winning of Independence*, 55–7.
69 Marr, 'Vietnam', 191–203.
70 George Pendle, *A History of Latin America* (London: Penguin, 1976), 183.
71 Thorne, *Issue of War*, 230–30.
72 Gabriel Kolko, *The Politics of War* (New York: Random House, 1968), especially 535.
73 Iriye, *Power and Culture*, 230–2.

Pacific only partly invalidated the United States' concern with getting Russia into the war. The Soviet invasion of Manchuria would probably have taken place in any case.[74] By the end of the war, the United States was certainly confident that it held a dominant position in the Pacific. Especially compared to the obvious problems of achieving a post-war settlement in Europe, the Pacific looked like becoming an American lake. As the American slogan in the war had it, 'to be specific, its our Pacific'.

The racist thread in the relationship between Japan and the United States was suddenly replaced by the new stereotype of Japan as 'the good pupil' and by Japanese Prime Minister Yoshida's notion of 'winning the peace' through American paternalism. The emergence of a Communist threat in Asia—as in Europe—helped reshape images in the Pacific as it did in the Atlantic. But the negative images left over from the Pacific conflict went deeper, and the foundations on which to build a new common ethos and alliance were far shakier.[75] With the rise of Japan as an economic power in the 1960s, the fragile basis of this friendship would once again become apparent.

Of course, the Europeans did return to their colonies but virtually every state and movement knew that there was no return to the political status of before the war. The United States loomed large in post-war calculations, taking over the dominant political and economic position in relation to Britain's old colonies, even in Australia.[76] Australia had emerged as a more important Pacific actor than smaller European nations such as Holland. As Britain failed to regain its past Pacific 'glory', Australia emerged as a genuinely independent Pacific actor.

In summary, by 1945 the basic pattern of politics in the Pacific had been revolutionized by the first Pacific war. Over 2.5 million Japanese had died; China lost 1.5 million soldiers and tens of millions of civilians. All Pacific societies suffered grievously, except for the United States, Canada, Australia, New Zealand, and Russia's far eastern territory. Some 4 million Indonesians reportedly died in a war-related famine.[77] Japan, the former dominant actor, was devastated, but its economy was reoriented to heavy industry in a way that would set the basis for its eventual rise to the status of an economic superpower.[78] In general the pace of industrialization and the move from the countryside to the cities was forced by the war, giving the United States a huge push forward and once again widening the gap between

[74] These issues are discussed in Kolko, *Politics of War*; Herbert Feis, *The Atomic Bomb and the End of World War Two* (Princeton: Princeton University Press, 1970). See also Thorne, *Allies* for a careful discussion.

[75] Dower, *Without Mercy*.

[76] Thorne, *Issue of War*, 198–225.

[77] Ibid., 258.

[78] Chalmers Johnson, *MITI and the Japanese Miracle* (Stanford, Calif.: Stanford University Press, 1982).

the developed and underdeveloped states.[79] Government ownership was extended and government became more closely related to people's expectations and daily lives. The groundwork was set for the startling success of the Pacific economies, even in the midst of the wars to follow.

In international terms, the high level of instability in the region was only partially changed by the short-term preoccupations with post-war recovery. The instabilities of decolonization, economic modernization, and superpower rivalry were still to come, and all of them only marginally less unstable influences than those that dominated the inter-war period. As James Joll noted, 'history moved too fast for our comfort'[80] as geographic, economic, and political time raced forward during the war. The Pacific may have been revolutionized, but it still could not live up to its name.

By far the most obvious change in international terms was the emergence of the two superpowers and the outbreak of their cold war. Most of the rhetoric of the Iron Curtain was Eurocentric and inapplicable to the Pacific. But the superpower confrontation was at least more simple than the inter-war diplomacy of confusion, even if it was less applicable in the Pacific than in Europe. What made the difference was the clear predominance of the United States, in terms of territory controlled, economic clout, and political influence. As an American official put it to a visitor from London, 'It is now our turn to bat in Asia.'[81]

79 Thorne, *Issue of War*, 251–2.
80 Cited ibid., 320.
81 Cited ibid., 206.

II

CULTURE AND IDEOLOGY

Culture and its often-related ideology can be seen as the basis of politics. In international politics the culture and ideology of states often lies at the heart of patterns of alliances and conflict. While conflict between East and West in Europe is not entirely ideological, it is certainly impossible to appreciate the depth and dimensions of the antagonism without understanding the ideologies that divide and unite. Similarly, the European Community and the special relationship across the Atlantic have deep roots in shared cultural and ideological experience. The notion of an Atlantic community is first and foremost cultural and ideological.[1] The economic and military systems that seem to dominate the relationship are mere products of those shared values.

Similar cultural and ideological factors are said to operate in attempts to organize the Arab world, and in other regional structures such as the Organization of American States. Yet these attempts at integration are often far less successful than in Europe and the North Atlantic, in part because, while certain cultural factors may indeed be shared, at the same time differences persist over ideology.

Thus any discussion of a modern Pacific community needs to begin with cultural and ideological factors.[2] To what extent are there cultural affinities among the peoples and states of the region, or is the pattern one of cultural pluralism? Do Pacific people conceive of themselves as 'Pacific', or do they have other, more dominant national and international perspectives? It is possible to appreciate the extent of the patterns of Pacific basin international politics only by understanding the basic patterns of cultural and ideological politics. This difficult task is rarely quantifiable and is approached here by assessing the patterns of language, religion, ideology, tourism, immigration, the arts, and social affairs in the region. While no pattern of Pacific-wide international politics emerges, there are important relationships that bind parts of the Pacific and other issues that create firm bonds with states and interests beyond the Pacific.

[1] Of course, the values are neither shared by all nor uniform, and have developed over time. See a discussion in A. J. P. Taylor, *Europe, Grandeur and Decline* (London: Pelican, 1987); Philippe Wolff, *The Awakening of Europe* (London: Pelican, 1987).

[2] The broader issues of regionalism and culture are discussed by Eric Wolf, *Europe and the People Without History* (Berkeley, Calif.: University of California Press, 1982).

5

Thinking Pacific

What is the Pacific basin: is it more than a geographic expression? As we have seen, a geographer has a neat answer to this question, and certainly a neater answer than is possible in defining what is Asia.[1] The historian has a similarly simple task, for we know that the Pacific was not known until a European navigator, Ferdinand Magellan, sailed across it and conferred a name on its vast waters. Yet for everyone else, the problems only begin with such answers. Unlike the debate over 'what is Asia', there is agreement on what is the Pacific. The real problem is whether the term should be anything more than a geographic label of convenience.

The politics of the Atlantic demonstrate that geographic concepts can take on important economic, political, and military significance. Although both oceans were 'discovered' within a generation of each other, there can be little doubt that the inhabitants of the lands along the shores of the Atlantic have managed to build genuine international communities. By contrast, few would argue that there is now a Pacific community in cultural and ideological terms. Perhaps a fairer question would be, are there signs of a developing Pacific community?

The terminology of international politics often reveals a great deal about the cultural and ideological bedrock. The term 'East Asia' is at least a geographically accurate description of where most people of the Pacific live. The more loose term 'the Far East' is now largely discredited as indicating a narrowly European perspective of the globe.[2] The older, Greek and Roman concepts of Asia Minor and Asia Major were no less ethnocentric and are thankfully virtually unused today. Yet they do draw on the Assyrian name 'Asia', which is at least ethnically neutral.[3]

The western Pacific, of course, has a much longer tradition of civilization, and thus self-definition. The eastern Pacific, loosely called 'the Americas', is

---

[1] 'What is Asia?' in *Far Eastern Economic Review* (12 February 1987); more generally, Edward Said, *Orientalism*, (London: Penguin, 1978).

[2] Of course the term continues to be used by such prestigious publications as the *Far Eastern Economic Review*, even though it is published in East Asia (Hong Kong). The term 'Middle East' has been adopted by most of the inhabitants of the region, even though it is another European-centred concept.

[3] 'Asia' and 'Europe' are both names of Assyrian origin, meaning 'sunrise, east' and 'sunset, west' respectively.

so-named because of a relatively obscure Spanish navigator, Amerigo Vespucci. This Pacific coast is almost never described as West America (as in East Asia), let alone the East Pacific. The islands between the great land masses of Asia and America derive their modern names primarily from European colonial experience, although many have been 'nationalized' since the 1970s.[4]

By force of historical usage, the term 'Asia' has become well understood as describing the area of the Eurasian land mass east of the Ural Mountains. Although it is culturally and racially meaningless, the term is at least understood. It has lost its pejorative connotation from colonial days, and has even been used at times by China and Japan as a way to appeal for anti-European unity. Yet some, including a modernizing Japan in the early twentieth century, saw the term as a synonym for backwardness.

If the term 'Pacific' is to have any meaning, it somehow must merge the meaning of Asia with that of America and the islands in between. Although the Americas, Australia, and New Zealand were once neo-Europes, with the emergence of the United States of America as a major power they have adopted some neo-American qualities while emerging as relatively unique societies. But the gap between the neo-Europes and Europe is small compared to the cultural and ideological divides of the Pacific.

PROBLEMS IN DEFINING CULTURES

Before assessing the roots of Pacific culture, it needs to be acknowledged that culture is constantly changing, especially in recent decades. The causes of change are diverse, and of course affect European or Atlantic communities as much as they do Asian or Pacific ones. Some countries, such as Laos, are more isolated from the causes of change. Others, like Japan, were once extremely insular but have become highly adaptive to modern trends for well over a century. A number of other states, such as Singapore, are new, with few 'national' cultural roots.

Perhaps the greatest force for cultural change is education. For some, such as Pacific island communities based on oral tradition, the introduction of literacy challenged existing political order and made available a wider degree of knowledge about the outside world.[5] When modern technological

---

4 Adrian Room, *Place Names of the World* (London: Angus & Robertson, 1987). Thus naming Pacific places is only a recent trend, and often suggests more wishful thinking than genuine reflection of reality. Few publications use the name, although the *Pacific Review* or *Pacific Affairs* have become increasingly trendy.

5 D. M. Topping, 'Identity and Literacy' in *Pacific Perspective*, 12/2, 41–3.

trends are added, the pace of education can increase and the range of information widens. Of course these trends can both break down small cultures in order to build wider, regional ones, as happened in Germany, and also break down larger cultures using the differing pressures of new ideas, as happened in the Arab world.

It is a sacred principle of such international institutions as Unesco that education is central to development and modernization. But that very education often smashes existing cultures and the most easily available replacement values are derived from the western world or, more specifically, North America and Europe. Once having opened a sealed cultural world, there is no controlling the types of breeze that will blow or the benefits and problems they will bring. The hopes for 'one world' through education often bring fragmentation and alienation, at least in the short term.[6] One-world publications such as Unesco's *Courier* are inevitably advertisements for diversity rather than unity. The reality is cultural pluralism at best, with only the vaguest sense of common reference points in the distance.[7] In the terms of the MacBride report on the new international information order, if there are 'many voices' it is hard to see how there will be 'one world', let alone one Pacific or even East Asian culture.

To complicate matters further, changes in culture happen unevenly. As sociologists remind us, the impact of the outside world will affect different people in different ways, and change at the level of the individual is not necessarily immediately evident at the level of a social system or entire culture. Depending on such factors as race, education, financial status, or even location of one's home, alien cultures can have very different impacts.[8] Such a syncretic process has been common in South-east Asia where Hindu, Chinese, Islamic and finally western culture struck different parts of society in different ways.

Even within individuals, the challenges leading to cultural change can be diverse. Especially among early generations experiencing the first impact of new cultures, the conflicting pressures can be acute. For example, the challenge of a dynamic western approach to power and technology tends to create a dominant culture of empirical thinking. In the period of transition from older cultures, confusion often results, especially where the results of technological success and modernization have not yet become fully apparent.[9] Thus it can be argued that, whereas Japan and Korea have adapted

[6] Sean MacBride, *Many Voices, One World* (London: Kegan Paul for Unesco, 1980); C. Geertz, *The Interpretation of Culture* (New York: Basic Books, 1973).

[7] 'The Cultural Global Village' in *International Herald Tribune* (16 October 1987).

[8] Koentjaraningrat, 'Intercultural Relations in Asia' in *East Asian Cultural Studies*, 16/1–4 (March 1977).

[9] Dargush Shayegan, 'The Challenge of Technology and Cultural Identity' in *East Asian Cultural Studies*, 16/1–4 (March 1977).

more smoothly to cultural change, many South-east Asian states have not. In part because of a stronger nationalism in these two North-east Asian states, they were better able to manage the process of cultural change.[10]

There is also the problem of knowing where to look for a Pacific cultural identity. There may well be such a phenomenon as a 'pan-Pacific person' haunting the corridors of regional organizations or inhabiting institutions such as Hawaii's East–West Centre. But these people, if only by virtue of their education abroad, wide travel experience, and often mixed ethnic origins, are atypical of their original society.[11] The more developed their home society, the more typical they are likely to be. Certainly the Eurocrat is a less peculiar person in Europe than a 'Pacrat' in the Pacific.

THE CULTURE OF LANGUAGE

Cultures change, especially under modern pressures of education and technology, but perhaps the most enduring and important indicator of cultural patterns is language.[12] In Europe, the imperatives of war and the web of immigration spread all the major European languages across the continent and across the Atlantic. English, and to some extent Spanish, remains dominant in the Atlantic community, although the situation within Europe is not as simple.

In theory, the European Community operates a system of language equality—a seemingly perverse process whereby as the Community expands so does the number of languages used and the piles of papers generated. In practice, the Community functions in English and French and most Eurocrats speak both. The West European system is, in fact, much like the United Nations, where there are five official languages and all members conform by speaking one of them. Officially at least, this is a more integrated system than in the EC and, considering the number of members of the United Nations, it does encourage far more co-operation.

Of course, the third model for international communication is the use of one language. Leaving aside the fringe adherents of Esperanto, the only language to have moved to such international status is English. Especially for states of the developed, capitalist community, the early lead of Britain and now the dominance of the United States has put English in this leading

10 Chie Nakane, 'A Comparative Analysis on Sociological Contexts in Asia' in *East Asian Cultural Studies*, 16/1–4 (March 1977).
11 R. G. Crocombe, 'The Pan-Pacific Person' in *Pacific Perspective*, 12/2.
12 David Crystal, *The Cambridge Encyclopedia of Language* (Cambridge: Cambridge University Press, 1987).

position.[13] To the extent that the Pacific is integrated along the lines of the international market economies, then it is logical that English should emerge as the integrative language of the Pacific. But simply because many people in the Pacific understand rudimentary English, that does not make them happy about its influence and many are reluctant to use it in business.[14]

Needless to say, there are a number of reasons to challenge this assertion of the dominance of English. In absolute numbers, of the four major languages in the region, English as the mother tongue is the smallest.[15] Chinese dominates, accounting for some 55 per cent of the population of the Pacific basin. Of course, Chinese is itself divided into major dialects, with some 750 million speaking the major dialect, Mandarin. Chinese is concentrated in China itself and there is only a significant diaspora in South-east Asia.

There are an estimated 15 million Chinese in South-east Asia, constituting a mere 5 per cent of the population. There are wide variations within states, for example Malaysia's population is some 35 per cent Chinese by origin, whereas less than 3 per cent of Indonesia is Chinese-speaking.[16] These Chinese are increasingly acculturated and are also divided by class and by the particular region of China from which they came. They are generally better off than the majority population and they do share a sentimental attachment to mainland China. The Chinese have also spread across the Pacific, with significant Chinese communities in major cities of the northern part of the eastern Pacific. Yet these American 'Chinatowns' are small by South-east Asian standards and at most are a thin bridge across the Pacific. The numbers of Spanish speakers along the Pacific coast of California, the largest of the various Asian communities in the United States, is three times that of the combined Asian communities. In 1970, 7.8 million United States citizens had Spanish as the mother tongue, compared to 6 million for German, 400 000 each for Japanese and Chinese, and 200 000 for Tagalog.[17] Nevertheless, the spread of English to Asia has not gone entirely unmatched by Asian influence in North America.[18]

The second-largest language group is loosely called 'Malay' and covers Malaysia and Indonesia.[19] It constitutes some 9.5 per cent of the people of

[13] Takao Suzuki, 'Language Barriers Between Japan and the Countries of Asia' in *Asia Pacific Community*, 27 (winter 1985).

[14] *Asiaweek* (2 August 1987).

[15] Numbers calculated from the appendix in Crystal, *Language*.

[16] Milton Esman, 'The Chinese Diaspora in Southeast Asia' in Gabriel Sheffer (ed.), *Modern Diasporas in International Politics* (London: Croom Helm, 1986).

[17] Crystal, *Language*, 36.

[18] *Los Angeles Times* (9 November 1987).

[19] More properly called Austronesian and with 500 languages including those in Polynesia, Micronesia, and South-east Asia.

the Pacific but hardly counts outside its heartland. The two countries agreed to a standard spelling in the 1970s but this has yet to take hold.[20] The third-largest language, Spanish, is spoken by some 9 per cent of Pacific people and is only somewhat more widespread. The dozen countries of Latin America are the core of this group and close to half the numbers are accounted for by Mexico. Although many people argue that Latin America is not yet a genuine part of the Pacific community, it does have language contacts across the Ocean. By virtue of the Spanish colonial experience, the language retains a foothold in the Philippines, albeit of ever-shrinking size.

Some 18 per cent of Pacific people speak a wide range of other languages, notably 6 per cent speaking Japanese, 3 per cent speaking Korean, and another 3 per cent speaking Vietnamese. The Pacific islands constitute a negligible percentage of the total population of the Pacific, but the region is perhaps linguistically the most complicated in the world. There are more than 2000 distinct languages, with the greatest concentration in New Guinea where few are spoken by more than 10 000 people.[21] But beginning with the influence of western missionaries, and now under the influence of new technologies of communication, this diversity is giving way to variations of pidgin English. For example, in 1981 Tok Pisin became the lingua franca of Papua New Guinea and, as English becomes a key to wealth and power, many of the tiny local languages have begun to die out.

Therefore we return to English, a language that 400 years ago was spoken by only some 7 million people on a distant, foggy island tucked away off the coast of western Europe. Now it is spoken as a mother tongue by some 9 per cent of Pacific people. These are concentrated in the United States, Canada, Australia, and New Zealand, but English also reaches across to Singapore where it is an official language and the Philippines where American influence is strong and English is spoken to some extent by 35 per cent of the population.[22] Calculated on a world-wide basis, and if the assessment is made by the working use of the language rather than simply as a mother tongue, English is the most widespread language. By such accounts, more people speak English than Chinese around the world, and certainly the language is used in far more countries.[23] It is estimated that one-quarter of China's billion or more brains were learning English by the 1980s. It also

[20] *South China Morning Post* (15 July 1987).

[21] S. A. Wurmn, 'Social and Political Roles of Some Languages in the Pacific Area' in *Asian*, 13 (October 1984).

[22] *International Herald Tribune* (3 December 1987).

[23] 1.4 billion speak English as opposed to 1.1 billion speaking Chinese, with English spoken in some 63 countries and Chinese in only 5. French is only spoken by some 220 million but it is spread in 40 countries. Details reported in the *Financial Times* (21 February 1987). See somewhat lower figures for all concerned in *The Economist* (20 December 1986); Crystal, *Language*, 287.

appears that when Japanese investors in South-east Asia conduct business in a foreign language they use English. By the 1980s the Malaysian campaign against the use of English had been stopped. English is increasingly recognized as the language needed to create a successful basis for international commerce.[24]

The reasons for the spread of English are closely related to the extension of first British and more recently American power. It has been assisted, so the linguists tell us, by the natural advantages of English, for it is a language that is easily spoken badly.[25] It is used as the official language of the European Free Trade Association even though none of its members speaks English as a mother tongue. Its Secretary-General says 'using English means we don't talk too much, since none of us knows the nuances'. Japanese firms like Nissan write international company memos in English. International aid agencies, international air-traffic control, and the International Olympic Committee communicate in English.

This very loose use of English is also its greatest strength in the Pacific. It is not so much that English is replacing indigenous languages, but rather that English is supplementing them. It is estimated that Japanese has some 20 000 English words in regular use.[26] Japanese advertising has a strong English tone, with words like *aisu kurimu* (ice-cream) and top-twenty songs with English titles. The culture of popular entertainment that seeks to adapt words from the United States or Britain has serious trouble in translating 'baby-baby love' and so adopts them undigested. English-language gibberish in Japanese advertising is well known for such things as the following advertisement for soft drinks: 'I feel Coke and sound special.'[27]

The variations of English even extend to the countries using it as a mother tongue. Canadians have long struggled with their mainly British heritage and American neighbour, producing such delicate compromises as 'tire centre'.[28] Australian English has adopted a number of Aboriginal words but the language has been mainly affected by Americanisms since the last half of the nineteenth century. Like Canadians, and unlike the United States, there is remarkable uniformity within the country. New Zealand's English in some senses has more in common with the English of the Falkland Islands than Australia and is certainly more British than American. Singapore's English, or 'Singlish', is rapidly evolving into a distinctive variant, borrowing heavily from Malay and Chinese.

---

24 *South China Morning Post* (15 July 1987).

25 Details in *The Economist* (20 December 1986); Robert McCrum, William Cran, and Robert MacNeil, *The Story of English* (London: Faber & Faber, 1986).

26 McCrum, *English*, 32. It is also noted that some Japanese words have made it into English, such as 'honcho'.

27 *The Economist* (31 October 1987).

28 Details ibid.

English is, of course, ever-changing and its contact with the Pacific has already helped enhance its vocabulary. From the colonial days there is 'amok' from Malaya and from China 'tea', 'kowtow', 'squeeze' and 'Shang-haied'.[29] From the Korean War the language has received 'brainwashing' and 'chopper'. The influence was first felt in American films, then in radio and television, all making their way back across the Pacific from California and Hollywood. The Vietnam War gave the English language 'napalm', 'fire-fight', 'domino theory', 'pacification', and 'air support', the euphemism for bombing. From the computer field, California's Silicon Valley has given the language 'interface', 'online', 'to access' and, of course, the need to be 'computerate' (computer literate). The newswires of Associated Press from the United States and Reuters from Britain have to 'translate' into each other's English.

The variations in the language are already well known, but they do at least allow basic communication and the partial demolition of the regional towers of Babel. There is certainly no evidence that a common language of commu-nication reduces conflict. Equivocation, lies, and babble flourish in English as much as any other language. But as an overlay to existing languages and cultures, English offers more scope for exchange of ideas and commerce. It is evolving into a two-tier language, with an International Standard as mostly an aspiration and a Local Alternative as the practice in many Pacific cultures. If, as seems likely, computer literacy is linked to knowledge of English, then English will be an important means of Pacific integration, but all the while retaining important regional characteristics. Thus there is no language basis for a Pacific culture, as there is across the north Atlantic, but there are distinctive sub-regional patterns and an overlay of global English.

RELIGION

While language is considered a strong guide to culture because all but the mute speak, religion is a less useful guide. Not everyone need be a believer. There is certainly evidence from the developed, western world that modern-ization tends to undermine religion and that much observance is more ritual than a genuine expression of belief. If some religions are less demanding, then they may be more easily adhered to, even though such adherence may be largely meaningless.

Europe has been the source of myriad religious wars as Christians massacred Jews, fought Muslims, and then the divided themselves into

---

[29] *Hobson-Jobson* (London: John Murray, 1903).

Protestant and Catholic factions. When colonizing the Americas, God and gold were main motivations and thus religion and its Christian conflict were brought to the New World. The Protestant British were squeezed between Catholic France in Canada and Catholic Spain in Latin America.

Since religious wars have largely given way to conflicts of ideology, religion has become a limited source of unity within Europe and between Europe and the Americas. In a world of rising Islamic fundamentalism, Christians tend to stress their common heritage and talk of ecumenism is rife. After the holocaust of the Second World War, even the Jews are included in a new 'Judeo-Christian' unity. Although most people in the Atlantic community are not active believers, they do now stress a common religious heritage.

The religious picture of the Pacific is much more fuzzy. The largest group of active believers is the Christians, comprising some 330 million people mostly in the Americas. Apart from the 35 million American Protestants, and others in Australia and New Zealand, the vast majority of these Christians are Catholics. Thanks to Spanish colonialism, Catholics dominate Latin America and the Philippines. Other significant Christian communities, for example in China or Korea, are also the result of European influence, but they constitute small percentages of modern East Asian societies.

The second-largest identifiable religion, and perhaps the most active, is Islam. Its adherents number over 170 million, with the vast majority in Indonesia, the world's largest Muslim state, several million more in Malaysia and the Philippines, and even some 3 million in China. Considering the recent wave of Islamic fundamentalism and increased Islamic consciousness, Islam is perhaps a more potent political force than any other religion in the Pacific. But only in Indonesia is it a predominant religion, and in Malaysia, where there are some 7 million Muslims, the religion is able to affect but not dominate society and culture, unlike in much of the Arab world.

The third significant religion is Buddhism, based mainly in South-east Asia. This religion came from India but as it spread east it was reshaped by local cultures.[30] It later mingled with Confucianism, a shadowy series of beliefs that many westerners classify as a religion. In principle, Confucianism is more a mixture of ancient Chinese cults, ancestral worship, state ritual, and moral precepts. Shintoism in Japan is also a similarly vague set of precepts and practices that only provide the loosest form of common beliefs.[31] If most of China and Korea are considered Confucian in the

[30] Geoffrey Parrinder, 'The Religions of Asia' in *The Far East and Australia* (London: Europa, 1986).
[31] Joy Hendry, *Understanding Japanese Society* (London: Croom Helm, 1987), ch. 7.

religious sense, then this is by far the most widespread religion in the Pacific. But in comparison to Christianity, Islam, or even Buddhism, Confucianism is a far less coherent and demanding system of beliefs. Certainly after decades of Communist rule in China, it is even harder to identify Confucianism as a religion.

In such an environment of liberal approaches to religion, there is much room for belief in a range of gods, ghosts, and gobbledegook.[32] Most of these practices, often called superstitions, are obsessed with the basics of life, birth, death, and marriage. To be sure, such practices are also common in the West, and the relative stage of modernization is little guide to the extent of these types of religion. Businessmen in East Asia seek commercial advice from the spiritual mediums much as many in the West watch their horoscopes or try not to walk under looming ladders. It is often said that some East Asian stock-markets have a heavy dose of spiritual intervention, as in the saying 'Red sky at night, index at its height.' In fact much of this superstition has parallels around the globe. The belief in witches is certainly shared, although Chinese and Koreans believe that a full moon is a time of happiness rather than dread.

In general, it is difficult to find a strong and general religious influence in the political process. In the early days, Islam was successful in South-east Asia because of its simple demands and its ability to merge with the mysticism of the people.[33] For some of the more active religions, as in the case of Islam, religion has helped exacerbate the problem of adaptation to westernization. The damage done to education and adaptation to modern technology, not to mention to women's rights and racial harmony, has on balance been detrimental to the modernization of Indonesia and Malaysia.[34] The new links to the Middle East rather than the West or East Asia have also probably helped isolate these states from the new political streams in the Pacific.

Much of the Islamic fundamentalism can be explained as a blacklash against the unsettling process of modernization. The non-Islamic peoples of the Pacific have often had less difficult adjustments to change. For example, Korea has seen major social changes as a result of a large growth in population, industrial development, urbanization, and economic growth. The experience of Japan's attempt to wipe out Korean culture and then of the superpower partition of the country shattered old beliefs and led to increased materialism. By 1970 less than half the Korean population were

---

[32] 'Gods, Ghosts and Gobbledegook' in *Far Eastern Economic Review* (4 January 1980).

[33] Koentjaraningrat, 'Family and Religion in Indonesia' in *East Asian Cultural Studies,* 13/1–4 (March 1974).

[34] 'The Power of Islam' in *Far Eastern Economic Review* (9 February 1979).

believers in a religion and a curious flourishing of fringe sects such as the Unification Church was apparent.[35] The new fervour was often channelled into nationalist causes, with religion of marginal value.

A similar process had already been visible in Japan during its process of modernization. The forces of economic modernization, including the American-inspired reform of the civil code, led to more nuclear families, greater mobility, and a trend towards the education of women.[36] But Japan remains a nation of believers. In fact, millions subscribe to more than one religion, leading some to ascribe to the Japanese an inflated sense of belief.[37] The religions no doubt give some sense of protection from the anxiety caused by high-speed change, while also making few demands. At its most basic, religion provides a sense of community, a value not always conducive to regional or international co-operation.[38] The habit of subscribing to an undemanding religion is also apparent in Thailand, where Theravada Buddhism dominates. But most people also worship other deities and trust in forms of magic.

Singapore is a fine example of the challenge of modernization being met by a syncretic religion that does not stand in the way of change. The more modernization is successful, as in Japan, the more religion is confined to private practices and declines as an active political force. Ritual and symbols continue, but the culture has been aptly described as a move from religion to 'moneytheism'.[39] The next step is to a 'rationality' culture where the common good is sought. Yet such rationality is also the culture of nationalism, not internationalism or a Pacific community. In the European or Atlantic worlds, a relatively common religious heritage had moved relatively early into the age of rationality, thereby helping build cultural and ideological bridges.

In the case of Christianity and the neo-Europes, there is a major divide between the Catholic and Protestant inheritance. The Protestant states are by far the most prosperous and also the least concerned with religion. Modernization has yet to come to most of Latin America and the Philippines, and in part the problem lies in religious principles, for example those preventing birth control. Yet as the deposing of President Marcos of the Philippines in 1986 made plain, the Church and its adherents of

---

[35] Tongshik Ryu, 'Religion and the Changing Society of Korea' in *East Asian Cultural Studies*, 11/1–4 (March 1972).

[36] Kuyomi Morioka, 'The Changing Family and Buddhism in Post-War Japan' in *East Asian Cultural Studies*, 11/1–4 (March 1972).

[37] Hori Ichiro, 'The Family and Religion in Japan' in *East Asian Cultural Studies*, 13/1–4 (March 1974).

[38] Hendry, *Japanese Society*.

[39] Tham Seong, 'Religion and Modernisation' in *East Asian Cultural Studies*, 23/1–4 (March 1984).

'revolutionary theology' can have a modernizing effect on their societies. Visits by the Pope to several Catholic states in a sub-region of the Pacific no doubt help break down national frontiers and stress internationalism. But Philippine Catholics are not seen by the Pope on a swing through Latin America, thereby emphasizing the dividing line down the Pacific Ocean.

The essential religious pattern in the Pacific is one of a region divided by religion, but by religions that are fading in importance as modernization marches forward, or else by religions that never were very demanding in the first place. Yet what has replaced these fading or minimal religions is often nationalism rather than regionalism or internationalism. They have also been replaced by political ideologies. Much like Confucianism, which contained principles of statecraft, or Christianity, which once thrived on a merger of State and Church, modern ideologies such as Communism are more demanding and have far greater influence on State policy. But the ideologies that swept China, Indo-China, and North Korea, covering over half the people of the Pacific, are best understood by a separate and more lengthy assessment of the evolution of political ideologies.

6

Decolonization

The ideologies of Pacific states have been shaped by a diversity of experiences. What is more, these experiences took place at different times, leaving the region divided by 'stage of development' as well as by ruling ideology. By 1945 it was only the neo-Europes of the Americas and Australia and New Zealand that enjoyed genuine independence. For most of East Asia and the Pacific islands, the pressing political issue was obtaining independence.

The way in which East Asia edged to independence had a major impact on the political system that emerged. Unlike the decolonization process in Africa, where there was enough in common between the individual states for some to call for pan-Africanism, in East Asia the diversity was too daunting. To call the East Asian process 'decolonization' is to suggest too much similarity in a process that left a wide range of ideologies in power. Of course, to some extent decolonization did leave many states with a common sense of grievance against the developed world. But the reactions to that grievance were so different that in the process East Asia imported and developed a wider range of political ideologies than any other part of the decolonized world.

It is even difficult to categorize the experience of decolonization. Most states did suffer some form of Japanese domination in the last phase of the war before 1945 and that experience did have the common impact of showing the vulnerability of white-man's rule. Those nationalist leaders who co-operated with Japan were not seen as quislings and the Europeans were surprised when the war ended and they themselves were not welcomed back as liberators.[1]

Broadly speaking there are those who fought for their independence, such as Vietnam, and those who waited more or less patiently for it to be granted, as in the Philippines. There are those who were more occupied than colonized, such as Japan, and those who never lost nominal independence, such as Thailand. There are those, such as China, that were never colonized in the orthodox sense, but rather were riven by civil war and partially invaded by colonial powers. Malaysia was colonized, but its civil war delayed the granting of independence. Of course the Pacific island states

---

[1] Evelyn Colbert, *Southeast Asian International Politics, 1941–56* (Ithaca: Cornell University Press, 1977).

were largely untouched by the first waves of decolonization, and they waited more or less patiently for their turn some two decades later.

JAPAN

Treating Japan in a section on decolonization is perhaps unfair. After all, Japan is unique among great powers in never having been successfully invaded, at least until 1945. Japan was also a major colonizer of others in Asia. Yet the American occupation of Japan did have some of the important ideological impacts of more orthodox colonialism.[2] In formal terms it reshaped the Japanese political system, and perhaps more importantly the defeat and occupation shocked the Japanese into new directions in foreign and domestic policy.[3] The formal surrender on 2 September 1945 brought to effective power General MacArthur, a man of definite opinions on how Japan should be run.

Under the guide-lines of democracy and decentralization, MacArthur and his staff wrote a new constitution, the judicial and administrative structures were recast, and labour relations were reshaped. Land reform was introduced and political prisoners were released. To be sure, there was hubris and incompetence in some of the American reorganization of Japan, but by and large their objectives were seen as benevolent.

The massive social changes engendered by the Americans were aggravated by the inevitable suffering of a people shattered by war. One of the few unifying political symbols to remain was the monarchy. Although the emperor 'came down from the clouds', he was seen to have retained his dignity throughout. This was as much a description of the emperor's personal plight as that of Japan as a whole.

According to the October 1946 constitution imposed by MacArthur, the emperor surrendered sovereignty and the Diet became the 'highest organ of state'. In practice, albeit not in name, Japan became a republic. Other articles of the constitution comprised an effective Bill of Rights. The bicameral structure of the legislature was retained but the House of Peers was replaced by a House of Councillors with much-reduced powers. Amendments to the constitution required a two-thirds vote of members in each House and had to be ratified by a referendum. Thus the demise of the Meiji constitution was complete, but the new American one was not without broad support.[4]

[2] Michael Schaller, *The American Occupation of Japan* (Oxford: Oxford University Press, 1985).
[3] Richard Storry, *A History of Modern Japan* (London: Penguin, 1968), ch. 10.
[4] Edwin Reischauer, *Japan* (New York: Alfred Knopf, 1981); Storry, *Japan*, ch. 10

By 1948 the attitude of the Americans had been altered by a fear of Communism and the rapidly cooling temperature of the cold war with the Soviet Union. The Chinese Communist triumph and then the Korean War galvanized the Americans into emphasizing rehabilitation and revival over reform. Thus there were second thoughts about dissolving the large industrial conglomerates and strikes were frowned upon more as signs of dangerous ideas than of democratic vigour.

Even the celebrated clause 9 of the new constitution, forbidding the creation of an armed force, was circumvented with the creation of a national police reserve and then a Self Defence Force that was to all intents and purposes an armed force.[5] The more conservative sectors of society welcomed this 'new realism' while many young people, the intelligentsia, and the working class opposed the new military orientation. The shock of the atomic bombing and military defeat had been a genuine catharsis and had altered the balance of forces in Japanese politics. The new sense of disillusionment with the United States was real, even though it may well have been provoked by important changes in the international environment.

The change in American policy was also the result of a desire to ease the economic burden of Japan. By 1948 it had proven impossible to obtain the agreement of the wartime allies for a peace conference on Japan, and the United States began granting more autonomy to Tokyo.[6] The zaibatsu re-emerged, 'purged' officials returned, and private trade with foreign countries was allowed. This process of rehabilitation was similar in motive and process to that taking place in vanquished Europe.

As in Germany, the process was made easier by the dominance of conservative politicians. Shigeru Yoshida was Prime Minister for seven years and presided over the economic reconstruction stimulated by the American campaign in Korea. National morale improved and a peace treaty was signed in San Francisco on 8 September 1951. Yoshida signed for Japan, recognizing the loss of empire, but the Communist states denounced the treaty. On the same day, Japan signed a security treaty with the United States, 'requesting' the retention of American forces, but on 28 April 1952, when the treaty came into force, Japan once again formally became independent.

CHINA

China might have been expected to regain independence in 1945 after the defeat of Japan, but prior to the Japanese occupation the Chinese themselves

---

5 Meiron and Susie Harries, *Sheathing the Sword* (London: Hamish Hamilton, 1987).
6 Roger Buckley, *Occupation Diplomacy* (Cambridge: Cambridge University Press, 1982).

had not been able to agree on a government or ruling ideology. Thus the end of occupation brought the civil war back to full flame. It was not until October 1949, when Mao Zedong proclaimed the People's Republic of China with the words that the Chinese people had 'stood up', that genuine independence was restored.

The extent to which this new Chinese revolution was more Communist than Chinese has been a topic of debate.[7] Clearly no country casts off its ancient heritage entirely, and certainly not if that heritage is as illustrious as that of China. But the Chinese Communist Party had demonstrated in its years of practice in the 'red areas' of China that it was determined to undertake a real revolution. Land reform and the reform of 'thought' were essential elements. Communism was not as opposed to Confucianism as it was to western capitalism, but Mao's peasant revolution did shatter traditional relationships of power.

Marxism-Leninism, on to which was grafted Mao Zedong thought, was a western ideology adapted to Chinese poor, peasant conditions. China had clearly taken the decision to modernize itself and its ideology, and by adopting a western ideology was suggesting just how deep had been the impact of the brush with western imperialism.[8] This change in China was not the direct result of colonialism as it had been in South-east Asia, but it was no less important. As East Asia's second and by far most powerful Communist regime, China was bound to take a leading role in the Communist versus capitalist confrontation that was coming to dominate international relations.

Yet, while most of China had 'stood up' in a Communist fashion, the civil war remained unresolved. The Guomindang's dash to Taiwan also meant a different type of revolution for the inhabitants of that island and the gradual evolution of a different political system. Considering the strong United States support for Chiang Kai-shek, it is not surprising that Taiwan became clearly oriented to the United States and the West.

Chiang also learned the lessons of the failed revolution of 1911. The move to Taiwan was burdened with pretensions to power in all of China, but at the same time the serious reforms of agriculture and modernizations of industry were precisely those enlightened steps that the Nationalists failed to take when they had their chance on the mainland.[9] Bolstered by American support, Taiwan evolved into what might be described as a non-Communist state with Chinese characteristics, ruled by an authoritarian regime but

---

[7] John K. Fairbank, *The Great Chinese Revolution* (New York: Harper & Row, 1986); John K. Fairbank (ed.), *Chinese World Order* (Cambridge, Mass.: Harvard University Press, 1968).

[8] Michael Yahuda, *Towards the End of Isolationism* (London: Macmillan, 1983), ch. 2.

[9] Ralph Clough, *Island China* (Cambridge, Mass.: Harvard University Press, 1978).

supported by the West. It was a curious, but soon to be potent, combination of political characteristics.

THE PHILIPPINES, INDONESIA, AND MALAYSIA

The path to independence in South-east Asia defies generalization.[10] Taking the easy ones first, the Philippines was already well on the way to independence before the Japanese occupation. The Philippines was colonized for longer than any other South-east Asian country and, what is worse, had the differing experiences of Spanish and United States rule. Not surprisingly, the Filipinos became the most estranged from their roots and in some ways the closest to western ways.[11]

Official independence in 1946 was granted to a nation that was ruled by an élite deeply influenced by United States power.[12] The basics of the relationship with the United States were accordingly maintained, including an agreement in 1947 on military bases and another on training of the Filipino armed forces. A 1954 agreement on 'free trade' continued to bind the Philippine economy to the United States. What was left was a discontented nationalist feeling that broke down into left–right debates as well as those between different minorities. The absence of real land reform ensured that, despite official independence, the Philippines remained an unstable and authoritarian-ruled place.

Indonesia might have ended up like the Philippines in many respects, but its struggle for independence followed a very different route. Indonesia had been transformed by the 350 years of Dutch rule into a far-flung nation focused on over-populated Java, but deriving most of its wealth from the outer islands. The 'Culture System' of agricultural products for export no doubt improved the wealth of the island, but also tied it into the international political economy. Indonesian society had been similarly recast by the colonial experience. Indonesian republicans tried to sneak into power in 1945 as Japanese rule collapsed. By the time the first Allied forces arrived in Jakarta in September, power had been seized in the ill-coordinated hands of local Indonesians.[13] British Indian troops acting for the Dutch gradually reasserted control but by November fighting was raging on a massive scale.

---

10 Milton Osborne, *Southeast Asia* (London: Allen & Unwin, 1985), 158.

11 D. J. M. Tate, *The Making of Modern Southeast Asia* (Oxford: Oxford University Press, 1979), ch. 5.

12 Alfred McCoy, 'The Philippines' in Robin Jeffrey (ed.), *Asia: The Winning of Independence* (London: Macmillan, 1981).

13 Anthony Reed, 'Indonesia' in Jeffrey (ed.), *Winning of Independence*, 142.

The returning Dutch attempted to rule by emphasizing federalism and minority interests, and thereby to 'hold the ring'. Although the concept of federalism made much sense for a country the size of Indonesia, it was unlikely to succeed if only because it was backed by Holland. Despite repeated attacks on the republicans, the Dutch could not obtain any significant popular support. Under intense United States pressure, Holland was forced to give up the fight in July 1949. Sovereignty was formally transferred on 17 August 1950 and the idea of federalism died with colonialism.

Perhaps the most lasting legacy of the bloody decolonization was the emphasis on national unity above all, and a pragmatic approach to nation-building that paid less attention to shaping sensible institutions of government. Dutch-educated nationalist politicians ruled the new state, but their claim to legitimacy was not unchallenged. Their patronage was limited and the bureaucracy was a less professional force than in other, for example British, colonies. This absence of strong authority and legitimate rule was eventually to lead to military government. Certainly the middle classes were unable to dominate and the state emerged as the dominant institution. Patronage dominated the legal system and Court factions fought for personal power that was derived from manipulation of the state.[14] It was a process of decolonization and a succeeding political system unique in the Pacific.

Malaysia might have come out looking more like Indonesia if it had not been for the fact that Britain was the colonial power. Britain returned after the war and established a Malay Federation in order to control separatist tendencies.[15] But non-Malays and the left challenged this British hand-over to its own trained local élite and a less than fully elected legislature. The main opposition came from the Malayan Communist Party with its deep roots in the Chinese community. In June 1948 a state of emergency was declared and the struggle was on in earnest. The conflict was at its worst in 1951 but gradually the disruption to the economy was minimized. At the same time, Britain co-opted wider sections of the Malay population into government. With the lessons of India and Palestine in mind, Britain helped forge a multiracial coalition, in part taking advantage of the disarray in the Chinese camp caused by the emergency. The merger of business interests and urban professionals laid the basis for a stabilized political system.

Britain became increasingly convinced that moderate constitutional parties were present. Federal elections provided a decisive win for an alliance party in 1955 and the determination to press for full independence grew.

---

[14] Karl Jackson and Lucian Pye (eds.), *Political Power and Communication in Indonesia* (Berkeley, Calif.: University of California Press, 1978).

[15] Lee Kam Hung, 'Malaya' in Jeffrey (ed.), *Winning of Independence*.

British opposition gave the alliance greater nationalist credibility and helped build national unity in order to convince Britain that stable government was possible. Compromise and conciliation among ethnic groups, coupled with special emphasis on the Malay language and Islam, held a tenuous coalition together. Independence in 1957 brought a parliamentary system with various safeguards to protect the Malayan ethnic patchwork. The transfer of power was smooth, with the significant numbers of Malays in the Civil Service moving up to take control. Strategies of economic development emphasized a free-market system and involvement in the international economy. Economic and social planning was stressed at home, as was land reform.[16]

Yet some awkward loose ends of decolonization were left over. These included the fate of Singapore, Brunei, Sabah, and Sarawak. Britain was looking for ways to divest itself of its colonial responsibility for these very different territories. But as Sabah and Sarawak were moved closer to union with Malaya, the Philippines and especially Indonesia opposed the move. The latter was always suspicious of the manner of Malayan independence, claiming it was merely an excuse for continuing colonial rule in another form. Co-operation with western and Chinese interests was seen as abandonment of the struggle. On 12 September 1963 the Malaysian Federation was created. Although Singapore was later to split off in 1965 to form the third Chinese state in the Pacific (the fourth, if Hong Kong is included), relations with Malaysia remained pragmatic.

It was the great success of the Malayan struggle for independence that a stable system emerged based on racial co-operation, when many would have bet on control being left in the hands of a limited, more chauvinist Malay coalition. The principles of consensus politics were relatively little practised in South-east Asia. The resulting, largely democratic political system joined its Commonwealth partners in retaining ties to the old colonial master but, unlike the neo-Europes, was determined to see itself as a non-white, developing state.

INDO-CHINA

Decolonization in the French territories of Indo-China followed the bloodier path of Indonesia rather than the more peaceful Malaysian model—only more so. The result was radicalization of an already-tough political system. Where Malaysia learned consensus, Indo-China learned conflict. Vietnam had always been the key to Indo-China and the post-1945 period was no

---

[16] Mark Rudner, *Nationalism, Planning and Economic Modernisation in Malaysia* (London: Sage, 1975).

exception. In the dying days of Japanese rule in 1945, Vietnamese independence movements were encouraged to take power. The humbling of French colonialists made a deep impression on Vietnamese nationalists, but in the end the humiliating experience only encouraged France to return in force.[17]

Before the French could return, the Viet Minh under Ho Chi Minh started their drive for power in August 1945. The Democratic Republic of Vietnam (DRV) was proclaimed on 2 September before Chinese and British troops arrived. Ho's ideology at that time had little place for class struggle and reflected a broad socialist-nationalist appeal.

With the return of the French, the Viet Minh were forced partly underground and partly into open rebellion. Their techniques of mass mobilization were developed and eventually radicalized as the war grew fiercer. France put the emperor Bao Dai back on the throne (he had abdicated in 1945) but France retained all essential power.[18] Ho's forces fought a classic guerrilla war, and when Chinese Communist forces triumphed in 1949 they provided more direct aid to Ho's struggle.

By 1954 when DRV soldiers took power in North Vietnam, it was inevitable that their restructuring of society would be radical. The polity had become polarized and the external environment of the cold war encouraged such extremist thinking. Although the 1954 Geneva Accords notionally made Vietnam in its two parts independent, the struggle for power in this essentially civil war was set to continue.[19] The emperor Bao Dai was deposed but the new rulers of South Vietnam refused to allow elections on the question of reunification.

This unfinished revolutionary pattern, despite formal independence, was also evident in the other Indo-Chinese states. Laos was always the most neglected of the three Indo-Chinese states—a remote world of interest only to the eccentrics in the French colonial system.[20] Laos remained a nation of subsistence farmers, despite two generations of contact with France. Geographic difficulties ensured there was little economic development and thus little real change in the political system. In fact, Laos was barely treated as an identifiable political unit.

Laos also had its brief flirtation with independence before the French returned, only to find itself with a notionally self-governing monarchy under a French union. The war in Laos between rival ideologies was not as fierce as that in Vietnam, nor was it resolved with the withdrawal of French power and the Geneva Accord. In fact, the creation of Laos as a political state

---

17 David Marr, 'Vietnam' in Jeffrey (ed.), *Winning of Independence*.
18 Stanley Karnow, *Vietnam* (New York: Viking, 1983), ch. 5.
19 Justus M. van der Kroef, *Communism in Southeast Asia* (London: Macmillan, 1981).
20 D. J. M. Tate, *The Making of Southeast Asia* (Oxford: Oxford University Press, 1979), ii. 404.

outran the far more confused political reality on the ground, for the sake of cartographic and diplomatic convenience.[21]

Cambodia, like Laos, remained a side-show to the main action in Vietnam. It was in fact French occupation that preserved Cambodia from being squeezed between Thailand and Vietnam and created an environment for modern Cambodian nationalism to prosper. Yet it was Japan that pushed King Sihanouk to proclaim independence, which France later softened to internal autonomy. In 1949 France granted independence except in external affairs, and in 1953 Sihanouk's pressure led to full independence as France retreated from the region. The remaining problem was the occupation of part of the country by Viet Minh forces and their allies, although they were notionally removed by the 1954 Geneva agreement.[22]

Although France had an impact on the intellectual élite of Cambodia, it had far less impact on the country's economy than it had in Vietnam. Cambodia remained a nation of peasant smallholders with only modest links to the international economy. Chinese small traders dominated local markets as they had for centuries. The French had not even made a significant impact by improving communications as many other colonial powers had done around the globe. When independence came, Cambodia found that it was still what it had been for centuries, 'either rulers, priests or peasants'.[23] In the final analysis, the legacy was of an unreformed monarchy and a delicate relationship with Cambodia's neighbours. As in much of the rest of French Indo-China, the result of decolonization was disarray, unstable government, and regional conflict.

PACIFIC ISLANDS

The process of decolonization has still not stopped in the Pacific. The last areas to obtain full independence have often been those more remote islands in the Pacific that have been cut off from the winds of change that blew through East Asia. The contrast to the East Asian experience of decolonization is stark. By and large the Pacific islands have made the transition to independence peacefully and with little outside involvement. Perhaps decolonization here, most of which took place in the 1970s, had the benefit of learning from the experience of others, in terms of the attitude of both the colonizer and the colonized.

Some territories, such as Western Samoa and Nauru, moved to

[21] Peter Lyon, *War and Peace in Southeast Asia* (Oxford: Oxford University Press, 1969).
[22] Michael Leifer, *Cambodia* (London: Pall Mall, 1967).
[23] Quoted in D. J. M. Tate *Southeast Asia*, 375.

independence in the 1960s. These two former German colonies had been under League of Nations and United Nations mandates held by New Zealand and Australia respectively. Western Samoa was the first of the Pacific islands to regain 'native sovereignty', in large part because of active local pressure.[24] Western Samoa's independence in 1962 included a peculiar arrangement whereby a *de facto* constitutional monarch for life was left in place until his death. Real power resided in a 47-member legislature composed primarily of elected tribal chiefs. Nauru obtained independence in January 1968 and maintained a unicameral parliament of just 17, with a President elected by the parliament.

The next country to obtain independence, and the first of the more populous Pacific islands, was Tonga, a state under British 'protection' since 1900. Its independence in June 1970 did not change the primacy of its King as head of state. Although a parliament of 23 was established, it had few political powers and the strength of traditional political order was based on tribal chiefs.

Fiji, the second most populous of the island states, also obtained independence in 1970, in October. But it was the first to suffer from serious political unrest, most of which was related to its colonial experience. The local Melanesians had been made a minority in their own land by the importation of Indians by the British to work the plantations. When the time came for independence the Indians held little of the land and complained about the insecurity of land tenure, while the Fijians were upset about Indian domination of commerce.

The complex communal system was addressed in the electoral system for the House of Representatives. The upper house, the Senate, was appointed by the Great Council of Fijian Chiefs, the Prime Minister and the leader of the opposition. Remarkably, this delicate modern political system, bequeathed by the colonial system, survived in its democratic form until 1987. A military coup then removed the Governor-General and established a republic that denied equal rights to the Indians. Fiji was rare among Pacific members of the Commonwealth for falling into military dictatorship.[25]

Papua New Guinea is by far the largest of the islands but it was not until September 1975 that it received full independence. It had been under the trusteeship of Australia since the collapse of German power during the First World War, after which Australia had taken a paternal interest in its closest neighbour. Papua New Guinea's transition to democracy was a smooth one and it soon settled down to the usual problems of domestic development and threatening neighbours, in this case Indonesia.

24 C. Hartley Grattan, *The Southwest Pacific Since 1900* (Ann Arbor: University of Michigan Press, 1963).
25 *Financial Times* (5 October 1987).

The Solomon Islands to the east were under British control before they obtained independence in July 1978. Their government was more decentralized than most, but with a unicameral parliament of 38 headed by a Prime Minister. This was a more modern example of the easy transition to independence, much like Kiribati which obtained independence a year later. Kiribati was established as a republic with a President elected by direct popular vote and a parliament of 36.

Vanuatu, which obtained independence in July 1980, was an uneasy clutch of territories held in an Anglo-French condominium. As different political systems of colonialism and tribal rule were mixed and matched, there were numerous political rivalries. The run-up to independence was marred by political unrest and attempts to form breakaway movements. In the end, a complex republican government was established and Vanuatu joined the Commonwealth. It has a 39-member unicameral parliament and a President chosen by parliament and the regional councils. The Prime Minister holds real power but, with some powers decentralized in order to satisfy regional interests, power is more diffuse than was the case in the Solomon Islands. For the time being the delicate political system has held, despite the inevitable difficulties bequeathed by confused colonial rule.

Of course, a number of territories in the Pacific are still under colonial rule. Some, like the Pitcairn Islands, are tiny and independence is not really an option. Others, such as the American trusteeship territories in Micronesia, are of strategic importance. By 1986 these territories were gradually formalizing relations with the United States and abandoning the fiction of United Nations control. The United States has already extended its territory to mid-Pacific with its integration of Hawaii. Referendums in the Marshalls, Palau, and the Federated States of Micronesia all opted for a status of 'autonomy in free association with the United States'. The Northern Marianas preferred an 'associated commonwealth' status much like Puerto Rico.[26] Although the Soviet Union and China have been critical of these arrangements, most other independent Pacific island states have been supportive. Some other islands, such as New Caledonia, are on their difficult way to independence, although their course has been delayed by serious ethnic and social problems, often created by colonial rule.

And then there are the odd ones but, such as Hong Kong and Macao. Both are to return to China, in 1997 and 1999 respectively, as Britain and Portugal voluntarily relinquish what have already been the loosest of controls. Portugal had been anxious to surrender control of its Chinese colony ever since the change of government in Lisbon in 1974. Britain, holding the far more important territory of Hong Kong, was slower to move.

[26] *The Economist* (5 July 1986).

China had never exerted particularly strong pressure on Britain to return Hong Kong, but pressure was steady. In the 1980s Britain decided that the Hong Kong problem was blocking a general improvement of relations with China and the prospects for access to the China market. In any case, the lease on the New Territories was running out in 1997 so that some new future for Hong Kong proper had to be found. With a more moderate leadership in power in China, which had opened the country up to the international economy, Britain eventually decided to return Hong Kong to Chinese control. The 1984 agreement represented the first time that any western government had handed over so many people, five million, to Communism, and a flourishing colony at that. This was not so much decolonization in the traditional form as irredentism by the largest and most successful colonizer of them all, China. The problem of making the differing systems of government in these territories fit within the legal framework of one China looks like being one of the most long-lasting colonial legacies in the Pacific.

Thus decolonization is not quite complete in the Pacific but the main part of the process is over. The implications for international economic and military affairs will be discussed in later chapters. But in terms of the kinds of political system left in place, it is clear that the Pacific patchwork has been further complicated. The process of decolonization has helped shape the diverse ideologies of the Pacific and helped lay the basis for deep national rivalries. Unlike the European or Atlantic worlds, where the evolution of political systems created far more common features between states (at least two types) and helped keep conflict under control, in the Pacific the diversity of ideologies led to even greater fragmentation.

7

Ideologies

Decolonization in the Atlantic community took place in the eighteenth and nineteenth centuries and by the modern era had over a century to establish regular patterns of international relations. By contrast, many states in the Pacific have only recently emerged as independent entities and the decolonization process is still unfinished. Not surprisingly, therefore, the dominant ideologies of the Atlantic states are more securely established.

Since 1945 there have been relatively few changes of regime and political system in the Atlantic community. To be sure, some southern European states have drifted in and out of military rule, as have most states in Latin America. But the changes have been far less fundamental than in the Pacific.[1] Not only has decolonization radically altered the political map, but some states have had revolutions, most notably in Indo-China. While the European community can be described as 'developed', until recently vast sections of the Pacific have been classed as the 'developing world'. Although the term 'developing' is usually applied primarily to the economic dimension, in the case of the Pacific many states have been developing both economically and politically.[2]

There are important differences between East and West in Europe or between Europe and some authoritarian regimes in Latin America, but the types of state are relatively clear-cut. Above all, there are close links between the political systems and ideologies of western Europe and many American states, and to a much smaller extent there are close links between the Soviet bloc and Cuba and Nicaragua.

In the Pacific world, there are far fewer links across the waters, and even fewer still within sub-regions. The ideological map of the Pacific is muddled. If states are divided up on the basis of Communist versus capitalist ideology, then the Communist world sweeps down from the north to include the Soviet Union, China, Mongolia, North Korea, and Indo-China. These states account for well over half the land and population of the Pacific basin, but they are divided among themselves on a number of grounds. Needless to

---

[1] Only Spain and Portugal can be said to have had major, enduring changes in political systems since 1945. Military rule in Greece and Turkey has been fleeting and the Latin American experiments with democracy seem fragile.

[2] Although this analysis will take into account the events from 1945, most discussion of political ideology in this section will focus on contemporary ideologies.

say, the so-called capitalist Pacific is also a very diverse bunch. Similarly, any division among states on the basis of authoritarian versus pluralist government will create even stranger bedfellows among the authoritarian regimes such as South Korea and China. States may slip in and out of authoritarianism without fundamentally changing their political culture.

It is perhaps more useful to fall back on the criterion applied in the European context, political culture. But even more so than in the European case, the Pacific basin has been affected by a number of political cultures and some coexist within a single state. Thus China and North Korea can both be seen as Communist and Confucian and are best discussed in both categories. Of course, it is impossible to assess all aspects of the ideologies of states in the Pacific and, as this study is primarily concerned with patterns of international relations, the main emphasis will be placed on ideology and political systems in relation to foreign policy.

EUROPEAN IDEOLOGY: DEMOCRATIC PLURALISM

The essence of such key institutions of the Atlantic community as NATO and the EC is a shared ideology. The ungainly term 'democratic pluralism' refers to a political system where there is a wide range of political parties and ideals, and where governments peacefully surrender power when defeated in general elections. The state also emphasizes the protection of individual rights, freedom of movement, and a respect for formal law. The economy gives a wide scope for market forces.

These political principles have evolved over centuries in central and western Europe and are all flexible enough to be adjusted in times of domestic and foreign crisis. Different West European or North American states emphasize different principles, but none can be violated for any length of time without fundamentally changing the nature of the dominant ideology. Stresses do appear in NATO because of the inclusion of non-democratic members. Similarly, Spain, Portugal, and Greece were prevented from joining the EC until they shed their military rulers.

In the widest possible interpretation of this democratic pluralist ideology in the Pacific, it can be said to encompass the states of North America, most of the south Pacific, Malaysia, and Japan. A number of other states are close to this model in many respects, including several Latin American states, the Philippines, Thailand, and Singapore. But only in the case of the first, more genuine group, can political ideologies be said to be shared to a sufficient extent to create genuine international bonds.

The key characteristics of these states have often led to them being described as members of 'the West'—as in the western alliance based in the Atlantic community. Clearly in geographic terms, when some of these states actually straddle the international date-line, such a description is next to useless. But in political terms it is true that these states do share some important aspects of their political ideologies, in the same way that states of the 'real' western alliance do.

The international bonds tying these states together are, of course, supported by a wider range of cultural, economic, and military ties. But the ease with which economic relations are maintained, or the willingness to provide military assistance and to perceive international threats in a similar light, are closely related to a shared political ideology. Thus when a coup in Fiji destroys the constitutional political system, as happened in May 1987, concern and advice is offered from states with similar ideologies in the Pacific and in western Europe.

But by and large the states of this 'democratic pluralist' community refrain from intervention in each other's political systems so long as these basic democratic and pluralist principles are maintained. Of course, there is concern that some states, such as Japan, have elections but no real change of government (in Italy coalition partners change more sharply). Others, such as the United States, may have changes of parties but the spectrum of opinion between the main parties is one of the narrowest in the democratic world. The dubious democracy of the Australian Governor-General being able to remove a Prime Minister, as happened in 1975, was a cause of some concern, but the Australian system of government was resilient enough to find its own solution.

Malaysia is perhaps the most unusual state in this category because of its status as a developing economy. Its politics remain mostly democratic and pluralist despite deep ethnic divisions. Although the country has a large Chinese community, the traditional political ideology of Confucianism is distinctly lacking in confidence when operating in a minority environment. In such conditions controversy is avoided and instead there is a tendency to opt out of the political process. Thus the Malays themselves dominate the political system, in accordance with democratic traditions bequeathed by the British.[3] One political party has been dominant since independence, but as part of a coalition government. The relatively wide powers held by the regional governments also help maintain democratic political pluralism in a divided state.

Despite the basic coincidence of these democratic pluralist political systems in the Pacific, there is remarkably little multilateral political co-ordination

---

[3] Gordon Means, *Malaysian Politics* (London: Hodder & Stoughton, 1976).

of policies. However, there are a number of close bilateral relationships which have a strong ideological overtone. Only the Commonwealth has any claim to be a political organization that helps develop contact between states with similar ideologies. The Commonwealth is based around the British Crown, and its members are far from consistent in adhering to democratic political principles. But with the recent exception of Fiji, all the Commonwealth's Pacific membership falls into the category of democratic pluralist states, at least in its broadest definition. It is a remarkable tribute to British and European values that the ideals of democratic pluralism and the Commonwealth itself should have survived colonialism to become a unifying force.

Yet the Commonwealth as an organization lacks real political weight and there has been no attempt to organize a Pacific sub-group. At times the Pacific states have expressed mostly common attitudes on issues of decolonization, but the focus of Commonwealth attention has mostly been outside the Pacific region. Thus the Pacific states sharing a democratic pluralist ideology are connected by mainly bilateral relationships, but by very little in the way of multilateral friendship. This is perhaps as much a function of geographic dispersal as a recognition that there is little to be gained from such co-operation. Unlike in Europe where the perceived threats from Communism or dictatorship are clear, in the Pacific opposing ideologies are much more distant. In the absence of a single major threat, it is easier and more comfortable for states to drift along on their own.

EUROPEAN IDEOLOGY: DEMOCRATIC CENTRALISM

Europe not only created democratic pluralism, it also developed the democratic centralism of Karl Marx as 'translated' by V. I. Lenin. The ideology of Communism as it was first known in Europe has shaped the other part of modern Europe across the great East–West divide. While not all states in Europe fit snugly into this bipolar scene, most of the so-called neutrals in reality bend to one side or the other. Whether it is pro-western, 'neutral' Austria, or pro-socialist, 'neutral' Yugoslavia, the ideological rift in Europe is important to these states for both domestic and foreign policy reasons. Of course there are also important differences among the Communist countries of eastern Europe, for example between reforming, market-oriented Hungary and the ultra-loyal Soviet ally, Bulgaria. But there is much that can be called common ideology.

The essential characteristic of a Communist system expressed in terms of democratic centralism is that the leading role of the Communist Party must remain unchallenged. The Party controls the state, which is much more interventionist in the organization of society. Group rights take precedence over individual rights and the rule of law must retain a strong socialist character. Market forces, though playing some part in economic reform, are always subordinate to central planning. Ownership is primarily the right of collectives or the state rather than individuals. International relations similarly emphasize central planning, and 'socialist internationalism' requires comradely support for fellow Communist Parties. The forces of history move 'forward' towards Communism and are not allowed to 'retreat' to capitalism.

The spread of this ideology to the Pacific came soon after it affected the Atlantic world. The Russian revolution of 1917 was swiftly followed by a Communist take-over in Mongolia in 1921. For much of the period before 1945 the model for Communism was the Soviet Union and Mongolia was the only other comradely regime in a hostile world. Stalinism was in command of the ideology and little account was taken of local Asian Pacific conditions.

Following the defeat of Japan in 1945, the wave of Communism spread to the Pacific as it did in Europe. By far the biggest ideological gain for Communism was the triumph of Mao Zedong's Communists in China in 1949. Measured by population, the Communist world suddenly became larger than the capitalist world. The People's Democratic Republic of Korea was actually proclaimed in 1948, before the People's Republic of China, but between 1950 and 1953 was torn by invasion and an internationalized civil war.

It was not until the establishment of the Democratic Republic of Vietnam in 1954 under the leadership of Ho Chi Minh's Communists that the Communist world expanded again in Asia. Unlike most European cases, or Korea, the Vietnamese Communists came to power like their Chinese comrades under their own steam and in a poor peasant country. With unification in 1975, Vietnam became the world's third largest Communist regime. Also in that year Kampuchea and Laos went Communist, extending the bounds of Communism in the Pacific when the ideology appeared to have stalled elsewhere around the globe. The apparent dynamism of Asian Communism suggested to some that the Pacific was becoming ideologically similar to the European world.

According to western domino theory the spread of Communism in Asia was seen as akin to Europe, where Soviet power extended a Communist threat by taking one country after another. Unlike in Europe where the Soviet Union was clearly in charge of the movement, in the Pacific the Communist movement was Hydra-headed. Not only was China seen as a more radical proponent of Communism, but the 'new Prussians' of Vietnam were yet another centre of independent-minded Communist expansionism.

Communism has undeniably been a dynamic ideology in the Pacific and, unlike in Europe, its opponents there can have little confidence that the 'threat' has been contained. While the cold-war lines in Europe have remained unchanged since 1945, the Communist world has made major gains in the Pacific. But the main flaw in such a simplistic notion of dynamic Communism is that when the irresistible force of the ideology ran into the immovable object of local conditions, it was the ideology that was transformed.

Of course, Communism in its Pacific variants is still Communism. None of the basic characteristics have been abandoned, although greater emphasis is placed on the development of the peasant economy than in Europe and most recently Chinese-led reform Communism has allowed greater scope for market forces. Yet this relative consistency in ideology has been disguised by major conflicts between the Communist states in the Pacific. The first large-scale military hostilities between the Soviet Union and China in 1969 and the full-scale wars between Kampuchea and Vietnam in 1978 and between Vietnam and China in 1979 have demonstrated just how little a basically shared ideology can be taken as a dependable guide to foreign policy behaviour. Although the causes of those wars will be discussed in later chapters, suffice it to say that the largely common ideology was insufficient to keep Communist from killing Communist.

One major difference from inter-Communist disputes in Europe is, of course, the fact that most Pacific Communists came to power under their own steam, and are strong enough to fight off a hegemonic Communist power. It was not just that China and the Soviet Union fell out over the best path to true Communism, but also that China, unlike Poland or Czechoslovakia, could thumb its nose at Soviet attempts to order affairs in the Communist world. Similarly, Vietnam's refusal to acknowledge Chinese suzerainty in determining ideology and foreign policy was supported by a battle-hardened army. Thus wars cannot disguise the existence of relatively common ideology, but nor is relatively common ideology a safeguard against warfare.

Although the inter-Communist wars have pitted China and Kampuchea against the Soviet Union and Vietnam, in terms of political ideologies there is an argument that China and Vietnam share a common Confucian tradition, along with North Korea. While it is true that Vietnam had been in the Chinese political orbit for centuries, it was also deeply affected by French colonization. Indo-China is the only part of the Pacific with a lower standard of living in the 1980s than in the 1930s. Interestingly, what all these states share is the French colonial experience. Vietnam in particular has a melancholy political culture that may only now be moving on from giving a priority to government to giving a priority to economics, as China had until recently done.[4] The success story of the other Confucian cultures so close to Vietnam suggests there is deep-rooted diversity in political cultures in the Pacific.

THE CONFUCIAN PACIFIC

Not surprisingly considering its great tradition, the Confucian world has also produced its own type of political ideology. What some call 'neo-Confucianism' is said to be a modern-day application of traditional principles of statecraft as practised under the old Chinese imperial orbit. One western political scientist compared the impact of Confucianism to that of Protestantism on the 'spirit of capitalism'.[5] The meaning of Confucianism for modern political systems is far from commonly understood, is difficult to define, and is even the subject of major research projects in East Asia. But it is said to be so important and unique that it gives East Asians an edge over other states with different ideologies and therefore lies at the heart of the Pacific challenge.

The Confucian political ideology is said to be one of government by a benevolent bureaucracy under a virtuous ruler.[6] One observer suggests the contrast between the ideology of 'original sin' in the West and the Confucian ideology of 'original virtue'.[7] In traditional China it provided for basic stability and eventually arrogance in the face of a superior western technology. But in its confrontation with western materialism it suffered little of the spiritual angst shown by many Muslims and Hindus. Especially as western imperialism only lapped the coasts of China, Korea, and Japan, Confucianism could remain the dominant ideology. And because Confucianism is agnostic, it could remain pragmatically concerned with the management of an unstable world.

At a minimum, there is more than one Confucianism. The more pure, historical concept had little time for the pragmatic orientation of merchants, a class much despised by the old Confucian élite. The more modern Confucianism, called vulgar-Confucianism by some, is what is usually

[4] Lucian Pye, *Asian Power and Politics* (Cambridge, Mass.: Harvard University Press, 1985), 244–6.

[5] Herman Kahn, discussed in 'Playing Fast and Loose with Confucian Values' in *Far Eastern Economic Review* (19 May 1988).

[6] Based on the innovative article by Roderick MacFarquhar, 'The Post-Confucian Challenge' in *The Economist* (9 February 1980). See a later, more elaborate, discussion in Roy Hofheinz and Kent Calder, *The East Asia Edge* (New York: Basic Books, 1982).

[7] Ronald Dore, *Taking Japan Seriously* (London: Athlone, 1987).

meant by followers of current vogues.[8] It is a system of paternalistic authority, which has more recently become mixed with nationalism. Confucianism leaves little room for western notions of a legally based political order. It shares with Communism a concern with the collectivity and group solidarity before the individual.[9] This is a patron–client political culture that does not regard paternalism as a pejorative term. Of course such dominant leadership naturally leads to the transformation of leaders into larger-than-life figures.[10]

It is clear that Confucianism is rarely articulated as a specific political strategy, because it is most often seen as a code of moral precepts or else a hodgepodge of pragmatic ideas drawn from ancient traditions that include Buddhism and Taoism. Certainly, morality is rarely debated, scheming is widespread, and infighting is rough. Wealth and religion were not considered alternative sources of power in this system so rival authority was not recognized. Only those formally in government could exercise power and thus the influence of pressure groups from outside the system was minimized.

In foreign policy terms, Confucianism is said to emphasize technocratic expertise and easy international contacts between élites relatively unfettered by pressure groups. It offers no reasons for solidarity as do other ideologies except on the grounds of creating the best environment for success. Loyalty on the basis of ideology, culture, or principles of almost any sort is not appreciated by a Confucian foreign policy. Yet success, if it is to be international, needs to make room for compromise for the mutual good. Confucianism is said to be better placed to accept such an argument than democratic pluralism, which puts a premium on outright victory.

Such principles are said to dominate politics in a wide range of Pacific states, including Japan, Korea, China, Taiwan, Hong Kong, Malaysia, Singapore, and, according to some, Vietnam. Yet it is clear that, especially as Confucianism has been around for so long in these states, it has had plenty of time to evolve into different, local varieties. The states have been in contact with different imperialisms and external ideologies, and they have often had their population-mix altered by immigration. The result is a multiplicity of Confucianisms.

Japan is perhaps the most important and difficult case to assess. Confucianism in Japan is often seen as a formal code-word for both anti-Communism and anti-Americanism, and in favour of closer co-operation with other Asians. On the one hand Japan is clearly a state with the outward

[8] *Far Eastern Economic Review* (19 May 1988).
[9] James Hsiung (ed.), *Human Rights in East Asia* (New York: Parragon, 1985).
[10] Pye, *Asian Power*.

appearance of western democratic pluralism. Yet in the search to explain why Japan has done so well in the modern world, numerous analysts have gone back to traditional roots in order to suggest a host of reasons why the Japanese system is basically unique. The Japanese themselves have fostered this image.[11] Obviously, to some extent all states are different and unique. Yet it is clear that many of the so-called unique Japanese practices in economic policy, for example in labour relations, are variations on more familiar Victorian paternalism as adapted at the turn of the century in United States economic policy.[12] What appears to be unique may instead be a natural stage of development that many developed western economies have long forgotten that they passed through.[13]

Of course it is also possible that some of the traits of early industrialization and its attendant political system will be retained in the Japanese political system for good cultural reasons.[14] The 'flexible rigidities' of paternalism may be more deeply engrained in Confucianism than it is in capitalism, and indeed Confucianism may be more deeply engrained in Japan than capitalism.[15] Yet there is certainly strong evidence of sharp competition and individualism in Japan, for example in its educational institutions and in the exploitation of subcontractors.[16] At least one prominent Japanese anthropologist has suggested that Japan is like a jellyfish, 'it has no bone but an internal order'. This pragmatic Confucianism stands in sharp contrast to China's firmer principles of social order.[17]

Even if the Japanese system is really several systems, all of which are changing, there are some characteristics of its Confucian variant that do seem important.[18] The remarkably steady succession of governments headed by relatively little-known rulers for short periods of time seems to have been a post-war pattern.[19] Thus decisions of government are built more on consensus, take time to be shaped, and are deeply affected by the interests of, and politics within, the all-powerful bureaucracy. The style of the bureaucrat sets the tone, with the attendant risk of policy drift.[20] Huge

---

[11] Peter Dale, *The Myth of Japanese Uniqueness* (London: Croom Helm, 1986).

[12] P. J. Buckley and H. Mirza, 'The Wit and Wisdom of Japanese Management' in *Management International Review*, 25/3 (1985).

[13] Ronald Dore, 'Reflections on the Learn From Japan Boom' in *IHJ Bulletin* (spring 1983).

[14] Ronald Dore, *Taking Japan Seriously*.

[15] Ronald Dore, *Flexible Rigidities* (London: Athlone, 1986).

[16] Roger Goodman, 'Japanese Education' in *The Pacific Review*, 2/1 (1988); Thomas Rohlen, *Japan's High Schools* (Berkeley, Calif.: University of California Press, 1983).

[17] Chie Nakane, *Japanese Society* (London: Weidenfeld, 1970).

[18] Joy Hendry, *Understanding Japanese Society* (London: Croom Helm, 1987).

[19] J. A. A. Stockwin, *Japan: Divided Politics in a Growth Economy* (London: Weidenfeld, 1982); Gerald Curtis, *The Japanese Way of Politics* (New York: Columbia University Press, 1988).

[20] Pye, *Asian Power*, 171–4.

economic power-houses maintain close relations with the bureaucrats and are less concerned about taking top political positions. Aversion to litigation is real, although possibly fading as greater experience is gained from the western-dominated international scene. The apt term 'flexible rigidities' encapsulates the idea that the Japanese system is both flexible and rigid at the same time—a nightmare for the analyst of comparative politics.

The condition of Confucianism in the Koreas is symptomatic of the problem with this amorphous ideology. Korea has been described as the 'Ireland of the east', with a people who are apt to become very combative just shortly after having seemed highly deferential.[21] Koreans certainly seem to have adopted a higher-risk political culture, in part because of a sense of living so close to disaster in the form of powerful neighbours.[22] In some respects, political legitimacy remains very much in question in both halves of the sharply divided, yet culturally unified country.

The Communist North remains deeply influenced by the ideology of centralism and socialism so common elsewhere in the more conservative Communist world. Although the South is more rigid and still more dominated by its military establishment than any other Confucian state, it has to be remembered that it is on a more or less permanent war footing. In the midst of this tension, the South manages to retain a far more pluralist political system than the North, although it also displays much of the paternalism and authoritarianism common elsewhere in the Confucian world. Like Japan, South Korea is run by bureaucrats and large corporations with close connections to the armed forces, civil administration, and banks. But in Korea the government is more active in directing the industrial process and therefore is more responsive to foreign pressures.[23]

By contrast, Taiwan is much more in the Japanese than the Korean mould. As a result of the lessons learned from the failure of the Guomindang in China, its closer relationship with the United States, and its greater ethnic diversity, Taiwan has become more pluralist than Korea and has made the cleanest break with its Confucian past. As in Japan the government plays a smaller role in the economic process and even more so than in Japan there is a major role for smaller private firms.[24] The political system remains repressive, but in the 1980s greater prosperity has brought demands for more political pluralism. Of course the state has actively intervened in the

---

[21] Ibid., 216.

[22] Ilpyong Kim, 'Human Rights in South Korea and United States Relations' in Hsiung (ed.), *Human Rights*.

[23] Richard Luedde-Neurath, 'State Intervention and Export-Oriented Development in South Korea' in Gordon White and Robert Wade (eds.), *Developmental States in East Asia* (Brighton: IDS Research Report, 16).

[24] Hofheinz and Calder, *East Asia*, 56–8.

Taiwanese economy and made special use of the banking system to direct the economy.[25] As in all the Confucian states, the notion of a self-regulating economy is clearly not accepted. But also like the others, Taiwan displays important distinctive variations on the Confucion principles.

Hong Kong is yet another special case, for reasons of its geographical location and its continuing colonial heritage. Britain's hands-off policy has contributed to a remarkably free-wheeling capitalist economy. This has developed in an atmosphere of minimal government except for the provision of basic social services. The state has stayed out of most economic policy. Yet unlike the democratic pluralist model there is no serious element of elected government and, as the 1984 agreement with China shows, fundamental decisions on the fate of the people can be taken without any serious democratic reaction.[26] This process can be seen as Confucian paternalism at its most pure, although in an economy that is more purely western and capitalist than anywhere else in the region.

Elsewhere in the Pacific, there are signs of Confucianism in parts of South-east Asia, but very limited parts at that. Singapore, like Hong Kong, is a more ethnically pure Chinese state than anywhere else in South-east Asia. Yet unlike Hong Kong, Singapore has a more classically interventionist, but mildly authoritarian, government when it comes to basic economic questions. A vibrant sector of small-scale industry flourishes at the economic base, but responds to state policy. As one might expect in a city-state, the ability of government to direct policy is relatively greater.[27] But unlike Hong Kong, political life is more pluralist and important.

Thus under a heavily western-influenced regime in Singapore, the political process of westernization has perhaps gone further than anywhere else in East Asia. Yet in economic terms the close involvement with western multinationals and the international economy is balanced by a highly interventionist, virtually socialist, policy at home. In economic terms, Hong Kong is closer to western ideas and further from Confucianism.

The picture of Confucianism as an ideology is unsatisfactory. Many states do qualify as practitioners but they retain distinctive characteristics even while sharing others. To some extent, 'Confucianism' is merely a convenient term to apply to a varied clutch of successful developing economies which happen to lie in the traditional Confucian zone but which are neither socialist nor democratic pluralist.

---

[25] Robert Wade, 'State Intervention in "Outward-looking" Development' in White and Wade (eds.), *Developmental States.*

[26] N. J. Miners, *The Government and Politics of Hong Kong* (Hong Kong: Oxford University Press, 1981).

[27] Hofheinz and Calder, *East Asia*, 58–60.

ASSORTED AUTHORITARIANISM

This fourth category is not really a category at all, more a catch-all for the remaining states of the Pacific that do not fit into the three main categories. They are concentrated in South-east Asia and Latin America. They are not democratic pluralist states or states run by a Communist Party according to the principles of democratic centralism. They often do look superficially like Confucian states, but usually the old benevolent paternalism is replaced by a harsher, often military, rule. Yet these states differ considerably one from another because of the idiosyncratic ways in which local political cultures have adapted to the challenge of modernization.

Of the three main South-east Asian states in this category, Thailand is perhaps the closest to the democratic pluralist model.[28] Like other South-east Asian countries, Thailand appears distinctive because of the way it has adapted to westernization while preserving a local culture that has already survived its relatively mild brush with earlier western imperialism. The Thai form of government is certainly not traditional and has been shaped by the particular preferences of the relatively narrow élite of the 1950s.[29]

Thai politics have been dominated by the armed forces but in recent years there are signs of a change to a more pluralist political system.[30] There is now a better balance among political groups, as in Malaysia, and the Senate in particular may be emerging as a place for more balanced politics. The growth of the lower, private sectors of the economy also suggests that real pluralism may be developing.[31] The economy is also increasingly open to foreign penetration and thus reliant on fluctuations in international market prices for Thai exports. The perceived threat from Vietnam's occupation of neighbouring Kampuchea adds to the need to rely on outsiders, and the United States in particular. But like many other developing countries have found when tied to the West but threatened by war, full, western-style democracy is difficult to develop.

A second South-east Asian authoritarian regime possibly in transition is the Philippines. Its booming economy was once held up as a beacon of success for developing states, but Philippine politics remains dominated by military power and crony capitalism. The deposition of Ferdinand Marcos in 1986 brought temporary relief and much hope of 'people power', but the

28 William Overholt, 'Thailand: The Moving Equilibrium' in *Pacific Review*, 1/1 (1988).
29 Ansil Ramsay, 'Thai Domestic Politics and Foreign Policy' in Karl Jackson, Sukhumbhand Paribatra, and J. Soedjati Djiwandono (eds.), *ASEAN in Regional and Global Context* (Berkeley, Calif.: Institute of East Asian Studies, 1986).
30 Ansil Ramsay, 'Thailand' in *Current History* (April 1987).
31 Tim Hindle, 'Thailand' in *The Economist* (31 October 1987).

real levers of power remained with the same small ruling class.[32] According to some the Philippines remains not far from a form of pluralist democracy, and it certainly has sufficient basis, by virtue of its close contacts with the United States, to develop such democracy. But like many developing states under loose military rule, the excuse of internal unrest is cited as a reason for not tackling the deep-rooted problems of inequality. In many senses the Philippines is a caricature of the extremes of the American system, with large doses of cynicism and idealism.[33]

The problems of inequality and the absence of political reform are probably more serious in the half of South-east Asia that is Indonesia. Clearly the 20-year rule of Suharto has run out of ideas. Notionally there is a multiparty system but, under the requirement that all parties abide by the state ideology of Pancasila, opposition is seriously curtailed. The appeal to religious and ethnic groups is prohibited and parties cannot maintain grass-roots organization between elections. The press is muzzled, especially when it reports on the cronyism at the top. With an economy split between isolated foreign ventures and an indigenous sector that is low waged, labour intensive, subsistence level, and based on mostly traditional techniques, there is little hope of externally stimulated change.[34]

Yet Indonesia has so far survived a bloody Communist uprising and endured the centrifugal tendencies of regionalism in the archipelago. Politics in Java remains the key, and this has been managed by master alchemists who have prevented the explosion of what ought to be a volatile mixture.[35] This presidential dictatorship in a diffused political system run by 'guided democracy' has survived a great deal, but has not achieved much more than survival. Guided democracy itself is an uneasy amalgam of western principle and local traditions of patron–client relations. Economic degeneration, bureaucratic ineptitude, and corruption are unchecked by a democratic system and the state is effectively run by a military bureaucracy.

Considering the differences among the political systems in South-east Asia, it is remarkable that the variously authoritarian ones plus Malaysia and Singapore could come together in ASEAN. Of course, unlike the EC, this is not an organization that demands much of its members' political systems since it is focused on economic co-operation. But the comparison to Europe is instructive if only to make the point that there are deeper political differences in South-east Asia. Whether that absence of a common political ideology is a main reason for the failure of ASEAN to integrate its members

---

[32] David Rosenberg, 'The Philippines' in *Current History* (April 1987).
[33] Pye, *Asian Power*, 125.
[34] John Andrews, 'Indonesia' in *The Economist* (15 August 1987).
[35] Lea Williams, *Southeast Asia* (Oxford: Oxford University Press, 1976), 253.

can be assessed only by looking at the organization's economic role, which will be considered later.

Curiously, at least in terms of political ideology, there may well be more that unites the three South-east Asian authoritarian states with the other guided democracies across the water in Latin America. Of the 11 Pacific Latin American states, one, Costa Rica, is a genuine pluralist democracy and one, Nicaragua, now falls into the democratic centralist category. The remaining nine are variants of authoritarian regimes affected by local conditions. Six of the nine—Ecuador, El Salvador, Guatemala, Honduras, Panama, and Peru—are particularly clear-cut versions of political systems where elected Presidents, juntas, and dictators swap chairs without changing much else. Of course some, such as Peru and El Salvador, have had elections. But more often than not the power of the armed forces looms large behind the pluralist façade. Guatemala has elections but no left-wing candidates; Peru has had radical left-wing military dictatorships and more recently a democratic government. The authoritarianism can be of the left or right, and it is usually far more blatantly military rule than anywhere else in South-east Asia. The junta type of authoritarianism is most characteristic of Latin American Pacific states.

Three other states stand out as closer to the milder authoritarianism of South-east Asia—Chile, Colombia, and especially Mexico. Chile had the most vibrant tradition of genuine democracy until the unrest of the early 1970s. A minority Marxist regime under Salvador Allende was eventually deposed in 1973 by a military coup, but the deep-seated democratic traditions have proven more difficult to eliminate. Superficially, the Pinochet regime has tolerated more opposition political organization, especially in the 1980s.

Colombia is a strange case of ineffective civil rule leaving terrorists and drug traffickers to lord it over vast parts of the state. The military is an important voice, but has stayed out of direct control for longer than almost anywhere else in Latin America. Radical policies have yet to be pursued and the armed forces remain deeply suspicious of deals with guerrillas. However, some form of guided democracy is possible under these circumstances.

Mexico is by far the largest and most important of the Pacific Latin American states. Its politics have been dominated by one party, the PRI, since 1929 and left-wing candidates did not stand until 1982. But in a curious electoral system that reserves most seats for the PRI, there is some scope for opposition parties to join the parliamentary system and to speak more freely. The PRI has been reasonably benevolent in the Asian mould, instituting land reform, trying to face up to the cancer of corruption, and tolerating opposition at the provincial and municipal levels. It is a system most akin to that in Indonesia, but with less of the one-man rule that has been so destructive in Jakarta.

Of course, all the Latin American states (except Nicaragua, and then only recently) are dominated by the presence of the United States. Although Washington sees no need for democratic systems in its own mould, it does see the need to encourage greater pluralism while not losing its economic and political dominance. It is often a delicate game to play, and one that helps keep Latin American political ideology diffuse and yet tied to the United States. While the occasional state, such as Mexico, may see ideological reasons to look across the Pacific for ideas on government for a developing state, most other Latin Americans have looked to their neighbours or to autocracies across the Atlantic in Spain and Portugal. With the new European democracy, these Latin Americans may well be encouraged to look for new ideas.

In general, the patterns of ideologies in the Pacific are far more complex than in the Atlantic. There are various groups of states, only some of which see transpacific links. In the Communist and Confucian worlds, most fellow members of a group are close by, but they are not necessarily to be counted as friends. The divisions, in both their ideologies and interests, has rendered ideology a poor guide to the foreign policies of these states. The development of a sense of Pacific community seems remote. Political fragmentation, but not necessarily isolation, means there is less Pacific order than disorder.

8

Culture and Place in the World

People and states may know where they are in the world in geographic terms, but that tells us little about ideological, cultural, and political alignment. In Europe, West Berlin is a fine example, albeit for very specific historical circumstances, of an entity that is ideologically 'of the West', but geographically in the East. In the Pacific, where so many neo-Europes have been planted and where colonialism or western influence was sometimes very strong, it is less easy to tell where states conceive their proper place in the world to be.

The states of the Pacific are also not of the same size or composition and thus are likely to look at the world in very different ways. The Soviet Union is a European power first and a Pacific power second. China is traditionally a continental power rather than one with a Pacific-orientation. The Americas were, of course, also part of the Atlantic community before they began paying attention to the Pacific.

Not all the states of the Pacific are ethnically homogeneous, and thus different groups within states may well view their place in the world in very different ways. Just as a Jewish diaspora in Europe and America has allegiances to Israel in the Middle East, so Chinese or Japanese abroad may not be fully integrated into their diaspora environments. Equally, attitudes of the host country to minorities may border on racism. At the very least societies can be deeply divided on ethnic grounds. States of the Pacific can be divided into those which see themselves as more or less independent and even isolated from their neighbours, and those which have close bonds with at least some neighbouring states. But not even the most regionally integrated state perceives itself to be part of a Pacific-wide political system.

HOMOGENEOUS STATES

Japan

North-east Asia has some of the most homogeneous states in the world. By far the most discussed and most important one is Japan, where 99.5 per cent of the population are Japanese and only some 0.5 per cent are ethnic Koreans. As a nation cut off from the world for so long, and one that moved so swiftly into modernization and imperialism, Japan has one of the most distinctive approaches to its place in the world. It is both a borrower of foreign cultures and an adept adapter of the imports—yet without importing the foreigners themselves.[1] Japan is a classical case of a 'self-strengthening' instinct.

Not surprisingly, the Japanese have been able to develop a mythology of their uniqueness.[2] A poll in 1983–4 showed that 80 per cent of Japanese thought they were one of the 'superior races' in the world.[3] To some extent this perception of uniqueness is typical of modernizing regimes feeling their way in what is perceived as a hostile world. European nationalism has also had its extremes in German nationalism and colonialist hubris. But unlike European states where living cheek by jowl with others for so long blurred cultural lines, Japan as an island has managed to hold on to its perception for longer. In fact, Japan is probably more culturally unified than almost any other state.

This sense of unity contributes to Japan's ambiguity about its place in the world. While modernization has meant some degree of integration into the world economy, enduring tradition has encouraged a sense of uniqueness.[4] The Japanese exhibit an obvious sense of superiority when dealing with foreigners. Not only do they sometimes mistreat, and usually mistrust, foreigners in their midst, they are also loath to accept them as Japanese even after several generations of intermarriage and residence in Japan. The notion of a 'hyphenated' Japanese, as there are Jewish-or Irish-Americans, is virtually unheard of. The term 'Japanese' is simply not used as an ethnic suffix, at least in Japan itself.

Japan's tradition of involvement with foreign countries has actually been relatively short and volatile. But the shock of the defeat in 1945 created the new, and still distinctive, version of Japan as an 'economic animal'. This tendency to look at other countries as markets rather than as how they might or should be changed from a Japanese perspective certainly contrasts with the more moralistic approach to international relations that is often demonstrated by western governments, and particularly by the United States.[5] Yet by the 1980s, under a new slogan of 'internationalism', Japan had begun to try to change its world-view. The task has not been easy.[6] The gap in cultural terms remains vast and although Japanese increasingly travel and

---

[1] Nathaniel Thayer, 'Race and Politics in Japan' in *Pacific Review*, 1/1 (1988).
[2] Peter Dale, *The Myth of Japanese Uniqueness* (London: Croom Helm, 1986).
[3] *Far Eastern Economic Review* (19 February 1987).
[4] Dick Wilson, *The Sun at Noon* (London: Hamish Hamilton, 1986), especially chs. 1, 14, 15.
[5] These points are developed in *Financial Times* (18 August 1987).
[6] 'Slogans, Images and Visions' in *Pacific Review*, 1/1 (1988).

live abroad they keep themselves apart and are particularly cautious about transferring decision-making outside Japan when they establish branches of Japanese multinational corporations.[7]

Thus, when looking at the world outside, the picture from Japan remains curious. Close neighbours such as the Koreans and Chinese are often disdained. They were occupied during the war and thus are often now seen as weak and inferior.[8] China may have been the 'elder brother' in cultural terms, but it is now seen very much as an older brother who fell on hard times because he was too slow and arrogant to react to new ideas from outside.[9] Unlike the Germans in Europe, who have come to terms with their responsibility for war, the Japanese seem unwilling to accept the validity of Chinese and other neighbours' complaints that Japan does not feel sufficiently guilty about its war record. Many Japanese see the Chinese reaction as an excuse for their own failure since 1945 and as jealousy of Japanese success.

The modernization of Japan has obviously transformed its self-image, but not entirely. One of the key ambiguities that remains for Japan is in understanding its place in Asia. There is a popular strain of opinion in Japan, embodied in Keitaro Hasegawa's *Sayonara Asia* published in 1986, that suggests post-war trends have cut Japan off from the Asian world, with the exception of Korea, much like a huge skyscraper in a slum is cut off from what takes place at its base. As we shall see, in economic and military terms this argument has only a grain of truth. But it is indicative of the extent to which Japanese know that they have made themselves into something very different from most of the states in their region.

This notion of isolation, of course, conflicts with the lingering aspirations for a Greater Asian Co-prosperity Sphere or with the milder version in the 1980s of making a 'contribution' to East Asian security.[10] Both notions, and especially that of the now unmentionable wartime doctrine, put Japan in the lead, but very much as part of an Asian challenge to the West. Yet it is clear that Japan's experience of Asia has demonstrated a lack of understanding as great as that displayed by western colonialism. Because of the wartime experience, Japan was banished from Asia for a while, in contrast to Germany which was quickly reintegrated into albeit both parts of Europe. Thus Japan's sense of unease over its proper role is made worse.

Some have suggested that the Sayonara Asia line is merely a stepping-stone back to the Co-prosperity Sphere, as the West drives Japan out of its

---

[7] *Financial Times* (4 December 1987).

[8] Susumu Awanohara, 'Japanese Talk Tough to Asian Neighbours' in *Far Eastern Economic Review* (3 July 1986).

[9] Wilson, *Sun at Noon*, ch. 15.

[10] *Far Eastern Economic Review* (24 March 1988).

own markets and cultural universe. Certainly the official line in Japanese foreign policy is a greater desire for integration in Asia, in terms of both North and South-east Asia, as part of a more natural 'contribution' to regional security. But Japan remains uneasy about new grand designs in foreign policy and is probably happiest not having to think about its new role in an age of declining superpowers. The tension between Japanese 'Gaullism' and the country's recent low profile is likely to grow more acute.[11]

The trend towards more regional thinking has developed in the 1970s, with the focus on the Pacific as Japan's natural region a compromise between regional and globalist concepts.[12] While Africa is generally neglected, and Latin America and the Middle East are seen as markets, Europe is still viewed as an ambiguous mix of markets and great traditions.[13] But Japan's approach to the Pacific, and indeed the general concept of a Pacific Century, has its roots in Japan's search for a way out of its dilemma over its place in the world. Both the plethora of Pacific organizations in recent years and their relative ineffectiveness form part of Japan's dilemma about its role in regional and global politics. While Europeans and Americans have had time to become accustomed to the problems of international interdependence, Japan has yet to resolve its own sense of place and importance.[14]

The emotional zigzags in Japan about its own sense of nationhood and place in the world have led some to become concerned about the growth of the 'new right' in Japan.[15] These new Volkists are particularly contemptuous of the Japanese bourgeoisie who are content to watch television instead of polishing their national souls to a *samurai*-like sheen. This intellectual identity crisis is also evident in assessing the West. The supposed lack of virtue and appreciation of aesthetics in the West provokes Japanese disdain. The Japanese seem especially concerned that western modernism 'destroys mankind by destroying nature' and thus needs to be saved by 'Japanese spiritual civilization'.[16] Even when Prime Minister Nakasone addressed the United Nations in October 1985 and spoke of international harmony, in Japanese his language was of different races.

Nationalism is an ideology that western countries also struggle to adapt to modernity in international politics. But the type of nationalism and patriotism of President Reagan and Margaret Thatcher is not the ultra-nationalism

---

[11] *Far Eastern Economic Review* (26 June 1986).

[12] Ronald Morse, 'Japan's Search for an Independent Foreign Policy' in *Journal of Northeast Asian Studies*, 3/2 (summer 1984); 'Japan and the Pacific' in Ronald Morse *et al.*, *Pacific Basin* (Washington DC: Center for National Policy, Paper 20, July 1986).

[13] Endymion Wilkinson, *Japan versus Europe* (London: Penguin, 1983).

[14] Nathaniel Thayer, 'Race and Politics'.

[15] Ian Buruma, 'The Right Argument' in *Far Eastern Economic Review* (19 February 1987).

[16] Michael Random, *Japan: Strategy of the Unseen* (London: Crucible, 1987).

or pride and prejudice that some of the Kyoto School of Japanese ultra-
nationalism propound.[17] Blood-purity is not an argument that any sensible
western politician would try to make in discussing modern nationalism. But
it is more popular to tell the Japanese that their economic miracle is due to
racial reasons than to talk about a talented bureaucracy. There does not
appear to be an intellectual or moral framework in which a response to
nativism is framed in Japan, apart from Marxism. Thus many Japanese are
inevitably drawn back to the myth of their own uniqueness, thereby making
it difficult for them to play a full role in a complex global disorder.

Korea

Korea, like Germany, is a nation divided by great-power politics. As time
takes its toll, the differences in outlook between North and South become
more real. It is one thing to recognize national unification as an ideal, but it
is quite another to abandon a way of life for the satisfaction of such
intangible nationalism. South Korea, like West Germany, is not prepared to
pay such a price for national unity.

Both North and South share the perception of being caught in the vice of
great-power politics. In traditional Korean international relations the pressures were 'merely' from China and Japan. Now there are two superpowers
who have joined the game. The Koreans gain some independence by their
ability to play off one ally against another in a hostile environment, and this
is particularly fruitful when the allies play politics with Korean allegiance.

Korea has been called 'the Palestine of East Asia' by virtue of its having
served as an invasion route for trampling rival empires. There are said to be
930 recorded invasions of Korea, counting from the tenth century. Yet,
unlike Palestine, Korea is remarkable for its ethnic homogeneity. The
differences between North and South are merely political and economic. As
in the case of Japan, this helps build a sense of national unity, although in
Korea's case it is clearly fragmented by contemporary international politics.[18] The tendency to 'nationalize' the ideas that are borrowed from others
is intense, precisely because of the regular threats and ethnic homogeneity.
For example, Confucianism was made more rigid and orthodox in Korea
than in China.

Korea's strong sense of national identification and paranoia also stems
from its relative lack of contact with the West. It was colonized, but by

[17] William Wetherall, 'Nakasone Promotes Pride and Prejudice' in *Far Eastern Economic
Review* (19 February 1987).

[18] Shim Jao Hoon, 'Koreans Turn to the West' in *Far Eastern Economic Review* (12 February
1987).

Japan. Interaction with the West is really only a post-war phenomenon, and the contacts experienced by North and South have been diverse. Therefore, whatever identification there is with the outside world, it is very different in the two parts of the country. Because of their antagonism towards Chinese and Japanese, South Koreans may now be happier to look to the Americas and Europe than to Asia. But even anti-Americanism is reportedly on the rise in the 1980s, as the limits on political reform are seen to be dictated by Washington as well as Seoul.[19]

The thread of 'economism' is not enough to give Koreans a sense of Asian solidarity, especially with their immediate neighbours. In some sense, the South Korean keenness for Pacific-wide co-operation (see Chapters 17–24) is a response to their uneasy sense of being Asian. In the 1980s the South Koreans have been going to great lengths to build bridges to Europe, probably because westernness is possibly a safer notion to aspire to than Asianness. For a country trapped in the cockpit of great-power rivalry, it is dangerous to be uncertain about one's place in the world.

China

China's view of its place in the world is hotly debated by observers of that once-great empire.[20] It was certainly the idealized vision of Chinese leaders in times past that they were the centre of the earth and that world politics was organized in a hierarchy flowing down from a pinnacle occupied by the Chinese emperor. Of course the reality was far less flattering to China, especially in times of dynastic weakness.

The most challenging period of weakness came with western pressure as has already been illustrated. The impact of western and Japanese imperialism, not to mention the challenges of modernization and Communism, all changed the élites' perception of the outside world.[21] The distress in having to adopt new visions of the world was seen best in the Chinese struggle over the best route to modernization. The key question was whether the modernization should be self-strengthening or accomplished with major foreign aid. China opted for the former, unlike Japan, and did so belatedly.

Whether China could ever have become as modernized as Japan is one of the great unanswered questions of Pacific history. The reality is that China remains a poor, peasant society. It is also a society with split views on the outside world, aware of what needs to be learned but also fearful of opening its door too wide to noxious outside influences. As Lu Xun noted,

19 *Wall Street Journal* (16 July 1987).
20 Details in Gerald Segal, *Defending China* (Oxford: Oxford University Press, 1985).
21 Michael Yahuda, *Towards the End of Isolationism* (London: Macmillan, 1983).

'Throughout the ages, the Chinese have had only two ways of looking at foreigners, up to them as superior beings or down on them as wild animals.'[22] Not surprisingly, in the period after 1949 China has swung its doors on their hinges, sometimes opening in one direction, sometimes in the other, sometimes opening individual doors more widely, and sometimes slamming virtually all of them shut.

China's mental map is as broad as that befitting a great power with greater-power aspirations. It pays attention to events far afield, for example in the Middle East, even if they have little direct impact on China itself.[23] Yet for all the talk of solidarity with other developing states, the Chinese remain as racist as any other haughty society, as testified by the periodic abuse of Africans in China.[24]

But above all China recognizes that its policy is deeply affected by the attitudes of the two superpowers: the only states since 1945 with the potential to do serious damage to China.[25] Thus China has honed its skills as a player of the great-power triangle and an assessor of superpower politics.[26]

While China's ability to play in the superpowers' league is limited for the time being, it is very definitely a regional power. Its conception of Asia is focused on its 12 neighbouring states, and that just about takes in all of Asia from Afghanistan to Korea. With a large overseas Chinese presence throughout South-east Asia its links extend to those parts of Asia with which China has no common frontier.

Despite such obvious wide-ranging perspectives, China is only dimly aware of its relative decline, even in its own region, and especially economically. Japan is still considered as 'little Japan' and Taiwan and Hong Kong are seen as parts of China. Its idiosyncratic and changing development strategy is a large cause of its relative isolation from Asia.[27] It is also a cause of wildly fluctuating perceptions of the outside world. More Chinese students go to the United States than anywhere else, but among the most educated western Europe is the most popular part of the world. A survey in 1988 apparently also revealed Japan to be the most popular country among the population as a whole, but the poll was carried out by the Japanese.[28]

China offers all manner of explanations for its weakness, but still seems

[22] Robert Thomson, 'China Looks Up and Down at the Big Noses' in *Financial Times* (12 July 1986).

[23] Yitzhak Shichor, *The Middle East in China's Foreign Policy* (Cambridge: Cambridge University Press, 1978).

[24] Thomson, 'China Looks Up'.

[25] Michael Yahuda, *Chinese Foreign Policy* (London: Croom Helm, 1979).

[26] Gerald Segal, *The Great Power Triangle* (London: Macmillan, 1982).

[27] Louise de Rosario, 'Isolation Led to China's Murky View of Neighbours' in *Far Eastern Economic Review* (12 February 1987).

[28] Kyodo in BBC, SWB, FE, 0123, A3, 5 (3 April 1988).

prepared to learn only from the West rather than from fellow Asians. Much like Japan, China tries to take advantage of its Asianness in building regional solidarity. But it is, at the same time, generally dismissive of Asia as being less important than the developed worlds of Europe and America. It plays on the Chineseness of overseas Chinese in order to attract their investment. But in practice the entrepreneurial capitalist who symbolizes the overseas Chinese is worlds away from his cousin, the bureaucratic factory manager in the People's Republic. Young, upwardly mobile Chinese professionals around the world have little in common with Beijing's socialist man. It is one thing for socialist man to accept the evident material prosperity of westerners, but quite another to accept it in fellow Chinese. This is not the best basis on which to build regional solidarity.

On the other hand, the Chinese of Taiwan have been able to move towards a more cosmopolitan world-view, although they remain deeply scarred by a sense of inferiority which results from diplomatic isolation. Compared to the new strength of Japanese identity and modernity, Taiwan seems curiously stunted. Its use of western names along with Chinese surnames is only one trivial sign of Taiwan's ambivalence about how Chinese and how western it is. The differences between generations and place of origin in China obviously have a great deal to do with the uncertainty in the Taiwanese self-image and place in the world.

Like West Germans visiting their relatives in the East, visits by Taiwanese to the mainland provoke feelings of regret and a sense of the increasing distance from their kinsmen. Yet Taiwan has been independent of China for longer than it has been united with the mainland. Although the evolution of another independent Chinese state recognized by the world is far from certain, it does seem increasingly likely as Taiwan develops an identity of its own.[29] Being Chinese is clearly no more a cause for unity than being Arab in the Middle East. For at least some Chinese, as for some Arabs, prosperity brings greater integration into a global culture and fewer ties to ancient backgrounds.

Thailand and the Philippines

Thailand is the only other East Asian state that has managed to retain its independence from western powers and thus remain more or less united. Yet 14 per cent of Thailand's population is Chinese, even though it has no common border with its great near-neighbour to the north. More

---

[29] Lillian Craig Harris, 'Towards Taiwan's Independence?' in *Pacific Review*, 1/1 (1988).

importantly, the cultural roots of the Thais run both west to India and east
to the rest of East Asia.[30]

Thailand remains on the border of the Pacific, looking more in than out,
and conscious of its position as an outsider. Yet so much of post-war Thai
history has been tied up with South-east Asia and the Pacific that over the
years it has become a more natural part of the region. Its political system is
derived from its close encounter with British and French imperialism, and
then with the even more pervasive United States since the 1950s.

Thailand, somewhat like Korea, is aware of its precarious position on the
pathways of great powers but, unlike Korea, is remote enough to have
survived with its independence intact. It remains a medium-sized state
paying close attention to its surroundings, but happier to be on the lip than
directly in the frying-pan of regional conflict.

The Philippines also lies on the fringe of South-east Asia in geographic
terms, but its people are overwhelmingly (over 95 per cent) Malay. This
unity is only punctured by a small Muslim Malay minority. The country's
fringe status in the region is enhanced by its Christianity and its closer
historical association with Spain and then the United States.

Thus even though Filipinos are undoubtedly of local stock, their view of
the world has been directed more across the Pacific than any of their fellow
Malay people. Coupled with the fact that their country is a relatively new
grouping of islands, it could be dangerous to look too much to other Malays
for fear of undermining the Filipinos' fragile sense of national identity.

Pacific Islands

Most of the islands in the Pacific, big and small, remain relatively ethnically
unified. Although they vary from white-settler-dominated Australia and
New Zealand to Melanesian Papua New Guinea and Micronesian Kiribati,
they have none of the deep domestic divisions of South-east Asia.

Some societies, such as those of New Caledonia and Fiji, have major
divisions resulting from colonial policy. The Indian majority in Fiji is distant
enough from India, unlike many South-east Asian Indians, that it has begun
to evolve its own image of Fiji, but this is still different from that of the
indigenous Melanesian Fijians. In New Caledonia the problem is similarly
intense, for the white settlers want control of the territory and close
association with France, which puts them in direct opposition to the 37 per
cent of the population that is local Melanesian and wants independence.

Apart from these special cases, the real splits in the region show up in the
different perspectives of isolated islanders. As in island South-east Asia,

30 *Far Eastern Economic Review* (18 February 1988).

basic geography has encouraged a fragmented world-view. Colonialism added an extra twist to this kaleidoscope, leaving different islands bewildered by different colonial traditions. Of course there always were basic differences between Micronesians, Melanesians, and Polynesians, providing fertile ground in which to sow discord.

Yet the islands are so small and far apart that they pose little threat to each other. The relative absence of rivalry makes it easier to promise international co-operation, albeit harder to find anything to co-operate about. The formation of the South Pacific Forum in 1971 was intended to build on what was common in the heritage and contemporary predicament of the region. The 14-member organization has so far remained more pious than practical, especially in the political realm. It has focused more on tourism and only peripherally on the far more important issue of trade. What is more, it remains dominated by the main Pacific islands of Australia and New Zealand.

GREATER INTEGRATION

Malaysia and Indonesia

Thailand and the Philippines stand out particularly clearly when compared to their fellow South-east Asians. Indonesia, Malaysia, and Singapore are all heirs to the great cosmopolitan traditions of the region and as a result they comprise a potentially lethal ethnic mix. Malaysia is the most volatile, with some 50 per cent Malays, 36 per cent Chinese, and 10 per cent Indians. Thinking Malaysian means thinking first in ethnic categories and thus there is little that can be called a Malaysian cultural unity.

The perception of place in the world varies from one community to another. For the Malays there are close relationships with the Indonesians but these barely stretch to the Philippines.[31] Yet increasingly the Malaysian Malays have come to see themselves as distinct from Indonesian Malays as Malaysia grows more prosperous. Similarly, Malaysian Chinese have distanced themselves from China as a way of proving that they are not Beijing's fifth column. But in reaction to their isolation from the motherland, Malaysian Chinese have also paid special attention to their culture, much like hyphenated Americans do across the Pacific. Indian Malays are tied more closely still to India, even in such matters as arranged marriages.

Malaysians, and indeed others in the region, began to 'look east' to Japan

---

[31] Suhainia Aznam, 'Malaysians Look Inward Before They Look East' in *Far Eastern Economic Review* (12 February 1987).

and Korea in the 1970s as prosperity seemed to come to North-east Asia before it came to the south-east. Yet wartime memories and the uncomfortable experience since with haughty Japanese business people in the region have kept the attitude towards Japan mostly hostile. South-east Asians have been ambiguous about their view of Japan: upset when they are paid insufficient attention, but concerned when the Japanese become too closely involved.[32] Anti-Japanese riots in Jakarta and Bangkok in 1974, and much less serious ones in the Philippines and Malaysia in 1984, indicate that there are very distinct limits on pan-Asianism as seen from South-east Asia.

Yet the notion of pan-Malay unity is also not taken seriously. With the Philippines already an outsider, Singapore a hard, mainly Chinese nut in the centre, and a number of territorial disputes in the region, the notion of unity seems remote. Although the Malays all speak a variation on the same language, their island geography has encouraged a fragmented world-view.[33] The notion of being an outsider, even in your own home region, continues to be common in island South-east Asia.

Indo-China

Indo-China is obviously deeply affected by the artificial unity imposed by French colonialism, and above all by the near-incessant wars since the departure of Japan in 1945. In fact, the very name 'Indo-China' suggests division between the worlds of China and India. The spread of Communism in 1975 to South Vietnam, Laos, and Kampuchea has added yet another confusing element to this already-self-obsessed part of the Pacific.

Laos certainly has the simplest world-view despite its divided ethnic composition. It remains tucked away, mostly out of the main line of regional conflict, and absorbed in its own traditional tribal conflicts. Its links to the region in the past have run through Thailand or Vietnam and now are mainly concentrated via the eastern route to Vietnam. In many respects Laos is like a remote Pacific island in its involvement in Pacific affairs, only it is a far more divided society than most island communities.

Kampuchea is less isolated but then it has also been more savaged by war and still remains divided. It is torn between traditional peasant isolation and orientation either to the Communist and Vietnamese worlds or westward towards Thailand. Although it is a relatively united society ethnically, its politics and world-view remain deeply divided and confused.

Vietnam remains the dominant Indo-Chinese state and the one most oriented to the outside world. It is also a relatively united society in ethnic

---

32 *Far Eastern Economic Review* (26 June 1986).
33 Milton Osborne, *Southeast Asia* (London: Allen & Unwin, 1985).

terms, 90 per cent Vietnamese, although its political wounds from years of war and civil war remain unhealed. It has been wrenched away from its traditional international orientation towards China by recent wars, and has therefore sought friends further north in the Soviet Union. This is an unnatural alliance in all but balance-of-power terms.

Vietnam, like other Indo-Chinese states, has been excluded and secluded from the dynamic economic and social change of the past decades in the Pacific, and thus has not developed a 'look east' policy like others in South-east Asia. Neither has it developed a western orientation, once again because of its political conflicts with both the French and the Americans. It is only part of the Indo-Chinese tragedy that Vietnam has been so isolated from the world around it.

Australia and New Zealand

The world-view of both Australia and New Zealand has been shaped primarily by their ethnic origins in Europe. Their older cultural links are to the UK and the Commonwealth, although they sit about as far from London as one can get. New Zealand is perhaps somewhat less touched by United States influence, and New Zealanders also suffer from a continuing inferiority complex towards their neighbours across the Tasman Sea. With the right to move to Australia whenever they wish, there is little to be gained from formal unity with Australia, and a lot of pride to be lost.[34]

Australia, with its fading sense of 'cultural cringe', remains confused about its position in the world. With its much-exaggerated 'culture' of 'no worries, relax', it likes to see itself as unique in an otherwise hurly-burly Pacific. This is not the pseudo-intellectualism of those who speak of a culture of 'dream-time', but more a recognition that success need not be based on the frenetic pace of Confucian culture.[35] In the long run, this emphasis on the 'quality of life' might be a more useful contribution to Pacific culture than the pressure to learn from 'Japanese uniqueness'. Whatever the case, there is undoubtedly a strong Australian sense of being distinctive, and a life-style certainly unlike that of the Asian Pacific.

The Australian view of the Pacific is confused, generally paying most attention to those furthest away in Japan and the United States. Australia sees itself as having special regional responsibilities, especially in the south Pacific, yet it has also never strayed much beyond an Australia-first policy. In some senses it is one of the few Pacific states to have genuine interest in what takes place across the vast expanse of Pacific waters, but it is also

[34] *Far Eastern Economic Review* (16 July 1987).
[35] Linda Christian, *The Ribbon and the Ragged Square* (London: Penguin, 1987).

very typical of the Pacific in its difficulty in developing a genuine Pacific perspective.

The Americas

The world-view of the United States, as befits a superpower, is global. Yet in ethnic terms its orientation is overwhelmingly European. The hyphenation in most Americans is with a European culture. The largest single 'minority' are blacks, all of whom originated across the south Atlantic. Some 7 per cent of Americans are of Latin American Spanish extraction, which gives a strong hemispheric focus. A mere 1 per cent of Americans are of Asian origin, with Chinese, Japanese, and Filipinos roughly taking an equal share. Public-opinion polls in 1987 continue to show that Americans see Europeans as their closest allies, and if anything the trend is towards seeing less friendship across the Pacific than in recent years.[36] Western Europe is seen as more friendly than Asia by a ratio of more than two to one. Japan is viewed as the only serious friend in Asia, with polls showing ambivalence about China.[37] What is more, as the steady pressure for trade protectionism has built up in the United States, it has been the Japanese and the Asians who have borne the brunt of American criticism even though the Europeans are also large contributors to the American deficit. What was even more disturbing, some of the American criticisms of Japan and other East Asians brought out the old racial stereotypes.

Yet, as will be suggested below, at least the Pacific part of the United States has established an increasingly important orientation westward to Asia. The reasons appear to be almost purely economic. The question remains whether this is merely part of a trend towards the globalization of United States foreign policy or an intrinsic interest in the Pacific on the scale of the more traditional Atlantic consciousness.

It is undoubtedly true that Asian-Americans are increasingly exploring their heritage and that their culture has added yet more spice to the American melting-pot.[38] But apart from a heavy concentration of people down the Pacific coast, the Asian communities remain much smaller than European, African, or Latin American immigrant communities. Unlike the Europeans in particular, they have been less willing to become involved in American politics. Asian communities have been conspicuously reluctant to

---

36 Poll by the Chicago Council on Foreign Relations, reported in *The Economist* (14 March 1987).
37 William Watts *et al.*, *Japan, Korea and China* (Lexington, Mass.: D. C. Heath, 1979).
38 *International Herald Tribune* (18 July 1987).

lobby the American government or to try to influence its foreign policy, in sharp contrast to Polish, Russian, Jewish, and Black Americans.

In almost no dimension of the United States' world-view can its priority be said to have shifted to the Pacific. To the extent that the transpacific links have been strengthened in recent years, this has been restricted almost entirely to economics. Even in 1987 a survey of voting records in the United Nations showed that most friends of the United States in Asia voted against it, while the West Europeans had some of the highest rates of similar voting to the United States. Only Japan scored 68 per cent agreement, whereas ASEAN states averaged 18 per cent.[39]

The other North American Pacific state, Canada, is a more divided society than the United States, but its divisions are between French and English and relate entirely to roots in European immigration and colonial policy. Canada has an even tinier Asian minority than does the United States. The orientation of Canadian policy, as with that of Mexico and much of Latin America, has been overwhelmingly to the nearby elephant that is the United States. As Canadian Prime Ministers are fond of noting, when the elephant rolls over, even inadvertently, their friendly mouse can get badly hurt. Canada and Mexico are closer to the United States than any other country, and thus feel especially vulnerable.

Other Pacific states in the hemisphere pay more attention to the United States than to any other great power, but otherwise most remain isolated from the currents of international affairs. When domestic unrest, for example in Nicaragua, gets out of hand, great powers including the Soviet Union do get involved and the region's problems become more internationalized.

Yet none of these international perspectives involves a look westward across the Pacific. Ethnically, these states are either overwhelmingly European, such as Chile, or a mixture of local Indians and Europeans, such as Ecuador, Colombia, Mexico, and Peru. By far the largest Asian ethnic minority is in non-Pacific Brazil. The only significant link, and a tenuous one at that, is along language and ex-colonial lines with the Philippines. The replacement of a Spanish-dominated world by one dominated by the United States is a trend shared across the Pacific, but so far it remains little more than a curiosity that catches the attention of sociologists and historians.

Clearly it is difficult to find anything like common world-views in the Pacific. Some states are very isolated and some prefer to look well beyond their region. Some states have ethnic links across the waters or with close neighbours and some are homogeneous. Only a few have deep traditions of thinking internationally, and those that do so today, such as China, Japan, and the United States, are divided among themselves, not to say divided by

---

[39] *Far Eastern Economic Review* (20 August 1987).

their own domestic dilemmas. Few people seem to think Pacific, let alone know or agree about what issues such thinking ought to encompass. One of the basic problems seems to be the diverse ethnic composition of the Pacific, for, at its roots, it is the ethnic heritage in the Atlantic culture that creates such cohesion as there may be.

9

Migration

Perhaps the most essential requirement for international integration is the integration of people. In Europe and across the Atlantic, such integration began in the fifteenth century and in a few hundred years had transformed a number of distant parts into 'neo-Europes'. Britain, Spain, and France were the main colonizers and laid the basis for the Atlantic community. Of the 70 million people who left Europe in the past 450 years, over 50 million went to the present-day United States.[1] All other migrations since the European Renaissance have been of much smaller proportions.

The colonial experience also moved people from one colony or coveted country to another. Thus millions of black Africans were taken in slavery across the Atlantic to Latin and North America. Indians from southern Asia were transported to Africa to work on plantations and before long began to transform the demographic balance in a number of countries.

Immigration has obviously been vital in shaping the modern character of the Americas and other neo-Europes. New cultures bring different political systems and economies, and of course reshape international relations. States with fully closed borders are rare, and even more rarely do such states flourish.[2] The Pacific basin has seen various types of migration but this has not led to the same degree of integration as occurred across the Atlantic. As has already been discussed, the Americas received millions of mainly British and Spanish migrants, starting in the fifteenth century. Although Spanish settlers reached the Pacific in that century, British settlers did not arrive in significant numbers until late in the nineteenth century. But certainly by the nineteenth century, migration from Europe had transformed the east coast of the Pacific.

Further west across the water, British penal policy, and later more orthodox emigration, planted neo-Europes in Australia and New Zealand. The only other major island to be heavily transformed by migration was Hawaii, which took in a significant, but still minority, white population from Europe and then the United States.

Thus the demographic links were stretched as far in the Pacific as they were in the Atlantic, but with a far less pervasive effect. The main reason for

[1] Thomas Sowell, *The Economics and Politics of Race* (New York: Quill, 1983).
[2] Alan Dowty, *Closed Borders* (London: Yale University Press, 1987).

this difference was the relative absence of a European or American presence in East Asia. Although half a dozen or so European empires trampled across East Asia, only Russia left behind significant numbers of its people. In fact, the number of Russian immigrants was not large in comparison to its European rivals, but the number of local inhabitants in the Russian Pacific region were few, so the European Russian presence was more significant. Elsewhere in East Asia, migration was more local, much like the movement of tribes within ancient Europe. Thus a Chinese minority drifted down to Vietnam and Thailand. In addition, the Thai, Lao, and Khmer people intermingled on the fringes of each other's states.

The only other significant pattern of migration before the twentieth century was that engineered by European colonialism. Although the scale of this change was rather small compared with the effects of hauling millions of Africans across the Atlantic, the demography of a number of Pacific states was radically altered. In some cases, as with British importation of Indians to Fiji or French transport of whites to New Caledonia, the locals became a minority in their own land. But the change was not as complete as in Australia or North America, nor was it comparable to many Latin American states where whites intermarried with local Indians to form new ethnic mixtures, for example in Colombia and Ecuador.

The country that was most complicated by migration was undoubtedly Malaysia. The predominantly Malay population was diluted under British rule with 10 per cent Indians and over a third Chinese. Many of the Chinese had already been in the region before the coming of European power, but the new, large influx was part of the old colonial game of divide and rule. Other Chinese were brought into other parts of South-east Asia, most notably in the Philippines and, of course, modern-day Singapore.

Thus the pre-twentieth-century demographic map of the Pacific was nothing like that of the Atlantic. Migration had spread white people along the eastern rim and out to parts of the south Pacific. But most of East Asia remained untouched by international migration and therefore unconnected across the water. East Asia also remained relatively untouched by local migration, with most people keeping to themselves and rarely intermingling on the scale of the closely packed Europeans.

TWENTIETH-CENTURY MIGRATION

The scale of migration in the twentieth century is clearly much smaller than in previous centuries. The traditional motives for migration, escape from persecution and hardship, and the hope for a better life elsewhere, have all remained. Certainly Chinese, Japanese, and then other Asian immigration to the United States and Canada in the late nineteenth and early twentieth centuries was due to a mix of problems at home and perceptions of good prospects abroad. But as has already been explained, these Asian minorities constitute barely 1 per cent of the United States population and less in Canada. Although their numbers are greater on the eastern rim of the Pacific, and especially in cities such as Los Angeles, San Francisco, and Vancouver, they remain a negligible portion of the total immigrant population. Certainly since 1945 there has been less Chinese and Japanese migration to the United States, although there were significant numbers from Korea, the Philippines, and Vietnam.

The most public and significant migration across the Pacific since 1945 has been of refugees from Vietnam. Beginning with the fall of Saigon in 1975, 300 000 Vietnamese refugees eventually made it to the United States.[3] A total of more than 650 000 reached the United States from Indo-China between 1975 and 1987.[4] These people provided both a formal and a very personal link to the experience of the Vietnam War and, as they were largely of Chinese descent, strengthened the Chinese presence in the United States. But as many people as the United States took in, they still barely added a fraction of a percentage point to the American population. Other Chinese, Filipinos, and Koreans came to the United States after the easing of some immigration laws in 1965. Between 1950 and 1974 some 210 000 people from China and Hong Kong moved to the United States and a further 110 000 went to Canada. The Philippines sent 300 000 to the United States and 41 000 to Canada. Japan sent 175 000 to the United States and 130 000 Koreans also made the trek.[5] In comparison to the millions of Mexicans who crossed the United States' southern border in that time, their influence on American demography has been negligible. Although the total immigration from Asian states is now higher than it is from Europe, the Asians are still barely on the league table of hyphenated Americans. They have certainly been remarkably absent from American politics, in stark contrast to European immigrants.[6]

Between 1975 and 1987 a further 183 000 Indo-Chinese refugees went to western Europe, 108 000 to Australia, and 110 000 to Canada. Japan took in only 5127, while a further 300 000 waited in camps around South-east Asia in 1987.[7] 'Compassion fatigue' had clearly set in after the initial wave of

[3] John Bresnan, 'Strengthening Human Ties' in *Proceedings of the Academy of Political Science*, 36/7 (1986).

[4] *The Economist* (1 August 1987).

[5] *Trends and Characteristics of International Migration Since 1950* (United Nations, Demographic Studies, 64, 1979).

[6] *Far Eastern Economic Review* (16 October 1986).

[7] *The Economist* (1 August 1987); *South China Morning Post* (19 July 1987).

resettlement in the 1970s.[8] China itself took in more Vietnamese refugees than did the United States. By 1978 China had taken in 250 000, mostly of ethnic Chinese origins. Another 265 000 came in by 1981.[9] This 'return to the motherland' is formally migration, but it is also unusual in that it reverses past migration patterns. It is also significant as part of a far larger trend of local migrations that result from the large number of active military conflicts in the region.

By far the largest migrations in the Pacific resulted from the Korean War and the Chinese Civil War. Much like the India–Pakistan conflict, the formation of new borders and rival regimes led to human tragedies on a massive scale. It is estimated that some 2 million Chinese fled Communist rule for Hong Kong and Macao after 1949. Only in 1980 was Hong Kong policy changed in an effort to staunch the flow by refusing illegal immigrants the right to stay. Between 1944 and 1949 some 1.8 million Koreans returned to Korea from Japan and another three-quarters of a million people fled from North to South Korea. During the war between 1950 and 1953 another 360 000 moved south.[10]

These movements of millions of refugees were part of an international trend of rearranging the world's population to cope with new political realities after the Second World War. Similar, more massive shifts were apparent in Europe, the Middle East, and South Asia. Few of the refugees travelled far, and most moved to, or stayed within, their cultural sphere. The demographic map of the Pacific was hardly altered.

Other major conflicts since 1945 have shown similar patterns in the Pacific. In the decade from 1947, some 270 000 Malaysians fled their homeland, Singapore taking in some 140 000. In 1960 about 100 000 Chinese left Indonesia after tough government legislation on dual nationality, and they were absorbed elsewhere in the region.[11] After the 1954 Geneva settlement in Indo-China, roughly 820 000 Vietnamese fled from north to south, many of them destined to move on again after the Communist take-over in 1975. By the 1980s the flow of people was no longer due to war, but rather to the search for employment—a trend well known in Europe as it too developed as a magnet for poorer migrants. In South-east Asia, Singapore took in 100 000 guest workers and Malaysia took over 400 000.[12] Of course, along with the new workers came new divisions over

[8] *International Herald Tribune* (19 June 1987).

[9] *International Migration Policies and Programmes*, (United Nations, Population Study, 80, 1982); *Population Distribution, Migration and Development* (United Nations, Expert Group on Population Distribution Conference, March 1983).

[10] *Trends and Characteristics of International Migration Since 1950* (United Nations, Demographic Studies, 64, 1979).

[11] Figures ibid.

[12] *International Herald Tribune* (15 December 1987).

politics and race. But these changes, as with the earlier ones, were mostly confined to the same cultural sphere and often involved consolidation rather than further fragmentation of ethnic groups.

Within South-east Asia itself there was a large movement of populations after the transfer of power within the Indo-Chinese states between 1975 and 1979. But few people actually settled in the countries to which they first fled. By the early 1980s Thailand still held the bulk of refugees that remained, close to 300 000, but it had already moved on at least a similar number or returned them to Kampuchea. By 1987 there remained 260 000 Kampucheans in camps along the border in Thailand, with some 120 000 more Indo-Chinese refugees in other camps.[13] Only a handful moved elsewhere in the Pacific, apart from the United States.[14] Japan was conspicuously closed to such refugees.

Of course, Japan remains one of the least diverse countries in the world. The poor treatment of foreigners is already well documented, especially in the case of the 680 000 Koreans who have lived in Japan for decades but are ignored by the race-conscious Japanese. They, like the other 100 000 foreigners living in Japan, have been angered by the Japanese practice of fingerprinting foreigners when they are registered.[15] In the 1980s there has been an increase in the numbers of foreigners drawn to the booming Japanese economy but, unlike the reaction in Australia, the Japanese authorities do nothing to encourage such movements of people. Most immigrants to Japan remain long-term 'residents' and continue to live on the fringes of Japanese society.[16] Apparently, Japan is unlikely to want to integrate culturally in the Pacific.

Although there are growing numbers of foreigners visiting Japan on business, the Japanese have long been particularly active in the United States. Over 10 000 Japanese live temporarily in the United States, yet as a group they are still less than 10 per cent of the Europeans. While the Japanese have difficulty integrating into American society and rely heavily on local Asians, the Europeans are far more adaptable to the American culture. Although the social life of Japanese in New York now makes the social pages of the local press,[17] it is still the Europeans who dominate. These human ties are obviously more related to culture than money.

The presence of foreigners in other countries has become a more volatile political issue in China, where economic liberalization since 1978 has

---

[13] *International Herald Tribune* (7 March 1987).
[14] *Trends and Characteristics of International Migration Since 1950* (United Nations, Demographic Studies, 64, 1979).
[15] *The Economist* (23 August 1986).
[16] *Far Eastern Economic Review* (18 June 1987).
[17] Bresnan, 'Strengthening Ties'.

resulted in the creation of Special Economic Zones. The idea behind these zones is to confine the 'noxious' influences of western 'bourgeois liberalism' to sealed-off enclaves. But as the purge of the Chinese Communist Party General Secretary Hu Yaobang in 1987 showed, the problems are not so easily contained. Although the reasons for the fall of Hu were far more complex than mere toleration of foreign influences, his fate was no doubt a sign that contact with foreigners can have a negative impact on local stability.

To some extent, Japanese influence in South-east Asia has provoked similar reactions. The problems with Prime Minister Tanaka's visit to Jakarta in 1974, when protests against Japanese influence forced him to change his travel plans, suggest that there are enduring and severe restrictions on the intermingling of different peoples. While Europeans may often complain about undue American cultural influence, American visitors are none the less actively sought.

Two countries that until recently unequivocally sought immigrants were Australia and New Zealand. Both countries, like the Americas before them, felt underpopulated and vulnerable in the modern age of more populous economic powers. But with growing international interdependence and domestic economic problems such as unemployment, the doors began to close. New Zealand has the particular problem of a significant Maori population and therefore a sensitivity to changing demographic balances. New Zealand has been attractive to neighbouring islanders for much the same reason as the United States beckoned to the Irish—economic prospects and new horizons.

Already, the nationals of the Cook Islands, Niue, and the Tokelaus have the free right of entry as New Zealand citizens and their populations in New Zealand outnumber those left behind. Immigrants from Tonga, Western Samoa, and Fiji have flooded in during the 1980s. Auckland now has the largest Polynesian population of any place in the south Pacific.[18] Five per cent of the Tongan population took 50 flights to New Zealand in 1986–7 and the New Zealand authorities had to crack down hard on the flow of immigrants. The doors to immigration, which have remained so tightly closed in most of the Pacific, now look like remaining shut in New Zealand as well.

Only Australia retains a relatively liberal immigration policy, and this despite an Aboriginal 'problem' of its own. Despite the 'fraying of the rope' that bound Australia to Britain, Australia has developed a distinctive identity that includes a curious mixture of English and American culture. The attitude towards immigration was always mixed, even in the 1950s

18 *Far Eastern Economic Review* (19 March 1987).

when most immigrants came from Europe.[19] Such ambiguity was not an uncommon sentiment in the neo-Europes, and especially not for one first based on the import of British convicts. But Australia remained almost unique in its determination to encourage immigration, and in the late 1970s the immigrants were mostly non-white and from the Pacific. By the 1980s Australia was still taking in some 80–90 000 immigrants a year, living up to its 'populate or perish' slogan of bygone years. But by 1987 only 2.8 per cent of its population was of Asian origin, with 76 per cent originally from Britain or Ireland and 20 per cent from other European countries.[20] While immigration figures fluctuate with economic prosperity, as a percentage of population Australia retains an admirable reputation for an open-door immigration policy.[21]

Australia is of course also very interested in business immigration, a scheme that by the 1980s was looking for an initial investment of $325 000 in order to 'buy' a passport. In the light of the exodus of money and people from Hong Kong in the run-up to the hand-over of power to China in 1997, such schemes were attracting easily assimilated and less burdensome immigrants. However, a more bizarre Japanese scheme to settle its old-age pensioners in Australia was running into more local Australian opposition, especially considering the wartime histories of many of these old-timers.[22]

Both Canada and Australia have in fact been the main beneficiaries in the 1980s of a 'brain drain' from Hong Kong and other uncertain economies in the Pacific, including Malaysia and Singapore. Canadian figures show that in 1987 1744 heads of family arrived, bringing with them $763 million.[23] Hong Kong is obviously providing the largest portion of these immigrants and is likely to provide the largest numbers in the remaining years of the century before the 1997 hand-over to China.[24] Certainly the earlier immigrants are some of the wealthiest and skilled ever seen, quite a change from previous movements of people in the region and unique in world migration.

Thus with the exception of the neo-Europes, few countries have a record of accepting immigrants and therefore changing the demographic patterns of the Pacific. Because the region remains ethnically divided, a basic inducement for integration is lacking. Japan, the economic power-house of the region, is a very different model from either imperial Britain or imperial Spain, both of which sent so many of their people abroad, or from the United States which accepted so many foreigners. In many cases such

[19] Linda Christian, *The Ribbon and the Ragged Square* (London: Penguin, 1987), ch. 4.
[20] *The Economist* (7 March 1987).
[21] *Financial Times* (30 March 1987).
[22] *Independent* (5 February 1987).
[23] *International Herald Tribune* (30 November 1987).
[24] *Far Eastern Economic Review* (18 June 1987).

regional diversity in the Pacific may make for more stable domestic politics, but it hardly encourages international contacts between countries or lays the basis of close international co-operation.

TOURISM

A less permanent, but in some cases no less influential, form of international contact comes with the phenomenon of international tourism. Tourism before 1945 was a rare event except for the wealthy. With improved communications and transport and greater prosperity came the greater interest in travel. Closer international economic contacts have led to more people travelling on business and the better provision of hotels and services for foreigners.

These trends were first seen in more wealthy and developed Europe and then spread both across the Atlantic and south to the Middle East. Travel to Asia and the Pacific was slow to develop in part because of the distances involved, and also because the area was marred by a number of wars. Business and leisure travel prefers to avoid war zones.

As the Pacific itself grew richer and somewhat more peaceful, it became more involved in the international travel market. But unlike Europe, where millions of people cross borders daily, the Pacific basin remains a relatively untravelled zone. By 1984 European countries such as France had over 34 million visitors and Italy had over 49 million. The vast majority of this travel was from within Europe, 82 per cent for France and 90 per cent for Italy. Even island Britain had over 13 million tourists, 55 per cent of whom were from Europe.[25]

The only comparable place for travel on such a scale is North America. Canada, with less than half the British population, took in over 13 million visitors in 1984, but 87 per cent of that total was from its American neighbour in the south. The United States had over 19 million visitors that year, of whom over 10 million, or 56 per cent, were Canadian. Thus the vast majority of those contacts were between neighbours, as in Europe.

No other Pacific state begins to approximate such levels of tourism, especially when measured in per-capita terms. Of course most states are not as wealthy and travel correlates very strongly with money. But even Japan, which by 1984 was wealthier than most European states, took in barely over 2 million visitors and sent only 4 million abroad. With a population roughly equal to that of Italy and France combined, Japan sent abroad less than 20

---

[25] All data in this section are from various annual volumes of *World Tourism* (World Tourism Organization, Madrid).

per cent of the number of Italian and French tourists. It received less than 20 per cent of the number of tourists who visited Britain, another island off the coast of Eurasia.

In some senses only the states of South-east Asia begin to approximate the volume of travel known in Europe. Close to 10 million visitors travelled to Thailand, the Philippines, Malaysia, and Singapore in 1984, but on a per-capita basis that is not very different from the Japanese figures. Tiny Hong Kong had about a third as many visitors in the same period and Singapore had more visitors than any other ASEAN member.

Most of the travel within the Pacific has therefore been within sub-regions. Most North Americans travel within North America and the vast majority of those Latin Americans who travel do so in their own region too. South-east Asians travel most heavily among themselves and Japan is the main traveller to both China and South Korea. Koreans rank third as travellers to Japan after the United States and Taiwan. In the south of the region the main travellers to Australia are from New Zealand and vice versa. These patterns, and the percentages, have been remarkably constant for over 20 years as the economies of the region have grown. Both Australia and New Zealand dominate the travel business in the south Pacific islands and have done so for decades.

The main travellers across the sub-regional divides in the Pacific are clearly the nationals of the wealthier states. Citizens of the United States are by far the most enterprising travellers. In 1965 the United States sent more than 500 000 people across the Pacific to visit other Pacific states, in 1971 it sent more than 1.1 million, and in 1981 the figure was more than 1.6 million. Japan was a clear second in this cross-Pacific experience, sending only some 90 000 out of its immediate region in 1965, 352 000 in 1971, but over 1.3 million in 1981. A long way down the list were Canada and Australia, with the latter's figure rising sharply to send 911 000 outside its immediate region in 1981.

Of course the populations of these states vary considerably in size and, when the figures are adjusted as a percentage of population, Australia is well in the lead with 5.9 per cent. Canada sent 1.1 per cent of its population outside of its immediate region, a figure marginally higher than Japan's 1 per cent and the 0.7 per cent for the United States. But New Zealand (2.4 per cent) and Singapore (1.1 per cent) each sent more than all but Australia on these per-capita calculations.

This pattern of very limited travel within the Pacific region as a whole shows little sign of change. Only a few states, such as Japan and Australia, have strikingly increased their percentages of travel within the region in the past decade. But in comparison to the heavily local travel in Europe, the Pacific figures are not particularly low in terms of distance travelled.

It is striking just how much this growth of Pacific travel, such as it is, is really part of a greater globalization of travel. Certainly the Europeans are more active travellers and hosts to North Americans than are the Pacific states. In 1965 the United States sent over 5.8 million visitors to the four main European states (France, Germany, Italy, United Kingdom), while sending around 435 000 to the top four Pacific states. More than 366 000 from the four main European states visited the United States in 1965 while Japan, with a population half the size of the European four, sent 46 000. In 1971 the United States sent over 6.5 million visitors to the four main European states while sending around 700 000 to the top four Pacific states. More than 735 000 from the four largest European states visited the United States in 1971, while Japan sent 313 000. In 1984 over 10 million Americans travelled to the main four European countries while only 1.1 million went to the top four Pacific locations. Yet over 2 million from the European four visited the United States while Japan moved ahead on a per-capita basis with 1.4 million visitors.

Japan received five times as many visitors from the United States as from the European four in 1965, four times as many in 1971, but only twice as many in 1984. In that year, the European four ranked as Japan's third-largest source of visitors after the United States and Taiwan. Europe was clearly becoming more important for Japan than in the past.

In 1965 the four major European states sent 21 000 people to Australia while Japan sent 4000. By 1971 the Europeans were sending 58 000 as compared to Japan's 16 000. In 1984 Japan sent 71 000, 7.6 per cent of the Australian total, while the European four sent 203 000—a smaller, but still clear, lead for the Europeans. Curiously, the United States, with a population roughly equal to that of the European four, sent 83 000 visitors to Australia in 1971 but only 139 000 in 1984. Thus the Europeans became more important for Australia than the Americans, but the Japanese did not.

Similar patterns of Europe's increasing importance compared to the United States are evident for many Pacific states. In 1971 Hong Kong used to take three times as many American visitors as those from the European four, but by 1984 it was taking less than twice as many. While the ratio for the Philippines remained more than 3.5 times Americans to these same four Europeans, in Thailand there were 50 per cent more Americans in 1971, but by 1984 the Europeans were more than twice as numerous. In Singapore in 1971 there had been 20 per cent more American visitors but in 1984 there were more than twice as many from the European four. In fact, by 1984 there were more visitors from the main European four than from the United States in Malaysia, Papua New Guinea, Singapore, Australia, Indonesia, and Thailand. However, there were more Americans in Hong Kong, Japan, Korea, New Zealand, the Philippines, and China.

This trend suggests a globalization of travel rather than a specific increase in travel within the Pacific. It is supported by travel trends for major Pacific travellers such as Japan. In 1974 Japanese citizens used to travel nearly 50 per cent more to the United States than to the four main Europeans. However, by 1984 Japanese travel to the four Europeans had almost caught up. Australia used to send three times as many visitors to the European four as to the United States but in 1984 it sent over four times.

Thus it is clear that these patterns of travel in the Pacific suggest the region is becoming a part of the global pattern of interdependence rather than developing a special regional character. These trends have a major impact on people's perceptions of their place in the world, for while the Europeans went through relatively gradual stages of nationhood, regional conscious-ness, and now global interdependence, the people of the Pacific are mostly skipping the intermediate stage. The shock of globalism is therefore more deep.

Developed countries such as the United States, Canada, Japan, Australia, Hong Kong, and Singapore have found the adjustment easier. But the newer entrants had a rougher time. In the 1980s China is perhaps the best-known example of mixed feelings about the bourgeois influences that stem from international tourism.[26] The Chinese have the added problem of adjusting to overseas Chinese visitors who are foreign, yet also too close for comfort. Tourism and contact with foreigners can breed as much disdain and hatred as it can friendship and peace. In Europe, for example, the proliferation of German tourists on European beaches well before their less energetic fellow Europeans often breeds dislike. Similarly the extravagances and finicky demands of European and American tourists in developing states engenders tension and sometimes scorn. The image of the 'ugly American' tourist has now been matched by a variety of European counterparts.[27]

The process of change encouraged by such contacts can go further still. The very poorest and most isolated of places, such as the Pacific islands, can find the shock of the twentieth century that comes with modern tourism quite traumatic for existing cultures and morals.[28] What is more, as tourism is so closely related to wealth, it affects different sectors of society in different ways. If the visitors come mainly for business, then the impact may be relatively confined, as in China's special economic zones, to take an extreme example. Yet if the country is small, such as Hong Kong or Singapore, travellers get everywhere and so have a greater impact. Because the states and societies in the Pacific are so different, the impact of travel is also diverse and uneven.

[26] *Financial Times* (12 July 1986).
[27] Donald Lundberg, *The Tourist Business* (Boston: CBI Publishing Co., 1980).
[28] For example, 'On Easter Island' in *Times Magazine* (15 September 1986).

Similarly, those who do the travelling are often of different types and so have varying effects on the societies they visit. The Japanese are well known for travelling in groups and keeping to themselves. Far more Japanese men travel in their thirties and forties, while female travel from Japan is mostly done at much younger ages.[29]

In fact, a great deal of modern travel does little more than skim the surface of the target countries. Resorts in Hawaii might as well be anywhere in the Pacific islands, and they often cater to package tours that by their very name aim to provide a uniform product that protects the traveller as much as possible from local conditions. If the purpose of the trip is business, to sit on a beach, or to 'collect' international sites for a scrap-book, the travel does little to improve international understanding. Few tourists are interested in local culture as much as they are in simply having a good time.[30]

Another form of visitor is the student or academic who stays for a few months or years. Yet these visitors are distributed mainly in the rich states of North America and Europe. The students follow the grants and fellowships, and hope to find new opportunities.[31] But as the Chinese, Filipino, or general ASEAN experience of a brain drain to the United States makes clear, many students do not return, leading to interstate friction. Many of those who do return often bring undesired ideas, not to mention bad habits or even diseases.[32] In general, this type of travel enhances the dominance of the Atlantic world, and helps if anything to fragment the Pacific community.

The globalization of international travel has undoubtedly taken place. But in the Pacific, as in other parts, it does not mean that the travellers obtain a better understanding of the country they are visiting that day. The impact may well be greater for the local who contends with the infrastructure that is in place to serve the visitor, but there is usually little real contact between visitor and visited.

[29] *Annual Report on Tourism, 1983/4,* (Prime Minister's Office).
[30] Emanuel de Kadt, *Tourism—Passport to Development* (London: Oxford University Press, 1979).
[31] Hamid Mowlama, *Global Information and World Communication* (London: Longman, 1986), ch. 8.
[32] *International Herald Tribune* (25 March 1988).

10

Communications and Culture

The impact of improved communications on the Pacific before 1945 is clear. The very coming of Western imperialism brought new technologies and the voyages of discovery themselves spurred further revolutions in communication. The new means of communication, whether it was faster ships, aircraft, or radio, all helped reshape the Pacific even more than they did the Atlantic and Europe in earlier years. If only because of the vaster distances in the Pacific, new communication technologies were even more instrumental in 'shrinking' the distances.

Since 1945 the pace of technological change has increased. While almost every significant new system was developed in North America or Europe, these soon made themselves felt in the Pacific world. The jet engine, satellites, television, and new fibre-optic cables not only brought the people of the Pacific closer together, they also brought the Pacific closer to the Atlantic.

While there has been much comment on the new technologies and the political integration of the Pacific, in reality the process has been far more complex. The new forms of communication have affected societies in different degrees. It seems that the more developed societies have, in fact, found themselves becoming more integrated with other parts of the developed world in America and Europe than with less developed states in the Pacific.

THE INTERNATIONAL POLITICS OF NEW COMMUNICATIONS

The people of the developed economies of the 1980s communicate with each other by everything from personal meetings to portable video-phones. In order to send complex data at high speeds and with reliable accuracy they need the most sophisticated channels of communication. Financial markets are some of the most demanding users of this technology and they have spurred the development of fibre-optic cables capable of sending over 40 000 simultaneous telephone conversations via laser light.[1] Not

---

[1] *International Herald Tribune* (6 December 1987).

surprisingly, these cables were first laid on the sea-bed of the Atlantic and only shortly afterwards in the Pacific. The cost of the Pacific system was twice that of the Atlantic, but that was a small price to pay to shrink the Pacific to a similar size.[2] At the same time, the far easier task of linking East Asian Pacific states with fibre-optics was well under way, but the first states to tie in were the more developed economies such as Hong Kong, Singapore, and Korea.[3]

Although modern communications help most states, they are primarily designed for the needs of the more developed countries and economies.[4] While it might seem clear that a fax machine, with its ability to translate images not merely words, would be a wonderful boon to developing economies, and especially those with ideographic scripts, such machines are highly dependent on a sophisticated communication infrastructure. Fax machines require the highest-standard communication cables and therefore are not necessarily a short-cut for developing states to skip the telex stage of communications.[5] The technological gap between developed and developing states is only closed by faster development. Thus the impact of new technology in the Pacific is uneven, with only the NICs able to make the leap into the fully modern world.

The technology of satellite communication is yet another field that reinforces the image of a divided Pacific. While the superpowers are obvious providers of such communications of the space age, few other states are able to play in that elevated league.[6] The Europeans' Ariane programme is evidence of how even the most developed economies find it difficult to support a sophisticated plan. Only China and Japan have pretensions to join this super-sophisticated club, but more often than not they join as national or global launchers of satellites, not in a Pacific-wide role. Ariane has taken payloads for the Australians, and the Chinese have offered to launch for the hard-pressed Americans and the pragmatic Australians.[7] By the mid-1980s even the Soviet Union was entering the international market for satellite launches, wooing South-east Asians and Australia.[8] With the Chinese and Soviet state-run satellite industries competing among themselves, and with the Europeans to launch Indonesian satellites, the trend was more to a globalization of international technology than to the evolution of a specific

[2] Ibid.; *Financial Times* (10 June 1986).
[3] *Far Eastern Economic Review* (29 May 1986); *Financial Times* (2 April 1987).
[4] Hamid Mowlama, *Global Information and World Communication* (London: Longman, 1986), ch. 5.
[5] 'The Search for an Edge' in *Far Eastern Economic Review* (19 February 1987).
[6] J. N. Pelton, 'Intelstat' in *Intermedia*, 14/4–5 (1986).
[7] *International Herald Tribune* (31 March 1988).
[8] *International Herald Tribune* (8 June 1987).

regional policy or pattern. Although many of these satellites serve transpacific roles, they are in fact part of a much wider trend of globalization of technology and communications.

Nowhere is this global rather than regional trend seen more clearly than in the rapidly changing world of personal computers. These paragraphs are written on a British machine with mostly East Asian components but oriented to standards set, and software written, in the United States. The printer is, of course, Japanese. On-line data are gathered from data bases in Britain and Europe, and via new cables from the United States. Such data bases include newspapers and wire-services from Japan and Hong Kong as well as Europe and America.

The world of personal computers is equally important for many Japanese, for the neo-Europes, and for the citizens of many of the NICs in East Asia. Not only do millions of people use these machines daily, but the clone-makers of Korea and Taiwan are important employers. Once again, however, the direct impact of these technologies of communication is minimal in the still-developing parts of the Pacific, not to mention its socialist component. The freer flow of information that is made possible by these new technologies is a particular challenge to the relatively closed societies of the Soviet Union, China, North Korea, and Indo-China. The failure to keep up with this new revolution in communications will only widen the gap between developed societies who are 'plugged in' and those who are not.

MASS COMMUNICATIONS AND CULTURE

The challenge of these new technologies varies depending on the level of development of the state, and the extent to which it has embraced the technology. A central question is whether this new technology is a new form of 'media imperialism' that forces conformity on the diversities of culture.[9] To be sure, the internationalization of the culture of the developed, mainly western, world has often led to a grievance about 'media imperialism', especially in television. While soap operas such as *Dallas* have a global reputation, few people outside of Japan know of the Japanese equivalents.

To some extent the new technologies which are dominated by Americans and Europeans do impose a set of common reference points for the mass media in the Pacific. But these reference points are primarily felt most sharply in the developed world that has access to the technologies of communication. This is a characteristic of developed states that unites them

[9] Sean MacBride, *Many Voices, One World* (London: Kegan Paul for Unesco, 1980). See also E. Katz and G. Wedell, *Broadcasting in the Third World* (London: Macmillan, 1978).

despite their place in different regions. The fear of media imperialism as expressed in the MacBride report has not been realized. Instead the reality has been a cultural pluralism where people are brought closer together but at the price of the loss of only some individual cultural habits.[10].

It is certainly far more difficult to argue that for these developed states there is a problem with technological determinism and domination of world information. Australia, New Zealand, Japan, Hong Kong, Singapore, and Korea are already active members in the international capitalist system and see few problems with international information 'slanted' towards their needs. For these states, as for the North Americans and Europeans, the technology is as much determined by the needs of market economies as the technology itself determines the needs of the society.

The more developed the society, the more it is able to maintain its own special national dimensions to its media. The Japanese press corps is notorious for its closed shops of 'lobbies' that exclude foreign journalists. The local press in Japan is tame by most western standards, although not in comparison to elsewhere in Asia. The Australian press is one of the roughest in the western world and such magnates as Rupert Murdoch have extended their empires into Europe and then America. The Hong Kong press covers a remarkably wide range of opinions and is often a mirror to its own free-wheeling society. In Singapore television has a high percentage of western content, but then that also represents a fair mix of the orientations and interests of its citizens.[11]

The broadcast material becomes increasingly home-grown as the state and society develop. American television is by far the most pervasive of the broadcasting exports to the region, but British television is also a major actor in the market. As other societies become more sophisticated in their home-grown product, as in the case of Australia, Hong Kong, Japan, and even Brazil, they too export television around the world.[12] This is a global market, not a regional one, and a market that depends very heavily on the level of development and political ideologies of the regimes concerned.

Most East Asian broadcasting systems operate on a variant of the British system. A BBC-type monopoly was first set up and only with the perception of excessive uniformity and demands from the society for greater variation was there a shift to commercial channels, as in Japan, Taiwan, and Korea.[13]

[10] The ambivalences between 'one-worldism' and 'media imperialism' are evident in most issues of the *Unesco Courier*. See a vivid example in the issue of July 1982. For a general discussion see Mowlama, *Global Information*.

[11] Erhard Heidt, 'Cultural Orientations in Television: The Singapore Experience' in *Internationales Asienforum*, 16/3–4 (1985).

[12] 'Television' in *The Economist* (20 December 1986).

[13] 'Asia in View' in *Far Eastern Economic Review* (5 January 1979).

But even more so than in Europe, broadcasting remains essentially under government control. So long as the channels remain primarily for entertainment rather than news, they are seen as less harmful and dangerous by the state. The steady diet is mostly of home-grown comedies and soaps, intermixed with sports. Most evidence suggests that local audiences prefer local soap operas to foreign ones.[14] As societies develop they become less dependent on foreign television and the local audiences have little problem in giving up *Little House on the Prairie* or *Dynasty*.

Despite the presence of several satellites to ease transpacific and transasian broadcasts, and such organizations as the Asian/Pacific Broadcasting union (ABU), there is little genuine transpacific television. The visit by President Nixon to China in 1972 was the first genuine transpacific extravaganza, but it was primarily an election show for Americans. Although the event had a major impact around the Pacific, its impact was more political than media. Most foreign journalists in the United States are from Europe and most remain based on the east coast.[15] The ABU has discovered that, although it can make use of the latest technology, it still ends up selling the usual hard political or disaster stories that it had previously criticized the media of the developed states for spreading.[16]

Most news remains local or confined to the immediate neighbourhood.[17] Detailed analysis has shown that United States and Japanese papers have different styles and content in keeping with their different cultures—the Japanese being more educational and less reportorial than the Americans.[18] Yet it is true that most genuinely international news agencies and broadcasters are from the developed states and they are the first into the market of the forthcoming international broadcasting channels.[19] Most events are covered by Visnews and UPITN in London and provide a world-wide audience. The attempt to establish an Asian Broadcasting Union in 1977 has not made any progress in its objective of fostering the exchange of regional news.[20].

While some international magazines, such as *Reader's Digest* or *Newsweek*, make an effort to 'localize' their issues, they still remain creatures of their American parents. The more influential journals, such as *The*

14 'Television' in *The Economist* (20 December 1986).
15 Hamid Mowlama, 'Who Covers America?' in *Journal of Communication*, 25/3 (summer 1975).
16 *Far Eastern Economic Review* (10 December 1987).
17 Mowlama, *Global Information* 38.
18 James Berninger and Eleanor Westney, 'Japanese and US Media' in *Journal of Communication*, 31/2 (spring 1981).
19 *Financial Times* (22 June 1987).
20 James Wei, 'Prospects for a Regional News Agency' in *Asian Culture Quarterly* 10/4 (winter 1982).

Economist, may be printed world-wide, but content is the same for all and remains under strict editorial control in London. Most major publications now make use of satellite technology to reach their markets more quickly, but few alter the content so much as the volume of their coverage of local events.[21] Thus the system seems pluralistic within the framework of common interests of developed, market economies. These are hardly media under the thumb of an imperial power. There is certainly nothing that can be called a Pacific or even an Asian approach to the media.

The deepest cleavage in the world of media is again between the developed and developing states. The less robust societies of the developing world are often more deeply traumatized by contact with the media of the developed world, even though the media may not be so instrumental in changing their societies.

South Korea is an interesting case because its society has moved from the status of a developing economy to that of an NIC relatively quickly. Its media have been heavily influenced by both the American and Japanese systems. The Japanese have been especially active in training staff, while the Americans have had the stronger cultural impact. Korean television has a strong diet of Japanese cartoons and American serials. Yet whether the Koreans take from Japan or the United States, the dilemma remains the same: how to take the good but not the bad.[22]

Korea has responded robustly to the challenge with domestic products. But most smaller developing states have been more seriously affected. For some of the Pacific islands in particular, the new technology offers the hope of building genuine unity and cultural awareness. But the temptation is to buy in cheaper and less local material. In the end there is no common Pacific culture, but rather a collection of the interests of the developed world, added to the very basic and fragile cultures of smaller, developing countries.[23]

The fear of domination on the part of Pacific islanders is mostly a worry about the impact of Australia. The decision by Papua New Guinea in 1986 to keep the Australian media from providing television to the island is evidence of a rearguard action. Of course, satellite dishes in Papua New Guinea allow the wealthy to obtain their foreign television if they so desire, and once again the division is drawn between rich and poor.[24] But the programmes they pull in are from Guam (United States influence),

[21] *Sunday Times* (London: 5 September 1987).

[22] Jin-Hwan Oh, 'An Inquiry into the Dynamics of Mass Communication Media in Cultural Exchange' in *Asian Culture Quarterly*, 10/4 (winter 1982).

[23] Chung Woo Suh, 'The Role of Mass Media for Cultural Exchange in the Asian-Pacific Region' and Georgette Wang, 'Cultural Exchange Through Television' both in *Asian Cultural Quarterly*, 10/4 (winter 1982).

[24] *The Economist* (23 August 1986); *New York Times* (18 October 1986).

Australia, and also Malaysia. The real influence of the outside world is also felt via another aspect of new technology, video-recorders. These machines, which are used primarily for 'time-shift' in the developed world, are means of obtaining the latest in western media culture at a cheap price in the developing world. They are also means for isolated ethnic groups, such as the Indians in Fiji, to reinforce their own culture with Hindi movies.[25] However, the tapes can also be of American soap operas, BBC drama, or Swedish pornography. The impact is that of global media in the developed world.

Thus the process of broadcasting brings the broadest impact for a western culture that is already pervasive elsewhere in the developed world. As states develop they attach themselves to this system, adding a little to the media *mélange* but rarely changing it except at the margins. The popularity of videos of Chinese kung-fu films is but one example of the trivial impact.

Allied to such pervasive broadcasting is the process of international advertising. This new form of multinational corporation has developed with the more general move towards service industries in the 1980s in the developed world. Advertisers have honed the skills of international sales pitches to capture locally targeted audiences.[26] The age of American domination of the advertising business has given way to a complex game of salesmanship between multinational firms. The world's largest in 1987, Britain's Saatchi and Saatchi, built its initial success on helping the British Conservative Party to power in 1979, 1983, and 1987. But even though such companies bring international skills to their trade, their success ultimately depends on the ability to understand and appeal to local markets by buying out local agencies. This is yet another form of narrowcasting: the targeting of small audiences with precise messages instead of the original idea of broadcasting to mass audiences.

The more developed states in the Pacific have found ways to narrowcast to themselves and therefore strengthen their own identity. So far, the less developed states have been less able to narrowcast and are therefore more subject to the power of international media blandness. The new wave of direct broadcasting systems offers the hope of true narrowcasting to small communities by poorer states, but also the risk that the more developed states will use the system to target more specific audiences around the globe.

Another example of narrowcasting is that in the relatively closed societies of the socialist Pacific. These states make strong use of the media to impose social control, shape ideas, and conduct campaigns. Unlike the states of eastern Europe, which are far more subject to the western broadcasts

---

[25] *Pacific Islands Monthly* (November 1985).
[26] Colin Cherry, *World Communications* (London: John Wiley, 1971).

beamed at them, the Pacific socialists states, with the important exception of southern China have virtually unchallenged control of their media channels. North Korean radios have only one station. Their people remain isolated from the rapidly sweeping trends in the international media world, and their sense of difference from the non-socialist Pacific is accentuated. As the European case suggests, it is unlikely that greater access to western media would break down these barriers, but in the Pacific there is little chance even to blur the lines.

Most broadcasting across international boundaries in the Pacific is likely to be of only marginal impact. Only in southern China is the divide between socialism and capitalism broken by broadcasts across the borders. More curiously, as rivalry between Communist states in the region has grown in the 1970s, the most pervasive cross-border broadcasting has been between these states. The Soviet Union and China have long broadcast to each other, and in turn used to jam each other's broadcasts. Only when Sino-Soviet relations improved in the 1980s did most of this hostile broadcasting and jamming cease.[27] For much of the 1970s the Soviet Union ran the most prominent international broadcasting network, and in that period China was rapidly developing the reach of its radio.[28] Also by 1970 North Korea had moved up to eighth place in the world broadcasting league. As the Sino-Vietnamese conflict worsened later in the decade, both sides stepped up hostile broadcasts, just as China began moderating the tone of its radio appeals to 'compatriots' on Taiwan.

The patterns of radio broadcasts already suggest that sovereignty is permeable in the Pacific, just as elsewhere, although geographic distance does help provide more protection for the state than in crowded Europe. However, the new broadcasting technologies of the last decade of the twentieth century promise even greater permeability of international frontiers. As messages can be beamed more efficiently from numerous satellites, so the technology of radio and television reception, and its portability, improves. The smaller dishes and less conspicuous receivers offer ways to break through the isolation imposed by some Pacific states.

For societies that depend on their ability to restrict information, the risks of the new freedom of the airwaves are great. Even for the more developed and more open societies of the capitalist Pacific, the new technology will widen the available information. The proliferation of private channels and narrowcasting via satellite will tend to fragment society and create common

---

[27] The Soviet Union maintained clandestine broadcasts such as '1st August Radio' appealing to the Chinese armed forces. Chinese circumvention of Soviet jamming was so sophisticated that for at least a decade it broadcast backwards to the Soviet Union.

[28] 'World Broadcasting' in *The Economist* (6 June 1987).

interests that cut across national boundaries.[29] The cultural and ideological patterns of the Pacific remain complex, but also increasingly subject to international influences.

INTERNATIONAL ARTS AND THE PACIFIC

The patterns of communication and the media in the Pacific clearly differ depending on the state's level of development, its ideology, and tradition. Simplistic notions about media imperialism by the developed West simply do not stand up to detailed inspection. Many of the more developed states of the Pacific share some trends with Euro-American culture, almost by virtue of their level of economic development. But in each of these cases, development also brings out more distinctive local cultures and blends them with the overlay of international, global culture.

It is obviously difficult to judge the importance of culture and the arts in shaping the politics of a state. Legend has it that Marshal Goering used to reach for his revolver every time he heard the word 'culture'.[30] But it was that famous French statesman Talleyrand who exhorted French diplomats to 'make them love France' and emphasis on culture was a key instrument. In more modern times, the emphasis on 'successor generations' leads states, especially in the developed world, to spend time and money educating younger generations from 'friendly countries' in their civilization.[31]

The line between culture and propaganda can be thin, as is evident from the differences in Europe over human rights and the definition of 'basket three' in the Helsinki Declaration of 1975. Yet the very existence of 'basket three', and the prevalence of cultural boycotts in international politics, for example against South Africa, suggests the importance attached to the cultural dimension of ideology and foreign policy. Cultural stereotypes are clearly barriers to understanding, but the invisible export of culture has also been described as 'invisible imperialism'. Governments feel that the spread of culture and art is useful, as is seen in the funding of such institutions as the Japan Foundation or the ASEAN Cultural Fund. The United States supports thousands of students studying in America and, more frivolously, cities are all too keen to twin themselves with others around the world. Yet this twinning process, as with the spread of culture in general, is far more global than Pacific. China's north-eastern port city of Dalian is twinned with Oakland in California and Glasgow in Scotland.

29 'Television' in *The Economist* (20 December 1986).
30 *Financial Times* (27 June 1987).
31 J. M. Mitchell, *International Cultural Relations* (London: Allen & Unwin, 1986).

The indigenous cultures of the Pacific are as varied as the types of people. The American Indian or Australian Aborigine cultures are of interest to small sectors of the community, not to mention anthropologists and art collectors, but they hardly represent the modern mass cultures of the societies around them. The true roots for these neo-Europes are the cultures of Europe and the way in which frontier living in the Americas transformed the values of the old world.

In almost every field of artistic life, the traditions are heavily European and the artistic communities are deeply affected by what still takes place in the cultural centres of London, Paris, and Florence. To be sure, the Europeans themselves are deeply affected by the newer cultural forms from the United States, and in turn ideas and symbols are transformed in Europe and returned to America. In the cinema, European 'art' films still excite the imagination of American artists. European film-makers, especially from France, Britain, and Italy have mass-audience support in North America in a way that is not felt for Pacific art. Only the Japanese and Australian film industries, and only selected artists at that, have a significant impact on the Americans. For reasons of language and culture, Britain remains by far the most influential foreign voice in the American film industry.

Similar, only more exaggerated, trends are evident in other artistic arenas where language is even more crucial. In the theatre, it is only the British who, as foreigners, sweep awards and audiences in the American market. In the literary world the trend is even more distinct, whether it is the popularity of John Le Carre and Frederick Forsyth, or the more up-market novels of John Fowles. Of course, many American films, plays, and books pass the other way across the Atlantic, but the point is that the flow across the Atlantic, and to Britain in particular, is far greater than for any other part of the world, including the Pacific. While Japanese and Chinese novels are translated for the more élite artistic market in the United States, the numbers of books remain a tiny fraction of even German, French, or Italian material. The translation of Russian material is far greater than that of Japanese. The key to all these trends is language and the doors to culture which it opens.[32]

In Latin America, language is also a crucial determinant of the flow of artistic content. The region's authors, particularly those specializing in 'marginal realism', draw their ideas from the peculiar local mix of Spanish and North American traditions, the pressures of authoritarian government, the Amerindian and African roots, and contrasting environments of wealth. It is a special literature—in fact one of the most dynamic of the developing world.[33] But its main international contacts are with the United States and

[32] *Statistical Yearbook* (Unesco, 1976, 1986). The problems in using these statistics are compounded by the fact that some countries use the same language.
[33] *The Economist* (13 June 1987).

Europe. International recognition comes from the translations into English and German, and of course the markets in the Spanish-speaking world. Needless to say, there is little that is truly Pacific in this lively Latin American literature.

Even in the field of music, the flow in the Americas remains overwhelmingly to Europe rather than Asia. In this dimension, language is barely a factor to be considered, and yet the hold that classical, European music retains on American concert halls is overwhelming. What is most revealing is the rise of Asians as great interpreters of the European tradition. Japanese and Chinese soloists increasingly appear on concert programmes, but the music they play is out of the grand European tradition. This is a trend to globalism of parts of international culture rather than the Pacificization of American culture. That one of the great operatic stars of the 1980s, Kiri Te Kanawa, should be a New Zealand Maori is symbolic of this trend.

In the field of popular music, the European voice in the Americas remains by far the loudest. While French, German, and Italian rock and pop music has failed to make a significant impact on the North Americans, the British and the Spanish have both had a major impact on their respective former colonies. No significant equivalent, even to the odd Swedish pop group, can be seen as influencing the Americas from Asia. Even the purchase of CBS records in 1987 by Sony, with contracts for Bruce Springsteen and Mick Jagger, shows that ownership of assets is very different from contribution to culture. Thus the sound of the last half of the twentieth century for most Americans remains mid-Atlantic, with barely the faintest resonance from the Pacific.

In the more decorative arts, the European impact on the Americas is less strong than it once was and at least in this field the impact of Asia has been greater. Certainly the American interest in the classical painting, sculpture, and architecture of Europe remains prevalent, as the contents of most museums will testify. Modern painting is much stronger in the United States, and the European influence somewhat diminished.

In architecture, the Japanese in particular have made their presence felt in recent years. The obvious characteristics of clean lines and stark shapes have been identified as typically Japanese.[34] Yet the use of pyramids and other universal symbols suggests the architectural trends are more global than regional or even national. The proliferation of skyscrapers and blocks of metal and reflecting glass are so ubiquitous in modern cities, especially in the developed world, that they hardly represent particular national styles. The success of Japanese and British architects in the United States, or

[34] *Financial Times* (11 May 1987).

Chinese-American ones in Europe, is part of the global overlay to certain aspects of international art and design.

Yet there are very sophisticated cultures in East Asia that have a tradition of great cultural achievement every bit as long as the people of Europe. That the Asians have barely affected the Americas is merely to point to the limits of transpacific cultural exchange, not to the absence of culture. The different artistic worlds of East Asia are far too complex to be discussed in detail, but what is relevant is the extent to which they are affected by trends from the world outside.

Chinese arts have bent depending on the prevailing political winds. The adoption of 'socialist realism' and then 'revolutionary styles', as in opera, had a great deal to do with the coming of Communism. In the more liberal atmosphere after the death of Mao Zedong in 1976, western influences were more apparent. Western theatre, music, and other visual arts were imported for observation and limited adoption. In some realms, such as cinema or literature, a degree of liberalism was tolerated in the later 1980s, and some films, like *The Last Emperor* even became joint ventures. But the firm and strict arbiter remained the Communist Party.[35] The impact on mass culture was minimal, despite the odd rock concert that attracted thousands of eager teenagers. The concern with bourgeois liberalism that came with western arts remained strong, and firm cultural control was retained by the Communist Party.

None of the other socialist states of the Pacific flirted with western art as much as China. They remain fixed in their local traditions with an overlay of revolutionary images and 'socialist', institutional architecture. As frames of mind change, not surprisingly the artistic manifestations of culture are also transformed.[36] It is only natural that, for socialist as well as for capitalist economies, contact with other ideologies and cultures brings changes in local artistic life.

It is too technologically deterministic to argue that the challenge of new technology subverts and destroys local cultures. The film industry is certainly a European and American invention, but it has been used by local East Asians of various persuasions to help develop their indigenous culture. The invention of computers creates new forms of literacy and increases the pace at which the written word can be produced. But such 'western' technology also allows local writers to produce more and allows poorer countries to reduce the costs of sustaining a modern artistic world. Literature remains a key expression of group identity and the introduction of foreign cultures has not at all meant the destruction of local cultures in the Pacific. It is true that

---

[35] *The Economist* (4 July 1987).
[36] Hidehiro Okada, 'Traditional Culture' in *Asian Cultural Quarterly*, 8/1 (spring 1982).

language has become more simple, but the ability to contact other members of one's group has expanded.[37]

The cultural pessimism about the ability to withstand the nihilism of dynamic western culture seems especially acute when considering the lost folklore and tradition after the coming of mass literacy.[38] Yet it is unfair to expect civilization to remain unchanged as history develops. This is as true of great civilizations, such as China, as it is of the smaller Pacific island traditions. What is undoubtedly true is that the smaller the tradition, the less robust it is likely to be in the face of direct external influences.

Thus there is no clear pattern of artistic practice in the Pacific. In the film industry there are huge differences between films, their subjects, and their stars.[39] To be sure, there is a fierce debate in artistic circles about national style. Is there something particularly English about Ealing comedies or French about the work of Truffaut? One prominent Filipino director rejects the idea that cinematic grammar is truly distinctive because 'the camera's eye is neutral'.[40]

What is most often shared, particularly among the developing economies, is the presence of only a few talented directors struggling to survive in a mostly rural, mass market. But even in Hong Kong the bulk of films are dominated by kung fu and comedy.[41] Many films are simply terrible imitations of often equally terrible western films. The most sophisticated films are only on the fringe in Hong Kong but, as in other developed states, they play to small audiences at home and abroad. Of imported films, 28 per cent were from the United States in 1983, while 22 per cent were from Europe's four largest countries and 8 per cent came from Japan.[42]

Japan, with its strong international reputation for cinema figures such as the director Kurosawa, presents a similar picture. Most films are produced for the local market (Kurosawa is more popular abroad) by four large production companies, and some, such as Nikkatsu, specialize in the vast soft–porn market. In 1983 the Japanese made 500 films, of which 70 per cent were soft porn. The Japanese market is mostly national and the types of film are certainly geared to local demands. The system of big commercial film companies keeps directors and actors in the same stable, endlessly perfecting the same film, thereby emphasizing technique over content. As in

---

[37] Anthony Burgess, 'A Talking Animal' in *Unesco Courier* (July 1983).

[38] Dargush Shayegan, 'The Challenge of Today and Cultural Identity' in *East Asian Cultural Studies*, 16/1–4 (March 1977).

[39] 'Cinemas in Asia' in *Far Eastern Economic Review* (3 May 1984).

[40] Ian Buruma, 'The Eye of the Camera Crosses National Borders' in *Far Eastern Economic Review* (26 March 1987).

[41] *The Economist* (4 July 1987).

[42] All statistics of this sort are from *Demographic Yearbook* (United Nations).

most countries, the age of television and video has hit the film industry especially hard, making it a less important aspect of Japanese culture.[43]

The Taiwan film scene is also dominated by local concerns, emphasizing historical epics and martial–arts films. It pays scant attention to international trends and in turn is paid scant attention by the outside world. American and Japanese influence is strongest, as is the case in Hong Kong. Yet with greater political liberalization, Taiwanese cinema has begun to develop its own quality directors, creating films with an eye to the more international and artistic market, as some Hong Kong and Japanese film-makers have done.[44] The Taiwanese experiments are particularly enlightening because they represent a struggle within an old culture coming to terms with isolation from the motherland, and new pressures from a powerful Japan and United States. The quest for self-definition is especially strong, thus producing an essentially national cinematic style, but with increasing contacts with a more cosmopolitan outside world of other developed states.

Other nationalist styles, but with differing degrees of contact with the outside world, are evident in both Indonesia and Australia. Indonesia's maturing nationalism has moved on from simple bans of American, Hong Kong, and Indian films. United States films made up 34 per cent of imports in 1983, compared to 13 per cent from the West European four, 30 per cent from Hong Kong, and only 1 per cent from Japan. Indonesians have begun to develop an indigenous industry that is viable because of the large local market. But that market is divided between town and countryside, and between developed and mostly unchanged life-styles. For the time being it is a style of film with little appeal to outsiders.[45]

Australia, on the other hand, can take advantage of its language to reach a larger market. As the boom of the 1970s showed very impressively, there was a distinctive Australian style of cinema that borrowed from American images but also from its British heritage.[46] Like the other front-rank film industries of the developed, western world, however, the made-for-television film market had taken its toll on local talent. Much like Hollywood, the images become more bland in order to reach a more universal television market and a more difficult international audience. Hollywood is, of course, in California but can hardly be classified as a specifically Pacific culture. Certainly in its early days it looked eastward across America and to Europe. It was one of the first great purveyors of global culture and as such can be seen as the initiator of the global trends more evident in the modern Pacific cinema.

[43] *Far Eastern Economic Review* (17 December 1987).
[44] *Far Eastern Economic Review* (26 March 1987).
[45] 'Cinemas in Asia' in *Far Eastern Economic Review* (3 May 1984).
[46] *Far Eastern Economic Review* (17 December 1987).

Smaller Pacific states have seen their cinema industry suffer because of insufficient local markets and the impact of modern video-technology. Videos ensure that films must be priced low. For example, Thai directors find it difficult to compete with Hong Kong productions that can be smuggled in on video, even though the government has officially banned the importation of films. Many of the governments have only their own people to blame, for the most efficient video-pirates are in South-east Asia.[47]

Thus Malaysia bans Indonesian films, South Korea and Taiwan ban Japanese films, and all are wary of American influence. South Korea, like the more developed countries in the region, has found that cinema is a declining form of entertainment as more people watch television and videos. The existing film industry shares much with Hong Kong in its Koreanization of western genres, but its exports cannot compete with more stylish Hong Kong varieties.[48]

For the larger states, television and the video-boom have helped bail out some failing film studios. But for the smaller states the ability to retain independence is made more difficult. Hong Kong, followed by the United States, has much the largest share of the official market for imported films. The spread of television and videos, as in more developed states, is by far the greatest challenge to the local film industry. The task of the censor and the nationalist is complicated by this new technology.[49] There is clearly a proliferation of styles and cultures in cinema, but taken together they are part of a global trend for developed states, and a difficult struggle with national identity for all.

The cinema remains the artistic form most symbolic of the new patterns of politics in the Pacific. In literature, where language is so crucial, there is not so much a pattern as deep fragmentation according to national styles. The odd attempt to promote regional cultural programmes in literature have failed to get beyond the platitudes.[50] Of course there are common themes in literature, many to do with adaptation to modernity, but each is expressed in a different way depending on the society under consideration.[51] To a large extent these problems are shared by all developing societies and were evident in the case of Japan well before 1945.[52]

---

[47] *The Economist* (31 October 1987).

[48] Thomas Doherty, 'Creating a National Cinema: The South Korean Experience' in *Asian Survey*, 24/8 (August 1984).

[49] John Lent, 'Film and Governments of the Association of Southeast Asian Nations', *Asian Culture Quarterly*, 12/4 (winter 1984).

[50] Mattani Rutmin, 'Modern Thai Literature' in *East Asian Cultural Studies*, 17/1–4 (March 1978).

[51] Shunsuke Tsurumi, *A Cultural History of Postwar Japan* (New York: Methuen, 1987).

[52] Michael Gibson. 'Clash of Art in Japan' in *International Herald Tribune* (23 December 1986).

Few East Asian states spend as much on the arts as do the governments in the United States and Europe. Japanese art is very much part of corporate culture, where large firms buy international items, such as the $39 million paid for Van Gogh's *Sunflowers* in 1987.[53] Japan's corporate power is used as a way of buying into the western world, but with little genuine affection for the artistic roots. The art is made to serve the corporate interest as part of a department store's feature on a European country, but it is a far cry from the palace dedicated to the arts that is a European museum.

Yet other aspects of the decorative arts have seen a greater Japanese interest in recent years. Fashion clothes and the decorative arts are perhaps the most notable areas where Japan has burst on to the scene, albeit with an austere rather than dazzling style. Most quality fashion still centres on Europe, and France and Italy in particular. The Japanese have arrived, bringing sharp lines, strong use of black and white, and a stress on quality of fabric.[54] In comparison to the weirder, more flamboyant European styles, Japan offers a more international and readily acceptable style to that tiny élite around the world that follows the fashion trends.

Indeed, the entire concept of fashion is confined to the developed world and modernization brings an internationalization of basic fashion. Japanese have won more major design prizes in Europe than anywhere else. Both Europe and Japan, more than the United States, share a concern for style and quality in design. This is most clearly seen in the clothing trade, but increasingly even in the motor trade with closer design collaboration in the 1980s.[55] The increasing eclecticism of Japanese style rather than the single form is a sign of both its vitality and its internationalism. The debates in artistic circles in Japan are as sharp as they are in Europe or the United States, but most discussion is remarkably transcultural, although there does appear to be a penchant among Japanese designers for the more practical rather than the speculative, and more emphasis on high quality and small scale.[56]

Most textile industries in the Pacific produce basic items for a local market, but at different times various East Asians have specialized in producing garments for the American and European markets. As part of the globalization of international trade, the 'rag trade' was encouraged by market 'needs' in Europe and America. Basic styling was done in Europe, production took place in East Asia, and markets were often dominated by the Americans.

Certainly the clothes worn in developed countries around the world seem

53 *The Economist* (2 May 1987).
54 'Asia Fashion' in *Far Eastern Economic Review* (11 October 1984).
55 *Financial Times* (28 August 1987).
56 See for example a discussion in *Time Magazine* (21 September 1987).

remarkably devoid of national culture. If it is true that dress defines people's roles and often bestows rank, it is clear that there is a move to a more international style, even in the least developed states.[57] It is not so much that China's Deng Xiaoping wore a Texan hat on his trip to the United States in 1979, but rather that the once-proud symbol of Thirdworldism, the safari suit, has been replaced by the more usual western business suit.

Men in the professions everywhere tend to wear sombre suits where the main variation is the number of buttons, the width of the lapel, or the flare on the trousers. Increasingly, professional women wear somewhat more stylishly tailored suits often in brighter colours, or modest skirts and blouses of quality material. Variations for climate mean some cultures tend not to wear neckties or jackets, but the development of modern heating and air-conditioning technology even smoothes out those differences. The less professional and/or the young wear the jeans and T-shirt seen first in Europe and then the United States. The more fashionable young look of the 1980s has spread from Italy through Europe, the United States, and now Asia, but is clearly an attempt at a universal look for young people in developed countries. All these styles for developed countries are supported by shelves of glossy fashion magazines and advertisements.

Of course, there are variations in developed countries on some cultural grounds, whether it is the hippie clothes of the 1960s or the outrageous coloured hair and leather and steel clothing of the 'new wave' in Britain and Europe in the 1980s. But as with *haute couture*, these fringe styles are filtered through the wider population in much-toned-down varieties.

Decorative styles in developing countries are wider, but seem inevitably to fade with development. The decline of the tattoo in the south Pacific was one of the first symbols of local culture to fade with development.[58] Modernization in China has brought the demise of the 'Mao suit', except as a potent political symbol.[59] Only the least developed states in the Pacific retain more distinctive national dress for everyday wear. Otherwise, clothing has become more functional than decorative, more universal than national.

In sum, the artistic world in the Pacific remains torn between global and particularist trends. No attempts at regional co-ordination of culture have so far been effective, although efforts have been made in the south Pacific, ASEAN, and socialist states.[60] On a global scale, the more developed societies find themselves increasingly tied into a process where they make

[57] Raymond Cohen, *The Theatre of Power* (London: Longman, 1987).
[58] Tunumafono Apelu Aiavao, 'Who is Playing Naked Now?' in *Pacific Perspective*, 12/2.
[59] *Far Eastern Economic Review* (8 August 1985).
[60] *Pacific Islands Monthly* (September 1985). The south Pacific attempt was tied up with French colonial policy (France picked up the tab) and was boycotted by a number of Pacific Forum states.

only a marginal contribution. The artistic world in particular remains dominated first by Europeans and then by Americans. For the developing states, there are international influences, but more often than not the art and culture remain more distinctly local and unchanged by international artistic trends. Finally, the socialist states of the Pacific remain more isolated of all, but with just as difficult a task of integrating Marxism with local traditions. Because art is to serve the revolution, it often turns out to be the most disappointing of the fragmented styles in modern Pacific art. But as a distinct series of styles, it merely accentuates these states' isolation from the faster-changing regional trends.

GODS, GANGSTERS, AND GAMES

The wide variety of social activities in any state is often a guide to where that state fits into international affairs. Equally, few things reveal more about societies and their cultures than their ways of 'hatches, matches, and despatches'. For close to a century now, the cultures of Europe and America have often looked upon these three basic phases of life in similar ways. For example, despite a variation of religions, marriage is usually made for reasons of romantic love instead of the previous system of arranged marriages. Yet this change has been slow to reach East Asia.[61] Even in Japan, nearly 50 per cent of marriages are arranged. Throughout most of non-Communist East Asia dowries are the norm, and this despite the increasing commercialism of marriages as states become more developed. Under such circumstances it is not surprising that intermarriage between races and ethnic types is frowned upon in most societies, only less so in more developed ones. At its most basic level the mixing of nationalities is limited by the enduring basics of different cultures attempting to keep to the old ways.

Much of birth, marriage, and death in Asia, as the world over, is governed by magic, omens, and portents. The more developed the society, the less pervasive the impact of mystic rituals. In East Asia they remain vibrant, even in the only recently developed societies such as Japan and Hong Kong.[62] Belief in the ability to predict the future—the basics of mystic ritual—is not confined to the poor, and business people take serious account of such advice for major decisions. One wag suggested, in a modification for the

---

61 *Far Eastern Economic Review* (5 May 1978).
62 'The Magic World of Omens and Portents' in *Far Eastern Economic Review* (4 January 1980).

Hong Kong stock-market of an old English folk saying, 'Red sky at night, Index at its height. Red sky in morning, a slump is-a-borning.'

Astrology is also common in western society, but not to the same degree as in East Asia. President Sukarno of Indonesia was said to make important decisions only on Wednesdays and Thursdays and to regard Saturdays as especially unlucky. Contractors on Hong Kong's mass transit railway made sure that work on tunnels or stations always began on certain red-letter days. Palm-reading is of course a universal practice, but the Japanese have now begun using computers to make the process electronic, and available at many street corners. The moles on the faces of Mao Zedong and Deng Xiaoping are said to be positive omens, even in Communist China.

The belief in such portents and mysticism is in itself not necessarily usual. But their persistence in the face of modernization does serve as a barrier to international exchange. They tend to emphasize localism and exclusivity, not to mention irrationalities. Thus there may be a sensible basis for ancient medicinal practices in China, but the hocus-pocus surrounding the process can stand in the way of medical change for the better. East Asia is moving slowly to the more scientific western culture, and the more slowly it moves—in the hope of hanging on to cultural roots—the more divisions between societies will persist. Equally, the sudden shattering of cultural roots may create conditions for alienation and revolution.

An even more difficult difference between the developed and developing portions of the Pacific is in their approach to corruption. It is undeniable that the scale of corruption as usually understood in western business practice is far higher in East Asia than anything seen in North America or western Europe.[63] While the Americans and Europeans have problems with insider trading in the financial markets, there are entire sectors of East Asian economies that function on insider information. While the organized crime of the Mafia is rife in Italy and the United States, Hong Kong and Taiwan have their triad gangs which have been exported to Chinese communities around the globe. While Europe has its drug rings, these rely heavily on the tough professionals in Latin America and the Golden Triangle of South-east Asia.[64]

This is not to suggest that the developing states of the Pacific are packed with more thugs than anywhere else, but rather that society operates by different rules, many of which conflict with the usual order in the more developed world. Some elements are perfectly recognizable, for example the Japanese Yakuza's control of gambling, prostitution, and pornography.

[63] Syed Hussein Alatus, 'Corruption in Asia: The Human Cost' in *Wilson Papers*, 17 (Washington DC: Wilson Center, 1983; Leslie Palmier, 'Corruption in the Western Pacific' in *Pacific Review*, 1/3 (1988).
[64] 'Crime: The Asian Connection' in *Far Eastern Economic Review* (27 December 1984).

Their way of working comes complete with ritual tattooing and the removal of fingers, but is recognizable as 'normal' thuggery by gangsters on the fringe of most developed societies. The main international dimension of the Yakuza syndicates is the drug trade. South-east Asian sources are tapped, using East Asian gangs, banks in Los Angeles, and markets in the United States. The Chinese gangs are the main links in this process and they too run their own rackets. During the Vietnam War the United States found its citizens tied into this traffic, but now the Chinese and Japanese have concentrated more on local markets and South-east Asia. Such genuine international co-operation in the Pacific used to include South Korea, but a crackdown since 1979 has shifted the market elsewhere, in part to Taiwan.[65] Many weapons are obtained in the Philippines and Thailand, and of course from the United States. Many of the women for the prostitution come from the Philippines, Thailand, South Korea, and Taiwan, and all can be found on the streets of East Asian capitals. Some 10 000 Thais alone send back home an estimated $1.5 million per month from their labours.[66]

Yet most of this crime, although it has international links, is carried out locally. The influx of refugees, as in 1975, created new problems by spawning extortion gangs, but these are usually confined to individual communities. Refugees of past wars, such as the Chinese Civil War, still operate a great deal of the heroin trade out of the Golden Triangle. These gangs are usually in touch with each other, but rarely operate in concert. This is a form of international contact that has mainly Pacific connections, but accounts for only a small portion of the individual gangster's business.

The more genteel pursuit of gambling is also closely tied up with gangsters, but has been assimilated into more normal life. The key to much official gambling, apart from the stock-market, is horse-racing, a sport brought by the British in imperial days. Such gambling is in some senses encouraged, for it is certainly a lucrative source of tax earnings.[67] Less legal forms of gambling, such as cards and cock-fights, are supplemented by casino machines and lotteries. Some towns, such as Macao, positively survive on the gambling trade.

Most games are legal and far less lucrative, but they are also less international. As with the Atlantic and European cultures, sport does not span vast distances very well. In Europe, the main sport remains football, known to the Americans as soccer. Certain parts of north-western Europe share rugby, and parts of north-eastern Europe share a mania with ice-hockey. Only the latter has strong transatlantic links with Canada and the United

---

65 Alec Dubo and David Kaplan, *Yakuza* (London: Futura, 1987).
66 Details ibid.
67 'Asia Takes a Gamble' in *Far Eastern Economic Review* (17 February 1978).

States, and even this is only a trend of the past two decades at most. American football has begun to attract a wider following in Britain, Germany, and Italy, but remains a marginal interest.

What is most international about sports is the regularity with which games are organized for international competition. But few of these competitions are genuine mass sports, with the exception of tennis. This remains essentially a mid-Atlantic sport although its premier tournaments are played around the globe. Three of the four major tournaments are played in London, Paris, and New York (the fourth is in Australia), and the top players are European and American. The recently established 'Pan-Pacific Open' is still dominated by European and American stars.

Other international sports include the wide range played at the Olympic games, from skiing to gymnastics. Hardly any of these are mass sports although they do draw large audiences on television and in arenas.[68] If jogging is considered a variation on the running competitions, then it has developed a mass appeal in recent years, although mainly in the United States. The range of competitions from local to regional and international level is vast, and often transcends political boundaries.

Sports in Pacific countries are even more fragmented, and local competitors are even less used to international competition on a regional basis. But with increased development and time for leisure, the sporting pattern does begin to approximate that in the Atlantic community. Some sports in the region have come from ancient traditions, such as martial arts or kite-flying. But most are derived from contact with Europe, such as football, baseball, cricket, and rugby.[69] The more restrained Go (*weiqi*), the great Asian board game, originated in China and is played in variations across the Sinitic zone. Mah-jong is far more popular, and is also played throughout the region.[70] But to some extent these traditional games have been replaced by new technological ones, the most notorious of which are pachinko, space invaders, and other arcade games.

By far the most widespread sport, however, is football, a game that links East Asians across the Eurasian land mass back to Europe rather than across the water to Australia or the United States. Football is also one of the few social and cultural links to Latin America. But apart from the football World Cup, there is no major international competition that bridges the Pacific. Even in the World Cup the East Asians are notoriously early losers, and they do not figure in the consciousness of Latin Americans as do the great rivals in western Europe.

[68] Trevor Taylor, 'The Seoul Olympics' in *Pacific Review*, 1 / 2 (1988).
[69] 'The Game's the Thing' in *Far Eastern Economic Review* (22 January 1982).
[70] R. C. Bell, *Board and Table Games From Many Civilizations* (Oxford: Oxford University Press, 1979).

Few other sports have such widespread support, but some do have more interesting international links. Baseball was introduced into Japan by the United States between the two world wars and has taken its place as a main attraction. The Japanese game has its local cultural characteristics, down to its deep bias against foreigners. Although some of best Japanese players have been 'tainted' by foreign blood, and some Americans play in the Japanese league, the Japanese have very much taken over the game as their own.[71] Yet few games are played between American and Japanese teams. There has been some friction as Japan and the United States compete in paying high salaries to certain stars, but in general the leagues keep to themselves.[72] There is no equivalent in baseball to the international ice-hockey competition across the Atlantic.

Yet Japanese leaders, unlike their European counterparts, have an advantage at summit meetings of western leaders, for they can at least understand the allusions to baseball made by American Presidents, even if the language of the reference needs to be translated.[73] Perhaps even more esoteric was the ping-pong diplomacy initiated by China in its opening to the United States in 1970. Despite the prevalence of Americans in many parts of the Pacific, no American national sports have caught on elsewhere. Certainly nothing compares with the more than 16 million Japanese who went to a baseball game in 1984 or the third of the population who claim baseball as their favourite sport.[74]

A more international, if more élitist, sport is golf, played by 63.4 million Japanese in 1983 and millions of others in Taiwan, Australia, and North America. Golfers from those countries take part in the international tour and, especially in women's golf, are among the top rank. Considering the importance of golf in the business world, the fact that it is played so widely in key states in the Pacific does have an impact on the way business is done. More of the main golfers and their tournaments are in Europe than in East Asia, but on balance it is a genuinely international pastime, and a 'language' that is as understandable in Europe as it is in America or Asia.

Two other, more peculiar, sports are played mainly in former British colonies. Rugby, which held its World Cup in New Zealand in 1987, brings together Europeans and mainly the inhabitants of the south Pacific, including Fiji and Tonga. Cricket is much more symbolic of imperial British rule and links Australia and New Zealand with Britain and the other main

[71] Saduharu Oh and David Falkner, *Saduharu Oh* (New York: Vintage, 1984); *International Herald Tribune* (14 May 1987).

[72] *International Herald Tribune* (12 December 1987).

[73] As happened at the Venice summit of 1987: *Independent* (10 June 1987).

[74] *Facts and Figures of Japan, 1984* (Tokyo: Foreign Press Centre, 1984).

cricket-playing former colonies such as the states of South Asia. It is a popular sport in Australia, as it is in India and Pakistan, but produces few genuine transpacific links. If anything the links, as with rugby, are to Europe rather than across the Pacific.

Perhaps the most genuine Pacific sport, for a brief time at least, was yacht-racing. The capture of the America's Cup by Australia, then its subsequent loss to the United States in 1987, was at least played out in Pacific waters. Although it fired the imagination of millions of sports fans in Australia and the United States, it remained a sport played only by the rich and famous. Its main players were also Europeans and North Americans, as well as Australians and New Zealanders.[75] Formula-one auto-racing is an equally élite sport, and the entry ticket again has more to do with money and technology. Yet, as in many other sports, it ties in Japan and Australia with Europe more than with the United States, except as part of the generally international auto industry.

A number of other sports are mostly confined to individual countries. Australian Rules football is self-explanatory. Japanese are great fans of sumo wrestling—they call it their national sport. It is so closely guarded that foreigners who compete run into barely disguised discrimination, such as confronted a Hawaiian-American star in the 1980s. Thai boxing is yet another sport whose name suggests the limits of its horizons.

Thus it is not surprising that there are few games played internationally in the Pacific. Of course, there are regional competitions, for example between south Pacific islanders where five sports are played.[76] The South-east Asians have their own games involving 18 sports, mostly won by whomever is the host nation.[77] There are also Asian games which stretch to the Gulf but not across the Pacific to the United States. The 10th Asian games were played in Seoul in 1986 and for the first time were won by the Chinese. Most of the sports are international, with the exception of taekwando and judo.[78]

In a similar way, the Olympic games are held from time to time in the Pacific, and in 1988 both its summer and winter sports took place around the rim (if Alberta is counted as Canada's Pacific hinterland). Some sports are dominated by Pacific people, including table tennis and badminton. But most are part of a wider international competition.[79] Of course the decision on where to hold the Olympics, and whom to include, has its share of Pacific as well as other political disputes and is closely tied to issues of national

---

[75] *The Economist* (7 February 1987).
[76] *Pacific Islands Monthly* (October 1985).
[77] *Far Eastern Economic Review* (12 October 1979).
[78] *Asiaweek* (19 October 1986).
[79] *Far Eastern Economic Review* (7 January 1988).

pride. The problem between North and South Korea over the Seoul Olympics, or the disputes between China and Taiwan over representation, are of course part of broader political disputes. Sport serves more as a forum for dispute than a fulfilment of its much-cherished objective of bringing people closer together.[80]

There is little that can be called unifying in Pacific terms about sports, especially in comparison to the Atlantic community. Although some sports do span a number of countries, they are more often than not European as well as American and East Asian. The odd bilateral link, such as that in baseball, barely begins to match the bilateral links across the Atlantic. In sports, as in other aspects of culture, the Pacific is fragmented. To the extent that it is tied into international linkages, they are truly global, and not genuinely Pacific or even seriously sub-regional within the Pacific.

FOOD AND INTERNATIONAL POLITICS

If 'you are what you eat', then the Pacific, even more that the Atlantic, has little unity. According to the theorists of food habits, the type of food consumed depends on the level of development and the specific geographic conditions. Food aversions and preferences fit with what is best for the nutritional and ecological welfare of the locals. Religious practice follows rather than determines these trends. Thus the Indians do not eat cows for sound reasons of efficiency and expense, and for the same reasons most inhabitants of the Middle East do not eat pork.[81]

Much like language and religion, food preferences help set cultures apart.[82] Of course, states do not go to war only for reasons of diet, but the types of food consumed are among the great demarcators of cultures and societies. Broadly, the Pacific has a few more differences in food habits than Europe and the Atlantic, but with increased development there are also international foods that are taking their place on Pacific menus.

From the south-western edge of the Pacific comes the influence of Islam and India. Islamic food laws developed where pig farming was uneconomic (pigs thrive on the edge of forested regions) and thus barely extended on to the mainland of Asia. In the Spice Islands chicken thrived instead, as did some beef. In fact, chicken is said to have originated in South-east Asia and made its way to Rome via the ancient trade routes. Naturally, spice formed a

[80] Taylor, 'Seoul Olympics'.

[81] Marvin Harris, *The Sacred Cow and the Abominable Pig* (New York: Simon & Schuster, 1987).

[82] Sidney Mintz, *Sweetness and Power* (London: Penguin, 1985).

basic component of the diet and the protein base was the near-ubiquitous East Asian rice. As wheat was the staple food in Europe and the Americas, so rice is a common ingredient in East Asian food.[83] Elsewhere in South-east Asia the rice and spice combination thrived, especially in conjunction with seafood, but the spice was mostly removed by the time the culture had spread as far as the more bland Philippine diet.

Further north in Asia are the two great food cultures of China and Japan. Both are also based mainly on rice, but China has five main styles of food, while Japan has developed its own distinctive style. Cantonese will eat anything (or so their neighbours say), Shanghainese like their food sweeter, and the Szechuanese have a taste for fierce spices, more in the Indian style. Like the Japanese, but unlike many South-east Asians, the Chinese have long used chopsticks to eat.

The Japanese, like the South-east Asians, had access to far more seafood than beef and thus are large consumers of fish. The northern part of China and the Koreas came under more Mongol influence and have more wheat products and beef. Yet their consumption of beef is nothing like that of the neo-European cultures in the Americas and Australasia. This strong link across the eastern and southern Pacific has been strengthened by the fact that the superior, lean New Zealand and Australian beef forms 20 per cent of the vast American ground-beef diet.[84]

These neo-Europeans are also hooked on that other peculiarity of their mostly North European forebears, milk. Few East Asians consume any significant quantities of milk or its products. They obtain their calcium from green leafy vegetables but developed taboos about milk because most of their people found it made them ill. The inhabitants of the smaller islands of Oceania never saw cattle until very recently and therefore never had to face the aversion to milk. These islanders preferred insects, as did many others in tropical climates where the insects provided protein that was otherwise scarce.

Thus some food, such as pig for Muslims or milk for Chinese, provoked sharp antipathy. While Chinese ate dog, the Inuit needed their dogs for hunting and haulage. However, few cultures ate other humans, except in the early state before tiny chiefdoms were established (as in Oceania). The exception was the Aztecs, but then they had few large sources of food as substitutes.[85]

Development and international contact has helped break down some of these food barriers (though, thankfully, eating people is wrong in most

---

[83] 'The Tastes of Asia' in *Far Eastern Economic Review* (30 December 1977).
[84] Harris, *Sacred Cow*, 126.
[85] Ibid., ch. 10.

cultures), as has ethnic-chic. The fast-food revolution from the United States spun off from beef into other foods such as chicken, pasta, and even sushi. Sake-flavoured chewing-gum is surely the worst of all worlds. Clearly the spin-off has become global, and their low cost makes such foods accessible to more than just the wealthy. Thus Hong Kong boasts the largest chain of Pizza Huts outside America, sushi bars are spreading across America and Europe, tofu is to be found in most supermarkets of the developed world, and even Japan has discovered bagels.[86] This process of internationalism is clearly complex, for beer from breweries that Europeans established in East Asia is now exported back to Europe and America as a premium product, often by companies owned by Pacific multinationals. The Swensen's ice-cream available in Hong Kong or Singapore has come a long way from Europe via America. The recent entry of Australian food multinationals into the take-over game says something about both the international nature of the global economy in developed states and the globalization of some tastes in food and drink.[87]

Apart from its importance as a major sign of cultural differences, food is not really a prominent cause of international conflict. The Japanese taste for whale meat does help keep Japan from agreeing to the international ban on whaling.[88] But in general, especially among the more developed societies around the Pacific, food is a product and symbol of national particularity, although food, like culture generally, does become flavoured by international fads. As European experience suggests, sustained economic development does not entirely destroy national eating habits.

THE POLITICS OF HUMOUR

Laughter, like eating, is a basic human activity that reveals a great deal about national culture. But what is perhaps most common about humour is its habit of putting other people down. Sometimes jokes focus on sex, bureaucracies, religion, and ethnic groups, but politics is never far from the surface. Yet the politics is often national and, even in the more visual art of cartoons, the allusions and images are often lost on foreigners.[89]

National politicians are always the butt of jokes. For example, the

---

[86] For a few of these cases see *Japan Times* (7 September 1986); *The Economist* (29 November 1986); *International Herald Tribune* (2 August 1986); *Independent* (15 June 1987).

[87] *The Economist* (12 September 1987).

[88] *The Sunday Times* (31 May 1987).

[89] Steven Lukes and Itzhak Galnoor, *No Laughing Matter* (London: Routledge & Kegan Paul, 1985); Khalid Kishtainy, *Arab Political Humour* (London: Quartet, 1985).

Filipinos recount that the favourite Marcos dance was 'one step forward, one step sideways, and two steps kickback.[90] In multiracial communities such as Malaysia, jokes often have a strong racial tone. One group parodies its rivals, using stock images of Indian money-lenders, Chinese shopkeepers, and Malay peasants.

Perhaps the finest political jokes are from the political cultures of eastern Europe, but the Communists of East Asia have not picked up the tradition. For the Chinese, humour is largely based on puns, making use of the wild possibilities of its multitonal language. The Thais have developed a national style of pun humour for the same reasons. Japanese puns are popular because of the homophones in speech which are distinguished in writing by different characters but, needless to say, such humour is not translatable.

The Indonesians have gone even further, establishing a national humour institute in 1979, but this has reportedly so far only arranged (rather boisterous) seminars. Like that of most of its South-east Asian neighbours, much Indonesian humour derives from the traditions of story-telling and its deeper peasant customs. Indonesian humour is said to retain much of its stylized tradition from the ancient puppet art, but in the modern age a great deal has deteriorated into slapstick. Indeed, slapstick will make people laugh around the world—what the Thais call a 'shallow funny-bone'. Of course, some laughter is from embarrassment rather than humour. This is related to what the Koreans call the 'east question, west answer' humour, when the reply is totally meaningless.

Thus Richard Hughes has aptly noted that humour remains national because of language barriers.[91] Asian servicemen going to Australia take a crash course in Australian humour, but it is of little use. Humour is also affected by ideology, for Chinese under Communism seem less liberated in their humour than the Taiwanese. As it is said 'a Communist with a sense of humour has no Party future'.

PACIFIC CULTURE

In terms of political culture, there is no Pacific. Nearly every way of assessing ideology and culture, from formal ideologies to language and food, reveals that the region is broken down into a number of important sub-regions. Compare this situation to Europe and the Atlantic world where far more, albeit not all, roots of political cultures are shared among states.

[90] This and following examples from 'Ho, Ho, Ho' in *The Far Eastern Economic Review* (6 January 1983).
[91] Ibid., 30.

Of course, unity in these terms is relative, but not only do the people of the Pacific show little evidence of present unity of thought, there also appears to be no trend towards greater integration. There are some links that have been established, for example between Japan and the United States in some aspects of political ideology, sport, and even language. But in comparison to British or even German relations with the United States, there is far more political-culture disunity than unity.

The main sub-regions of the Pacific follow relatively conventional geographical lines. The Americas and Australia and New Zealand remain a world unto themselves, with still predominant links to European culture. The north–south cultural links in the Americas are not quite as firm, but are certainly more robust than any ties across the Pacific. The main exception is, of course, the bonds, between the neo-Europes of Australia and New Zealand and their fellow new states in the Americas. If there is a real Pacific in cultural terms, that is about as far as it extends across the water, and such links owe more to European colonialism than anything else.

The second major sub-region comprises the states of ASEAN. Although they share cultural characteristics such as food with their neighbours in Indo-China, they are deeply divided from them by political ideology. The large movement of population across these frontiers in recent years is unlikely to blur the lines, for few of the refugees have been resettled in the region.

China remains a great cultural sub-region on its own. Although it is not as dominant in the area as it once was, its impact in terms of ideology and cultural practice remains strongly felt. Its long isolation from anything but its own internal debates or the Communist world, as well as its under-development, helped cut it off from the new trends elsewhere in the region. With greater economic integration in the Pacific, China may possibly open its doors to outside political culture.

While North Korea can be classified in much the same way as China, South Korea is best seen in the very different mould of Japan, Taiwan, Hong Kong, and Singapore. All these states have been rapidly modernized. They all retain distinctive cultural dimensions, but all have been more active in cultural exchange. They even have commonalities in political ideology. Yet the integration is not nearly as close as in the Americas, as is evident from language, food, and exchange of populations.

Island Pacific remains diffuse in cultural terms, leaning in different directions depending on the islands' own traditions and their current dominant power, be it the United States, France, or Australia. As developing micro-states, they are isolated and most often ignored, but are still washed by the tides of cultural change in the Pacific.

The main waves that reach almost all the region, except for its Communist portions, are the global trends of cultural internationalism. In a fragmentary way the ideals of European politics have split the region into Communist and non-Communist states. But as we have seen, these divisions have already developed their own subdivisions. The more genuinely international ideas have come with international travel. Cultures of language, food, art, and sport have broken down in marginal ways, leaving an overlay of superficial globalism. Cities, hotels, and cars may look alike around the world, but the culture that produced them remains very distinctive.

In the West European and Atlantic cultures political similarities are supported by rough cultural unity. In the Pacific the similarities are barely skin deep. To the extent that they exist, they are a function of greater economic development and integration in a global, rather than specifically Pacific, community. The links of tourism are international, and make Europe as much a part of the Pacific as the North Americans. Perhaps the talk of a Pacific community should be balanced with discussion of a Eurasian community. As more states like South Korea or Taiwan develop, they join this global community, but do little to enhance the creation of a Pacific community.

The dominant powers in these political cultures are difficult to judge. The United States, with its leading role in the globalization of ideology and culture, must be considered the main Pacific power. It has benefited from the spread of European colonialism and established close links with states on the eastern rim of the Pacific, as well as with Australia, New Zealand, and the NICs. By contrast, Soviet influence is felt on the western fringes of the Pacific, linking with North Korea and the states of Indo-China. Although the ties in political terms are as strong as America's are with its friends, in cultural terms there are virtually no ties that bind. This is a major weakness in the Soviet position in the Pacific.

China is the third major cultural power in the region, but mostly for historical reasons. Since 1949 it has exerted little lasting cultural influence on any state except North Korea, and if anything the gap between China and its neighbours is growing in cultural terms. The level of development in many states takes them further away from Chinese influence, although in some aspects of language and food they remain close.

Japan is perhaps the most ambiguous of these powers, for its is the most developed state in East Asia, but is remarkably isolated from the region. It has forged, and seems to desire, few links in cultural terms with other Asians or even non-Asians in the Pacific. Like the Soviet Union, it exerts power in the region for other reasons, but has little of the deep-rooted influence that flows from ideology and culture. The pride that Japan takes in its exclusivity may well shut the country off from taking a leading role in the Pacific.

Thus the Pacific remains fragmented. Lines of influence do run across its waters and around its rim, but they are mostly bilateral and isolated. They certainly do not constitute a community on anything like the West European or Atlantic scale. While there is an overlay of some common features, these are the result of globalism and global interdependence rather than the creation of a Pacific community. In that sense, Europeans are as much a part of the Pacific as the Americans.

III

THE MILITARY DIMENSION

Some of the earliest effort at 'thinking Pacific' were the result of military considerations. Strategists of military affairs are usually quick to perceive sweeping geopolitical trends and the need to control vast areas for reasons of 'security'. Not surprisingly, all great powers since the fifteenth century have turned to the Pacific at some time, either out of fear, or a calculation of opportunity. Yet the first genuine Pacific-wide war was not fought until the first half of the 1940s, when Japan swept all rivals from its region only to find itself in turn pushed back home and then occupied from 1945.

Since then, military issues have figured prominently in the painting of patterns in Pacific international politics. In fact, until the 1970s the Pacific was perceived primarily in military terms. With rapid economic growth around the Pacific in the 1970s, and with the control of some Pacific conflicts, the military dimension began to take second place to economic affairs.

Nevertheless, there is nothing like a military crisis to focus the minds of leaders on the policy essentials. Therefore it is important to assess military affairs in the Pacific for evidence about the main patterns of international relations in the region. The central questions to be asked are: what are the areas and reasons for conflict around the Pacific; how is force used in conflict; and what are the reasons for co-operation in alliances or in arms control?

Once again, by comparison with the clear-cut patterns in Atlantic and European affairs, the Pacific is far more complex. It is useful to distinguish between conflicts that have more or less terminated, those that are unresolved but broadly under control, those that are still hot, and those that threaten to break the surface. The more co-operative aspects are best assessed by looking at the reasons for, and nature of, alliances (old and new), and the patterns of arms control. In conclusion, the overarching patterns of balances of power and international security can be identified.

What is perhaps most striking about conflict in the Pacific is the fact that virtually none of it is best examined through a Pacific-wide lens. The conflicts are best explained either in terms of sub-regional issues, or else with reference to broader, global aspects of the superpower balance. It is therefore impossible to identify what some observers have called a Pacific 'security complex'.[1]

Nevertheless, there are a number of distinctive features of military affairs in the Pacific. The balance of power is less dominated by the superpowers, China is an independent and growing military power, Japan is potentially a major power but under self-restraint, there have been a wide range of wars as part of the decolonization process, and territory has changed hands in the

---

[1] On the security complex concept see Barry Buzan and Gowher Rizvi, *South Asian Insecurity and the Great Powers* (London: Macmillan, 1986).

various wars in East Asia. But the region has also seen other, more pacific, trends. There has been a reduction in military conflict, a distinctive type of arms control has emerged in parts of East Asia, there has been a declining role for nuclear weapons, and in general there has been a shift to greater multipolarity as the superpowers decline in importance. All these aspects make the events in the Pacific distinctive and worthy of analysis, even though they do not constitute a coherent, region-wide pattern.

11

Past Conflicts

Few conflicts in the Pacific since 1945 can be said to have fully ended. The two great wars of the region, in Korea and in Indo-China, are nowhere near as hot as they once were. Although the Korean War remains unresolved and tension between North and South is apparent, this conflict is best treated as a war to be completed. On the other hand, the conflicts in Indo-China have been through a fundamental change of character. Until 1954 the main conflicts were the struggles by local states against French imperialism. For the next 20 years the dominant conflict was the civil war in Vietnam, which subsequently spilled over into the surrounding Indo-Chinese states. The conflicts since 1975 have tended to be between neighbouring states in a clash of local nationalisms. Thus it is possible to concentrate on the second war in Indo-China (the first has been considered in Chapter 6) as a more or less terminated conflict. In the period after 1975 the patterns of conflict and co-operation in Indo-China are drastically altered, even though the legacy of the two decades before 1975 continues to affect the policies of Pacific states.

INDO-CHINA, 1955–1975

The Geneva Conference which opened in 1954 took place in the midst of an East–West cold war and against a background of confused local politics. The Korean War had stumbled to a stalemate, leaving all sides with a feeling of having made the best of a bad situation. The sense of a draw rather than a victory was calculated by the superpowers in global terms, but by China, Japan, and the Koreas far more in local terms. Clearly, not everyone was playing the same game by the same rules.

The situation in Indo-China was different again. Unlike in Korea, the latest round of fighting there involved a last-ditch effort by France to retain its colonies. The Vietnam War was further evidence that the age of European military power had passed in East Asia and that guerrilla tactics employed by a poor, peasant army could triumph over a more sophisticated, but distant and only partially committed, modern power. However, the war also showed that such military triumphs by developing states came more easily when there was significant assistance from like-minded allies. Chinese and Soviet aid to the anti-French forces was essential, but not sufficient to ensure North Vietnam's victory. Thus the Indo-China conflict looked something like the Korean War in that the overlay of the East–West conflict helped determine who fought on which side.

From 1955 the conflict moved into its next phase—local struggles for domestic power—with a significant degree of external intervention. So while the overlay of East–West conflict continued to apply, the nature of the domestic conflict changed. In all three Indo-Chinese cases, Vietnam, Laos, and Cambodia, the struggle involved Communist forces fighting guerrilla wars, but only in the case of Vietnam was there large-scale and direct involvement of the United States in support of its ally, the Republic of Vietnam (South Vietnam).

In Laos, the Geneva Conference failed to end the struggle as warring parties fought for control. The Pathet Lao was a Communist force created by the Vietnamese and also supported by China. It provoked other local factions involved in the conflict to accept a neutralized Laos but forces supported by the United States saw such neutralism as little but a cover for Communism.[1] The fiercest fighting took place between 1960 and 1962 and was brought to an end by another unofficial agreement in Geneva which had been cobbled together by the United States, the Soviet Union, and China.[2] Laos was to become neutral, but all sides seemed to recognize that the *de facto* result would be partition while the main conflict was waged in Vietnam. By 1963 the Pathet Lao ruled the north-east portion of Laos bordering on Vietnam and China, while the Souvanna Phouma regime held the rest. From 1964 United States aid to Souvanna Phouma increased as the Americans looked for additional ways of pressuring Vietnam and protecting American interests in Thailand.[3]

With the increased tempo of the war in Vietnam, the Vietnamese took a more prominent role in Pathet Lao affairs in order to secure their supply routes down to South Vietnam. The United States increased the scale of its bombing of Laos in order to cut the supply lines but, as American power in Vietnam faded, the Pathet Lao extended its control over the country even further.[4] An agreement in 1973 between the Pathet Lao and the Vientiane government on a coalition, as the Americans and North Vietnam reached agreement in their war, did not last long. The defeat of the American-supported regime in Saigon in the spring of 1975 brought about a collapse of power in Vientiane as well.

[1] Arthur Dommen, *Laos* (Boulder: Westview, 1985); Hugh Toye, *Laos: Buffer State of Battleground* (Oxford: Oxford University Press, 1968).
[2] Gerald Segal, *The Great Power Triangle* (London: Macmillan, 1982), ch. 2.
[3] Martin Stuart-Fox, *Laos* (London: Frances Pinter, 1986), ch. 1.
[4] Dommen, *Laos*.

The new Communist regime in Laos owed a huge debt to Vietnam. As the split between China and Vietnam grew wider, Laos found itself surrounded by a hostile Thailand, a sullen China, a distracted Cambodia, and a far-too-friendly Vietnam. By paying the price of Vietnamese dominance, Laos was able to retain nominal independence and peace. Laos was the only one of the three Indo-Chinese states which found itself basically at peace in 1975. But it also found itself isolated and tucked away from the new wave of prosperity sweeping the East Asian rim of the Pacific. Laos was confined to the Communist part of East Asia, but by virtue of its alliance with Vietnam, it was not open to the reformist ideas that were soon to sweep Communism in China. Laos more or less won peace, but at the cost of remaining very poor.

Neighbouring Cambodia obtained independence from France in 1953 before the Geneva Conference, and power was held by Prince Sihanouk. Unlike in the case of Laos, in Cambodia the United States, China, and the Soviet Union were more or less resigned to Sihanouk's neutralist and populist politics and were unwilling to make major efforts to topple him.[5] But by the the mid-1960s, as the war in neighbouring Vietnam escalated, politics in Cambodia became more polarized. Left-wing pressure from local Khmer Rouge Communists helped push Sihanouk into breaking diplomatic relations with the United States in May 1965.[6] Yet Sihanouk also failed to pursue reform at home and the left remained opposed to his regime.

However, Vietnam, which was the main support for the Khmer Rouge, refused to sanction major attacks on Sihanouk because his neutral line allowed them to pursue the main effort in South Vietnam using Cambodian bases. In 1970 disputes among the conservative Khmers led to a coup by Lon Nol that brought to power a more right-wing regime, and Sihanouk fled to China. But this was not a simple process of polarization because the Sino-Soviet split meant that Sihanouk was unlikely to be as favourable to the Soviet Union as he was towards China. In fact, Moscow maintained diplomatic relations with the Lon Nol regime until its end in 1975. What is more, as Vietnam and China became estranged, the leftist cause in Indo-China was further fragmented.

The main rebel movement inside Cambodia was controlled by Pol Pot. He argued for pushing the revolutionary struggle even faster, and rejected the more cautious approach that best served the Vietnam-first argument made by the North Vietnamese. At least in the initial stage between 1970 and 1975 it is difficult to argue that China was Pol Pot's main supporter. The

---

[5] Ben Kiernan and Boua Chantou, *Peasants and Politics in Kampuchea, 1941–1981* (London: Zed Press, 1982); Ben Kiernan, *How Pol Pot Came To Power* (London: Verso, 1984).
[6] Michael Vickery, *Kampuchea* (London: Frances Pinter, 1986), ch. 3.

primary explanation for Cambodian events is to be found in internal politics, and in the polarization encouraged by events in neighbouring Vietnam.[7]

The escalation of the American bombing campaign in the Vietnam War, as part of its effort to transfer the bulk of the ground fighting to South Vietnamese forces, meant heavy bombing of North Vietnamese supply routes through Cambodia. The corrupt Lon Nol regime ruled only parts of the country and, much like Laos in the first half of the 1970s, Cambodia was essentially partitioned, awaiting the resolution of the main action in Vietnam. The Cambodian side-show was concluded in 1975 when Pol Pot's forces marched into Phnom Penh and declared 'year zero'. But unlike the situation in Laos, the radical policies of the new regime resulted in disputes with its neighbours, and new wars in the region. The fact that the new regime was supported by different, and increasingly antagonistic, Communist regimes meant that the local basis of dispute was aggravated. Clearly the regional balance of power had shifted with the defeat of the forces supported by the United States. But the inter-Communist rivalry was to be every bit as bloody.

Vietnam was clearly the focus of the Indo-Chinese conflict, and the pace-setter for its neighbours. As France's grip failed in the 1960s, the United States grasped the ring by supporting South Vietnam in opposition to the Communist north. The Geneva Conference declaration of elections on unification was rejected by the United States and South Vietnam as, since most of the population lived in the North, it was bound to produce a pro-Hanoi vote. In the 1950s the United States had attempted to shore up the regime in the South by helping fend off northern-supported rebels. This was also a time of American support of regional defence schemes such as SEATO, created by the Manila Pact of September 1954.

In the American perception, China was the main regional threat to its ally, South Vietnam. With the Sino-Soviet split in the early 1960s, China was seen as the more active and dangerous part of a divided Communist camp. The Soviet Union was also a threat in its support for Hanoi, but it was at least possible to do business with Moscow.[8]

During the 1960s the United States gradually slid into a land war in Asia. Support for South Vietnam increased, especially after 1964, with matching if not equal escalation on the Communist side.[9] By the beginning of 1968

---

[7] Vickery, *Kampuchea*.

[8] Segal, *Great Power Triangle*, ch. 4.

[9] The literature on the war is vast, but for a range of analyses see Stanley Karnow, *Vietnam: a History* (New York: Viking, 1983); R. B. Smith, *An International History of the Vietnam War* (London: Macmillan, 1985), George Kahin, *Intervention* (New York: Alfred Knopf, 1986); Gabriel Kolko, *Anatomy of War* (Toronto: Pantheon Books, 1985).

there were more than half a million American troops in South Vietnam—easily the largest deployment of American troops outside the United States.

Yet for all its troops, and modern technology, the United States was unwilling and to some extent unable to win the war in Vietnam. Opposition at home, and from European allies concerned about the reduced attention to NATO, hampered the American war effort. North Vietnamese resistance was fierce and support from its allies kept flowing. American tactics did not build support in the 'hearts and minds' of the population in the South and the regime was allowed to stumble on unreformed and corrupt.

The principle behind the American engagement in South-east Asia was to demonstrate the credibility of its promise to defend its allies from Communism. Unfortunately, the audience for this didactic war—that is, other allies in the area and around the world—were not convinced that South Vietnam was worth saving or that the United States had set about the task in the best way. The transfer to Indo-China of European and Atlantic notions of deterrence and containment was considered inappropriate. The western military alliance was founded on the need for democratic societies to defend themselves from external threat. That seemed a far cry from defending corrupt dictatorships which depended on outside support in what looked very much like a civil war.

Once the United States had made such a commitment to South Vietnam, and then realized in 1968 that it could not win the war, the question became how to get out without allowing 'dominoes' of allies to tumble elsewhere and without America's prestige around the world suffering a body-blow. The 1973 Paris Accords between the United States and North Vietnam allowed the United States to withdraw its troops from the war, but the triumph of the North over the South in 1975 made it clear that the damage to the American position was irreversible.

Of course, the result could have been more devastating for the United States and the Pacific. War between the United States and North Vietnam's patrons in China and the Soviet Union was avoided, despite the fact that Chinese air-defence troops fought in the North and Soviet aid shipments were destroyed in American bombing raids on northern cities and ports. The Soviet Union provided more than 80 per cent of the military aid Hanoi received and, by deterring the United States from adopting more adventurous war plans, ensured that Vietnam could fight the war on its own terms. China was more active in the war, and for a time in 1965–6 looked like repeating the Korean experience. But both the Chinese and the Americans had learned the lessons of the Korean War and successfully communicated caution in crisis.[10]

[10] Allen Whiting, *The Chinese Calculus of Deterrence* (Ann Arbor: University of Michigan, 1975); Gerald Segal, *Defending China* (Oxford: Oxford University Press, 1985).

In 1971 the United States played its most sophisticated geopolitical games in the post-war period in an attempt to get out of the Vietnam War without losing too much honour. The grand strategy, as formulated by Henry Kissinger, was to improve relations with China and the Soviet Union, thereby encouraging both Communist allies of Hanoi to force an amicable deal in Indo-China.[11] But both China and Soviet Union merely considered the American proposals on their own merits, and declined to press Vietnam into anything that prevented it from winning the war.

Clearly the overlay of East–West relations that had been so crucial in previous conflict in Indo-China had been replaced by a more complex picture of multipolar great-power relations. Although the so-called great-power triangle had been in operation well before 1971, in fact ever since the Sino-Soviet split, it was only in the 1970s that the United States tried to use the rift in the Communist world as a way out of its Vietnam quagmire. That the effort failed does not obscure the fact that great-power conflict in the Pacific was no longer bipolar.

The importance of the Vietnam War goes well beyond the fact that it was the most costly war, in human and financial terms, since 1945, that it was the most extensive American military engagement at any time since 1945, that it did serious damage to America's economy, self-confidence, and credibility, and that it helped formalize the transition from a bipolar to a multipolar world. The map of Indo-China was transformed. What were two semi-neutral states and a divided Vietnam became three Communist states with Vietnam the world's third-largest and third-most-powerful Communist state. The year 1975 is clearly the second-most-important time of change in the Pacific balance of power. One state South Vietnam, disappeared, one state, North Vietnam, expanded, and two states, Laos and Cambodia, changed regimes from neutralist to Communist.

Other South-east Asian states were forced to readjust their international perspectives. SEATO was shown to be a hollow alliance and eventually died in 1977. The shock of war and defeat was too much for this Asian version of NATO. SEATO's failure also shattered any illusion that an alliance structure in the Pacific could be maintained along Atlantic lines. Thailand now found itself on the front line in the struggle against Communism, and Malaysia, the Philippines, and Singapore now stared across the South China Sea at a set of Communist regimes. Unlike the situation in Europe, the front line in Asia had moved since 1945.

As far as the great powers were concerned, the main loser was clearly the United States. It had committed a large proportion of its conventional power

---

[11] Henry Kissinger, *The White House Years* (London: Weidenfeld, 1979); Tad Szuc, *The Illusion of Peace* (New York: Viking, 1978); Seymour Hersh, *Kissinger: The Price of Power* (London: Faber & Faber, 1983).

to a land war in Asia and had been unable to win. Its withdrawal showed there were limits to a superpower's ability to use its military force, even against poor, peasant countries. The United States could not use its military power to order events in the western Pacific, or at least not short of total war. More positively for the United States, it was clear that great-power crisis management could be effective in limiting wars. Although there were problems in communications, and times of high tension, the great powers kept the war limited. After the Korean experience of a direct clash between China and the United States, the Vietnam experience could be considered progress.

The other superpower, the Soviet Union, had perhaps done best out of the 20 years since 1955. It did not get dragged into the wars. Despite the complexity of local conflicts, the Soviet Union was only occasionally embarrassed, as in its continued recognition of Lon Nol in Cambodia. Military aid was not quite as fulsome as the local Communist forces wanted, but then they received all that they needed. The lesson for Moscow was that military aid and superpower deterrence could work to improve the Soviet position in the world. The Soviet Union had gained merely by keeping a low profile, while America's international reputation plummeted elsewhere in the developing world as a result of its 'adventurism' and 'gunboat diplomacy'. Opposition to United States policy was also increased in, from the Soviet perspective, the far more important European theatre. The European left was critical of American 'imperialism' while the right was worried about the damage done to NATO and the international economy by a distracted and drained United States.

In 1975 China could also be pleased that it had helped eject the United States from Asia. It could hope that the American withdrawal would also loosen the strings on Taiwan, but it feared that, if the United States only retreated offshore and not back across the Pacific, Taiwan would become more, rather than less, important. More worrying still, a defeated United States would be less useful in holding off the perceived Soviet threat to China. When the Vietnam War first began, there was no Sino-Soviet split to speak of and the United States was the common enemy. While the Soviet calculation remained the same throughout the war, China changed its mind in the early 1970s and improved relations with the United States. It therefore ensured that the defeat of the United States in Vietnam was a mixed blessing.

China could also be pleased that there were now more Communist regimes on its frontiers. But once again, the Sino-Soviet split had taught China that not all Communists were the same. If these regimes were more pro-Soviet than pro-Chinese—and Laos and Vietnam looked very much like that—then their triumph may not have been in the Chinese interest. Certainly, a triumphant Vietnam was more powerful, confident, and independent of China than in 1955, and less likely to resume the subservient relationship that China liked to remember from its idealized vision of traditional East Asian foreign policy.

From a Pacific-wide perspective, the Vietnam War had a major impact. The United States became less directly involved in Pacific security, if only because fewer of its men were dying in western Pacific jungles and fewer ships and aircraft had to cross the waters to supply its military forces. The retreat from the Asian land mass encouraged the United States to think about the Pacific in more naval and offshore terms. This more detached perspective may have been productive in the long term but, in more immediate and military terms, it marked a decline in the United States' Pacific perspective.

The war had brought the Soviet Union closer to the states of Indo-China, and to Vietnam in particular. The absence of other Communist states in the region had made China more important and had left Soviet foreign policy with fewer options. The addition of new Communist regimes, and especially one such as Vietnam which was prepared to offer the Soviet Union military facilities, was a major spur to the Soviet Union to think Pacific. The expansion of Soviet military power around the globe was already under way, but the events in the Pacific presented the Soviet leaders with a greater success and more prospects there than anywhere else in the developing world. The victory of North Vietnam certainly provided the Soviet Union with much-needed naval facilities. And it happened in a region that had otherwise been stony ground for Soviet influence. To be sure, some Pacific states were scared by Soviet success. But others, such as Indonesia, were henceforth to feel a greater need to get on with Moscow as a legitimate actor in the region.

The Vietnam War had little direct impact on China's Pacific perspectives. It saw the war very much in regional terms and in its already well-established framework of trying to retain dominant influence in South-east Asia. The rise of the Soviet Union and the fall of the United States as Pacific powers was, as has already been suggested, seen as having ambiguous implications for Chinese security. But to the extent that the war encouraged China to build bridges to the United States, it did help span the Pacific and create a stronger Chinese Pacific-consciousness. But China had always understood that the United States was important, even though in the past it was seen as more a threat than an opportunity.

For other Pacific states, the Vietnam War had a varying impact. South Korea, Japan, and, further south, Taiwan, Hong Kong, and some South-east Asian states had benefited from the increased American investment that was necessary to support the war effort. The United States came to the western Pacific for the defeat of Japan, stayed for the Korean War, and then built a huge economic and military infrastructure to support the drawn-out Vietnam War.

Yet all these states were concerned with the loss of American credibility that came with defeat in the war. The fear, especially in South Korea, was that the United States would retreat from Asia and leave them to the mercy of the local great powers, all of which were Communist. As it turned out, these states benefited by the war because, having lost its foothold in South Vietnam, the United States then decided to place greater emphasis on these remaining friends.

It is perhaps the greatest paradox of the American defeat in Vietnam that it resulted in the long-term strengthening of its economic involvement in the Pacific. But the added involvement of the Soviet Union in this new Pacific world also ensured that the politics of the region would be more complex. The rise of the fifth-largest Pacific military power, Vietnam, also made calculations of the future balance of international security far more difficult. The geopolitical shifts that followed the end of the war in Vietnam meant that a truly pacific Pacific was an even more remote prospect than it had ever been.

12

Hot Conflicts

By the late 1980s there were only two major Pacific conflicts where the guns had not yet fallen silent.[1] Vietnamese troops still sat in occupation of Kampuchea, while rebels from the former Khmer Rouge regime waged low-level guerrilla war against the Vietnamese-supported regime in Phnom Penh. Just to the north, China kept up the pressure on Vietnam as the two sides exchanged artillery fire and their troops fought the occasional skirmish along the frontier.

By comparison with the previous levels of conflict in the region, the Pacific was more at peace than at any time this century; more peaceful, too, than the Middle East, torn by devastating, and still-continuing, wars. Both of the still-hot conflicts were cooling and rapidly approaching the category of 'controlled conflicts'. But both were still relatively young conflicts, although with obvious roots in history and in the earlier post-1945 Indo-Chinese wars.

CONFLICT IN KAMPUCHEA

The defeat of the United States and its allies in the three Indo-Chinese states in 1975 brought to an end the second phase of the local struggle. But within barely four years of their triumphs, three of the region's Communist states would be at war again, with the Communist superpower, the Soviet Union, anxiously looking on. The events of post-war Europe had shown there was nothing surprising about Communist brothers falling out, and the Sino-Soviet split had shown just how dangerous the conflict could become. But few expected the intensity, not to mention the swiftness, of the wars between Communist states in Indo-China.

Various explanations have been offered for the war between Vietnam and

---

[1] The Central American war between the Contras and Nicaraguans is obviously also a hot conflict, but is far more a hemispheric and possibly an Atlantic conflict than a Pacific one. The protagonists rely on the United States, Cuba, and the Soviet bloc for assistance. All Soviet aid comes via Europe and no substantial aid comes through Pacific waters. To be sure, there is some combat along the Pacific coast, but the waters might as well be a small lake than an ocean reaching Asia. On the Pacific option see *Jane's Defence Weekly* (27 June 1987).

Kampuchea, as it was known after 1975.[2] No single explanation is adequate, but as the Sino-Soviet conflict suggests, ideological rivalry mixed with underlying nationalism is a potent mix. It is also undeniable that the previous phase of the war, when the United States added to the trauma of the region with its heavy campaign of bombing, helped lay the basis for the post-1975 conflicts.[3] But as upsetting as the bombing of Cambodia, as it was then known, undoubtedly was, it was not as destructive to the national political fabric as the disputes within Kampuchea, including those between Vietnamese Communists and Pol Pot's Khmer Rouge.[4] Pol Pot's followers derided the pro-Vietnamese Khmer Communists as 'Vietnamese in Khmer bodies'. These groups had different strategies, power bases, and alliances in international politics.

Following the victories of 1975, the Communist powers were well aware that there were 'gains' to be made. China's traditional view of the region led it to believe that the removal of American power would enhance its own role. The Soviet Union believed that it had earned the friendship of the local Communists by virtue of its steadfast material and spiritual support. Vietnam itself was aware that it was the Pacific's third-largest Communist power and had its own aspirations for special relationships with its fellow Indo-Chinese.[5] This is not to say that conflict among the Communists was inevitable, only that it was highly likely.

On the principle that the best defence is offence, and because it was already paranoid about Vietnamese intentions, Pol Pot's Khmer Rouge regime took a firm line from the start on the question of the withdrawal of Vietnamese troops from Kampuchea. Both sides also established border-liaison committees, even though they took different sides in the still-looming Sino-Soviet split.[6] But in 1977 Pol Pot led Kampuchea into ever more violent border clashes with Vietnam and both sides escalated hostilities and demands for support from Communist allies. Kampuchea obtained more military aid from China even though Beijing was not pleased to see the conflict get out of hand.[7] China perceived that growing polarization gave it a closer ally in Kampuchea, but less leverage in Hanoi. The Pol Pot regime was becoming increasingly radicalized as its policies at home were clearly failing. This

2 Robert Ross, 'Indochina's Continuing Tragedy' in *Problems of Communism* (November 1986).

3 William Shawcross, *Sideshow* (New York: Simon & Schuster, 1979).

4 Ben Kiernan, *How Pol Pot Came to Power* (London: Verso, 1984); Elizabeth Becker, *When the War was Over* (New York: Simon & Schuster, 1986).

5 Nayan Chanda, *Brother Enemy* (New York: Harcourt Brace Jovanovich, 1986).

6 See several essays in David Elliot (ed.), *The Third Indochina Conflict* (Boulder, Colo: Westview, 1981).

7 Evelyn Colbert cited in Ross, 'Indochina's Tragedy'.

regime, in its perverted revolutionary zeal, earned the unenviable record for slaughtering more of its citizenry than anyone since Hitler.

By February 1978 the Vietnamese had decided to sort out their Kampuchean neighbours and install a more pliable regime.[8] Vietnam's actions were rooted in its basic desire to order Indo-Chinese events, but also in the specific problems posed by a radical and aggressive Kampuchean neighbour.[9]

The Soviet Union was willing to support Vietnam for a number of reasons. Not only was Vietnam demanding little more than diplomatic and material aid—something it had done to Soviet advantage for decades—but Vietnam also offered Moscow access to military facilities in Vietnam, including the American-built naval base at Cam Ranh Bay, and the prospect of improving its strategic position in the Pacific.[10] Although the Soviet Union did not begin to get regular access to Vietnamese bases until 1979, the bait was clearly being dangled in front of the Soviet Union for some time before.[11] What is more, the growing Chinese support for Pol Pot made Moscow more anxious to balance Chinese influence and keep Beijing from dominating Indo-China. Economic costs aside, the international costs of such Soviet support were minimal because of the increasingly poor reputation of the Pol Pot regime, and a general sense that its genocidal actions against its own people left it with few sympathizers ready to weep over its demise.

The obvious distaste that the Pol Pot regime evoked in the outside world's minds also made ASEAN's reaction to Indo-Chinese events more difficult. Most states did not want to see a powerful Vietnam, but it might be a useful counterweight to an even more powerful China. The only good reason for the continued existence of the Pol Pot regime was that it would keep the Communist states preoccupied with each other and leave those nearby, such as Thailand, relatively safe.

China faced the harder choice and as the major supporter of Pol Pot found these dilemmas increasingly acute. Deteriorating Sino-Vietnamese relations (see below) and the long-standing Sino-Soviet dispute made China and Kampuchea natural allies. But as the Kampuchean tail wagged the Chinese dog with increasing vigour in 1977 and 1978, China discovered that an independent Kampuchea was as much a problem for China as it was a counterbalance to Vietnamese and Soviet power.[12] Nevertheless China

[8] Chanda, *Brother Enemy*, ch. 7.

[9] William Duiker, *Vietnam Since the Fall of Saigon* (Athens, Ohio: Ohio University Press, 1985).

[10] Leszek Buszynski, *Soviet Foreign Policy and Southeast Asia* (London: Croom Helm, 1986), ch. 4.

[11] Chanda, *Brother Enemy*, 397.

[12] Chanda, *Brother Enemy*, ch. 8.

continued to pour aid into Kampuchea and was unwilling, and perhaps unable, to press Pol Pot to adopt more moderate policies.

All the pieces on the board were shifted on 25 December 1978 when Vietnamese troops rolled into Kampuchea, and by 11 January 1979 they had established a new regime in Phnom Penh under Heng Samrin. Vietnam had extended its power, and to a lesser extent so had the Soviet Union. China and Thailand were the main losers, the latter becoming a haven for refugees fleeing Vietnamese troops and the front line across which the defeated Khmer Rouge and the triumphant Vietnamese fought out border skirmishes.

CHINA AND VIETNAM

The course of the Kampuchean conflict in the 1970s is very closely intertwined with Sino-Vietnamese relations. Although much of the pace of the Kampuchean events was determined by the domestic policies of the Khmer Rouge, the role of outsiders also had an important impact. The two other main actors, China and Vietnam, were both reacting to Kampuchean events, but were also determined to pursue their separate interests.

The extent of the separateness of these interests can be traced back to ancient history, but more immediate evidence of disputes is to be found in the course of the first two phases of the Vietnam War and Hanoi's feeling that China's support was both inadequate and manipulative. From 1975 until the Chinese attack on Vietnam in February 1979, China and Vietnam drifted to war for obvious, but far from inevitable, reasons.

The first reason for war was no doubt the fact that China found itself dragged into taking Kampuchea's side in the Vietnam–Kampuchea conflict. China wanted to see Indo-China either under its own influence or, at a minimum, not under Vietnamese control. At its most basic, this view resulted from China's great-power aspirations and a conflict of interests with Vietnam.[13]

Had Vietnam not sided with the Soviet Union in the Sino-Soviet split, China might have been less antagonistic to Vietnamese predominance in Indo-China. But similarly, had China not been so anti-Soviet, it might have looked on Vietnam's leanings as less significant. Both sides had powerful

[13] Robert Ross, *The Indochina Triangle* (New York: Columbia University Press, 1988); Charles McGregor, *The Sino-Vietnamese Relationship and the Soviet Union* (London: IISS, Adelphi Paper, 232, 1988); Chang Pao-Min, *Kampuchea Between China and Vietnam* (Singapore: Singapore University Press, 1985).

reasons for suspicion, but this suspicion also fed paranoia about each other's intention which soon ran out of rational control.[14]

Another contributing factor was Vietnam's treatment of its own Chinese population. In the spring of 1978 Vietnam began restricting the rights of Chinese by limiting the activities of Chinese traders and then undertaking a collectivization drive. The traditional fear of a Chinese fifth column was fed by China's attempts at the time to make better use of its Chinese compatriots around the world in supporting Chinese policies. Not surprisingly, the new pressures on the ethnic Chinese led to a flood of refugees, mainly to China. By May 1978 China had terminated its aid projects to Vietnam and in July the two countries were fighting minor border clashes.[15]

This rapid deterioration of relations was in many respects an accelerated version of the slide to war along the Sino-Soviet frontier in the 1960s. The Soviet Union was clearly a major part of the Chinese concern, especially since Vietnam joined Comecon in June and signed a Friendship Treaty on 3 November. For Vietnam, these were sensible precautions before a war with Kampuchea and in expectation of heightened tension with China. For China, they were red rags provoking deeper fears of Soviet encirclement of China.

Another interested observer, the United States, had its part to play in the Vietnamese tilt to the Soviet Union. It was always going to be difficult for any American administration to normalize relations with Vietnam so soon after its victory over the United States. The Carter administration was probably more to blame than Vietnam for America's failure to improve relations with Hanoi, but under any circumstances the time was probably not ripe.[16] The failure to heal the breach meant that Vietnam had little option but to move closer to Moscow.

The deterioration in Sino-Vietnamese relations and the inexorable move to war saw the United States and China drawing closer together. Against a background of escalating Vietnamese–Kampuchean clashes, China accepted the revised American terms for normalization of relations.[17] Deng Xiaoping visited the United States and Japan just after Vietnam had invaded Kampuchea and it seemed clear then that China had decided to attack Vietnam in the near future. Deng heard nothing on his trip to dissuade him from his venture and on 17 February 1979 the Chinese troops struck.[18]

---

[14] Gerald Segal, *Sino-Soviet Relations After Mao* (London: IISS, Adelphi Paper, 202, 1985).

[15] Gerald Segal, *Defending China* (Oxford: Oxford University Press, 1985), ch. 12.

[16] Chanda, *Brother Enemy*, chs. 5, 9.

[17] Zbigniew Brzezinski, *Power and Principle* (New York: Farrar, Straus & Giroux, 1983); Jimmy Carter, *Keeping Faith* (London: Collins, 1982); Cyrus Vance, *Hard Choices* (New York: Simon & Schuster, 1983).

[18] Bruce Burton, 'Contending Explanations of the 1979 Sino-Vietnamese War' in

The war went badly for China and on 16 March it was forced to withdraw without Vietnam having been taught the lesson that China intended.[19] Vietnam was not forced out of Kampuchea, nor was it forced to run to Moscow for assistance. China's military instrument was too blunt and rusty to force panic in Hanoi, and Beijing had to reassess its position.

REASSESSING THE INDO-CHINESE CONFLICTS

The defeat of China at the hands of Vietnam in their short border war was the most damaging loss suffered by the People's Liberation Army (PLA) since the 1969 engagements with the Soviet Union. It was to be a major impetus to reform of the Chinese armed forces and a reason for the ensuing strategy of caution in Chinese foreign policy.[20] The eventual *détente* between China and the Soviet Union in the 1980s was achieved largely because of the Chinese decision by 1980 that its heavily anti-Soviet policy was too costly. The knee-jerk reactions that had caught China in the Indo-China tangle were only recognized with the shock of the war.

The new reality that China faced in the 1980s was most unpleasant. It 'lost' Kampuchea as an ally and now had to help shore up Thailand, which was not even a Communist state. All of Indo-China was now under Vietnam's sway, and with that came Soviet power, influence, and military bases. China ran supplies down to Khmer Rouge rebels and its allied opposition movements on the Thai border with Kampuchea. Until 1985 China could have some hope that its support for the rebels might pay off in the long run. The strategy was to bleed Vietnam sufficiently to force its withdrawal. The bleeding would be assisted by extra pressure from the Sino-Vietnamese frontier and to that end China kept tension high.

But from the time of the 1985 spring offensive by the Vietnamese, the Khmer rebels were confined to the furthest reaches of Kampuchea nearest Thailand and ceased to pose a major threat to the Vietnamese occupation. Although sporadic clashes took place (most reports of the scale of success were exaggerated), it was clear that the war had wound down. China was

International Journal, 34/4 (autumn 1979); Danile Tretiak, 'China's Vietnam War and Its Consequences' in *China Quarterly*, 80 (December, 1979); Harlan Jencks, 'China's "Punitive" War on Vietnam' in *Asian Survey*, 19/8 (December 1979); King Chen, 'China's War Against Vietnam, 1979', in *Journal of Northeast Asian Affairs*, 3/1 (spring/summer 1983); Segal, *Defending China*, ch. 12.

[19] Segal, *Defending China*; Jencks, 'China's Punitive War'.

[20] Ellis Joffe, *The Chinese Army After Mao* (London: Weidenfeld, 1987); David Goodman *et al.*, *The China Challenge* (London: Royal Institute of International Affairs, Chatham House Papers, 32, 1986).

concentrating on its domestic programme of modernization and its foreign policy priorities were for improved relations with the Soviet Union.

To be sure, China continued to view the Kampuchean conflict as the main obstacle to Sino-Soviet *détente* and to that extent maintained the linkage that had so dominated its foreign policy of the 1970s. China insisted that it would not normalize relations with the Soviet Union unless Moscow pressed Vietnam to withdraw from Kampuchea. While the Soviet Union could not do so publicly for fear of losing its bases in Indo-China, it could 'encourage' Hanoi to be more positive. Soviet pressure for economic reform in Vietnam, demands that Soviet aid be spent more effectively, and the decision to discuss the Kampuchean question in the biannual Sino-Soviet talks were all forms of coercion on the Vietnamese.[21]

Although by 1987 China had yet to force a withdrawal of Vietnamese troops from Kampuchea, it certainly had stopped the rot in its regional foreign policy. Vietnam was feeling increasingly under pressure to loosen its grip on Kampuchea, and its success in containing the rebel threat suggested that it might be possible for Vietnam to begin to extricate itself from day-to-day control in Phnom Penh. From Hanoi's point of view the continuing conflict was tragic, especially considering the suffering of its own people in more than 40 years of near-constant war. The incentive to get out of Kampuchea and begin development and reconstruction at home was great. But the question was, what degree of independence could Vietnam tolerate for Kampuchea, without giving China a sense that pressure on Vietnam had proved successful?

For the Soviet Union, the Indo-China problem not only was a drain on its budget, but also slowed up Sino-Soviet *détente* and prevented the Soviet Union from making inroads into ASEAN.[22] The Vietnamese occupation of Kampuchea also prevented the Soviet Union under Gorbachev from playing a more active role in Pacific co-operation. It was not even a simple Soviet calculation of whether to support socialist as opposed to non-socialist economies, for Communist China made it plain that Soviet influence in the region would be stunted unless it resolved the Indo-China issue.

The United States, after having invested so much in the fate of Indo-China in the 1960s, had become one of the least involved states in the region. While it nominally supported the Kampuchean rebels and prevented the seating of the Heng Samrin regime at the United Nations, its main purpose was to

---

[21] Gerald Segal, 'Sino-Soviet Detente' in *World Today* (May 1987).

[22] Donald Zagoria (ed.), *Soviet Policy in East Asia* (London: Yale University Press, 1982); Gerald Segal (ed.), *The Soviet Union in East Asia* (London: Heinemann, 1983); Georges Tan Eng Bok, *The USSR in East Asia* (Paris: Atlantic Institute, Atlantic Papers, 59–60, 1986); Gerald Segal, 'The Soviet Union and the Pacific Century' in *Journal of Communist Studies* (autumn 1987).

shore up the defence of Thailand. To that extent, Chinese and American interests coincided. But unlike China, or even Japan, the United States saw little reason to make a major effort to resolve the Indo-Chinese conflict and restore stability. A certain wariness, even fear, of Vietnam and the Soviet Union on the part of ASEAN members and China was clearly in the United States' interest.

The ASEAN states themselves were divided in their views of the Indo-China problem. Some, such as Thailand and the Philippines, took a harsher view of Vietnamese intentions and held out for non-recognition of the Vietnamese-backed regime. Others, such as Indonesia and to some extent Malaysia, saw the integration of Vietnam and the other Indo-Chinese states into a wider South-east Asian stability as more important. These states saw China in a less benign light and regarded Vietnam and the Soviet Union as useful counterweights. Yet none of them except Thailand was especially concerned about the level of conflict that existed in 1988, although all would have preferred to see the fighting over with a resolution reached.[23]

The linchpin of the ASEAN strategy had been support for the coalition of Kampuchean rebel forces led by Prince Sihanouk which was formed in June 1982. Yet rebel difficulties were barely concealed by this fig-leaf, for the hated Khmer Rouge were still the only effective fighting force. Vietnam's partial military defeat of the rebels in 1985 helped reduce Khmer Rouge dominance, but the Communist members of the coalition still had the power to veto any possible compromise with the Vietnamese regime.

By 1989 this latest Indo-Chinese war finally seemed to be winding down. Under pressure from the Soviet Union, Vietnam made repeated concessions. In the run-up to the Sino-Soviet summit in May 1989, pressure was increased for a settlement of Indo-Chinese problems. A Sino-Vietnamese dialogue was begun in 1989, and in April of that year Vietnam agreed to withdraw all its troops by October 1989. Although some details concerning the supervision of this transition needed to be resolved, it was clear that the conflict was becoming less international. To be sure, it was likely that fighting would continue inside Kampuchea but, like many previous rebel movements in South-east Asia, this one looked like gradually fading away. The Kampuchean conflict was the only active conflict in the Pacific, but was at its lowest point of tension since the end of the Second World War. This represented progress, of a sort, towards a more peaceful Pacific.

---

23 See a broad analysis of differing perspectives in the 1980s in Claude Buss (ed.), *National Security Interests in the Pacific Basin* (Stanford, Calif.: Hoover Institution, 1985); Donald Hugh McMillen (ed.), *Asian Perspectives on International Security* (London: Macmillan, 1984); Charles Morison (ed.), *Threats to Security in East Asia-Pacific* (Lexington, Mass.: D. C. Heath, 1983).

13

Controlled Conflicts

For the first 25 years after the Second World War, East Asia experienced the most severe and intense international conflicts. While few of those conflicts continue as hot wars, they have not yet been fully resolved. The flammable material is still on site and, while it may take more than just an isolated spark to re-ignite the fires, the risks remain. The three main conflicts of this type, between the two Koreas, between China and the Soviet Union, and between China and Taiwan, can be assessed in terms of the causes of the conflict, the course of the conflict, and the extent to which the conflict remains unchanged by shifting balances of power.

KOREAN CONFLICTS

Korea has been called the 'Palestine of East Asia' by virtue of its strategic location. Certainly Japan has viewed it as its natural sphere of concern, sometimes seeing Korea as a dagger pointing at the heart of Japan. A Korean proverb describes Korea as a prawn, whose back is liable to be broken by the movements of the great-power whales around it.[1] In the twentieth century there have been at least four whales to contend with and the prawn has literally been snapped in half.

Korea had been occupied by Japan for most of the twentieth century until the defeat of Japan in the Second World War reopened the question of who should rule this strategic zone. With China split by a civil war and Japan defeated, there were only two powers left in North-east Asian waters. The United States and the Soviet Union had not given a great deal of thought to Korea after the war, with the former more involved in Japan and the latter more concerned about China. Thus an American proposal to divide Korea at the 38th parallel was made more out of compromise and convenience than from a consideration of history or justice.[2]

Unlike divided Germany in Europe, which was a vanquished nation, the Koreans were mere Asian pawns in what was to all intents and purposes a

---

[1] Brian Bridges, *Korea and the West* (London: Chatham House Papers, 33, 1986).
[2] Peter Lowe, *The Origins of the Korean War* (London: Longman, 1986), ch. 1.

mainly European-focused cold war. With most of the people in the South and most of the industry in the North, a divided Korea made no local sense and was a recipe for war. The causes of that war have been exhaustively debated by specialists—for it was the the first major war of the post-1945 world and, until the Vietnam War, the bloodiest.[3]

The formation of two Koreas was driven by the global rivalries of the superpowers and facilitated by the disarray in Korea itself. Yet neither Korea was satisfied with the division of their country and the superpowers were less than explicit in defining the limits of tolerable change. The fine-tuning of maps that took place in post-war Europe was carried out in an atmosphere of relatively careful crisis management. The sloppy communication and relative disregard of East Asia left the locals there free to upset the not-so-carefully-laid plans of the great powers.

To complicate matters, another great power, China, had traditionally (before the twentieth century) been the dominant influence in Korean affairs. The assumption of power by a Communist regime determined to capture the Chinese nationalists supported by the United States in Taiwan made for a parallel of sorts with the situation in Korea. As the Chinese Civil War drew to a close in 1949, China's interest in Korea resumed, but ran the risk of colliding with China's primary aim of completing the unification of its own country.[4]

The outbreak of the Korean War on 25 June 1950 seems to have been the result of the North Koreans 'jumping the gun' that was primed by Soviet aid and Chinese support. But considering the background of tension and confusion in the region, it is difficult to be sure that any single state perceived the causes of the war in the same light. The North hoped for a swift victory that would be over before the United States and its allies could respond. They very nearly succeeded. The South Koreans held on only just long enough for the United States to organize reinforcements and allied support under the cover of the United Nations, which it dominated. Ultimately some 15 nations gave material support to the United States.[5] The Communist forces were

---

3 Ibid.; Bruce Cumings, *The Origins of the Korean War* (Princeton: Princeton University Press, 1981).

4 Allen Whiting, *China Crosses the Yalu* (Stanford, Calif.: Stanford University Press, 1960); Robert Simmons, *The Strained Alliance* (New York: Free Press, 1975).

5 Robert O'Neill, *Australia in the Korean War* (Canberra: Australian National University, 1981), who notes the following states: Australia, Belgium, Canada, Colombia, Ethiopia, France, Greece, Luxembourg, Netherlands, New Zealand, Philippines, Thailand, Turkey, South Africa, and United Kingdom; medical units from Denmark, Italy, India, Norway, and Sweden. Of the total casualties, South Korea suffered some 1.3 million, the United States 142 091, other United Nations troops 17 260, and Communist countries a total estimated at 1.5–2 million: David Rees, *Korea: The Limited War* (London: Macmillan, 1964).

driven back across the 38th parallel and up to the Chinese frontier at the Yalu River.[6]

The Chinese had warned the United States about crossing the 38th parallel but the messages were not taken seriously. The Chinese intervention in force in November pushed the United States back, and the war settled down to a slugging match around its original starting-point at the parallel.[7] The sapping stalemate, followed by a new Soviet foreign policy under Stalin's heirs in 1953 and a new American foreign policy under Eisenhower, brought the war to an end with an armistice.

It is difficult to decide who wins and who loses a war that ends pretty much where it started. For the Koreans, the war proved that reunification could not be brought about by force. While it may have been 'worth a try' in 1950, before there was much tradition of division, by 1953 too high a price had been paid for maintaining that division for anyone realistically to suggest another try. The division of Korea was just as unreal as in 1950 but, with the movement of population that accompanied the war and the status that each government had earned by surviving it, the notion of division became more acceptable. Much like the effect of the Berlin crises in Europe, the Korean War stabilized the region by showing that, however unnatural the status quo might be, the parties concerned and their allies were willing to fight for what they held dear.

The fact that stability in the cold war in the Pacific, as in the Atlantic, required a crisis on this scale to make the point was ultimately satisfying to the superpowers. The United States had demonstrated its credibility as an ally, and the credibility of those of its European allies who fought for their system as they promised to do in the 1949 NATO pact in Europe. Deterrence of threat in the primary theatre in Europe was reinforced by shedding mainly Korean, Chinese, and American blood in North-east Asia.

Although the United States did not fight the war primarily for its importance in Pacific affairs, the war did reinforce its military presence on the Asian mainland. The defeat of the Guomindang in the Chinese Civil War had, to all intents and purposes, driven the United States off the Pacific end of Eurasia and forced it to concentrate on Japan. The Korean War swiftly brought the United States back, in part as a forward defence of its main interests in Japan.

The Soviet Union had managed to stay out of direct combat, although it reportedly provided, at a price, air cover for Chinese cities and a large portion of the equipment for the Communist side of the war. Like the United

---

[6] Lowe, *Korean War*, ch. 7.

[7] Rosemary Foot, *The Wrong War* (London: Cornell University Press, 1985); Gerald Segal, *Defending China* (Oxford: Oxford University Press, 1985), ch. 6.

States, the Soviet Union showed it was willing to defend its regional interests, although the focus on East Asia was an unwelcome distraction from the main European theatre. The war also created closer allies for the Soviet Union out of China and North Korea, which has depended so heavily on Soviet support. This laid the groundwork for the most successful era of Soviet East Asian policy.

China was perhaps the only major great-power loser from the war. While China did demonstrate its resolve to defend its own frontiers and support an ally in North Korea, these were not tasks that before 1950 China had felt were especially pressing. The Chinese priority had been unification of all China and peaceful reconstruction. The war meant that the United States interposed its Seventh Fleet in the Taiwan Straits and that China had to bear the cost in human and economic terms. China was left poorer, more reliant on the Soviet Union, more hostile to the United States and Japan, and still without control of Taiwan and the offshore islands.

The course of the Korean conflict since 1953 has been punctuated by periodic crises, but nothing on the scale of the 1950–3 war.[8] As these crises developed, for example over the north Korean attack on the United States intelligence-gathering ship *Pueblo* in 1968, the great-power whales of the region kept the waves to a minimum. Although local events were the main cause of such crises, the pattern of crisis management had a great deal to do with the overarching pattern of great-power politics. However, these interlocking patterns kept changing, and so kept creating instability.

The fundamental realities of the Korean conflict remain the same today as in 1950. There is a genuine cold war—a sort of 'no war, no peace'—but one that generates more heat than anywhere in the 'home' of the cold war in Europe. The two Koreas are squashed into a small peninsula where modern weaponry makes both sides highly vulnerable. Most people in North Korea live within 320 km of the frontier and the capital Pyongyang is only 150 km away. Seoul is a mere 50 km south of the frontier, within artillery range of the North or three minutes' flying time. With both societies moving rapidly away from their agricultural base towards industrialization and city life, both are even more vulnerable than they were in 1950. War is not a sensible option for either side.

The balance of military power has remained tense but reasonably stable. Both sides have increased defence spending as their economies have developed, but the better growth rates in the South make its defence burden progressively easier to bear.[9] While the North has a quantitative advantage

---

[8] Donald and Janet Zagoria, 'Crises on the Korean Peninsula' in Stephen Kaplan (ed.), *Diplomacy of Power* (Washington DC: Brookings, 1981).

[9] The question of the military balance is tackled in a number of ways by different analysts. For a sampling see Georges Tan Eng Bok, 'Arms Control in Korea' in Gerald Segal (ed.), *Arms*

in most categories of weapon, it does not have the sort of decisive advantage that could make war seem winnable. The South has advantages in quality of equipment and training, as well as the presence of some 40 000 United States troops, including their tactical nuclear weapons. Chinese forces withdrew from the North in 1958.

The North has made a speciality of the threat of unconventional war, deploying the world's largest commando forces of 80 000.[10] It also built tunnels in the 1970s under the demilitarized zone in an effort to break the military stalemate. And it has used terrorism in its attempts to destabilize the South, for example by blowing up the South Korean Cabinet in a bomb attack in Rangoon in 1983 and a South Korean passenger aircraft in mid-air in 1987.

Despite the obvious military tension on the Korean peninsula, the chance of conflict is reduced by the unwillingness of the superpowers to contemplate another war in Korea. The United States is primarily concerned with the peace and security of its economically prosperous allies, Japan and South Korea, and sees no advantage in coveting the territory of North Korea.[11] It was notable that, in the amendment proposed by United States Senator Sam Nunn in the 1980s to reduce United States troops strength in Europe, the troops in Korea were to be left in place. The previous plan by President Carter to withdraw United States troops from Korea was seen as destabilizing and was also criticized for sending the wrong kind of signal to North Korea.[12] Much like the discussion of troop withdrawals from Europe, the problem the United States and its allies face in Korea is how to reduce the defence burden without cutting the quality of the deterrence that made economic prosperity in the South possible.

The Soviet Union is equally satisfied with the status quo and would regard any war as likely to destroy its chances of building bridges to other East Asian states. A war might demand new evidence of comradely Soviet loyalty to the North that would upset Japan in particular.[13] China is certainly not interested in supporting North Korean adventurism. In the 1970s its closer relations with the United States meant that it had even less patience for North Korean attacks on the South. While China and the United States remain on opposite sides on the Korean issue, this has mainly been because

Control in Asia (London: Macmillan, 1987); Doug Stuart (ed.), *East Asian Security* (London: Gower, 1987).

10 Statistics from *Military Balance* (IISS).

11 Harold Hinton, *Korea Under New Leadership* (New York: Praeger, 1983).

12 Bridges, *Korea and the West*, ch. 5.

13 Gerald Segal, 'The Soviet Union and Korea' in Gerald Segal (ed.), *The Soviet Union in East Asia* (London: Heinemann for the RIIA, 1984); Ralph Clough, 'The Soviet Union and the Two Koreas' in Donald Zagoria (ed.), *Soviet Policy in East Asia* (New Haven: Yale University Press, 1983).

of Chinese fears of losing the friendship of the Pyongyang regime in the Sino-Soviet conflict. When Sino-Soviet relations began to improve in the 1980s, China and the Soviet Union both colluded in keeping North Korea under control. The leverage that the North once had on its Communist patrons, playing one off against the other to maximize their support, was declining.[14] Also, by the late 1980s China was doing trade with the South worth close to $2 billion annually, far more than with its ally in the North. Even the Soviet Union had established formal trade ties with South Korea.[15]

Japan has long been an economic great power, especially for Korea, but militarily Japan is now far less significant than at any point since the nineteenth century. Korean–Japanese relations remain ambivalent, especially on the question of possible Japanese rearmament. Koreans were the first to suffer the last time Japan militarized and the United States is clearly preferable to Japan as a military guarantor.

Clearly none of the great powers has an interest in further conflict in Korea. The risks of war must be considered minimal, although new sparks might yet fly from unrest in the South or the succession to Kim Il Sung in the North. The local states still have enormous scope to make mischief, and therefore upset the uneasy status quo beloved of the great powers. Much like the division of the two Germanies, the unnaturalness of the division of the Koreas diminishes with the passage of generations. Social systems evolve in different ways and new traditions are developed behind the barbed-wire and despite the divided families. Not all nationalities are inevitably united in single states—witness the Arab nation or the Latin American world. Because such a division also straddles one of the major 'East–West' divides of the cold war, the Korean conflict is now more stable. However, the division and the tensions that still flow from it do little to help foster any sense of Pacific-consciousness.

THE SINO-SOVIET CONFLICT

The rivalry between China and its northern neighbour is one of the oldest in the Pacific, although the protagonists have changed shape and ideology over the centuries. Since 1945 and the mopping up of Japanese forces on the Eurasian land mass by the largest Eurasian power, the Soviet Union, China has faced only one major land-based challenger. In 1949, when the Communists came to power in China, they hoped for genuine independence, if

---

[14] Gerald Segal, 'Sino-Soviet Detente: How Far How Fast?' in *World Today* (May 1987).
[15] This process is discussed in Gerald Segal, 'Taking Sino-Soviet Detente Seriously' in *Washington Quarterly*, June 1989.

not a return to the grandeur of the pre-western-imperialist age. But while sea-based western imperialism and even offshore Japanese power could be controlled, the Soviet Union was firmly fixed to the northern reaches of the Pacific basin and perched on the roof of China.

The other reason why there was no return to the past was that the ideological inclinations of the Chinese and Russian actors had changed. Both were now nominally united in their Communism and opposed to the United States, Japan, and America's other allies in Europe and the Pacific. Thus the fundamental tensions that have dogged the great-power politics in the post-war Pacific were set. China was an ally of the Soviet Union, but also potentially a natural rival. China was at first dependent on Soviet assistance, for example in the Korean War and also in facing nuclear threats from the United States. But China also hoped to cast off the shackles of such alliances of necessity with what it still saw as a European power.

On 14 February 1950 Mao Zedong signed a treaty of friendship, alliance, and mutual assistance in Moscow which included a Soviet pledge to surrender rights to the Manchurian railway and hand over the Port Arthur naval base to China. There was no explicit entangling military alliance, but Soviet aid during the Korean War was that of a close comrade in arms.

The reasons for the falling out of the two Communist giants were primarily related to the changing Chinese approach to revolution at home and Moscow's difficulty at the time in accepting that any Communist state could pursue an independent path of development.[16] Military matters were not a primary cause of the dispute, although the two sides did differ on such issues as the Sino-Indian War of 1962, the Cuban missile crisis of the same year, and the Soviet Union's cautious line on supporting world revolution and using its nuclear weapons when challenging the United States in crises. In 1963, when the Soviet Union signed the Partial Test Ban Treaty with the United States and Britain, the Sino-Soviet split was publicly acknowledged.

The ensuing contest for leadership of international Communism was clearly won by the Soviet Union. China was frustrated that its more radical policies found less appeal among fellow developing states when they were offered rival, and more materially useful, Soviet aid to keep them out of the Chinese camp. Even in the neighbouring Vietnam War where China committed some of its anti-aircraft troops, Beijing was unable to defeat Soviet influence. The one exception to this pattern was quirky and lonely, European Albania.[17]

The militarization of the Sino-Soviet conflict began only in 1964–5 after

[16] Donald Zagoria, *The Sino-Soviet Conflict* (Princeton: Princeton University Press, 1962); John Gittings, *Survey of the Sino-Soviet Dispute* (Oxford: Oxford University Press, 1969).

[17] William Griffiths, *Sino-Soviet Relations* (Cambridge, Mass.: MIT Press, 1967); Gerald Segal, *The Great Power Triangle* (London: Macmillan, 1982).

the failure of efforts to arrive at a new *détente* following the purge of Nikita Khrushchev. Of course, the roots of the dispute along the frontier between the two countries extend back to the seventeenth century and the imposition by Russia of the so-called 'unequal treaties' on a fading Chinese empire. But in reality the modern frontier dispute was about Chinese pride and its determination to have the Soviet Union deal with it as an equal. As the Sino-Soviet dispute became more serious across a range of domestic and foreign policy issues, both sides looked at their long and open frontier and realized the extent of their vulnerability. China was the first to raise the boundary question in 1963 and negotiations began in Beijing in February 1964. The increasing radicalism and anti-Sovietism of China during the Cultural Revolution led many in the Soviet Union to believe that China was unstable and liable to rash actions. A buildup in Soviet forces began in the mid-1960s and was soon more than matched in men, but not material, by China.[18]

The Soviet invasion of Czechoslovakia and the restatement of the credo that the Soviet Union reserved the right to intervene in a a socialist state to 'safeguard the revolution', the so-called Brezhnev Doctrine, was perceived as a threat by China. In the paranoid mood of the Cultural Revolution, China decided to 'teach' the Soviet Union that China was not Czechoslovakia and could not be pushed around.[19] On 2 March 1969 Chinese troops apparently ambushed a Soviet patrol on Chenbao (Damansky) Island, killing tens of Russians. On 15 March the Soviet Union responded with a stunning demonstration of military superiority, killing hundreds of Chinese soldiers.

There were by far the biggest border clashes, although some had taken place before and others would continue until well after 1969.[20] But apart from the loss of life, this conflict is important because it was the first between two nuclear powers and along a wide-open frontier whose spaces were increasingly being filled with both soldiers and equipment. From the Soviet point of view, the main danger was of an uncontrolled China adding a second front to the main Soviet concern in Europe. From the Chinese point of view, the main problem was how to convince the Soviet Union that China could credibly defend itself and its idiosyncratic revolution.

The Soviet Union tried to convince China to sit down again and negotiate about the border, thereby limiting the risks of escalation and the need for further Soviet commitment. China refused to negotiate, despite Soviet-orchestrated border incidents in the summer of 1969.[21] The Soviet Union

18 Thomas Robinson, *The Sino-Soviet Border Dispute* (Santa Monica: The Rand Corporation, 1970).

19 Gerald Segal, *Defending China*, ch. 10.

20 Alan Day, *China and the Soviet Union* (London: Longman, 1985).

21 Richard Wich, *Sino-Soviet Crisis Politics* (Cambridge, Mass.: Harvard University Press, 1980).

then stepped up the pressure by letting it be known around the world, but especially in the United States, that it was contemplating a 'surgical strike' against Chinese nuclear-weapons sites. These threats constituted the Pacific's version of the Cuban missile crisis, and by October China was scared enough to sit down and talk about the frontier.

Although the events of 1969 resulted in comparatively little loss of life in comparison to the contemporaneous Vietnam War, like the Cuban crisis they carried the very real risk of war between two nuclear powers. As such, this Sino-Soviet border conflict must rank as the most dangerous Pacific crisis since 1945.

It was also 1969 when the United States discovered that it too had a role in this major new conflict in the Pacific. The belated discovery of the diplomatic possibilities of the great-power triangle, and the open discussion of its implications by Henry Kissinger and President Nixon, added a global dimension to what had been at first a regional, Pacific problem.[22] The growing 'strategic co-operation' between the United States, Japan, and China was perceived by the Soviet Union as a major threat. The talk of China as 'the sixteenth member of NATO', as well as American arms sales to Beijing, fed the paranoia of the Soviet Union about its vulnerabilities in the Pacific. The United States may have lost the Vietnam War, but it had gained a sizeable 'ally' in China.

As a result of this management of friend and foe the most important push yet was given to the arms race in the Pacific. In the decade from 1969 the Soviet Union invested 80 per cent of the increase in its military expenditure in upgrading its capabilities in the Pacific. By the end of that decade it had deployed between one-quarter and one-third of all its military power in the region, and most of this was aimed at China. There were more Soviet troops manning the Sino-Soviet frontier than in all of eastern Europe. Soviet military hardware in the region was soon to be of the first rank, infrastructure was developed, and extensive fortifications built.[23]

By 1979 Soviet deployments had reached 52 divisions, while 78 divisions were deployed on the Chinese side by 1980. Sporadic border incidents were reported until 1980, but with very little loss of life. The publicity given to the incidents that did take place varied according to the political winds of the day. They were used as political symbols in a far more complex Sino-Soviet dance. Just as the increased military tension had followed the increase in tension along other dimensions of the Sino-Soviet relationship, so a real decline in the military tension awaited a broader *détente*.[24] Slowly but

[22] Henry Kissinger, *The White House Years* (London: Weindenfeld, 1979).
[23] Details from Gerald Segal, *Sino-Soviet Relations After Mao* (London: IISS, Adelphi Paper, 202, 1985); Gerald Segal (ed.), *The China Factor* (London: Croom Helm, 1982).
[24] Gerald Segal, *Sino-Soviet Relations*, 'Sino-Soviet Detente', and 'Sino-Soviet Relations: The New Agenda', in *World Today* (June 1988).

steadily that *détente* developed in the first half of the 1980s. Sino-Soviet trade grew by leaps and bounds as Soviet technicians returned to China to help in the modernization and refurbishment of old Soviet equipment and the construction of new plants. In almost every aspect of the original split, some improvement was apparent. The Soviet Union had finally broken the spell cast by Sino-American co-operation in the 1970s.

Sino-American disputes over Taiwan and the generally more assertive Reagan foreign policy helped drive Sino-Soviet *détente*. To be sure, real disputes continued between the Soviet Union and China, most notably over the Soviet occupation of Afghanistan and Soviet support for the Vietnamese occupation of Kampuchea. But there is no doubt that a degree of military *détente* between the Soviet Union and China followed the generally improving atmosphere.

The scale and manner of this military *détente* is outlined below, but suffice it to say there has been a process of tacit arms control under way since 1982. China pulled back many of its troops from the frontier, and cut its armed forces by a million men between 1985 and 1987. Similarly the Soviet Union has thinned out its 50-odd divisions by placing them on a lower level of readiness. In July 1986 the Soviet leader Mikhail Gorbachev offered China important concessions in order to improve relations. The East Europeans were allowed to resume Party-to-Party relations with China, and Moscow accepted the Chinese claim that the eastern border between the two countries ran through the centre of the main channel of the border rivers, not along the Chinese bank as had previously been argued. Extensive contacts along the frontier developed as both sides decentralized economic decision-making as part of their economic reforms.[25] Gorbachev also decided to withdraw his troops from Afghanistan, and put pressure on Vietnam to reform itself and improve relations with China. Most impressive of all, in December 1988 Gorbachev announced that 200 000 Soviet troops would be withdrawn from the Far Eastern theatre. Gorbachev then travelled to Beijing in May 1989 for the first Sino-Soviet summit in 30 years. The visit also marked the restoration of Party-to-Party relations.

If the Sino-Soviet split and the tensions of 1969 had been the most important shift in the Pacific military balance since 1945, then the *détente* of the 1980s was of nearly equal importance. Yet China remained deeply concerned about the potential Soviet threat and the Soviet Union remained uneasy about Chinese power and China's proclivity for forging alliances with other Soviet rivals. The Soviet Union still deployed more troops and nuclear power in the Pacific than anywhere outside Europe. Although, by the mid-1980s, the focus of Soviet concern in the region was America's power

[25] *The Economist* (24 October 1987).

rather than China's, in terms of sheer numbers and military geography, China still posed the most significant threat to Soviet power in the region. Similarly, any increase in Soviet influence in the Pacific was mostly to the detriment of China. Not surprisingly the basic roots of rivalry remained.[26]

For its part, China still committed more troops for defence against the Soviet threat than against any other. Border incidents still took place, but only one has been reported since 1980, apparently as part of the complex *détente* process following the 1986 Gorbachev initiative. The American challenge under Reagan to the Soviet Union, China's own defence modernization, and the general process of *détente* along the frontier all helped decrease Chinese fears.[27] But there could be little doubt in the minds of Chinese strategists that shared socialism with the Soviet Union was no protection from military threat.[28]

The Sino-Soviet confrontation was nearly as important for others in the Pacific basin. The United States undoubtedly benefited from the massive rip in the flag of Communism. The drawing off of Soviet military strength to cope with the threat from China eased the burden on Europe and NATO. China's preoccupation with the Sino-Soviet dispute eased the pressure on Japan, Taiwan, and other American allies in the Pacific. The redirection of the Chinese military instrument to confront the Soviet Union accentuated the difference between warring Communist and prospering capitalist states in the Pacific.

Yet the risks of uncontrolled war between Russia and China were of serious concern to non-Communist Pacific states. Rivalry in Korea might have led to competition to arm Pyongyang. The wars in Indo-China might have spread to Thailand and ASEAN. In both cases the stability and economic prosperity of the western Pacific would have been undermined, forcing the United States to resume a higher military profile. The extreme scenario of a Sino-Soviet war brought the risk of United States involvement in support of China, with all the obvious dangers of a global nuclear holocaust.

For the smaller states of the Pacific, the shifting of great-power balances that resulted from Sino-Soviet rivalry was generally welcome. Japan was at first concerned that America's renewed interest in the China factor would mean that it was neglected by the United States. However, by the 1980s the

---

[26] Robert Scalapino, 'Asia in a Global Context', Harry Gelman, 'The Soviet Far East Military Buildup', and J. J. Martin, 'Thinking about the Nuclear Balance in Asia' all in Richard Solomon and Masataka Kosaka, *The Soviet Far East Military Buildup* (London: Croom Helm, 1986).

[27] Ellis Joffe, *The Chinese Army After Mao* (London: Weidenfeld, 1987); Ellis Joffe and Gerald Segal, 'The PLA Under Modern Conditions' in *Survival* (August 1985).

[28] Harry Gelman, *The Soviet Far East Military Buildup* (Santa Monica: The Rand Corporation, 1982).

possibility of Sino-American strategic co-operation had diminished. Similarly, South Korea, Australia, New Zealand, and the ASEAN states were increasingly reassured that the United States was not hopping into bed with China and ignoring its other, older allies in the region.

The smaller Communist states of the Pacific at first found the Sino-Soviet split useful as a way to squeeze more aid out of their patrons. Vietnam and North Korea were past masters at this game and both suffered in the 1980s as Sino-Soviet relations improved. The Chinese and Soviet desire for *détente* forced these smaller Communist states to compete for the favours of the Communist giants, instead of vice versa. North Korea felt the pressure for compromise with South Korea, and Vietnam, Kampuchea, Laos, and even Mongolia came under Soviet pressure to improve relations with China. The maturing of the Sino-Soviet conflict was clearly good for the stability of the Pacific region.

CHINA AND TAIWAN

The conflict between China and Taiwan can be seen as part of either the unfinished Chinese Civil War or the unfinished East–West conflict between capitalism and Communism. Neither description is complete, if only because the nature of the conflict is still changing. It has been more than 25 years since both sides seriously fought, but it would be rash to say the use of force can be ruled out in the future.[29]

The end of the war with Japan in 1945 merely brought into the open the barely disguised Chinese Civil War between the Communists and the nationalists of Chiang Kai-shek's Guomindang. With American support, Chiang's forces swept into Communist strongholds. But Chiang's regime remained fundamentally corrupt, and unwilling to undertake the necessary reforms to ensure effective rule over all of China. The Communists under Mao Zedong overran the Guomindang and in 1949 Chiang fled to the offshore island of Taiwan, taking some 1.3 million people with him, including 600 000 troops. The population of the island had been overwhelmingly Chinese ever since 1800. China's rulers had, since 1661, brought increasing numbers of Chinese to the island.

In 1949 Chiang took control of Taiwan, but he also instituted land reform and economic development that might have saved his regime on the mainland had it been implemented there. With strong American support and investment, Taiwan became increasingly able to stand on its own. But the

29 Lillian Craig Harris, 'Towards Taiwanese Independence?' in *Pacific Review*, 1/1 (1988).

United States still gave crucial military assistance, and from 1950 used the Seventh Fleet to protect Taiwan from Chinese attack. While both China and Taiwan claimed there was only one China (Taiwan's legislature retained notional members for all of China's provinces), the United States effectively acted as if there were two Chinas.

In April 1950 the Communists seized the large island of Hainan off the southern coast, which many saw at the time as a prelude to an invasion of Taiwan. But the outbreak of the Korean War and the interposition of the United States navy between the two Chinas stymied any attempt to seize Taiwan. Neither side viewed the civil war as over, and in 1953 the Communists began mopping up some tiny nationalist-held islands off the Chinese coast.[30] In September 1954 the South-East Asia Treaty Organization (SEATO) was formed and on 2 December Taiwan and the United States signed a mutual-defence pact. China shelled the offshore island of Quemoy and in January 1955 seized the Dachen Islands from Taiwan. On 29 January President Eisenhower signed the Formosa Resolution passed by the Congress, pledging United States protection to Taiwan and military aid for the protection of the offshore islands.[31]

While China felt it was making progress in retaking some territory from Taiwan, it was also increasingly aware that the United States was the main military problem. However, although the Soviet Union was willing to support Chinese aspirations, it was not keen on pushing the United States too far and causing another war so soon after the end of the Korean conflict.

In 1958 the Chinese once again tested the waters of the Taiwan Strait by shelling Quemoy in order to enforce a blockade and then surrender. But the United States again supported Taiwan and threatened to take action against China if it did not lower the threat. For a brief time the artillery exchanges and the air war were savage, but China soon backed down when it realized that it would be unable militarily to breach the protective barrier. Yet another, even briefer, crisis erupted in 1962, but at no stage was China able to take any more territory.

With its military position guaranteed, Taiwan settled down to a dash for economic development fostered by the United States and Japan. By the 1970s the economic miracle had transformed Taiwan into a shining example of export-led economic growth and prosperity. With China itself torn by the Cultural Revolution and taking on both superpowers at the same time, Taiwan seemed to be holding its own quite nicely.[32]

---

[30] J. H. Kalicki, *The Patterns of Sino-American Crisis* (Cambridge: Cambridge University Press, 1975); Bruce Swanson, *Eighth Voyage of the Dragon* (Annapolis: Naval Institute Press, 1982).

[31] Segal, *Defending China*, ch. 7.

[32] Ralph Clough, *Island China* (Cambridge, Mass.: Harvard University Press, 1978).

But the 1970s were also a period of great shock to the Taiwanese system. The Sino-American *détente* of 1971 and the Shanghai Communiqué in 1972 at the end of the Nixon visit to China led to an American agreement that there was only one China. But it was not until 1979 that the United States exchanged diplomatic relations with China, following an agreement to sever diplomatic relations with Taiwan and wind down arms sales to the island. Yet the 1979 Taiwan Relations Act passed by the United States Congress allowed for *de facto* diplomatic ties and 'business as usual'.

China still refused to pledge the non-use of force against Taiwan but by the 1980s China was working harder at the peaceful reunification of the island with the mainland. Under the supremely pragmatic banner of 'one country, two systems', China even offered Taiwan its own independent armed forces and currency so long as it officially became part of Communist China. The Taiwanese rejected the offer, wary of the regular changes of mind by Chinese leaders in the past, and seeing little reason to swap their hard-won prosperity for the righteous poverty of the mainland.

Of course, the allure of being part of one China, and the more moderate policies of the Deng Xiaoping leadership on the mainland, made the Chinese offer more attractive. Yet the differences between the two systems, and the passage of the generation used to power on the mainland, meant that the Chinese appeal was fading more than it was growing in the 1980s. The Reagan administration in the United States was true to its anti-Communist principles and, while holding Sino-American relations on an even keel, improved *de facto* relations with Taiwan.[33] While official United States arms sales to Taiwan were cut back in the 1980s, the United States allowed private firms to sell increasing amounts of arms and above all to license production arrangements on Taiwan.[34]

China became increasingly displeased to find that time was not inevitably on its side. For one thing, it had been outmanoeuvred by the United States. Chinese officials, including Party leader Hu Yaobang, asserted that China would not rule out the use of force against Taiwan, and if need be the modernized Chinese navy, air force, and marines would be ready to take the island by the twenty-first century.[35] While China could be pleased that it reached an agreement with Britain in 1984 on the return of Hong Kong, there was nothing inevitable about one Chinese state—witness the separate existence of Singapore. It is doubtful whether a China that worked so hard to be seen as a more peaceful and rational state, a suitable home for

---

[33] Jonathan Pollack, *The Lessons of Coalition Politics* (Santa Monica: The Rand Corporation, 1984); also, see generally David Shambough, 'China's America Watchers' in *Problems of Communism* (May 1988).

[34] *Jane's Defence Weekly* (4 July 1987).

[35] Gerald Segal, 'As China Grows Strong' in *International Affairs* (spring 1988).

international investment, would be willing to throw it all away for the sake of the principle of unification. Certainly a forceable unification might well destroy whatever economic benefit could be obtained from closer relations with Taiwan.

For the time being in the mid-1980s China was unwilling to rock its modernization boat by taking an active and even adventurous line on Taiwan. It still noted that the Taiwan issue was an obstacle to normal Sino-American relations, much as it insisted that it had three obstacles in its relations with the Soviet Union. But it was difficult to see what realistic options China had to retake Taiwan, especially with the growth of a new political generation on the island. The new Taiwan-born generation was less opposed to a genuine declaration of independence in lieu of the present fiction of a regime awaiting return to government over all of the mainland.

Most other states in the Pacific are happy enough with the status quo and would be concerned at any use of force by China. Taiwan is an important trading partner for the United States, Japan, South Korea, Australia, and the ASEAN states. These states have had lengthy experience of living with the *ad hoc* arrangements. None would be pleased to see the sphere of Communist control extended, and the ASEAN states in particular would worry about such expansion and the looming presence of a militarily successful China. Nor would the Indo-Chinese Communist states be pleased to see an expanding China, fearing that they would be next on the list of scores to be settled. Although the Communist states have all regularly supported the idea of one China under Communist control, in the light of the Sino-Soviet rift none would be pleased to see China succeed and strengthen its power. The removal of the major irritant in Sino-American relations would also add to the pressure for more Sino-Soviet *détente*.

While China may once have had prospects of regaining Taiwan in the 1950s, the opportunities seem increasingly remote. It is impossible to judge the ever-changing military balance as both Taiwan and China modernize their forces.[36] To some extent the Taiwanese calculation regarding China is like that of China towards the Soviet Union: a wise strategy will merely raise the cost sufficiently to move the enemy on to another target of opportunity. Certainly, with the cessation of Chinese shelling of offshore islands in 1979 and the evident economic success of the island, there can be little reason for Taiwan to do much else but get on with business and await developments on the mainland. The Taiwan–China struggle has moved on from a bitter civil war to a faintly tense, but probably fading, international conflict.

---

[36] Martin Lasater, *The Taiwan Issue in Sino-American Strategic Relations* (Boulder, Colo.: Westview, 1984).

14

Potential Conflicts

War can, of course, break out at almost any time and in almost any place. For the professional soldier, there is a duty to determine where war is most likely to occur and, when it comes to planning for defence, to err on the side of caution. For the more detached observer, such worst-case thinking about potential conflict needs to be distinguished from more careful analyses of the prospects for conflict. In the nuclear age, the need to avoid war between the major powers has helped create the phenomenon of the 'cold war'; a conflict, but one that is not fought except in simulated war-games or in competitive military expenditures.

Europe is the home of the original cold war, and of course the origin of numerous studies of the East–West military balance. While prudent observers of the Pacific could envisage a variation on the European version of a superpower clash in that region, there are also numerous other potential disputes, some of which may sometimes generate new crises. The patterns of security in the Atlantic and Pacific are different in many vital ways, and most clearly in that there is no overarching pattern of conflict in the Pacific as there is in the Atlantic. Although there are important linkages between local security issues and those on the global level, there are also far more numerous small conflicts than in the Atlantic theatre.

SUPERPOWER CONFLICT

The conflict between the superpowers is often described as an 'East–West' conflict, deriving its geographic images from the European and Atlantic theatre where the Soviet Union and its allies are to the east while the United States and its West European allies are to the West of the ideological dividing line in Europe. Of course, in the Pacific, the Soviet east lies to the west, while the American-led West is to the east. This is only one of the more trivial, but symbolically important, differences between the superpower balances in the Pacific and Atlantic theatres.[1]

---

[1] J. D. B. Miller, *Asia and the Pacific* (New York: Institute for East–West Security, Occasional Paper, 4 1985); see articles by Seizaburo Sato and Kenneth Hunt in *Convergence and Divergence in East Asian and Western Security Interests* (London: IISS, Adelphi Paper, 216, 1987); Michael Leifer (ed.), *The Balance of Power in East Asia* (London: Macmillan, 1986).

More importantly, the superpowers have come close to war more often in the Pacific than in the Atlantic since 1945. The conflicts in Korea and Vietnam are only the most notable cases where the superpowers supported opposing sides. Soviet citizens were killed by American attacks in both wars and tens of thousands of Americans were killed by Soviet-made weaponry. However, the superpowers never found themselves as close to direct conflict as they were during the Cuban missile crisis or the various turret-to-turret confrontations in Berlin. Even the Middle East War of 1973 brought the two superpowers to a higher state of military alert than any conflict in the Pacific.

Nevertheless, the Korean and Vietnam Wars were probably more damaging to superpower relations than any other major post-war conflict. Only with the end of the Korean war was it possible to begin superpower discussions on disarmament. The Vietnam War stifled superpower *détente* and complicated the early arms-control agreements of the 1970s. The Soviet-supported Vietnamese invasion of Kampuchea in 1978 was seen in Washington as yet another sign of Soviet perfidy and helped destroy the SALT 2 agreement.

Yet crises in Korea after 1953 were increasingly well controlled by the superpowers and not allowed to harm grander Soviet–American strategies of *détente*.[2] The complicating factor of China's involvement in the offshore islands crises with Taiwan in the 1950s was controlled by the United States and the Soviet Union.[3] Even during the Vietnam War the superpowers were eventually able to conclude the first SALT agreement and, as American involvement in the war began to wind down, clink glasses at the high point of *détente* in the early 1970s.[4] Although these wars complicated superpower relations, they were eventually kept from contaminating the atmosphere when both superpowers saw strong reasons for strategic *détente*. Such insulation of their relations from regional confrontations was more possible in the Pacific than in Europe because, with the exception of Japan, the Pacific allies were seen as less important.

Another major difference between the superpower confrontation in the Atlantic and the Pacific is the absence of such clear lines of demarcation in the latter. Unlike in the European arena, the superpowers do actually touch

---

[2] Donald and Janet Zagoria, 'Crises on the Korean Peninsula' in Stephen Kaplan, *Diplomacy of Power* (Washington DC: Brookings, 1981).

[3] J. H. Kalicki, *The Pattern of Sino-American Crisis* (London: Cambridge University Press, 1975); Alexander George and Richard Smoke, *Deterrence in American Foreign Policy* (New York: Columbia University Press, 1974); Gerald Segal, *Defending China* (Oxford: Oxford University Press, 1985), ch. 7.

[4] This process is best documented in Henry Kissinger, *The White House Years* (London: Weidenfeld, 1979); Seymour Hersh, *Kissinger: The Price of Power* (London: Faber & Faber, 1983).

frontiers in the Pacific, in the Bering Strait. But the northern wastes are not of primary strategic concern as they contain a tiny population and their geography is forbidding. Only in Korea does the United States station troops that help defend an American ally, which directly confronts a Soviet ally bordering on the Soviet Union. Yet the Soviet–Korean frontier is only 20 km long and North Korea hardly serves as a strategic glacis as do the East European states in the Soviet Union's far west.

United States forces were developed in strength in South Vietnam in the 1960s, but most of them had been withdrawn by 1973 and all American personnel left the country in 1975. In mainland South-east Asia, only Thailand receives large-scale American support, but this entire area is as far from the Soviet frontier as Morocco. Vietnam and Moscow's other Indo-Chinese allies are more akin to Cuba and North Yemen than to eastern Europe in the Soviet strategic calculation.

Thus it is difficult to know where the lines of 'containment' and conflict in the Pacific cold war should be drawn. Although it is true that it took some time, and most notably the 1948–9 and 1961 Berlin crises, the 1956 Hungarian crisis, and the 1962 Cuban crisis, to etch the lines so deeply in Europe and the Atlantic, the degree of uncertainty about political geography was never as great in Europe as it was in the Pacific. Most observers would now agree that one of the main causes of the Korean War was the absence of a proper Soviet understanding of the American commitment to defend Korea. The Vietnam War in the 1960s had a great deal to do with American attempts to prop up what it perceived to be toppling dominoes in East Asia and to halt the Communist advance there.

But perhaps the crucial difference between the balances of power in the Pacific and the Atlantic is the presence of China. Until the 1960s the United States perceived China as part of a solid Sino-Soviet alliance. Despite the Sino-Soviet split, many Americans still perceived China as the more radical wing of Communism, but essentially an ally of Soviet interests.[5] Joint Sino-Soviet support for Vietnam in the 1960s was seen as a case in point. It was not until Sino-Soviet border clashes in 1969 and the Kissinger–Nixon reassessment of American foreign policy that China came to be viewed as potentially a genuinely independent power. China might even be helpful in the confrontation with the Soviet Union. Chinese Communism was then reinterpreted in a more moderate light and was found to have its own national drives and interests—a trend that in practice did not show itself clearly until the Deng Xiaoping reforms of the 1980s.

The transformation of China from being an ally of the Soviet Union to being an enemy was the single greatest strategic loss suffered by the Soviet

---

[5] Gerald Segal, *The Great Power Triangle* (London: Macmillan, 1982).

Union since 1945. It was not the result of anything orchestrated by the United States, but clearly the Soviet need to redirect spending to the Pacific theatre to meet the Chinese threat was of huge benefit to the United States. As the old, and nearly universal, adage has it, 'the enemy of my enemy is my friend'. Equally, and nearly opposite, the slow but steady *détente* in Sino-Soviet relations in the 1980s has reduced Soviet anxiety and beefed up defence spending, and represents the single most important improvement in the Soviet strategic position in the Pacific since 1945. Once again, the United States was not responsible for this shift. Its relative position in the Pacific has not apparently suffered to any great extent.

In military terms, there is no strictly bipolar confrontation in the Pacific. China has certainly turned the old two-power balance into a triangle since the 1960s, and the growth of Vietnamese power in the 1970s has made it even more difficult to calculate a South-east Asian balance of power. Japan used to be a military power in the Pacific, but since 1945 has eschewed a military role outside of its own immediate security zone. Although Japan's booming economy is able to support the world's third-largest defence budget, unlike in the case of China the force that Japan has acquired has not been used in anger against any other state. Thus the Pacific theatre is more complicated than the Atlantic one, but not as complicated as it was before 1945.

Another major difference between the Atlantic and Pacific arenas is the relatively more diffuse nature of the superpower tension. In Europe, the lines of confrontation have been immortalized by Winston Churchill as an 'Iron Curtain' that hangs across the heart of Europe. There is no similar drapery in the Pacific, except for the heavily fortified Korean frontier, which bears some resemblance to the inner-German frontier. Otherwise, the most heavily fortified frontiers in the Pacific are between Communist states, rather than between Communist and capitalist ones.

The real dividing line of superpower influence, especially since the triumph of Communism in Indo-China in 1975, runs through the waters dividing eastern Eurasia from its offshore islands. Japan, Taiwan, and the Philippines are the states closest to the mainland that are oriented towards the United States.[6] In contrast to the Atlantic system, which has its dividing line on land, any assessment of a superpower balance in the Pacific must be primarily in naval and nuclear terms.

Whereas in Europe the sign of the American commitment to its allies is very visible—troops in barracks and tanks rumbling across fields—the near-total absence of American land power in East Asia makes it harder to provide

---

[6] Thailand is of course an American ally on the mainland; Malaysia leans to the American side and has both continental and islands parts.

symbols of deterrence and friendship. What is more, the traditional strength in Soviet military power has been its land-based forces. Thus, in the Pacific the Soviet Union is less of a threat to the United States and also less able to take on the United States in a way that plays to Soviet strengths. In order to confront American power, the Soviet Union must go to sea—precisely the arena of American strength. In any case, most Soviet ground forces are deployed against China.

It is difficult to suggest that either superpower has a usable military advantage in the Pacific.[7] Much as in Europe, a rough balance of deterrence has existed for decades, although any calculation of such a balance must be imprecise at best.[8] The essential basis of this deterrence is the global nuclear balance of terror. Most Soviet ICBMs are based east of the Urals but are targeted on the United States.[9] By the 1980s the Soviet Pacific Fleet had become Moscow's largest, and a significant proportion of its SLBMs were based out of Pacific ports. They were part of Soviet forces in the Pacific but their task was global.[10] Similarly, the United States deployed most of its intercontinental nuclear weapons at sea and the majority were based in, or regularly traversed, Pacific waters. These forces were only properly considered part of the Pacific balance of power in the sense that the global balance determined the Pacific balance.

Because of this distinction between global and regional missions, it is impossible to identify the numbers of troops that the Soviet Union and the United States deploy against each other in the Pacific. In terms of troops deployed abroad in the Pacific region, the Soviet Union has some 60 000 in Mongolia but fewer than 8000 in all of the rest of the region. By 1991 the Soviet Union promises to remove all but 10 000 of its troops in Mongolia.

By comparison, the United States deploys some 140 000 of its 520 000 troops stationed abroad in the Pacific and East Asia, 33 000 of whom are afloat. However, at least one estimate suggests that a mere 14 per cent of the United States defence budget in 1987 was for the defence of the Pacific.[11] The total force in the Pacific is less than half the number deployed in Europe, although the naval contingent represents more than half the total number of

---

7 Barry Blechman and Robert Berman, *Guide to Far East Navies* (Annapolis: Naval Institute Press, 1983).

8 Malcolm McIntosh, *Arms Across the Pacific* (London: Frances Pinter, 1987).

9 Robert Berman and John Baker, *Soviet Strategic Forces* (Washington DC: Brookings, 1982).

10 Harry Gelman, 'The Soviet Far East Military Buildup' and J. J. Martin, 'Thinking About the Nuclear Balance in Asia' both in Richard Solomon and Masataka Kosaka, *The Soviet Far East Military Buildup* (London: Croom Helm, 1986).

11 Francis Fukayama, *Soviet Civil–Military Relations and the Power Projection Mission* (Santa Monica: The Rand Corporation, April 1987); *Far Eastern Economic Review* (12 May 1988), 20.

American servicemen afloat (32 000 are with the army in Korea and Japan, 42 000 are with the Seventh Fleet, 38 000 are marines, and 37 000 are with the air force).[12] Japan hosts some 2400 American army personnel, 7400 from the navy, 26 000 marines, and 16 600 airmen. Korea hosts 29 000 army and 11 000 air-force personnel, while the Philippines hosts 5300 navy personnel, 660 marines, and 9400 from the airforce. The navy also deploys some 4900 in Guam and the air force deploys 4200 others. Some 250 other air-force personnel are based in Australia, 29 926 along the Pacific coast of the United States, and a further 10 800 in Alaska.

A comparison of naval forces also reveals some American advantages, but none that confers any decisive ability to defeat the Soviet Union. As the American Pacific Command stated, in the early 1980s the American position in the Pacific was better than it was in the NATO theatre.[13] At least according the IISS in London, the balance in Europe provides no side with a usable military advantage.[14] The United States' two fleets in the Pacific regularly deploy seven aircraft-carriers as compared to the two, far less impressive, Soviet carriers.[15] The Soviet Union has a greater total number of surface ships as a result of a major naval buildup in the 1970s. But since 1980 the Pacific fleet has remained roughly the same proportion of the total Soviet navy, while being modernized.[16] By the mid-1980s there was a new emphasis in Soviet naval strategy on deployment closer to home and fewer operations in the Third World.[17] The Australian Foreign Minister said in April 1988 that the Soviet Pacific Fleet was spending up to 50 per cent fewer days at sea than in the late 1970s.[18] The emphasis in Soviet military strategy remained more in Europe than Asia; even the Pacific fishing fleet was resupplied and crews changed with flights from European Russia via Ireland and Panama. Under the Reagan administration, American naval power was also increased to restore the relative, albeit minor, American advantage.[19]

There are, moreover, a host of strategic disadvantages that limit the Soviet Union's ability to take on the United States at sea. While it is true that combat close to Soviet shore-based facilities will minimize the American carrier advantage, the United States has bases and allies all along the Eurasian coast, stretching 16 000 kilometres from the Aleutians to Australia.

12 Statistics from *Military Balance* (IISS).

13 John Collins, *US–Soviet Military Balance, 1980–1985* (Oxford: Pergamon, 1985), 144.

14 See various issues in the 1980s of the IISS' annual publication, *Strategic Survey*.

15 For details see Peter Hayes *et al.*, *American Lake* (London: Penguin, 1987), appendix E.

16 Anthony Preston, 'The Changing Balance in the Pacific' in *Jane's Defence Weekly* (20 September 1984); 'The Pacific: Still America's Lake?', *East–West Papers*, 8 (July 1987).

17 *International Herald Tribune* (23 October 1987).

18 *International Herald Tribune* (13 April 1988).

19 Robert O'Neill, 'The Balance of Naval Power in the Pacific' in *Pacific Review*, 1/2 (1988).

The only significant Soviet bases in the Pacific are those facilities in Vietnam and Kampuchea obtained after the defeat of the United States. However, Soviet facilities are not permanent and are no match even for American facilities in the Philippines. The Australian Defence Minister pointed out in 1987 that the Soviet bases would not survive day one of a war and are more important as a political symbol.[20] With the winding down of Soviet naval operations in the Indian Ocean, the need for Cam Ranh Bay has not grown.

The Soviet Union once had access to bases in North-east China but surrendered them in 1954. The primary mission of Soviet naval forces now seems to be to protect its northern territories from American attack and above all to guard its sea bastions in the Sea of Okhotsk for the safe launch of SLBMs. But perhaps the greatest weakness of Soviet naval forces in the Pacific is the difficulty of getting the navy out of the sea bastion without being tracked by the enemy. The narrow choke-points make it highly likely that the Soviet fleet will remain bottled up in wartime.[21]

The idea of threatening sea-lines of communication further south in South-east Asia is unlikely to be a Soviet priority.[22] In economic terms, these sea lanes, especially through the Malacca Strait, are vital for Japanese oil and the trade on which the prosperity of many states is built. Yet in wartime the free passage of ships is also vital to the Soviet Union for reinforcing its Pacific flank.[23] Some estimates indicate that up to 80 per cent of Soviet supplies for its Pacific coast come by sea and the difficulties in developing the trans-Siberian rail links suggest that the Soviet problem is a long-term one.[24]

The United States made use of the Malacca Strait during the Bangladesh War but is particularly interested in a less observable route from Guam to the Indian Ocean and Diego Garcia. The Malacca Strait is too shallow for secret passage of submarines, while the Ombei-Wetar and Lombok-Makassar Straits in Indonesia, as well as the Timor Sea, do allow such secret passage. New Trident submarines make the use of all such channels less necessary, and therefore the task of Soviet trackers even more difficult.[25]

The United States relies heavily on its bases at Clark Field and Subic Bay in

[20] *Far Eastern Economic Review* (18 June 1987).

[21] Anthony Cordesman, 'the Western Naval Threat to the Soviet Military Presence in Asia' in *Armed Forces Journal* (April 1983).

[22] Hayes, *American Lake*, ch. 16.

[23] Michael Leifer, *Malacca, Singapore and Indonesia* (Alphen ann den Rijin: Sijthoff & Noordhoff, 1978).

[24] Allen Whiting, *Siberian Development and East Asia* (Stanford, Calif.: Stanford University Press, 1981).

[25] Ibid., Michael Leifer, *Indonesia's Foreign Policy* (London: Allen & Unwin, 1983): Yaacov Vertzberger, *The Malacca–Singapore Straits* (London; Institute for the Study of Conflict, Conflict Paper, 140).

the Philippines to help keep open these sea lanes. Up to 70 ships a month refuel and resupply at Subic Bay. Clark is the base for the 13th Air Force, which is responsible for the western Pacific and Indian Ocean. Fifty per cent of world oil traverses these waters, as does 80 per cent of Asia's trade with the United States and Japan.[26] However, the two bases are only rented from the Philippine government and the existence and terms of the lease are regularly debated. Perennial unrest in the Philippines makes these United States bases unreliable in the long term.

In times of superpower cold war, a war in which no shots are fired, these bases retain more political than military roles.[27] The United States understood this basing game much earlier than the Soviet Union, establishing its string of bases down the coast of East Asia by the early 1950s.[28] While the improvements in modern technology made such bases less critical, the growing American presence, and the war in the Vietnam, reinforced the argument in favour of forward bases. The change in the United States' definition of the adversary, which came with *détente* with China and the retreat from Vietnam, led to a debate in Washington about Pacific bases. But the triumph of Vietnamese Communism and the Soviet use of Indo-Chinese bases kept American attention focused not too far off shore in the western Pacific, and not surprisingly the decision by President Carter to remove troops from South Korea was quickly revoked.

But despite the growth in Soviet and American naval power in the Pacific, it is hard to argue that the Pacific has slipped closer to superpower conflict than in the immediate post-war period. By the late 1980s there were no major wars in the region where the superpowers were actively involved in supporting opposing adversaries. The United States had virtually no troops on the East Asian mainland and the role of a more independent China ensured that both superpowers were uneasy about calculating a possible winning coalition for war. By the 1980s even the Soviet Union was talking of a Helsinki-like arms-control measure for the Pacific (see below), while the United States and its friends were more concerned with ensuring a peaceful atmosphere for economic development.

For all these positive trends, there were some distressing signs of possible conflict. As part of a more forward American naval strategy, United States naval exercises in the Pacific, such as Fleet Ex-85, operated carrier battle groups close to Soviet waters. The Soviets protested, but also carried out their own exercises by flying simulated bombing missions against American

---

[26] *International Herald Tribune* (3–4 May 1986).

[27] *The Economist* (14 November 1987).

[28] William Feeney, 'The Pacific Basing System and United States Security' in William Tow and William Feeney (eds.), *US Foreign Policy and Asian-Pacific Security* (Boulder, Colo.: Westview, 1982).

carrier groups.[29] Other reports suggest that, with increased military use of outer space, the south Pacific rivalry of the superpowers takes on new importance. The so-called 'gateways' for satellite interception available in the Pacific give the region new importance in the age of 'star wars'. But for the time being, such matters of importance to the Pacific remain far in the future and the concerns of the 1980s are far more mundane.[30]

Although similar naval manoeuvres take place regularly in the Atlantic, there were few strong signs that the Soviet Union was prepared to challenge the United States' dominance of the Pacific as it sometimes did in the Atlantic. In the mid-1980s there were some suggestions of new Soviet interest in the Pacific islands, but it was difficult to point to any obvious Soviet 'gains'.[31] Disputes between the United States and some Pacific islands had their origins in the United Nations Law of the Sea Conference, which created exclusive economic zones 200 miles out from even the tiniest coral atoll. The refusal of the United States to pay more for fishing rights in island waters led to bad feeling, which was aggravated when the Soviet Union signed a fishing accord with Kiribati in 1985 on terms favourable to the islanders. A Soviet deal giving landing rights to Aeroflot in Vanuatu soon followed.[32] The military coup in Fiji in 1987 removed a government that was interested in similar accords with the Soviet Union.[33]

For all the flurry of activity in south Pacific waters, most of the events there seemed to be related to American determination not to provide the minuscule amounts of extra money needed to keep the islands happy. The risk of an island 'going Communist' could not be discounted entirely, but the real threat was from the domestic unrest in individual islands as a result of local inequalities, rather than from something fomented by the Soviet Union.[34]

In sum, the superpowers are clearly the most important military powers in the Pacific. But it is difficult to claim that there is anything that can be called a 'superpower balance' because their zones of influence are not nearly as clearly identifiable as they are in the Atlantic. In any case, any such balance is best described as 'western Pacific' because, despite the Soviet submarine

[29] William Arkin and David Chappell, 'Forward Offensive Strategy' in *World Policy Journal* (summer 1985); William Arkin and Richard Fieldhouse, *Nuclear Battlefields* (Cambridge, Mass. Ballinger, 1985), ch. 7.

[30] *International Herald Tribune* (7 July 1988).

[31] *International Herald Tribune* (21 January 1987); W. T. Roy, 'The Soviets and the South Pacific' in *Asia-Pacific Defense Forum* (winter 1985–6).

[32] Malcolm Macintosh, 'Fish Bone of Contention' in *Guardian* (12 June 1987); *Asiaweek* (24 August 1986).

[33] *Jane's Defence Weekly* (23 May 1987).

[34] Coral Bell, 'The Security of Pacific Ministates' in *Asia-Pacific Defense Forum* (winter 1985–6).

threat, the reach of Soviet power barely extends beyond that of shore-based aviation. If there is any element of a balance, it is derived from the overarching global superpower balance of terror. This is not to suggest that the superpowers are irrelevant in Pacific military terms, or, indeed, that the Pacific is irrelevant to the two superpowers, but rather that their role needs to be understood in specific conflicts where more complex local balances of power can be identified.

POTENTIAL HOT SPOTS[35]

Conflicts can break out for a wide range of reasons, only some of which are immediately apparent beforehand. Sometimes, force is used merely for financial gain, as is evident in the continuing problem of piracy in the Malacca Strait.[36] But most conflicts are pursued for political reasons and regularly run the risk of involving interested neighbours and powers.

One of the most peculiar conflicts in the Pacific is a tiny dispute between the two superpowers over their mutual boundary. The frontier at the Bering Strait was not set clearly in the 1867 agreement by which the United States purchased Alaska from Russia. Although there is no population problem involved, the two superpowers began negotiations in 1981 to resolve the issue. Talks were inconclusive and were ended in 1983, only to be resumed again in 1984. The dispute mainly concerns the possible exploitation of mineral resources, but it has also been distorted by the overarching state of superpower relations.[37]

A similar dispute also simmers between Canada and the United States over waters in the Hectate Strait near Alaska, the continental shelf in the Beaufort Sea between Alaska and the Yukon, and the Juan de Fuca Strait dividing Washington state and the province of British Columbia. As with the Soviet–American dispute, these arguments are over potential mineral rights and to some extent immediate fishing rights. Most recent of all is the dispute over the famed North-west Passage. Canada claims these Arctic waters to be its own, while the United States sees them as international waters. In 1987 Canada decided to acquire new submarines to patrol the disputed waters, although it was always unlikely that they would fire on their United

---

[35] This section does not consider conflicts which have already broken out into war since 1945. Nor does this section include discussion of such issues as the Sino-Indian conflict, which involves a non-Pacific power as a major protagonist.

[36] *International Herald Tribune* (25 May 1987).

[37] The discussion of this and the following territorial disputes depends heavily on Alan Day (ed.), *Border and Territorial Disputes* (London: Longman, 1982); Henry Degenhardt, *Maritime Affairs—A World Handbook* (London: Longman, 1985).

States ally. This was more a question of national pride, and a real concern with dangers of pollution, although often couched in terms of protecting the northern approaches to the Atlantic.[38]

Canada also expressed a new interest in Pacific waters through its 'three-ocean' policy, which took in the Pacific and the Atlantic as well as the Arctic passage between the Atlantic and Pacific. The growth of the American Pacific navy has helped attract Soviet submarines closer into the North American coast and in 1987 Canada decided to deploy an independent task force in the Pacific for the first time. Some ships were even transferred from the Atlantic to the Pacific, marking a new balance in Canadian defence policy that had already been evident for a decade in American strategy.[39]

In fact, most of these potential disputes involve a mixture of pride and perceived economic potential. Certainly the series of Latin American disputes along the Pacific coast has strong doses of these two potentially lethal components. Since the nineteenth century, Argentina and Chile have disputed the ownership of the small islands of Picton, Lennox, and Nueva at the eastern entrance to the Beagle Channel off Tierra del Fuego. The territory had long been under Chilean control but Argentina formally claimed it in 1967. Argentina was concerned both with the prestige and principle of its nationalist claim and with the strategic and economic value of the sea that would be controlled by the extension of a 200-mile limit around the islands.

In addition, with the islands under Chilean control, Argentina argued that access to its key naval base at Ushuaia would be severely restricted. In 1971 both sides accepted international arbitration and the International Court of Justice ruled in favour of Chile in 1977. Argentina rejected the ruling and both sides then made warlike gestures. Talks in 1978 reached only partial agreement and in December both sides accepted mediation by the Vatican. In 1981 Chile accepted the Papal proposals but once again Argentina rejected them. Further border tension in April and September 1981 resulted in yet another round of talks and further threats in 1982.

Argentina's sudden occupation of Britain's Falkland Islands in 1982 raised Chilean fears that it would also resort to force to support its claim to the islands in the Beagle Channel. But the British victory, apparently with tacit Chilean support, and above all the end of military rule in Argentina, led to moderation in Buenos Aires. After yet another round of Vatican mediation, on 5 October 1984 both sides accepted a deal that confirmed Chile's possession of the islands, gave Argentina some oil and mineral rights, and confirmed existing claims to Antarctic territory.

---

[38] *News Brief* (Royal United Services Institute, July and August 1987).
[39] *Peace and Security*, 2/2 (summer 1987), 16.

Further up the continent, a more complicated conflict simmers away. Bolivia had been landlocked ever since the war of 1879–84 when Chile seized the port of Antofagasta and the surrounding area. Luckless Peru joined the war to support Bolivia, but instead lost its southern provinces of Tacna and Arica to Chile. Tacna was regained in the 1929 Treaty of Ancon.

Bolivia's relations with Chile have barely improved since. Diplomatic relations were severed in 1962 when Chile was accused of reducing the flow of the Lauca River. Relations were resumed in 1975 and Chile offered Bolivia a narrow corridor to the Pacific in exchange for territory in Bolivia's south–west. Peru complained that this was a violation of the Ancon Treaty, which prevents the transfer of the mineral-rich former Peruvian territory to a third party without Peru's consent. The deal also collapsed because of Chile's unreasonable demands, and in March 1978 relations between Bolivia and Chile were once again severed.

Further to the north, 300 000 sq. km of the Amazon basin in northern Peru are claimed by Ecuador. Spanish manipulation of the natural frontier had left Ecuador without access to the Amazon or any other major waterway. After a brief war in July 1941, the Rio Protocol of January 1942 delimited the frontier in Peru's favour. Argentina, Brazil, Chile, and the United States acted as guarantors of the settlement, but Ecuador remained dissatisfied and in 1960 declared the 1942 accord null and void. Peru, having already been defeated in wars to its south, and having already lost territory to Bolivia and Chile, was unwilling to compromise with its weaker neighbour, Ecuador. In any case, the guarantors were reluctant to reopen the matter and rejected Ecuador's claim.

In subsequent years Peru claimed that Ecuador illegally seized some border posts and in January 1981 fighting broke out in the Condor Mountains. In the five-day war, Ecuadorean troops were driven back and a ceasefire was arranged by the Organization of American States. Periodic reports of oil finds in the contested territory have raised the stakes but Ecuador simply lacks the power, or the external support, to change the status quo. Sporadic clashes continue and may yet develop into something more dangerous as Brazil asserts control over its territory further west in its conquest of Amazonia.[40]

What is most striking about these conflicts in the Pacific Americas is the total non-involvement of any state from across the Pacific. Unlike many other conflicts in the western Pacific, these disputes have remained small-scale and of interest only to states of the region.

[40] These disputes are discussed in Peter Calvert, *Boundary Disputes in Latin America* (London: Institute for the Study of Conflict, 1983); M. Morris and V. Millan, *Controlling Latin American Conflict* (Boulder, Colo.: Westview, 1983); H. Munoz and J. Tulchon (eds.), *Latin American Nations in World Politics* (Boulder, Colo.: Westview, 1984).

To be sure, there are some other Pacific conflicts which are only of narrow, regional interest. Australia and Indonesia reached agreements on their maritime border in 1971–2 but they did not include a 250 km stretch south of Timor because it was still under Portuguese control. Nor was agreement reached on the line dividing Australia's Christmas Island and Java. Talks ended in October 1981 without success. The discovery of oil in 1983 in Jabiru off north-western Australia again brought these issues to a head. Indonesia proposed that a median line be accepted, but Australia preferred following the continental shelf—a notion arguably abandoned in the UNCLOS agreement. Australia's argument was weakened by the fact that it signed a fishery pact with Indonesia in 1981 that also accepted the median-line principle.

By contrast, the question of East Timor did involve the interests of outside powers, although not to any great effect. The April 1974 revolution in Portugal led to the decision to give up the colony of East Timor. While the local population was split in a civil war, in which 60 000 died, Indonesia took control in December 1975 to pre-empt the consolidation of power by Fretilin, an independence movement. The territory was integrated into Indonesia in August 1976. It was never officially recognized by the United Nations, but the United States, Australia, New Zealand, and in practice most other states have recognized Indonesia's claim in an effort to keep on good terms with Indonesia.

The East Timor issue has almost disappeared because there are no powerful spokesmen or supporters for the local population. By contrast in the clash between Japan, China, and Taiwan over disputed islands where there are strong supporters of the opposing sides, there are other reasons for keeping the dispute under control. The uninhabited Senkaku (Tiaoyu) Islands and other smaller islands are 320 km west of Okinawa and 160 km north-east of Taiwan. The 1951 peace treaty between the western allies and Japan at San Francisco included the Senkakus in the Ryukyu Islands, which reverted to Japan on 14 May 1972 under the terms of the United States–Japan treaty of 17 June 1971.

Yet on 30 December 1971 China declared that these islands were part of Taiwan and therefore part of China. Taiwan had already claimed the islands on 11 June 1971 and declared them to be incorporated into Taiwan in February 1972. The question of the islands was raised, but left as an issue in dispute, when China and Japan negotiated their Peace and Friendship Treaty of 12 August 1978. China thought it best not to push its claim for the sake of Japanese friendship and closer economic relations. Yet China trots the issue out from time to time when it wishes to remind Japan and the world of Japan's imperial past and unreasonable contemporary behaviour.

The dispute between Malaysia and the Philippines over North Borneo, or the Malaysian province of Sabah, is yet another case of principle and territory traded off against wider interests. On August 1977 the Philippines renounced its claim for the sake of ASEAN unity, and the Aquino government did the same in 1987.[41] Both Malaysia and the Philippines now undertake joint border patrols to prevent piracy and drug trafficking. Malaysia has also encouraged the moderate Philippine line by cutting off aid to Muslim Moro rebels in the southern Philippines.

Ever since the creation of ASEAN, the member states have shown remarkable restraint in controlling old disputes for the sake of a common good—economic progress. Nowhere is this spirit better evident than in the Strait of Malacca. In 1969 both Indonesia and Malaysia claimed 12-mile limits and yet both sides managed to reach agreement on the boundary despite the fact that one-third of the 960 km of the strait is less than 24 miles wide. In 1971 the two sides jointly announced that they did not see the waters as international and in 1972 they announced a ban on ships greater than 200 000 deadweight tons. With more than 90 per cent of Japan's oil and much of the region's shipping passing this way, few states accepted this declaration apart from China. The United States, Australia, and Britain took a low-key position, unwilling to damage their role as *de facto* allies of Indonesia and Malaysia.[42]

At the United Nations Law of the Sea (UNCLOS) discussions, both Indonesia and Malaysia abandoned their stand on the strait in favour of the archipelago principle.[43] Singapore was especially anxious to obtain reaffirmation of the principle of freedom of navigation, which was essential to its continuing prosperity. Malaysia had previously grown anxious that the archipelago principle would hamper links between peninsular Malaysia and Borneo. Indonesia was particularly concerned that, given the shape of its country, a patchwork of scattered islands, it had to exert some control over the dividing waters. The concept of 'archipelagic status' was enshrined in the 1982 UNCLOS treaty, as was the right of 'transit passage', thereby achieving a compromise that pleased the particular, and the diverse, interests of ASEAN states.[44] The compromise was also especially pleasing to other archipelago states in the Pacific, such as Fiji, Papua New Guinea, the Philippines, and the Solomon Islands.

While most of these disputes have faded from the foreign policy agendas of Pacific states, a few other issues have not. In the north-west Pacific there is still an unresolved dispute between Japan and the Soviet Union over

---

[41] Lela Garner Noble, *Philippine Policy Towards Saba* (Tucson: University of Arizona Press, 1977); *Asiaweek* (27 November 1987).

[42] Vertzberger, *Malacca-Singapore Straits*; Leifer, *Malacca, Singapore*.

[43] Leifer, *Indonesia's Foreign Policy*, 143–6.

[44] Ken Booth, *Law, Force and Diplomacy at Sea* (London: Allen & Unwin, 1985).

islands off the north-eastern tip of Hokkaido. Etorofu and Kunashiri are generally recognized as part of the Kurile chain which currently belongs to the Soviet Union. To the south of these two islands lie the Habomai group and Shikotan. The combined land area is about 5000 sq. km and had a population of about 17 000 at the end of the Second World War. About half fled at the time of Soviet occupation, and the remainder were interned and later forcibly repatriated to Japan between 1947 and 1949.

The history of this dispute is complex.[45] The Soviet Union's claim is based on vague wartime agreements, especially at Yalta. Japan points out that the islands were not specified in the agreement and that in any case Japan was not party to the Yalta agreement. The Soviet Union refused to sign the 1951 peace treaty at San Francisco but began talks on a separate peace. Talks broke down in 1956. The Soviet offer to return the Habomais and Shikotan had at first been accepted by the Japanese government, but then refused because it did not include all four island groups. The complexities of domestic Japanese politics had a great deal to do with this change of mind.[46] As part of the 1956 restoration of Soviet–Japanese relations, the Soviets agreed to return the southern two if a peace treaty were agreed.

Soviet policy hardened after 1956 and a deal was linked to the withdrawal of the United States from Japan.[47] The Soviet Union opposed the 1960 Japan–United States security treaty which allowed the continued American military presence in Japan. In treaties in 1968 and 1971 Japan obtained the return of the Bonin, Volcano, and Ryukyu Islands from the United States. In 1978 the Sino-Japanese friendship pact was interpreted in Moscow as an anti-Soviet gesture and attitudes hardened even more against compromise. Fishing disputes in 1977 were resolved by accords but fishermen found operating in disputed waters were still detained. Japan then went on to claim that the Soviet Union was building up its forces on the northern islands, including Shikotan, which had not been militarized since 1960.

Apart from the fishing rights, and the symbolism of an accord between the United States and its main Pacific ally, Japan, the northern territories are of some strategic value to the Soviet Union. Soviet control of the islands makes it even vaguely plausible that in time of conflict Soviet ships could exit from the Sea of Okhotsk to the Pacific, whereas if the islands were under hostile control they would be even more bottled up than they already are. With the shift to a policy more focused on defending the sea bastions, the islands

---

[45] Wolf Mendl, 'The Soviet Union and Japan' in Gerald Segal (ed.), *The Soviet Union in East Asia* (London: Heinemann, 1983).

[46] Donald Hellmann, *Japanese Foreign Policy and Domestic Politics* (Berkeley, Calif.: University of California Press, 1969).

[47] Gregory Clark, 'The Cold War Goes On and On for Tokyo and Moscow' in *International Herald Tribune* (12 June 1986).

became more important as yet another link in the chain preventing the entry of hostile enemy craft. Nowhere else does the Soviet Union face such a powerful military threat so close to such a vital base.[48] While a compromise along the lines of that offered in 1956 seems possible, the Soviet Union will have to 'regurgitate what it has swallowed', something it has rarely done since 1945. The Soviet Union needs to be convinced that there is a reward for territorial compromise—a motive very evident in its previous concessions in Pacific territorial disputes. It has already returned territory to neighbouring China on more than one occasion since 1949, the latest being the promised return of islands along the river frontier, as mentioned in Mikhail Gorbachev's 1986 Vladivostok speech.

China is also involved in two other simmering disputes, both involving its former ally Vietnam. As inheritors of French Indo-China, Vietnam claimed the Paracel (Xisha) and Spratly (Nansha) Islands in the South China Sea, while China claimed them as traditionally Chinese. For more than 15 years after the French withdrawal from Vietnam, South Vietnam held both groups and even removed Chinese residents from the Paracels.[49]

In 1973 South Vietnam awarded oil concessions to western companies that in part encompassed the Spratly archipelago. The South incorporated the area into one of its provinces in September and drilling revealed exploitable deposits.[50] China protested and in January 1974 took the only kind of action it could—against the northern Paracel group. China seized the islands while South Vietnam was too weak to act, while the North and the Soviet Union were still nominally allies, and while the United States was courting China.[51] It was a masterful piece of low-risk war that made it plain that China would use force to regain what it claimed as its own.

In the 1970s all China could reach was the Paracels, but in the 1980s it began expanding the reach of its navy. Aircraft and ships were increasingly sent down to the Spratlys. These lie 500 km from the Philippines, 500 km from Vietnam, and 1050 km south of China's Hainan Island. All the islands in the group are tiny, with the largest being only 90 acres, but they command the sea passage from Japan to Singapore. Oil has been discovered at Reed Bank and has been developed by the Philippines since 1979. Taiwan keeps a garrison at Itu Abu and in 1971 fired on Philippine fishing boats. The Philippines set up a military command post on Palawan in 1976 and by 1978 had a garrison on seven of the islands. In 1978 an agreement was signed with

[48] *Far Eastern Economic Review* (10 September 1987).
[49] Marwyn Samuels, *Contest for the South China Sea* (London: Methuen, 1982).
[50] Ronald Keith (ed.), *Energy, Security and Economic Development in East Asia* (London Croom Helm, 1986).
[51] Details in Gerald Segal, *Defending China*, ch. 11.

Vietnam to settle the issue peacefully, and a similar accord was signed with China in 1979.

With the Philippines in command, Vietnam had grown less worried about a Chinese attack. Yet growing Chinese naval power and poor Sino-Vietnamese relations made a Chinese attack more likely. Of all the potential disputes, by the 1980s this was the one that looked most likely to spark into open war, as had happened in the Paracels in 1974.[52] Indeed, in March 1988 China took advantage of its new *détente* with the Soviet Union to attack Vietnamese troops in the Spratlys and inflict hundreds of casualties. Like the 1974 operation, little territory was acquired, but the principle of Chinese determination to take what it claims was reinforced. Since the islands sit astride vital sea routes for the growing trade of the Pacific, China's pursuit of its principles was seen as dangerous and perhaps even a harbinger of a more potent Chinese military power in the years to come.

As the Spratly incident shows, although the Pacific has grown more pacific in recent years, there are a number of disputes that can wreak havoc on regional stability. Most of the least understood potential crises involve maritime disputes, and particularly all down the coast of China. With increasing interest in the new law of the sea and the potential exploitation of sea-bed resources, such disputes may well figure even more strongly in the future.[53] The complex disputes between the states of North-east Asia are good examples of the new, but as yet mostly low-key, conflict.[54] Even further away in the future are the potential disputes over the mineral rights at the 'bottom' of the Pacific in the Antarctic.[55] But conflict over the Antarctic, as indeed with many other disputes in the Pacific, involves far more than merely the states of the Pacific and therefore is resolved or exacerbated on a global level.

[52] Gerald Segal, 'As China Grows Strong', *International Affairs* (Spring 1988).

[53] Mark Valencia, 'Troubled Waters' in *Far Eastern Economic Review* (31 March 1988).

[54] For example, the Japan–South Korea disputes over Takeshima (Tokdo) and Danjo islands, the former held by South Korea and the latter by Japan, but both disputed.

[55] Sir Anthony Parsons, *Antarctica: The Next Decade* (Cambridge: Cambridge University Press, 1987); *Far Eastern Economic Review* (11 February 1988).

15

Alliances

One of the most striking features of the Atlantic world, and especially the north Atlantic, is the matching alliances that formalize military relationships. The cold war appears in a number of vivid symbols, most notably the wall in Berlin. But the acronym NATO and the name of the Warsaw Pact are equally recognizable symbols of the post-war division of the Atlantic world. Although no similar alliances stretch across the south Atlantic, Latin American states are linked northward to the United States in the Organization of American States.

The Pacific world has never been neatly tied in alliance knots. Of course, it is the Atlantic alliances which are the unusual ones, for the notion of wide-ranging multilateral alliances in peacetime was virtually unheard of before the founding of NATO in 1949. The alliances in the Pacific are more the normal kind of loose bilateral ties, almost all of which are dominated by one major ally. Thus there is no single pattern of security in the Pacific, but rather a quilt-like set of overlapping patterns, some of which have faded and been replaced with new ones.

FADED ALLIANCES

While no post-war Atlantic alliance has been terminated, three of the main underpinnings of Pacific security have been shattered by changing political circumstances. Not surprisingly, as the Pacific balance of power has shifted so dramatically since 1945, it was predictable that the structure of security and alliances would move with the times.

Perhaps the most important post-war Pacific alliance was that between the two largest Pacific states, China and the Soviet Union. After lengthy negotiations in December 1949 and January 1950, a 30-year Treaty of Friendship, Alliance and Mutual Assistance was signed on 14 February 1950. The two sides also agreed that by the end of 1952 the Soviet Union would withdraw from the joint administration of the Manchurian railway and the naval base at Port Arthur. The third component of their pact was a promise of long-term Soviet credits to China to buy heavy equipment.[1]

[1] John Gittings, *Survey of the Sino-Soviet Dispute* (Oxford: Oxford University Press, 1969).

The mutual-assistance treaty was the result of sometimes-acrimonious negotiations as two proud peoples and Parties struggled to align against a common enemy—Japan and the United States—while trying not to have to spend too much in doing so. Both countries had been devastated by the war, but a shared ideology and a perceived common threat cemented the alliance structure. Both pledged that 'the other party would immediately render military and other assistance with all the means at its disposal' if either country should be attacked by Japan or its allies. This key clause was successfully tested in the Korean War later in 1950, when the Soviet Union provided the necessary military aid to support the Chinese intervention. Although China paid for some of the aid, it was worth over $2 billion, including 1000 aircraft and support for the Chinese war industries.[2]

The war, and the delay in normalizing Soviet–Japanese relations, also postponed the Soviet withdrawal from Port Arthur. But by 1954 it was agreed that the Soviets would finally pull out in 1955 and increase their economic aid to China. In this honeymoon period in Sino-Soviet relations, Moscow became closely involved in all sectors of the Chinese economy, establishing new plants and aiding reorganization of the armed forces while the two countries co-ordinated their foreign policies. The Soviet Union even helped China develop nuclear weapons.

From the Soviet perspective, this alliance with China was part of the cold war, and a key assurance of the Soviet eastern flank, well before the formation of the Warsaw Pact in 1955. Although China was involved in Warsaw Pact consultations, there was no similar attempt to build a Pacific alliance network around China, North Korea, North Vietnam, and Mongolia. The Soviet priority remained Europe, especially as East Asia become calmer in the mid-1950s.

As has already been explained, Sino-Soviet relations deteriorated in the late 1950s over a number of domestic and foreign policy disputes. By the 1960s the two states were nominal allies but fighting each other in small border skirmishes. The alliance was in *de facto* operation when both states supported North Vietnam in the 1960s, but officially 'united action', such as one might expect from normal allies, was avoided. After the major Sino-Soviet border clashes in 1969, even the remains of the *de facto* alliance were buried as China drifted off into what was to become a different *de facto* 'strategic partnership' with the United States.

The Sino-Soviet alliance was only officially terminated in April 1980, 30 years after it officially began. On 3 April 1979 China announced that it would not extend the treaty and the Soviet Union officially regretted the decision. Moscow also revealed that it had made various offers to China in the 1970s to sign non-aggression treaties and other pious statements.[3] But

---

[2] Alan Day, *China and the Soviet Union* (London: Longman, 1985), ch. 1.

[3] Gerald Segal, *Sino-Soviet Relations After Mao* (London: II SS, Adelphi Paper, 202, 1985).

China did take up the Soviet offer to discuss an agreement about principles governing their relations. The formal talks officially began on 17 October 1979.

Neither side had illusions that they could return to the alliance of the 1950s, and the early rounds of talks were really forums for propaganda exchanges. At the time, China was particularly anxious about the concentration of Soviet troops along the frontier and Soviet support for Vietnam's occupation of Kampuchea. That China agreed to talk less than a year after the Vietnamese victory suggested China realized it needed some kind of understanding with the Soviet Union. However, the Soviet invasion of Afghanistan in December 1979 led China to suspend these new negotiations.

When China agreed to resume talks on 5 October 1982, the sessions were for a time called only 'discussions'. By now China had merely added a third obstacle to the agenda, Afghanistan, yet carried on quietly improving relations while biannual talks continued. In February 1987, following the conciliatory speech by Mikhail Gorbachev in Vladivostok in July 1986, specific border talks were resumed and initial agreement was reached in 1987. The biannual normalization talks reflected the general mood of Sino-Soviet relations. In May 1989 Sino-Soviet relations were normalized with the summit meeting in Beijing, even though no formal agreement on the frontier had yet been announced.

For all the progress since 1985, Sino-Soviet relations were not headed back to the alliance of the 1950s. Their 1950s alliance was clearly an historical oddity. It was unlikely that two Communist great powers sharing a long, vulnerable frontier would ever return to such friendship unless there was a common sense of threat. The pre-1945 Pacific suggested such a configuration of forces was unlikely, except for a fleeting period. The post-1945 events confirmed such an assessment, although it also suggested that a modicum of co-operation was equally natural. In the uneasy, and inevitably complex, balance of power in the Pacific, a close and long-lasting alliance between two such great powers made little sense.

THE MANILA TREATY

The formation of the Sino-Soviet alliance was perceived by the United States as a major building block in the Soviet structure of alliances. America had responded to what it saw as the Soviet consolidation of its bloc in Europe with its own—called NATO. But in the Pacific it was far more difficult to know how to meet the 'Sino-Soviet challenge'. Support for South Korea and other friends in the Pacific (see below) was achieved without a formal alliance. But with the defeat of France in Indo-China, and the appreciation of the nature of global security, the United States felt a need for a more formal alliance of its own in the Pacific, especially as a way to involve France and Britain, who were excluded from ANZUS (see below).

The cobbled-together response was the Manila Treaty, a brain-child of Secretary of State John Foster Dulles, conceived with the lawyer-like zeal of a true believer in the alliance strategy in the cold war.[4] The South-East Asia Treaty Organization (SEATO was set up by the 8 September 1954 Manila Pact (the South-East Asia Collective Defence Treaty) and was composed of the United States, Britain, France, Pakistan, Australia, New Zealand, Thailand, and the Philippines. Only two states were South-east Asian, as many as were from Europe. France withdrew from military co-operation in 1967 and ended its financial contributions in 1974. Pakistan withdrew in July 1972.

In the 1950s there was some sort of common perception of the Soviet Union and China as the main threats to a western political and economic system. China was seen as the main Soviet ally, and in fact the most active member of the partnership that also egged on Vietnam and various other Indo-Chinese Communists. But SEATO members found it difficult to agree on the best strategy to meet this challenge, and the extent to which they should become actively involved in assisting threatened states in Indo-China, who, after all, were not even members.

SEATO never made much practical sense and was more a public-relations organization. Certainly in comparison to NATO, it lacked a regular, unified command. It was geographically divided, ruled by a motley collection of governments, and its members were not always agreed on the locus of the main threat. When crises did emerge, as in Laos in 1960–1 or Vietnam in the following years, and despite Australian assistance in the Vietnam War, there was never any question of a combined SEATO operation. What made NATO work was common political objectives, and the absence of such common objectives in the Pacific was the very reason for the failure of SEATO.

The demise of the organization was only formally agreed on 29 September 1975 (effective 30 June 1977), when the defeat of the non-Communist Indo-Chinese regimes made a mockery of SEATO and the perception of the Chinese threat was reduced. In any case, the members had all changed their outlook on the regional balance of power in the intervening 20 years. Britain and France had, of course, almost completely retreated back to Europe. The extent of their out-of-area operations was Africa, the Middle East, or the south Atlantic. The United States remained in the Pacific, but had since improved relations with Communist China, and retreated from most land-

---

[4] Richard Barnet, *The Alliance* (New York: Simon & Schuster, 1983), 160–1.

based commitments in Asia. Yet the United States did join with Australia and New Zealand in restating a vague commitment to the security of SEATO states and most especially to Thailand and the Philippines.[5]

Pakistan was of course never a Pacific, let alone a South-east Asian, state, and had also vastly improved its relations with China in the interim. Australia and New Zealand were part of ANZUS and were chastened by the Vietnam experience from seeking grandiose military engagements beyond their relatively safe south Pacific. Only the Philippines and Thailand felt left out by the demise of SEATO, but then they both had bilateral defence relations with the United States. They had both also begun to focus more clearly on non-military confrontation. They sought to safeguard security through economic development, and to that end concentrated on ASEAN as a viable regional body.

The demise of SEATO was a recognition of new balances of power in the Pacific. The division of the 'Communist threat' into Soviet, Chinese, and Vietnamese components made it impossible to agree on a common enemy. The retreat of American power from mainland Asia made East Asian states less willing to rely on the United States. The death of SEATO, as with the somewhat earlier death of the Sino-Soviet alliance, made it even more difficult to think militarily in comprehensive East Asian, let alone Pacific, terms.[6]

TAIWAN AND THE UNITED STATES

The major shift in Pacific military equations caused by the changes in Chinese foreign policy not only helped shatter SEATO, but also helped reduce what was once a major link in the United States security chain in the western Pacific—the United States–Taiwan alliance. But unlike in the case of SEATO, the severance of the United States–Taiwan link was an explicit goal of China in its improving relations with the United States. The process is still not entirely complete, and can be achieved only if, and in the unlikely event that, China regains control of Taiwan.

The United States link to the Guomindang regime that rules Taiwan can be traced back to the Chinese Civil War and the American determination to defend the anti-Communist forces. With the defeat of the Guomindang and its retreat to Taiwan, the United States also uneasily shifted its wartime

[5] T. B. Millar (ed.), *Current International Treaties* (London: Croom Helm, 1984).

[6] See a general discussion in Barry Buzan, 'The Southeast Asian Security Complex' in *Contemporary Southeast Asia* (February 1988); Michael Leifer, *Asean and the Security of South–East Asia* (London: Routledge, 1989).

alliance with mainland China to a cold-war alliance with offshore Taiwan. It was a poor second choice, and one that did serious harm to the United States' strategic position in the Pacific.

Yet in the atmosphere of the cold war the United States took itself closer to Taiwan and further from China. With the outbreak of the Korean War, President Truman ordered the Seventh Fleet to protect Taiwan from China and the United States built up Taiwan as a defence bastion in the early 1950s. American assistance to the Taiwanese economy laid the groundwork for the booming NIC that Taiwan became in the 1970s.

The commitment to Taiwan was strengthened in 1954—much like the foundation of SEATO—in the wake of the French defeat in Indo-china. A treaty between the United States and Taiwan on 2 December 1954 provided an American commitment to defend Taiwan and some offshore islands. This came in the midst of the first of a series of offshore islands crises when China threatened, and in some cases took, islands that were once held by Taiwanese forces. In the 1954–5 crisis, as well as in 1958, the United States provided active military assistance and successfully deterred China from any more aggressive action against Taiwan.[7]

At best, this was an uneasy alliance. Taiwan wanted more forceful United States support in recovering the mainland. While the United States was anti-Communist, it realized that the Chinese clock could not be turned back—Chiang Kai-shek had missed his chance. Yet neither was the United States prepared to allow China to regain control of Taiwan, for that would be seen as irresolution in the face of Communism. Taiwan was defended just as South Korea, West Germany, and eventually South Vietnam would be with direct United States assistance.

So long as the United States saw China as part of a Sino-Soviet Communist bloc, there was little chance that it would dump Taiwan in favour of a deal with China. Only when the Nixon administration improved relations with China, and distinguished between Soviet and Chinese Communism, was there something worth deserting Taiwan for.[8]

The diplomatic dance that led to full normalization of Sino-American relations is too complex to document here. In the Shanghai Communiqué signed during the Nixon visit to China in February 1972, the United States agreed that there was only one China. This was not yet a normalization of relations, for that had to wait for the shock of the American shift of friends to sink in. The pro-Taiwan lobby was active in Washington, but to little

[7] J. H. Kalicki, *The Pattern of Sino-American Crisis Management* (London: Cambridge University Press, 1975); Alexander George and Richard Smoke, *Deterrence in American Foreign Policy* (New York: Columbia University Press, 1974).

[8] Martin Lasater, *The Taiwan Issue in Sino-American Strategic Relations* (Boulder, Colo.: Westview, 1984).

avail. It was clear that the United States was moving to full diplomatic relations with China.

China demanded three concessions from the United States regarding Taiwan—severence of diplomatic relations, cancellation of all existing treaties with Taiwan, and withdrawal of all United States forces from the island. The trick for the United States was to sever all outward signs of alliance with Taiwan, while maintaining the essence. On 15–16 December 1978 China and the United States announced that diplomatic relations would be resumed on 1 January 1979.

While this one-China policy officially brought the United States into line with the position of the Soviet Union, in reality the United States was trying to keep Taiwan as a quiet ally while making use of China as a 'card' against the Soviet Union. For the time being, China was happy to make common cause with the United States, for it was locked in combat with Soviet-supported Vietnam. The United States could not adopt a formal alliance with China, but certainly there were strong voices in the Carter administration for doing so.[9] It was at this time that Western discussion of China as the sixteenth member of NATO, and a prospective purchaser of western arms, made the Soviet Union especially anxious about a Sino-American strategic alliance. The concern reached its peak in the Carter administration, and only faded with the new Reagan administration in 1981.[10]

But the ambiguities in the United States' relationship with Taiwan did not end with the 1978 accord. Congress passed the Taiwan Relations Act in March 1979 and President Carter signed it on 10 April. It stated that any attempt to resolve the Taiwan question by other than peaceful means would be considered 'of grave concern' to the United States and required the United States to assist Taiwan with sufficient self-defence capability. It also specified that Taiwan was regarded as an independent state for immigration purposes. The American Institute in Taiwan which opened on 16 April 1979 was staffed by Foreign Service Officers temporarily on leave from the State Department, and the members of the Co-ordination Council for North American Affairs (the Taiwan embassy) had full diplomatic privileges.

Although the United States officially withdrew its military personnel in accordance with its termination of the Mutual Defence Treaty, American advisers remained in civilian clothes. What is more, the Reagan administration was more supportive of the Taiwan regime and continued to sell arms to the island.[11] On 17 August 1982 the United States and China

[9] Banning Garrett, 'The United States and the Great Power Triangle' in Gerald Segal (ed.), *The China Factor* (London: Croom Helm, 1982).

[10] Gerald Segal, 'The Soviet Union and the Great Power Triangle' in Segal (ed.), *The China Factor*.

[11] Michael Yahuda, *Towards the End of Isolationism* (London: Macmillan, 1983), ch. 5.

agreed that arms sales to Taiwan would gradually be reduced. In the meantime, China had been pursuing a more positive approach to Taiwan, offering it near-total independence under the banner of 'one country, two systems'.

Yet Taiwan and the United States resisted Chinese carrots and sticks and maintained a low-key policy that helped sustain Taiwan as a pro-capitalist state. Formal arms sales gradually declined, but sales by 'private' American corporations increased and a growing range of military equipment was sold under licence for production in Taiwan. China had normalized relations with the United States and obtained the formal severance of the United States–Taiwan alliance. But most of the reality of the alliance, including the *de facto* independence of Taiwan, was maintained. Unlike the other dead alliances in the Pacific, this one lived on past its official termination. Although the political rationale—opposition to Chinese Communism—had changed, the need for a friendly, independent Taiwan remained.

JAPAN AND THE UNITED STATES

The United States has more bilateral alliances of one form or another in the Pacific than anywhere else, but the patchwork may give a false impression of a coherent 'security system'. The reality is a mess of tangled lines of alliance. The lines needs to be flexible, or else they would snap with the pressure. But they are also sturdy enough to take the United States to the coast of East Asia, ensuring that the waters behind are clear of danger. This position was attained with the defeat of Japan in 1945 and basically has not changed since. It is not for nothing that both critics and ardent supporters of the United States refer to the Pacific as an 'American lake'. It is nothing short of remarkable that such a string of alliances should be maintained despite the major shifts in the Pacific balance of power.

Without doubt the key ally, in whose shadow all other states are eclipsed, is Japan. Once the defeated imperialist of the Second World War, now the second-largest economic power after the United States itself, Japan is a vital ally and symbol of what can be done for the welfare of citizens of countries under American protection. The association with Japan has gone so far that leading Japanese like to boast of their membership of 'the West'. They certainly have earned a seat at the top economic tables. Yet for all its gigantic economic and political proportions, Japan remains a curious military dwarf. It is more dependent on the United States than France or Britain and, unlike Germany, Italy, and other NATO states, has few friendly allies to help balance American power. It is in this very inequality of the alliance that the problems begin.

The United States–Japan alliance has it roots in the American occupation and the San Francisco Peace Treaty that returned full sovereignty to Japan. It was the United States that gave Japan its special constitution, and especially Article 9, forbidding it from making war and restricting the type of forces it could maintain. Attempts to demilitarize West Germany were formally abandoned in the mid-1950s because of the need to fill the gap in NATO. In the Pacific, the United States signed a string of mutual-assistance pacts with friendly states in the early and mid-1950s, and Japan received its version in 1954. But *de facto* rearmament had already begun with the Korean War. It was certainly clear at that time that Japan was a key base for American operations in Korea and that Japan could benefit economically from the forward American military position. Along with the signing of the peace treaty in September 1951 came a Japanese–American security treaty, which allowed for American defence of Japan and the right to station forces there.

Yet under the terms of the March 1954 Mutual Defence pact, Japan was to build a self-defence force with American finance and expertise. The Japanese declined conscription and showed little enthusiasm for the project.[12] They also declined to send Japanese abroad in anything vaguely like a military role and left the struggle against Communism to the Americans. Neutralism appealed to many in Japan, but in practical terms the United States would not permit it. In any case, American protection provided the foundation for Japanese growth that was not overburdened by much defence expenditure.[13]

The dilemmas of the alliance for Japan were clear: how independent could it be without spending on defence, but why spend money on defence when the United States would bear the burden?[14] Japan was extremely vulnerable to economic blockade—for example its economy could be shut down in weeks if oil supplies were stopped from the Gulf—and yet Japan had no independent means or apparent willingness to solve its weakness. The legacy of the Second World War, which started over such strategic calculations, was still too powerful. The dilemmas for the United States were equally clear: why give Japan a free ride on defence that was not tolerated of European allies, but was Japanese rearmament a process the United States could control? Thus when Japanese and American policies diverged, these dilemmas in the alliance became more acute.

---

12 Meirion and Susie Harries, *Sheathing the Sword* (London: Hamish Hamilton, 1987).
13 Nathaniel Peffer, *The Far East* (Ann Arbor: University of Michigan Press, 1968), 509–10.
14 Radha Sinha, *Japan's Options for the 1980s* (London: Croom Helm, 1982).

In 1960 the security treaty was renegotiated, giving Japan more favourable terms for its bases, especially in Okinawa.[15] The bases became vital to the American war effort in Vietnam, but also became a focus for Japanese opposition to the war and the United States. It was not until 1972 that the United States gave up control of Okinawa, while still retaining its bases. But the two big shocks that President Nixon delivered to Japan in the early 1970s—recognition of China and floating exchange rates—forced Japan to re-evaluate its alliance with the United States. President Nixon also called on all its Pacific allies to bear more of the defence burden as the United States pulled back from the land war in Vietnam. The number of United States installations in Japan was reduced from 2800 in 1952 to 125 in 1970. The result was a more balanced relationship and a spur to the greater internationalization of Japanese foreign policy.[16] Sino-Japanese links were to be the main new trend.

But the 1970s was also a period of growing Japanese concern with the expansion of Soviet military power in the Pacific.[17] If Japan was serious about genuine foreign policy independence, then it would have to increase its own defence spending and rely less on the United States. Although Japan expanded its Self-Defence Forces, deployed twice as many destroyers as the United States in East Asia, and supported the world's third-largest defence budget, it was still far from having a force capable of independent defence of its home territory, let alone offensive action.[18] For a supposed great power, it remained alarmingly vulnerable to having its resources cut off and its trade routes severed.[19]

By the mid-1980s Japanese defence spending had begun to creep above the notional 1 per cent of GDP limit that had been set in the 1970s. Especially under Prime Minister Nakasone in the 1980s, there was an attempt to meet some of the United States' demands that Japan was not spending enough on defence. In comparison to European spending levels in NATO, Japan was taking a free ride on the American defence budget. Yet in an era of growing Japanese–American trade rows, many Americans realized that it was not wise to drive Japan to a more independent foreign policy, for fear of stoking the fires of Japanese nationalism.[20] In 1980 for the first time United States

[15] A. J. Gregor and M. H. Chang, *The Iron Triangle* (Stanford, Calif.: Hoover, 1984).

[16] J. A. A. Stockwin, *Japan: Divided Politics in a Growth Economy* (London: Weidenfeld, 1982), 248.

[17] Edward Olsen, *US–Japan Strategic Reciprocity* (Stanford, Calif.: Hoover, 1985).

[18] J. M. W. Chapman, R. Drifte and I. T. M. Gow, *Japan's Quest for Comprehensive Security* (London: Frances Pinter, 1983); and Harries, *Sheathing the Sword*, ch. 25.

[19] On the energy dimension see Ronald Keith, *Energy, Security and Economic Development in East Asia* (London: Croom Helm, 1986).

[20] Daniel Okimoto, 'Chrysanthemum Without the Sword' in Martin Weinstein (ed.), *North East Asian Security After Vietnam* (London: University of Illinois Press, 1982).

and Japanese forces held joint exercises, although proposals for more permanent integration of commands on the NATO model have been sidelined. Most Japanese military equipment has been American,[21] and the United States almost seems happier with a pliant, if miserly ally, even one that leaks high technology to the Soviet Union, than with the more uppity, yet defence-conscious West Europeans.[22]

From the Japanese perspective, this was an alliance better not mentioned, but better still not challenged. Even when former American ambassador Edwin Reischauer admitted in May 1981 that American ships had been armed with nuclear weapons when they visited Japanese bases, the Japanese managed not to ban American ships in support of the sacred post-war Japanese principle of a non-nuclear Japan.[23] The arrangement was to ignore the contradiction so long as it did not have to be faced officially.

Japan, like Britain on the other side of Eurasia, remains a crucial unsinkable aircraft-carrier for the United States. But unlike Britain, Japan has no multilateral alliance within which it can help minimize its dependence on the United States. At least for the time being it has chosen the diplomacy of the merchant rather than that of the warrior.[24] Yet Japan remains very much aware of the Soviet threat, and its vulnerability to having resources such as oil cut off. It has a remarkable ability to rely on others for defence and to assume a low profile in all but international economic affairs in the hope that no one will do anything as nasty as severing its energy supplies. This is a unique, but ultimately risky, strategy.

Thus Japan strongly supports its Self-Defence Forces and trusts the United States and other Western allies. Japan has increasingly taken comfort from its role as a member of a wider western alliance, and not merely a dependency of the United States.[25] Furthermore, Japan can get away with spending only a quarter as much of its (albeit much larger) GDP on defence as Britain. But this very dependence can be taken as a major reason why the Japanese–American alliance is stronger than the European bonds, for Japan and the United States have little choice but to rely on each other. The war in the Pacific 45 years earlier is a warning of what might happen if their alliance should ever collapse.

[21] Reinhard Drifte, *Arms Production in Japan* (Boulder, Colo.: Westview, 1986).

[22] *Far Eastern Economic Review* (10 September 1987).

[23] Edwin Reischauer, *My Life Between Japan and America* (New York: Harper & Row, 1986).

[24] The distinction is by Harold Nicolson, quoted in Shinkichi Eto, 'Japanese Perceptions of National Threats' in Charles Morrison (ed.), *Threats to Security in East Asia-Pacific* (Lexington, Mass.: D. C. Heath, 1983).

[25] Malcolm McIntosh, *Arms Across the Pacific* (London: Frances Pinter, 1987).

OTHER BILATERAL ALLIANCES

If Japan is the main link in the American security chain, then Korea is the key
to the lock. Certainly Japan has traditionally regarded Korea as the route
along which Eurasian threats reach the Palestine of East Asia.

South Korea, like Japan, had its present political system established by the
United States and was garrisoned by American troops.[26] Unlike Japan,
Korea was attacked by Communist forces, although to some extent South
Korea was defended because it was the gateway to the far more important
Japan. The United States suffered over 142 000 casualties in the Korean
War, more than in any other post-war conflict except the Vietnam War.[27]
Thus the 1954 defence treaty, which came into force on 17 November was
signed with South Korea as part of a series of such bilateral pacts around the
Pacific.

Leaving aside the aberration of Vietnam, the Korean conflict is the most
comparable to the NATO and Atlantic context. South Korea is the only
American Pacific ally since 1975, apart from Thailand, to share a border
with a Communist state. Like West Germany, South Korea would like to
have a reunified state but sees too many benefits from its present separate
and protected status as part of the community of western-oriented states.[28]
South Korea is the only country in the Pacific whose armed forces belong to
an integrated military command with the United States that is anything like
comparable to the NATO structure.[29] And of course there has been a
consistently higher level of tension on the Korean peninsula for longer than
anywhere else in the Pacific.

Because of this high level of tension, and regular incidents in and around
the inner-Korean frontier, the United States has maintained a 'trip-wire'
strategy.[30] Much like the inner-German frontier, the strategy is to deter an
aggressor by threatening to trigger an American involvement if the trip-wire
is activated. The 30 000 ground troops and over 11 000 United States
air-force personnel based in South Korea as a deterrent constitute the
second-largest American deployment in the Pacific. But like the larger
commitment to Japan, it has also not been without controversy.[31]

[26] Gregor and Chang, *Iron Triangle*.

[27] Peter Lowe, *The Origins of the Korean War* (London: Longman, 1986), 218.

[28] Sang Woo, 'The Roots of South Korea's Anxiety About National Security' in Morrison
(ed.), *Threats to Security*.

[29] Brian Bridges, *Korea and the West* (London: Chatham House Papers, 33, 1986).

[30] Donald and Janet Zagoria, 'Crises in the Korean Peninsula' and William Zimmerman,
'The Korean and Vietnam Wars' both in Stephen Kaplan, *Diplomacy of Power* (Washington
DC: Brookings, 1981).

[31] Gerald Curtis and Sung-joo Han, *The US–South Korea Alliance* (Lexington, Mass.: D. C.
Heath, 1983).

The South Korean–American alliance, like all others in the region, was upset by Sino-American and Sino-Soviet *détente* in the 1970s. If the enemy was less evil, then there appeared to be less need for an entangling alliance. Although these sentiments were raised in Europe and Japan, they were less strong in Korea where the sense of threat remained acute. The problem for South Korea was how to appear receptive to new ideas of *détente* without lowering its guard. Thus abortive inter-Korean *détente* moved in parallel with the ups and downs of *détente* between the West and the Communist powers.

The downswing in superpower *détente* in the late 1970s was matched by a strengthening of United States and Japanese relations with China, the state that sent millions of 'volunteers' to war in Korea. China was still the main supporter of North Korea (see below) and could exert influence on the North to improve relations with the South. But the United States was unable to cajole China into using its influence, for Beijing feared losing out to Moscow in the Sino-Soviet competition in Pyongyang. Thus the Korean–American alliance took the strain of diverging interests between the superpower patron and the local South Korean interests.

It was therefore not surprising that President Carter sought to improve relations on the Korean peninsula. But he adopted a perverse strategy of promising to withdraw American troops prior to any more general accord.[32] As with many other decisions in this often-chaotic presidency, the promise was eventually withdrawn. Yet it was in some respects at least a formal, if abrupt and therefore destabilizing, recognition that the United States was a Pacific power, but not an Asian power.[33] The anomaly of maintaining troops only in Korea remains stark.

The succeeding Reagan administration upgraded the defence of South Korea to an area of 'vital interest' and a great deal of reassurance was provided to the Koreans about American reliability.[34] The United States increased the scale of its joint exercises with South Korean forces and these 'Team Spirit' manoeuvres became an increasing source of tension in inter-Korean relations.[35]

In the 1980s, when the United States was supporting its ally with renewed vigour and Sino-Soviet relations were steadily improving, North Korean leverage on China diminished. China, and to a lesser extent the Soviet Union, developed a vast covert trade with South Korea. The Soviet Union

[32] Joo-Hong Nan, *America's Commitment to South Korea* (Cambridge: Cambridge University Press, 1986).

[33] Edwin Simmons, *Korea to Kampuchea* (London: IISS, Adelphi Paper, 216, 1987).

[34] Peter Hayes *et al.*, *American Lake* (London: Penguin, 1987), 134.

[35] Young Whan Khil, 'The Two Koreas' in Young Whan Kihl and Lawrence Grinter (eds.), *Asian-Pacific Security* (Boulder, Colo.: Lynne Rienner, 1986).

and China found it easier to make overtures to South Korea as its booming economy was increasingly attractive to more reform-minded Communists in Moscow and Beijing. These shifts in the strategic balance, unlike the events of the 1970s, strengthened the United States–South Korea alliance.

The challenges to this alliance were now coming as much from internal South Korean politics as from external realignments.[36] In a successful economy with a growing middle class and increased demands for democracy, questions were raised about the American role in supporting the military regime and in suppressing opposition. Although the United States denied that it played such a role in internal South Korean politics, American support was vital to the regime. The latest round of liberalization in 1987–8 was clearly supported by the United States, much as it had been in the Philippines in 1986. The real test for this alliance was now how South Korea could be allowed to become more democratic, and perhaps also independent, as how it was defended against a Communist threat. This was an alliance problem virtually unheard of in Europe for 40 years, but it was symptomatic of the special kind of alliances in the Pacific. As one perceptive observer has suggested, American alliances in the Pacific appear impressive, but much like its first city on the Pacific coast, San Francisco, these American alliances are built on fault lines that seem doomed to constant, perhaps devastating, shifts.[37]

The other unsinkable American aircraft-carrier in the Pacific, or according to the geographic metaphor the other fault line on which the American string of alliances is built, is the Philippines. This former American colony has had American forces on its territory since 1898 and an American base at Clark Field since 1902. Unlike the American bases in Japan and Korea, Americans feel 'more at home' in the Philippines and have been more directly involved in local politics.

Upon its return to the Philippines and the defeat of Japan, the United States granted independence but demanded a 99-year lease, rent-free, for 23 bases. The 1947 treaty was the basis of the massive American presence until it was revised in 1959, the leases being shortened to 25 years, and then again in 1979, the lease on Clark and Subic being extended for five years. In 1951 a Mutual Defence Treaty was signed, a forerunner of the alliance system that the Americans would try to build in 1954–5.[38] The bases, especially at Subic Bay and Clark Field, are America's largest outside of home territory and are the most vital in protecting Pacific sea lanes.[39] With the defeat in

---

36 Far Eastern Economic Review (12 May 1988).

37 Coral Bell, US Military Power in the Pacific (London: IISS, Adelphi Paper, 216, 1987).

38 William Feeney, 'The Pacific Basing System and US Security' in William Tow and William Feeney (eds.), US Foreign Policy and Asian-Pacific Security (Boulder, Colo.: Westview, 1982).

39 International Herald Tribune (3–4 May 1986).

Vietnam, and the new Soviet naval presence across the water in Indo-China from the late 1970s, the Philippine bases assumed even more vital importance. The United States ceded most of the territory of the bases to the Philippines in 1979, but retained control of vital sections.

Although the importance of the bases has grown since the 1970s, they have become even more caught up in the instability of Philippine politics. The United States is the second-largest employer in the state after the Philippine government, but became a focus of opposition when it was seen to be supporting the fading, corrupt Marcos regime. Much as in South Korea, the dilemma for the United States was how much independence should be granted to, or could be forced upon, their ally without jeopardizing the vital bases.

The United States has paid an increasing amount in military and economic aid to the Philippines, most of which Washington regarded as rent. The latest agreements, which govern the American presence until 1991, provide for $900 million spread over five years. Yet this remains a small portion of the estimated $8 billion it would cost to relocate the bases. The real threat remains domestic unrest, and it was to that end that the United States helped remove President Marcos in favour of Corazon Aquino in 1986. Although the threat from Communist rebels has barely been controlled, there was some hope that the damage caused by Marcos' 'crony capitalism' could be repaired and the economy put back on a better footing.

This kind of close involvement in the domestic politics of allies is in part a function of an alliance between a superpower and a developing state. It is certainly not evident in the United States' alliances with NATO states or even Japan. It remains the major problem in the United States–Philippines alliance and, unlike the alliance with South Korea, is not balanced by a shared perception of an imminent, common enemy. The necessity to make the alliance with the Philippines work is strong, but not quite as strong as in North-east Asia.

Few of the other American bases in the Pacific are either as close to Asia, or as complicated by significant local opposition. In mid-Pacific there is the American state of Hawaii. Further out towards Asia, on the same longitude as Melbourne, is Guam—part of the American Trust Territories that include the Marianas and the Caroline and Marshall Islands. These often barely populated islands are politically the near-ideal base, free of hostile neighbours and relatively free of hostile natives. Many were former colonial holdings of faded European powers which the United States picked up in its slog through the islands in the Second World War.

One of the more difficult of these otherwise unbothersome islands is Palau, a tiny speck strategically located 500 km from the Philippines and 3000 km from Japan. Unfortunately for the United States, its 15 000 people have refused to go quietly the way of most of the other United States Trust Territories and adopt a Compact of Free Association with the United States. The locals object to the militarization of their island and the stationing of nuclear weapons. The United States plans to expand Palau's role as a refuelling and support base for naval and air operations in the western Pacific.[40] From the American point of view, Palau would be the best replacement for the Philippine bases if they should be forced to move.

It is unlikely that the United States can be forced to surrender its collection of bases in the western Pacific. There is simply not sufficient population on these territories, or powerful enough hostile neighbours, to force the United States back to its own side of the Pacific. Thus even if the far more vital bases in South Korea or the Philippines might be lost, the United States will retain its core of military power in the western Pacific. In that sense, American power in the Atlantic is more vulnerable than it is in the Pacific. Apparently the only really secure base is a sparsely populated colony or a distant bit of sovereign territory.

AMERICA'S MULTILATERAL ALLIANCES

Despite the difficulty in constructing multilateral alliances around the changing balances of power in the Pacific, there have been some attempts which have not entirely collapsed. While it is true that the United States has mostly given up the search for comprehensive 'macro-security networks' in the Pacific, there are still some who try to keep the hope of a Pacific NATO alive.[41] But the emphasis on bilateral alliances remains dominant.

To some extent, the need for a comprehensive, multilateral security system has diminished with the improvements in the technologies of war and communication. Especially as the United States is not waging war on the Asian continent, there is less need for the massive support that bases can provide. Intelligence can now be gathered adequately from space, and AWACS surveillance aircraft have vastly increased range. What is more, as the American definition of the adversary has changed, the need to be prepared to wage war in Asia has diminished.[42] Coupled with the enduring

---

[40] McIntosh, *Arms Across the Pacific*.

[41] Contrast the regionalist perspectives of Masashi Nishihara, *East Asian Security* (London: The Triangle Papers, 30, 1985); Donald Hugh McMillen (ed.), *Asian Perspectives on International Security* (London: Macmillan, 1984); and the more macro-oriented Tow and Feeney (eds.), *Asian-Pacific Security*.

[42] Feeney, 'Pacific Basing System'.

problems of independent-minded allies and the emphasis in the region on the diplomacy of the merchant rather than of the warrior, the argument for bases and a co-ordinated alliance has faded.

To be sure, the new emphasis on naval and offshore power still requires a network of bases. But the United States retains sufficient reliable friends and enough territory that it controls on its own to make a NATO-like structure unnecessary. The southern link in this system is one of the few surviving multilateral military alliances in the Pacific, ANZUS.

When negotiations began in 1950 for the treaty linking Australia, New Zealand, and the United States, it was already clear that New Zealand would have simply been happy enough to obtain a unilateral American statement promising to protect New Zealand, much as Washington had given to the Canadians in 1938.[43] Even after the ANZUS pact was agreed, New Zealand felt it necessary to reach a public bilateral agreement with Australia that they would help each other in case of attack.[44] But ANZUS finally came into effect in April 1952 in a treaty that met Australia's desire for a more formal and multilateral arrangement. The course of the last world war and the retreat of British power had left Australia more convinced than ever that the United States had to be the new strategic partner.[45] From the United States' point of view, it is instructive that highest-grade intelligence has been shared with only two Pacific states, Australia and New Zealand.[46]

The main American desire was to ensure that it had secure bases in the southern Pacific, as in the Pacific part of the Second World War, and to safeguard lines of communication. The United States was not particularly worried whether Australia and New Zealand wanted to take a leading role in the immediate affairs of smaller south Pacific islands. New Zealand trained soldiers from Fiji while Australia airlifted Papua New Guinean troops to Vanuatu in 1980 and raised and trained the Papua New Guinea armed forces.[47] Australia has also funded listening posts in such places as the Solomon Islands.[48] But ANZUS was never a front-line alliance, being as far from the nearest conflict with Communists in South-east Asia as Chad was from the Brandenburg gate. It is true that America's ANZUS partners sent

[43] Ranesh Thakur, *In Defence of New Zealand* (Boulder, Colo.: Westview, 1986); Michael McKinley, 'ANZUS' in Khil and Grinter (eds.), *Asian-Pacific Security.*

[44] H. W. Degenhardt, *Treaties and Alliances of the World* (London: Longman, 1981); L. Ziring and C. I. E. Kim, *Asian Political Dictionary* (Oxford: ABC Clio, 1985).

[45] Henry Albinski, *The Australian–American Security Relationship* (London: University of Queensland Press, 1982).

[46] Peter Wright, *Spycatcher* (New York: Penguin, 1987), 276.

[47] Henry Albinski, 'The US Security Alliance System in the South West Pacific' in Tow and Feeney (eds.), *Asian-Pacific Security.*

[48] *Jane's Defence Weekly* (7 November 1987).

troops to Korea and Vietnam, but it was not done formally as an ANZUS operation. All three stayed out of any major confrontation with Indonesia, apart from one in 1964–5, which was in any case regarded as a state leaning to the western camp.

Seldom tested as a multilateral alliance, ANZUS was always little more than a nominal cover for a bilateral American–Australian relationship. The Americans regularly took a harder line on the Chinese and then Soviet roles in the Pacific. There were also differences of opinion on how much the Americans should spend to keep the other south Pacific islanders from causing problems by inviting foreign influences, and how much the ANZUS members should contribute to such out-of-area operations as the Gulf.[49] Australia and New Zealand were also consistently wary about how much defence co-operation could be considered with Japan.

The United States continued to be primarily interested in its ANZUS partners as a place for friendly port calls and above all for listening posts and communications bases as a vital link in the global American system.[50] For Australia, American access to these facilities was not an excessive price to pay for overarching security in an otherwise peaceful environment. Although Australia has at times been very exercised about threats from France, Russia, Japan, China, and latterly the Soviet Union, by the 1970s most direct threats were seen as remote.[51] The real problems were those of maintaining regional stability so as to promote economic exchanges and access through vital straits.[52] Australia gradually came to see the Americans as much in economic as in military terms.[53] The nature of ANZUS was changing.

The publication of the Australian Defence White Paper in March 1987, based on the Dibb report, marked a new stage in Australian defence.[54] The orientation was now to defence in depth, focused more on the home region.[55] The _de facto_ strategy was one of 'denial', and in some senses it mirrored the low-key Japanese strategy. Australia planned to rely on America's intelligence and its nuclear umbrella, and the ability to buy weapons off American shelves.

[49] See Robert O'Neill and D. M. Horner (eds.), _Australian Defence Policy for the 1980s_ (London: University of Queensland Press, 1982) for a discussion of these differences.
[50] Desmond Ball, 'US Installations in Australia' in Claude Buss (ed.), _National Security Interests in the Pacific Basin_ (Stanford, Calif.: Hoover Institution, 1985).
[51] Norman Harper, _The Great and the Powerful_ (London: University of Queensland Press, 1987); more specifically, Ross Babbage, _Rethinking Australia's Defence_ (London: University of Queensland Press, 1980).
[52] Robert O'Neill, 'Australia's Perception of Threats to their Security' in Morrison (ed.), _Threats to Security_.
[53] T. B. Millar, 'Australia and the Security of the Pacific Basin' in Buss (ed.), _National Security_.
[54] Ross Babbage, 'Australian Defence Policy Review' in _Pacific Review_, 1/1 (1988).
[55] _Financial Times_ (20 March 1987); _Far Eastern Economic Review_ (19 June 1986).

This step back from alliance entanglements, except for the immediate defence of Australia, meant that by 1984 ANZUS had all but become a bilateral Australian–American affair. Further problems in ANZUS came with the election of a Labour government in New Zealand that acted on public pressure for a ban on all nuclear-powered and nuclear-armed ships. The Americans, fearing the spread of what it called the 'Euro-disease' of anti-nuclearism, took a hard line in warning that such a policy would remove New Zealand from ANZUS. In June 1986 the American Secretary of State declared that New Zealand was no longer considered a member of ANZUS, although it remained a friend.[56]

With more than 40 per cent of the American navy nuclear-powered, and the risks of sending the wrong message to other allies, this firm American line was almost inevitable.[57] But given New Zealand's already acute sense of distance from the rest of the world's conflicts, it was equally inevitable that New Zealand would not take kindly to being pushed around by a super-power ally.[58] Australia ultimately sided with the United States on this issue, but it was clearly not as upset as the United States.[59] While New Zealand was prepared to leave the treaty in limbo, Australia still felt the need for formal links to the United States.

As ANZUS staggered on, a number of other less formal multilateral military co-operation projects were under way. Although SEATO had collapsed in 1977, the South-east Asia Collective Defence Treaty of 8 September 1954 (the Manila Pact) which set it up was still not formally defunct. A number of its members continued to mount small-scale operations for a wide range of reasons. In 1971 the RIMPAC naval exercises based in Hawaii tied in the United States, Canada, Australia, New Zealand, and later Japan. In 1986 such exercises also involved Britain in an operation that some in the United States were hoping might lead to a Pacific NATO.[60] But the presence of Britain, let alone the location and scale of the exercises, suggested more a political stunt than a serious military operation or the precursor to a more formal alliance.

Before 1967 and its withdrawal east of Suez, Britain had been a significant military presence in the Pacific. As part of its military commitment to the defence of Malaya, it had entered into the Anglo-Malaya Defence Agreement (AMDA) on 12 October 1957. It was intended to tie together some Pacific Commonwealth states as they gained independence. Australia and

56 *International Herald Tribune* (18 June 1986).
57 Dora Alves, 'ANZUS In 1985' in *Asia- Pacific Defense Forum* (winter 1985–6).
58 Richard Kennaway, 'The Interests and Policies of New Zealand' in Buss (ed.), *National Security*.
59 McKinley, 'ANZUS'.
60 *Observer* (15 June 1986).

New Zealand associated themselves with this arrangement in 1959.[61] Australia had been looking for firm western security links in the Pacific, and thus had joined SEATO. But AMDA did not include the same members as SEATO, and remained a loose consultative framework rather than an effective alliance.

In November 1971 it was transformed into the Five Power Defence Arrangement (FPDA) including Singapore. Clearly the anchor of the alliance had shifted from Britain to Australia, which took over parts of the British role in reassuring Malaysia and Singapore. Yet with the demise of SEATO and trouble in ANZUS, by the 1980s the FPDA remained the only multilateral military alliance in the Pacific, and one which included non-Pacific Britain rather than the United States. Britain also provided troops for the defence of Brunei on the basis of five-yearly 'contracts', the first one in 1983.

FPDA exercises included the regular operation of Australian naval ships in South-east Asia.[62] They continued in 1986 even with the New Zealand navy, although the United States suspended similar exercises because of the anti-nuclear row.[63] But the FPDA seemed to be a less serious attempt at building multilateral security. The presence of Britain suggested a more symbolic venture, or at best a general reaffirmation that, in the modern age, deterrence of threats was a global strategy.

The FPDA seemed to fit better with the series of bilateral and multilateral efforts that many western-inclined states have pursued in the western Pacific since the victory of the Indo-Chinese Communists in 1975 and the withdrawal of Britain from east of Suez after 1967. Malaysia and Indonesia had been exercising together since 1959 and Malaysia and the Philippines since 1967. Singapore and Indonesia had joint exercises against smugglers in 1974. In 1975 New Zealand, Malaysia, and Singapore held joint exercises of mechanized infantry.[64] But these intermittent exercises were far from constituting a regular pattern and permanent command structure as in NATO. Similarly, Sino-American military co-operation, for example in the establishment of a joint listening post in China to monitor the Soviet Union, was an act of convenience that fell far short of full strategic co-operation. Co-production deals on weapons between China and various West Europeans was in a similar category, and held no more significance than the Soviet agreement in 1987 to refurbish China's main steel plant producing

[61] Chin Kim Wah, *The Defence of Malaysia and Singapore* (Cambridge: Cambridge University Press, 1983).

[62] Albinski, 'US Security'.

[63] *The Times* (16 August 1986).

[64] Robert Rau, 'Southeast Asian Security in the 1980s' in Tow and Feeney (eds.), *Asian-Pacific Security*.

Chinese military equipment.[65] Ultimately, the security concerns of the local actors were too diverse and too changeable for the building of broad, multilateral alliances.[66]

SOVIET AND CHINESE ALLIES

With all these complicated and intertwining western alliances, it is surprising to find fewer equivalents in the Communist Pacific. It is not purely propaganda when the Soviet Union denounces the FPDA, RIMPAC, and other naval exercises as an attempt to create an interlocking pattern of Pacific alliances.[67] There are few formal inter-Communist alliances in the Pacific, and most of those which do exist involve the Soviet Union.

Yet the essence of any alliance is a number of important *de facto* alignments. The Sino-Soviet alliance has already been discussed, and *de facto* the Vietnamese and Chinese were in alliance for much of the Vietnam war. Without a publicly formal accord, Chinese and Soviet air-defence troops fought in North Vietnam and suffered casualties.

In China's earlier venture beyond its frontiers, in Korea, it was reportedly operating under the terms of a formal, albeit secret, accord.[68] China certainly shed a great deal of blood in defence of its Korean ally—a million casualties at a rough estimate. In most respects, the Chinese guarantee to North Korea remains as much in force as it did over 35 years ago. But it was only in 1961 that a formal security pact—China's only surviving agreement of that sort—was signed with North Korea. What has really changed since the Korean War is China's willingness to tolerate North Korean adventurism and a risky policy that might distract China from its modernization and bring it into conflict with the United States.

But as has already been discussed, the changed balance of power resulting from the Sino-Soviet rift gave Pyongyang increased leverage by allowing it to play one ally off against the other. Only when both Communist powers pursued *détente* with the United States, or with each other, was North Korean leverage reduced. By the later 1980s it was quite clear that both China and the Soviet Union would not allow North Korea to begin another round of fighting if they could help it. Both alliances with North Korea were

[65] *Jane's Defence Weekly* (19 December 1987).

[66] See the series of local arguments in Morrison (ed.), *Threats to Security*; McMillen (ed.), *Asian Perspectives*.

[67] For example, *Krasnaya Zvezda* in BBC, SWB, SU, 8254, A3, 2 (4 May 1986); various reports on Moscow Radio in 8293, A3, 1–3 (17–20 June 1986).

[68] Gerald Segal, *Defending China* (Oxford: Oxford University Press, 1985), ch. 6.

for the defence of territory, not a blank cheque for the North Koreans to ruin the domestic and foreign policies of their patrons. Alliances, especially informal ones, are only as good as their coincidence of interests.

The longest coincidence of interests for the Soviet Union and an East Asian state has been with Mongolia. Its 1946 pact was Moscow's first in the post-war Pacific and was fairly forthright in promising Soviet support if Mongolia was attacked. At this time, before the founding of the People's Republic of China, this pact was as much a part of Stalin's bilateral pactomania, as seen in eastern Europe at this time, as it was specifically aimed at a perceived threat. In February 1966 a newer Soviet–Mongolian security treaty was signed, which this time was clearly aimed at the Chinese threat. It was the basis for the stationing of large numbers of Soviet troops in Mongolia and was perceived by China as part of a Soviet attempt to encircle it in Asia.

Yet this was clearly a time of ambiguities in alliances in the Communist Pacific. Both China and the Soviet Union signed security pacts with North Korea in 1961, while trying to restrain North Korean adventurism. Neither Communist power had a public agreement with North Vietnam, despite providing huge military supplies in the war against the United States and South Vietnam. And of course, the Soviet Union and China itself were still nominal allies while killing each other's soldiers along the frontier.

The main problem for the Soviet Union in the mid-1960s was what structure was to be devised to replace the failed Sino-Soviet alliance. In the 1960s the Soviet Union sought a formal series of friends in Asia, mainly to counteract China, and in 1969 Leonid Brezhnev proposed an Asia-wide collective security scheme.[69] Only India and Mongolia expressed any interest, and the Soviet Union found other socialist states wary of upsetting China by joining. But from 1975 Vietnam found its relations with China deteriorating. When war seemed likely and the United States and China were making progress in normalizing relations, Vietnam turned to the Soviet Union for formal support.[70]

A 25-year treaty was signed on 3 November 1978 that promised only 'mutual consultation' if either signatory was attacked. Neither side was apparently under any illusion that this was anything but a pact of convenience only reluctantly accepted by Vietnam. The Soviet Union obtained another formal ally as a counterweight to China. Vietnam obtained more formal protection against China before Hanoi invaded Kampuchea. Its

---

[69] Donald Zagoria (ed.), *Soviet Policy in East Asia* (London: Yale University Press, 1982); Gerald Segal (ed.), *The Soviet Union In East Asia* (London: Heinemann, 1983).

[70] Leszek Buszynski, *Soviet Foreign Policy and Southeast Asia* (London: Croom Helm, 1986).

attempt to balance the treaty with more economic co-operation with Japan failed, and Hanoi found itself deeper in political hock to Moscow.

Vietnam was later to find itself under Chinese pressure in 1979 and, in an effort to relieve some of the burden, apparently traded Soviet access to bases in Indo-China in exchange for increased financial aid. By the late 1980s Vietnam was costing the Soviet Union some $5 million a day in aid and a great deal in international prestige, especially with China and in South-east Asia. A Soviet calculation of burdens and benefits from this alliance had to be finely balanced.

As a result, Mikhail Gorbachev began pressing Vietnam to reform at home and improve relations with its neighbours, including Thailand and China. As part of its effort to improve Sino-Soviet relations, the Soviet Union began discussing the Vietnamese problem at the biannual talks with China and sent the Soviet Foreign Minister on a tour of the region in 1987. Vietnamese reforms were begun at the end of 1986 and by early 1989 Vietnam had promised to withdraw its troops from Kampuchea, thereby reducing the Vietnamese drain on the Soviet economy.

If this relationship was an example of what alliances could bring, the Soviet Union was unlikely to be enthusiastic. Of course, if relations with China and ASEAN could improve while the Soviet Union retained its Indo-Chinese bases, as appeared likely by 1989, then the balance sheet would look far better. With the emphasis in Moscow on economic modernization at home, even for a Communist state an alliance balance sheet in the red can be tolerated only for a limited period.

Thus Gorbachev amended the Asian collective security scheme in a major speech at Vladivostok in July 1986. Instead of building an anti-Chinese alliance, the idea was to formulate an Asian version of the European Helsinki and CSCE scheme of regional security. Like at Helsinki, the Soviet Union was willing to recognize the North American states as legitimate members of the regional scheme. While the Soviet Union was really proposing a strategy to improve its own image in the region, and especially towards China, this new scheme was at least a far more positive attempt to forge genuine Pacific-wide ties. But unlike Europe, there were no real salient issues that could be realistically negotiated between relatively coherent groupings of states. The same diversity that ruined attempts to form opposing alliances in the Pacific would no doubt harm efforts at building regional security.

PATTERNS IN THE ARMS TRADE

One of the best guides to alliances and alignments is the amount and types of weapons provided to friendly regimes.[71] While the gathering and analysis of arms-transfer statistics is notoriously complex, it is possible to identify major trends and patterns of international relationships.[72] The most striking trends in the Pacific are the decline in the overall trade of weapons and the variable pattern of main purchasers and sellers.

When wars raged in East Asia, the area was a booming market for arms transfers. In 1955 East Asia and Oceania took 48 per cent of total transfers of major weapons to developing states and the figure remained at that level until the early 1960s.[73] Although the absolute value of transfers has increased to the present day, in constant 1985 dollars, other markets increased faster. In the 1960s the region took around 25 per cent of all transfers to developing states and by 1975 the figure had dropped to 10 per cent. In the 1980s the figure hovered in the low teens, making it by far the smallest regional arms market in the developing world.

The major arms suppliers to these developing states in East Asia and Oceania have been the superpowers. In 1951–5 the United States held 64 per cent of the market in major arms while the Soviet Union took 24 per cent, China 3 per cent, and the big four West European exporters 4 per cent. The Soviet Union's share rose to 46 per cent in 1966–70 as it poured weapons into Vietnam. However, by the first half of the 1980s it was back down to 25 per cent of the market. The American market share only regained its early 1950s peak in the first half of the 1970s when it was trying to stand the South Vietnamese armed forces on their own two feet. By the first half of the 1980s its market share had fallen to 46 per cent.

While overall Chinese arms sales increased sharply in the 1980s, its share of its home region fell to 2 per cent. In common with most exporters, China was concentrating on the lucrative Middle East. The real surprise for true believers in a Pacific world that has little place for the Europeans was the rise of West European arms sellers to the Pacific. Their market share climbed to 10 per cent in the early 1970s and 15 per cent in the early 1980s.

The developing states were obviously the main market for arms transfers. Not quite comparative figures for overall arms transfers to the region reveal

---

[71] Andrew Pierre, *The Global Politics of Arms Sales* (Princeton: Princeton University Press, 1982).

[72] Ibid.; Anne Gilks and Gerald Segal, *China and the Arms Trade* (London: Croom Helm, 1985).

[73] Michael Brzoska and Thomas Ohlson, *Arms Transfers to the Third World, 1971–85* (Oxford: Oxford University Press, 1987).

a similar pattern.[74] East Asian and Oceanic states imported 40 per cent of all weapons in 1967 and 35 per cent in 1972, but only 17 per cent in 1975 and 15 per cent in 1980 and 1985. Their exports were a mere 4 per cent of world totals in 1971 but under 1 per cent in the 1980s. In the period 1967–76 the region took 28 per cent of total arms transfers and by 1981–5 the figure was down to 10 per cent. As wars slowed down or terminated, arms transfers fell off. The best form of arms control was ending wars.

In the 1967–76 period the United States was the main supplier to Taiwan, Cambodia, Indonesia, Japan, Korea, Laos, Malaysia, the Philippines, Singapore, Thailand, South Vietnam, and its ANZUS allies, while the Soviet Union held the lead only with China, North Korea, North Vietnam, and Mongolia. But by the early 1980s the West Europeans had strengthened their position, especially in Singapore, and were leading the markets in Indonesia and Malaysia. The Soviet Union became the main supplier to Kampuchea and Laos, while holding a lead over the United States, but not the West Europeans, in the China market.

In line with the decline in conflict in the Pacific, the United States' supply of weapons to its NATO allies in Europe, which had been only 60 per cent of the total to East Asia in 1967–76, was 30 per cent greater than to East Asia. The Soviet Union found its support for Vietnam and North Korea was relatively more costly, rising from 45 per cent of its transfers to Warsaw Pact allies in 1967–76 to 60 per cent in the first half of the 1980s. These figures suggest that European states were more involved in the Pacific arms market than ever before while the interest of the United States had waned. This trend may reflect America's less military-minded view of the region, or simply the increased interest and attractiveness of the West European sellers.

The main markets were of two types. In the 1967–76 period they were the states at war, with the Vietnams taking 56 per cent of the market, the Koreas 16 per cent, and Taiwan 9 per cent. In the first half of the 1980s it was wealthy but peaceful Japan which took 20 per cent, just ahead of Vietnam on 19 per cent, the two Koreas on 15 per cent, and Taiwan on 14 per cent. Weapons were increasingly acquired for deterrence rather than use.

With this trend towards less war and more of a weapons-for-deterrence strategy, it was not surprising that some East Asian states became more active arms suppliers themselves. Japan could have been a major force in the market but prohibited from doing so by its constitution. The growing Japanese defence industries suggested that, like the West Europeans, Japan might soon become a major arms supplier, thereby further reducing the American market share.[75] Some developing states, notably China, were

[74] *World Military Expenditures and Arms Transfers* (United States Arms Control and Disarmament Agency, various volumes, especially 1979 and 1987).

[75] Drifte, *Arms Production.*

already taking a far more active part. However, for China, by the mid-1980s apparently the world's fourth-largest arms exporter, and the other East Asians such as the Koreas and Singapore, the main markets were further afield. Although all these states produced most of their equipment for their own forces, they, like the rest of the arms traders, found a lucrative market in the war-torn Middle East. A more peaceful Pacific was less important as an arms market for any major exporter, even the locals.

In sum, there is a maze of alliances in the Pacific, most of which are oriented to and run by the United States. There has never been a comprehensive security scheme for the Pacific, and if anything the course of events since 1945 suggests this has become even less likely. The balances of power have shifted more radically than in any other region and thereby destroyed or destabilized the foundations of most alliances.

The United States retains far more allies in the Pacific than the Soviet Union or any other state. Japan keeps a low profile, leaving the United States to bear the burdens. Most American allies are dissatisfied with American leadership and, with the exception of Japan, Australia, and Korea, are not strong supporters of the relationship. Yet they all retain friendly ties with the United States. This suggests that the New Zealand model of alliance on its own terms may yet be as attractive to many states as the United States feared.

16

Arms Control and Disarmament

Since the Second World War the Pacific has led the way in the number of war-deaths. Nearly half the total of 17 million such deaths since 1945 have been in East Asia.[1] Wars in Korea and South-east Asia have been some of the most vicious in the modern era. Apart from this sad record, some states are also facing serious internal security problems. The resulting increase in military spending by Pacific states is obvious. But arms races are unlikely to solve problems of insecurity, indeed they often help exacerbate tension.

In the Atlantic world, these problems of war and arms races have been addressed through arms control.[2] Of course, arms control remains a way of enhancing state security, but it is based on the notion that international or common security can contribute to national security. The Pacific has had virtually no experience of formal arms control.

However, it would also be wrong to see arms control as the exclusive preserve of Europeans or of the superpowers. At its most fundamental, arms control is 'restraint internationally exercised upon armaments, whether in respect of the level of armaments, their character, deployment or use'.[3] Thus arms control is concerned with everything from controlling the numbers of troops and weapons to establishing demilitarized zones, arranging for confidence-building visits to enemy manoeuvres, or bringing outside observers to monitor troop disengagement. There is nothing ethnocentric about this idea.[4] It is simply sensible in most cases to help control the risks and scale of war by limiting the implements of destruction. If parts of the Pacific are at war, then it makes sense to try to limit or end those wars. It would be a regrettable act of 'ethnic-chic' to suggest that arms control has no place in the Pacific.

---

[1] Figures include civilian deaths as a result of war, with an estimated 4.5 million in East Asia and 1.9 million in South Asia.

[2] Barry Buzan, *Introduction to Strategic Studies* (London: Macmillan, 1987), pt 2.

[3] Hedley Bull, *The Control of the Arms Race* (London: Weidenfeld, 1961), p. ix.

[4] It has been suggested by some developing states in Asia that arms control is a superpower or European idea and thus that it is ethnocentric to discuss it in the Asian context. At best this is a semantic argument; more likely it is a rhetorical flourish. In 1985 alone, India held talks with five other non-aligned states in Delhi explicitly about arms control (27–9 January), and discussed such detailed matters as enhancing verification procedures with Sweden in October–November. For a critique of ethnocentrism see Ken Booth, *Strategy and Ethnocentrism* (London: Croom Helm, 1979); Gerald Segal, 'Strategy and Ethnic-chic' in *International Affairs*, 60/1 (1983–4).

Of course, it would be ethnocentric to suggest that arms control as developed in the European and superpower context is directly applicable to the Pacific. In fact, such Pacific arms control as has already developed shows signs of forming a distinctive pattern. Instead of focusing on formal agreements, with all the related problems of counting weapons and agreeing verification, Pacific arms control has tended to be more informal, but at times no less successful than its European variant. What is more, Pacific arms control is usually more concerned with conventional than with nuclear weapons, and with confidence-building measures and demilitarization than with the reduction of weapons.

THE ACHIEVEMENTS OF PACIFIC ARMS

There have been remarkably few formal arms-control agreements in the Pacific since 1945, and even fewer that are still worth the paper they were written on. In the two most important relationships in global times, the superpower balance in the Pacific and Sino-Soviet relations, there has been no significant formally agreed arms control. Yet the powers in the Pacific have not been entirely dismissive of arms control. Some agreements have been enshrined in documents, and others have emerged tacitly.

The most formal arms-control regime is the 1968 Non-Proliferation Treaty (NPT). Although this is not strictly a Pacific treaty, it does have special implications for arms control in the region. Three states in the area have a nuclear weapons capability, the two superpowers and China. Only two, however, have signed the NPT. China denounced the treaty as an attempt to impose superpower hegemony.

In recent years China has become a *de facto* adherent of the NPT. It has accepted IAEA safeguards in civilian nuclear co-operation agreements with other countries and has taken a more positive approach to verification.[5] The latest adherent to the NPT is North Korea, which also suggests strong Soviet interest coinciding with that of China to control the Korean conflict. The signature was a precondition of the Soviet sale of a nuclear-power plant to North Korea.

China and Japan have also played their parts, informally, in controlling the nuclear risks in the Pacific. China has developed a wide range of nuclear weaponry, but with small numbers in each category. It therefore has little available surplus for cutting and minimizes the threat to its neighbours. Of

[5] Reinhard Drifte, 'China and the NPT' in Joseph Goldblatt (ed.), *Non-Proliferation* (London: Taylor & Francis, 1985), 45–55; Gerald Segal, 'China and Arms Control' in *World Today* (August 1985).

course, some of China's smaller neighbours will feel threatened even by China's minimal deterrent.

Japan had imposed upon it, and then warmly adopted, the non-nuclear principle. Japan has promised not to acquire nuclear weapons and, as the only victim of a nuclear weapon fired in anger, it has a particular sensitivity to becoming nuclearized. Although it clearly has the economic and techno-logical capability to develop a first-rate nuclear arsenal, Japan has foresworn the option and therefore reduced the incentive for others to go nuclear.[6] Of course, Japan shelters under the American nuclear umbrella, however tacitly.

A more formal agreement, on the eastern edge of the Pacific, is the treaty for the prohibition of nuclear weapons in Latin America. It was signed in February 1967 at Tlatelolco in Mexico and came into force at first for Mexico and El Salvador in April 1968. Its purpose is to ban the testing, use, manufacture, production, or acquisition of nuclear weapons in the region. Argentina has signed but not ratified the treaty and Brazil, Chile, and Trinidad and Tobago say they would be bound by it only when all the other Latin American states have ratified it. Cuba and Guyana are the only states that refuse to sign. All five nuclear powers have agreed to the protocol respecting the terms of the treaty. While the treaty has not been a complete success, at least there has been no proliferation of nuclear weapons to this eastern side of the Pacific.

In part because of this relative success for multilateral arms control, a similar idea has been tried more recently in the south Pacific with the signature of the Treaty of Raratonga for a South Pacific Nuclear-Free Zone. It was first proposed by Australia in 1983 to a meeting of the South Pacific Forum and was formulated in general principles at a Forum meeting in Tuvalu in 1984. At Raratonga, Cook Islands in 1985, the heads of govern-ment of the Forum came up with a draft agreement.[7] The treaty, which entered into force in December 1986, intends to prevent the deployment of nuclear weapons on the territory of states in the area, but would not ban their transit through the zone. Nor would such a partial nuclear-free zone make the south Pacific a nuclear-safe zone, as weapons can be targeted on the region from thousands of kilometres away.[8]

The treaty had its roots in growing concern about French nuclear testing in Tahiti and the increased risks of nuclear war affecting the one region of

---

[6] Reinhard Drifte, 'Diplomacy' in J. W. M. Chapman, R. Drifte, and I. T. M. Gow, *Japan's Quest for Comprehensive Security* (London: Frances Pinter, 1983).

[7] *International Herald Tribune* (30 May 1986).

[8] F. A. Mediansky, 'The South Pacific Nuclear Free Zone' in *Asian-Pacific Defense Forum* (winter 1985–6).

[8] *Far Eastern Economic Review* (15 May 1986).

the world that had hoped to escape a nuclear holocaust. The row in ANZUS over port visits by American nuclear-armed and nuclear-powered ships was part of this process. Not surprisingly, therefore, the United States, France, and Britain refused to abide by the terms of the treaty, while the Soviet Union and China promised to do so.

A more successful, but not specifically nuclear, arms-limitation treaty was the Antarctic Pact of 1959, which entered into force when it was signed by 12 states in 1961. It banned the militarization of this remote region of 13.7 million sq. km which holds three-quarters of the world's store of fresh water. The signatories to the pact agreed to defer all territorial claims until 1991 while scientific research was carried on. A number of islands were claimed by more than one state and there were disputes over fishing and mineral rights.

The 12 original signatories included a wide range of states, as befits the location of the Antarctic on the fringe of the Atlantic, Pacific, and Indian Oceans. Of the 12, six were Pacific states (Australia, Chile, Japan, New Zealand, and the two superpowers), four were European (France, Britain, Belgium, Norway), and the others were Argentina and South Africa. Of the eight others who later signed the pact, seven were European and the other was Atlantic-facing Brazil. The existing Antarctic claims include the major Pacific territories of Chile, New Zealand, Australia, and France, while the only unclaimed area lies between the claims of New Zealand and Chile. The Antarctic treaty is a tribute to what arms control can do if it gets under way before a region is militarized. But the treaty has also benefited from the Antarctic's remoteness, and from the high cost of maintaining a claim by scientific research for anyone but a wealthy nation. While some members of the non-aligned organization in the Pacific have opposed this carve-up of the Antarctic, they do not see the issue as a priority and lack the means to exploit the region.[9]

The superpowers have also agreed to two minor measures that can be classed as confidence-building arms control. In 1972 they agreed to help reduce incidents at sea and in 1985 they agreed with Japan to help assist air safety after Soviet aircraft shot down a civilian Korean airliner. Both agreements remain in force and have been useful in their own, minor way. Both sides see clear limits but a useful role for measures in these essentially technical spheres. Neither superpower has an interest in conflict arising from uncontrolled disputes and tensions. Because the East–West division in the Pacific is less clear than in Europe it is all the more important to ensure mechanisms for limiting misunderstanding. This basic confidence-building exercise is often a first step to ensuring the stability necessary for future *détente* and more formal arms control.

[9] *Far Eastern Economic Review* (15 May 1986).

Perhaps the most formal arms-control measures in the Pacific were those agreed as part of the end of the Korean War in 1953. The armistice of 27 July 1953 created a demilitarized zone that nominally remains in force today. Four states were appointed as part of a neutral supervizing commission, and all were from Europe (Sweden, Switzerland, Poland, and Czechoslovakia).[10] However, the zone has been repeatedly violated and there have been more than 30 years of very frigid cold war between North and South Korea. Arguably, arms control helped control a conflict to the limited extent that both parties desired, but in practice, it has not done a great deal to advance the cause of peace in the region.[11]

The most important *détente* in inter-Korean relations has come about because of changes in the wider balance of power and especially the periods of *détente* in great-power relations. South Korea only dropped its version of the Hallstein Doctrine in 1973 and established diplomatic relations with states who had similar ties with the North. By 1980, when Kim Il Sung was arguing for 'one country, two systems', he was moving in large part because China had offered similar terms to Taiwan.

Further south, another series of arms-control agreements existed fleetingly in the various phases of the Indo-China conflict. The 1954 Geneva Accord managed the difficult process of the withdrawal of French troops. But it proved a dismal failure in controlling future conflict. The essential problem was that the Geneva agreement tried to freeze a conflict that was unresolved. Crucially, the agreement was also undermined by the United States, which was hostile to neutralism in an area where it perceived a 'Communist' threat. Further agreements in Geneva in 1962 attempted to organize the politics of Laos in particular, and were similarly unsuccessful.[12]

The Paris peace agreements of 1973 punctuated yet another phase of the Vietnam War. American troop withdrawals were part of a package that was also supposed to restrict the flow of arms from North to South Vietnam. But the agreement was never observed in its essentials, except in that it allowed the United States a modicum of honour when it departed the war.

In 1989, when Vietnam essentially was pushed by the Soviet Union into withdrawing from Kampuchea, Vietnam decided to go without a formal agreement. It merely proposed that those countries that supervised in the agreements of the 1950s be called back into service in 1989. This unilateral arms control was even more pragmatic than the fig-leaf of United Nations supervision at the time of the Soviet withdrawal from Afghanistan, earlier in 1989.

---

10 Brian Bridges, *Korea and the West* (London: Chatham House Paper, 33, 1986).

11 George Tan Eng Bok, 'Arms Control in Korea' in Gerald Segal (ed.), *Arms Control in Asia* (London: Macmillan, 1987).

12 Anne Gilks, 'Arms Control in Southeast Asia' in Segal (ed.), *Arms Control*.

However, such pessimism about the results of formal arms control in Asia ignores the less formal achievements. Sino-Soviet relations have begun to benefit from tacit arms control in the form of confidence-building measures such as the thinning out of troops along the border and withdrawals to create *de facto* demilitarized zones. The thinning out of Soviet divisions has, depending on how the counting is done, reduced the actual number of Soviet soldiers on the frontier by about 80 000.[13] China officially cut its armed forces by 1 million men by 1987, so that there has been at least an equal reduction in combat troops from the Chinese side. Such measures have achieved more than the long-running MBFR process in Europe, albeit without formal agreement. In March 1987 China and Mongolia began talks on confidence-building measures along their frontier, but only after the Soviet Union had announced a unilateral withdrawal of more than a division of Soviet troops from Mongolia.[14] In December 1988 Mikhail Gorbachev announced that the Soviet Union would withdraw all but a division of troops from Mongolia by 1991 as part of a reduction of 200 000 troops in the Far Eastern theatre. In this tacit, virtuous circle of arms control, China was reportedly planning to cut a further 500 000 soldiers from the PLA rolls.

PROBLEMS WITH PACIFIC ARMS CONTROL

Most types of arms control have never been easy to achieve, even in the decade of superpower *détente*, the 1970s. In the more than 20 years that arms control has been a main item on great powers' agendas, since the 1963 Partial Test Ban Treaty, there has emerged a voluminous literature on the problems and prospects for arms control. Most discussion has focused on the political roots of the negotiations, the problems of what to count, and the difficulty of counting anything at all. While these issues are important, they are not necessarily the main problems dogging arms control in the Pacific. In their order of importance, there are six main difficulties in reaching arms control in the Pacific.

---

[13] Details on the balance of forces in Gerald Segal, *Sino-Soviet Relations After Mao* (London: IISS, Aldephi Paper, 202, 1985). The precise number of troops in the Soviet divisions is a matter of much controversy, but the fact that the number of Soviet divisions has remained constant and that their state of readiness has been reduced is relatively uncontested. Basic figures are in *Military Balance* (IISS).
[14] BBC, SWB, FE, 8516, i.

The Complexity of the Political Roots of Conflict

Arms control of any sort is pre-eminently a political process. It is pursued as an element of a state's security policy and must essentially be judged by whether it enhances first national security and second international security. Weapons are instruments of policy. It is competing politics which lie at the root of conflict, and weapons can be limited only if there is a more basic political will to compromise.[15]

In European and superpower relations the conflicts are real and important, but because of the overhanging nuclear threat both sides have settled for what is essentially a stable balance of competition and coexistence. By contrast, in many parts of the Pacific the political conflicts are often still hot, or just cooling. Wars are being fought and a great deal of blood has been shed during the past generation.[16]

Broadly speaking, two types of conflict in the Pacific can be outlined. First, there are the active wars, which are probably least susceptible to arms control because the political causes of conflict are unresolved and the combatants are still shedding each other's blood. The South-east Asian wars seem to fall into this category. Secondly, there are conflicts which seem to be under control and may be approaching European levels of controlled tension. These include the superpower balance in the Pacific and the Sino-Soviet conflict. The Korean conflict seems to hover somewhere between the two types, with a great deal of emotion becoming moderated by the passage of time. Nevertheless, conflict can easily flare up again as a result of domestic or foreign changes.

Clearly, successful arms control in the Pacific is more likely in specific areas where rivalries have begun to stabilize. What is more, the complexity of the politics of each conflict is distinctive, making a Pacific-wide approach to arms control unlikely.

The Balance of Power

The balance of power in Europe is essentially that between the superpowers and their alliances. Despite the presence of a nuclear-armed France or Britain, deterrence in Europe is a relatively simple equation of two major power blocs. Multilateral arms control, in the form of limits either on arms sales or on deployments, is easier to discuss, if not to achieve, because each side knows where the other stands and which forces should be counted.

In the Pacific there is no simple balance of power. Therefore multilateral

---

[15] Gerald Segal, 'Introduction' in Segal (ed.), *Arms Control*.
[16] Masashi Nishihara, *East Asian Security* (London: The triangle Papers, 30, 1985).

arms control is harder to achieve than bilateral arms control. There are significant superpower forces in the Pacific, but then there are also substantial Chinese and Vietnamese armed forces. There are in fact several balances of power and needless to say this is a nightmare for multilateral arms control. Do the superpowers merely count each other's forces or must allowance be made for the Chinese threat to the Soviet Union? But then is not China potentially a threat to the United States as well? How are Soviet 'swing' forces to be counted: are they to be included in a Pacific or European balance? Can Vietnam be counted as part of the Soviet camp? A messy picture indeed, and one that essentially defies any region-wide arms control.

The Pace of Modernization

In the European and superpower balance, the states concerned are all relatively modern and prosperous. While many do have domestic problems of development and intercommunal strife, these are comparatively few and far between. In any case, they rarely cause international problems across the East–West divide. The problems of Ireland and Turkey, or Poland and Czechoslovakia, are not a major cause of East–West conflict.

Pacific states are far less uniform. First, there is the unique case of Japan: a wealthy, developed economy with a relatively stable political system. Others, like the NICs are booming economically, but under rough-and-ready political systems. Yet others, such as most of the ASEAN states, are less developed, and many have serious domestic problems.

The poorer Pacific states have an even wider spectrum of domestic problems that can be said to result in international conflict. The Vietnam War was a bloody civil war that drew in various great powers on both sides. In its most recent phase it concerns the radical domestic politics of the Khmer Rouge in Kampuchea and Vietnam's attempt to install a more amenable regime in Phnom Penh. The Taiwan–China conflict is an unresolved civil war.

These, and indeed myriad other internal problems, are in large measure concerned with debates over the path of modernization. None of these issues looks like being easily resolved and therefore no swift end to conflict is likely. If the conflicts remain acute, there will be little room for meaningful arms control.

Defence Culture

Arms control is a 'game' that Europeans have been playing for a century or more in various guises. While it is true that none of the agreements concluded has lasted for long, states have seen a rationale for at least temporary relief from the pain of conflict. Therefore the defence policies of European states have come to accept formal arms control, and especially the notion of limiting arms races, as a useful instrument of policy—a component of defence culture.[17] For states with a tradition of operating in the state system and respecting certain aspects of international law, the concept of formal arms control that restrains arms races is almost natural.

In the Pacific, there is no such tradition. There is an instinctive rejection of 'colonial laws' and 'legacies of imperialism'. It is true that a great deal of this rhetoric is self-serving, often masking great-power aspirations by Pacific states. But there is a deeply held belief that rules are made by the powerful to control the weak and by the old to control the young. For young states with optimistic dreams, arms control is often seen merely as a charade to slap them down and to maintain the status quo.

Of course, this is not to suggest that Pacific states have pursued uncontrolled arms races and deployed forces without concern for reducing tensions. Tacit limitations on arms transfers to various regional conflicts have been a feature of regional politics since the Korean War. But it is striking that the defence cultures of Pacific states have not seen the necessity for formal arms control. As a result of broader assessments of 'balances of power' and the costs of unrestrained arms races, states in the Pacific have tacitly accepted restraint on weapons and tension. By focusing on western conceptions of arms control, the important events in the Pacific can easily be misunderstood.

Verification

Because sensible arms control is not a matter of trust, agreements must be verifiable. This essential feature of European and superpower arms control has held up many negotiations and destroyed others. Negotiations at the level of START, a comprehensive test ban, or even MBFR, spend vast amounts of time devising intricate verification procedures. The tragedy of the obsession with verification debates is that unless every possible loophole is sewn up many leaders are not flexible enough to see the overriding need for a deal. The obsession with formality and legality can destroy an agreement that is otherwise politically sensible.

Needless to say, most Pacific states have not come anywhere near such detailed arms-control negotiations. The type of arms control they have

---

17 Gerald Segal, 'Defence Culture and Sino-Soviet Relations' in *Journal of Strategic Studies* (June 1985).

undertaken has usually not been formal and has therefore not required formal verification. The recent Sino-Soviet tacit arms control is a case in point. Thus both side do not get bogged down in confidence-sapping disputes over verification. The protagonists concentrate instead on the main issues—is tension reduced, is confidence built, is war unlikely?

This informal approach, with little need for ambitious verification measures, makes sense in an area where few states have the capability to undertake sophisticated verification measures. Not only is the area to be covered so vast in Asia, but there is also the vexed question of who is going to do the verifying in an area of so many diverse states and interests. Japan is undoubtedly capable of verifying agreements, and indeed has offered to do so for the United Nations and the superpowers. But in part because of the legacy of Japanese imperialism and overwhelming economic influence, other states of the region are unlikely to depend on Japan to help guarantee their security.[18]

Most of the states are less developed and cannot afford the complex verification hardware, much of which is space-based or at least dependent on sophisticated technology. In most cases it will not do to rely on the superpowers for verification, for they have an axe to grind in most conflicts and will be regarded suspiciously by local states, especially those anxious to preserve their independence. For example, China, one of the few states that can deploy its own rudimentary verification technology, such as satellites, has been wary of being too dependent on the United States' surveillance of Soviet military forces. The other obvious verification option, the United Nations, has proven ineffective since it was first used in the Indo-Chinese conflict. The United Nations remains a mirror for global disunity.

The Advantages of Perceiving Threats

For many states in the region, arms control appears inopportune at a time when leaders want to focus the public's attention on external threats and the need to increase arms spending. In both Korea and Japan, arms control could be useful precisely as a way of enhancing security. But such an option is not encouraged by local leaders, and is further undermined by blatantly propagandistic offers of arms control from the Soviet Union. In Japan, for example, confidence-building measures are often seen as concessions to the Soviet Union, since they might be taken as recognition of Soviet occupation of the northern territories. They might also be thought to undermine the delicate consensus on the need for increased defence expenditure.

[18] *Daily Yomiuri* (22 February 1985); *The Times* (31 January 1985).

PROGRESS IN PACIFIC ARMS CONTROL

In the past decade, there has been a flood of arms-control proposals in the Pacific, but few have been more than propaganda gestures. The least practical proposals are those for so-called Zones (ZOP). These proposals are based on the assumption that a particular region has only to get rid of the superpowers or other extraregional powers and all will be quiet and peaceful.

The ASEAN Zone of Peace, Freedom, and Neutrality (ZOPFAN), declared in 1971, has been largely ignored. It was an admirable but unlikely effort to keep their zone free of the surrounding great-power conflict. Combatants in South-east Asia have murdered millions in the decade and a half since the proposal was made.

The ZOPFAN idea remains an aspiration rather than a policy. With the partial success of the Raratonga Treaty, the supporters of ZOPFAN tried again to raise the issue in the form of a nuclear-weapons-free zone. At a meeting of ASEAN Foreign Ministers In June 1987, the United States made clear that it was strongly opposed to any such treaty. As ASEAN was closer to war zones, had a more cynical experience of arms control, and had some members highly dependent on the United States, the idea was effectively side lined, much to relief of the United States.[19]

The Soviet Union has also come up with a variant on the ZOP. In the 1970s the Soviet Union proposed an Asian collective security scheme which was essentially an attempt to organize Asian states in a containment ring against China. Moscow found few supporters and the idea was gradually dropped. In the early 1980s, and especially since 1985 under Mikhail Gorbachev, the Soviet Union has revised its proposal. In a major speech at Vladivostok in July 1986, Gorbachev relaunched the initiative, even offering the United States a place in a Pacific, Helsinki-like process. But as Soviet officials made clear at the time, such grandiose plans were for the long-term future and took second place to more specific overtures to Japan and China.[20]

The Gorbachev initiative for an Asian Helsinki was an attempt to break up what the Soviet Union perceived as an anti-Soviet coalition organized by the United States in the region. The European Helsinki process in 1975 had caused the Soviet Union problems primarily in the sphere of human-rights violations. But in the Pacific this was unlikely to become an issue for fear of harming western relations with China as well as with some of the recently favoured, but less than democratic, NICs. The advantages for the Soviet

---

[19] *Independent* (17 June 1987); *Far Eastern Economic Review* (2 July 1987).
[20] For an early statement before Gorbachev see Soviet Government Statement in BBC, SWB, SU, 8242, A3, 1–3 (23 April 1986); *Pravda* in 8263, A3, 1–2 (12 May 1986).

Union of an Asian Helsinki would be similar to those in Europe—recognition of existing frontiers and allied regimes. Yet the problems with such a proposal are even larger than in Europe, if only because of the lack of identifiable blocks and the lack of an agreed status quo.

The Soviet Union's unilateral withdrawal of some troops from the border with China suggests that a more fruitful course of arms control is bilateral or small-scale multilateral. But the experience of Vietnam and Kampuchea in the late 1980s suggests that formal negotiations are rarely the route to arms control. Despite several types of talks on how to get Vietnam out of Kampuchea, the route eventually chosen was a unilateral Vietnamese withdrawal without a formal agreement.

Perhaps the most serious arms-control proposal to reduce the risks of accidental war in a specific zone is the portion of the 1982 Law of the Sea Treaty that seeks to ensure the free passage of ships through straits and limits the right of passage of warships into certain coastal waters.[21] Although the treaty is not yet in operation, and many of its features merely codify sensible existing practice, it does represent a useful accord for an area such as the Pacific with so many potential naval disputes. If, as some have argued, the idea of the Exclusive Economic Zone is extended to include a ban on anti-submarine warfare (the so-called ASWEEZ), then the superpowers and China will have an even greater need to ensure the smooth operation of arms control in the Pacific. It is true that the United States has not signed the treaty, but the vast majority of Pacific states have done so and wish to see it implemented. Like the NPT, this is not an Asian arms-control measure. But unlike the NPT, it is one that the developing states want. As a result, it may end up being one of the most observed of any arms-control agreements in the Pacific.

A much more promising, partly formal, bilateral arms control arrangement also seems to be taking shape on the Sino-Soviet frontier. There are a variety of proposals on the table. China has urged Moscow to withdraw troops several hundred kilometres back from the border to build confidence. Moscow has replied with its own ideas for Helsinki-type confidence-building measures. In practice, both sides have engaged in *de facto* arms control and lowered tension along the frontier. The reopening of border-demarcation talks in February 1987 and the subsequent rapid progress have been paralleled by the *de facto* negotiations along the frontier by soldiers from both sides to resolve local problems as they arise. China and the Soviet Union seem ready for a formal agreement to codify the détente that is already under way.

Perhaps the most dangerous bilateral conflicts are along the Kampuchean-

---

21 Ken Booth, *Law, Force and Diplomacy at Sea* (London: Allen & Unwin, 1985).

Thai frontier and the inner-Korean border. The former is a relatively new state of affairs and until most recently has seen heavy fighting as Vietnam pounded rebel bases along and across the border. Both Vietnam and Thailand proposed a scheme of demilitarization but any specific deal will have to await a military defeat for the Vietnamese or, more likely, for the rebels. For now, both sides want the demilitarization to take place on the other side of the frontier. It appears increasingly clear the Vietnam is gradually establishing control and a semblance of quiet in Kampuchea. Once again the arms control, when it comes, is often sweeping and unilateral. Thus a formal demilitarization of the frontier might soon be a sensible codification of a new and less dangerous status quo.

Along the Korean border a demilitarized zone was established in the 1953 armistice. In fact, the demilitarization has never been observed. Both sides have subsequently have proposed ways to create genuine demilitarization, but the process founders on a number of issues, including the basic question of who is to do the negotiating. While North Korea refuses to talk to the South on such matters, the South Koreans seek recognition by way of negotiations. Although some slight progress has been made on other bilateral issues, notably on humanitarian problems, there has been no arms-control progress. The United States has also proposed that North Koreans send observers to the annual United States–South Korea Team Spirit exercises on the model of the Helsinki accord on confidence-building measures. But Pyongyang has so far refused.

Finally, there has also been some spin-off for the Pacific from the superpower arms-control process in Europe. Negotiations on limiting intermediate-range nuclear forces (INF) have long been complicated by the presence of Chinese nuclear weapons and the allocation by both superpowers of some parts of their arsenal for anti-China roles. In the SALT 1 agreement the Soviet Union was granted a *de facto* 'China quotient' in its long-range weaponry so as to meet a perceived Chinese threat.[22] The United States originally conceived of its ABM shield for an anti-China role and this led to the eventual ABM treaty as part of SALT 1.[23]

In the 1970s the Soviet Union began deploying the SS-20, an INF weapon targeted both on western Europe and East Asia, as well as in a 'swing' mode capable of hitting both theatres. Following the deployment of NATO's INF weapons in the early 1980s, the superpowers began negotiating an agreement on limiting and then completely banning INF weapons.[24] The question

[22] These issues are discussed in Gerald Segal (ed.), *The China Factor* (London: Croom Helm, 1982).

[23] On these treaties see Lawrence Freedman, *The Evolution of Nuclear Strategy* (London: Macmillan, 1980).

[24] Richard Solomon and Masataka Kosaka, *The Soviet Far East Military Buildup* (London:

arose whether the superpowers should retain some 100 weapons in the Pacific
to deal with the more complicated balance of power in that region. The
Soviet Union told China that the SS-20 was targeted on Japan and United
States forces, while it suggested to the United States and Japan that they
were needed in anti-China roles. The Soviets offered to scrap these final 100
INF weapons if the United States would remove its weapons on ships and
bases just off Eurasia.

In July 1987 Mikhail Gorbachev agreed to scrap the 100 weapons,
thereby accepting an INF ban on land in Eurasia but not at sea. Thus
Europe and Asia were to be free of these weapons, but not the Atlantic or
Pacific. Yet the agreement was held up because of a dispute over German
INF weapons—thus reiterating the point that, at least on the nuclear and
superpower level, regional security could not be separated from global
security. When a deal was finally signed in December 1988, what began as
European arms control had become a major agreement affecting nuclear
weapons in East Asia as well. In arms control, there was no Pacific-thinking,
but rather much 'Eurasian-thinking'.

PROSPECTS FOR PACIFIC ARMS CONTROL

The obstacles to arms control in the Pacific are still daunting. Parties to
conflict are either not interested in any form of arms control or simply see it
as a way of obtaining enhanced national security rather than mutual
security. Nevertheless, it is clear that genuine, if limited, arms control has
taken place in the Pacific, and is likely to do so in the future. The problem of
arms control is often merely in the eye of the (mostly western) observer.
Pacific arms control has more often than not been informal and bilateral,
and has stressed confidence-building measures rather than the reduction of
weapons.

The conflicts least likely to make use of arms control are the region's hot
spots such as Indo-China. It would be comforting to believe that agreements
could be reached that would control the movement of rebels and their arms
across international frontiers, or neutralize certain states in order to contain
conflict. But what seems more likely is that the conflicts will be fought to
clearer conclusions. Once a new, more stable political order is established,
then some form of arms-control measures plays a part. Peacekeeping in the
style of the United Nations has already been proposed and could help by
demilitarizing conflict zones and observing disengagement accords.

A less unstable, but still emotive, type of conflict is that such as between

Croom Helm, 1986); Hiroshi Kimura, 'Arms Control in East Asia' in Adam Garfinkle (ed.),
Global Perspectives on Arms Control (New York: Praeger, 1984).

North and South Korea. There have already been proposals for arms control placed on the negotiating table. In the Korean case there are in fact old agreements which have been neglected. The conflict seems increasingly ripe for two types of arms control: confidence-building measures; and the thinning out of forces in border regions, or even their genuine demilitarization.

The degree of optimism about the implementation of these measures hinges on the extent to which the conflict is seen as dormant and both sides are prepared to compromise. In Korea, a powerful argument can be made that arms-control and confidence-building measures are needed urgently to control escalation. But there are obvious uncertainties over the future domestic politics on both sides of the frontier. The great-power supporters of the two sides are interested in maintaining the non-violent status quo, but the failure of talks in 1986 on confidence-building measures suggests this may not yet be a fruitful area for arms control.

The most stable set of conflicts are those between the superpowers in the Pacific, and between the Soviet Union and China. These three great powers are already well on their way to a 'mature' relationship of competition and coexistence. The superpowers have the most training in this sort of *détente* and have already begun to reach formal regional arms-control arrangements. Of course, both superpowers have far less surplus weaponry in the Pacific than in Europe, and there is therefore less scope for arms control that involves the actual reduction in numbers of weapons or troops.

What is more, in comparison to Europe there is one important incentive to confidence-building measures lacking in East Asia—the Soviet Union has little major interest in obtaining international recognition of borders in East Asia. The disputed territories are not 'sovereign states', but rather land incorporated into the Soviet Union itself. The Soviet Union has nothing as substantial to offer as it did in Europe. There are no Japanese left on the disputed northern territories and thus there is no eager American ally, such as West Germany in Europe, interested in pushing for compromise. On the contrary, Japan is fearful that any arms control will merely enshrine its loss of the northern territories. Thus many of the practical underpinnings of *détente* in the Helsinki style are lacking.[25]

But such confidence-building measures are most likely to be fruitful if they are bilateral and applied only to very specific circumstances. What is more, experience suggest that informal measures are often easier to achieve and more far-reaching than the laboriously negotiated formal measures. For example, Sino-Soviet relations have matured in recent years, largely because China has adopted a more balanced and defensive foreign policy strategy. If this process continues, there is some reason to expect some formal agreement

[25] Reinhard Drifte, 'The Superpowers and Arms Control in Asia' in Segal (ed.), *Arms Control*.

on demilitarization and confidence-building measures on both frontiers. Confidence-building measures, as in the CSCE, will of course require formal agreement. But talks are already in progress on both fronts where these issues have reportedly been raised. What is more, the two sides have already gone a long way to reducing numbers of troops along their common frontier. Demilitarization and thinning out of forces by the Soviet Union and China can be seen as a prime example of the most likely and important type of Pacific arms control.

There seems to be a distinctive approach to nuclear weapons in the region—states almost close their eyes and pretend that the weapons do not exist. The Japanese pretend that American weapons do not exist by not asking the Americans whether their ships carry nuclear weapons. The Chinese rarely talk about their arsenal, while claiming they do not pose a threat to anyone. It is therefore not surprising that in this environment the formal measure of the NPT is not the main arms-control regime. In a sense, the Pacific states have gone beyond the need for only formal agreements and have recognized the advantages of informal nuclear-arms control.

In the final analysis, two aspects appear most starkly on the Pacific arms-control agenda—informal rather than formal accords, and confidence-building rather than more complex and precise measures. The process of arms control is clearly useful to Pacific states, but they go about it in a less legalistic and less formal way. That seems like a sensible strategy for coping with the inherent change and uncertainty in the region's conflicts. Flexible arms control based on unstated self-restraint seems to be the hallmark of the Pacific approach.

PATTERNS OF PACIFIC SECURITY

There never has been, nor is there now, anything comprehensive enough to be called 'Pacific security'. While there are undoubtedly many regional security balances within the Pacific, there is no wider pattern to the balances of power, conflicts, alliances, or arms control. Although the Second World War that so shaped the politics of the Atlantic began and ended in the Pacific, it left a far more diverse set of military relationships there than it did in Europe.

There are major differences between the two worlds of the Atlantic and Pacific. The Pacific remains less important for both superpowers than the Atlantic, although some American rhetoric would have the world believe otherwise. There are few direct clashes of superpower interests as in Europe and the cold war has translated badly to the Pacific idiom. The Atlantic world has one main balance of power, while in the Pacific there are several. There are two main superpowers in the Atlantic world, while the Pacific has several great powers. In the European confrontation of blocs all major states pull their military weight, while in the Pacific there are vastly more unequal defence burdens. The Atlantic world is almost entirely at a kind of peace called 'cold war', while the Pacific has seen many hot wars and is only now cooling down. The Pacific had seen some early and very violent manifestations of decolonization, while the Atlantic world's obsession with the cold war was particularly unsuitable as an explanatory model of Pacific international insecurity. In the Atlantic world there is a relative balance of forces between the superpowers, while in the Pacific the United States is far more dominant.

There are a number of reasons for these differences, most of which have strong roots in the pre-1945 patterns of Pacific politics. The manifestation of these differences can be seen clearly in the special roles of the main actors in the Pacific. The United States finds itself in a far more favourable position in the Pacific, with a string of bases and friends hard up against the long Eurasian coast. Eastern and central Pacific waters are hardly contested by any adversary, unlike the Atlantic where there is a more active Soviet fleet and a Soviet ally, Cuba, in the American backyard. While it is true that the United States has 'lost' more friends in the Pacific (China, Laos, South Vietnam, and Cambodia), it is arguable whether these developing states were ever America's in the first place. Certainly the United States retains the friendship of most Pacific states, and nearly all the wealthy and fast-developing ones.

The Soviet position is far more perilous and unsuccessful. Its military forces have grown rapidly in the region, but remain trapped in defence of a highly vulnerable Sino-Soviet frontier with virtually no buffer states. Its naval power remains bottled up in home bases or highly vulnerable in an isolated base in Indo-China. It has barely benefited from the American 'loss' of states in the region. China was only briefly an ally before becoming an enemy and then more independent. Vietnam remains an ally of convenience and by the 1980s a drain and problem for Soviet foreign policy. Kampuchea and Laos are clearly lesser liabilities and also allies of an even more remote kind.

China has no equal in Europe and is the single most important reason for the differences between the Atlantic and Pacific worlds. It has changed its foreign policy so often, and shifted the regional and global balance of power as a result, that the creation of stable patterns of security has proved impossible. China's new independent foreign policy of the 1980s has undoubtedly improved its stature in the region. China now has more friends and fewer security concerns than ever before. Yet it remains the great wild card of Pacific security, for it is far from clear that as China grows strong it will also remain passive and unbothersome to its neighbours. Like Germany it remains a society with unresolved national claims, but unlike Germany it may well have the independent power and incentive to satisfy its irredentism.

Japan must be the second major reason for the peculiarity of Pacific security. Like Germany it has risen from its defeat in the Second World War. But unlike Germany it has never fully come to terms with its war-guilt and has been far more anti-military than West Germany.[26] Japan has pioneered what has become known as the Yoshida Doctrine of the diplomacy of the merchant rather than the warrior. Thus Japan remains more deeply dependent than any developed western state on American goodwill and its defence shield. This is in some ways a force for peace through economic rather than military confrontation. But it also makes Japan hostage to American good behaviour. Japan has avoided entanglements of arms control and debates over relations with the Soviet Union to an extent that many Europeans would envy.

These very distinctive qualities of domestic and foreign policy have helped create a number of different patterns of security in the Pacific. The over-arching one—the global balance of the superpowers—is obviously similar to that in Europe. Because of the balance of terror, which in part depends on intercontinental-range weapons based in the Pacific, the superpowers avoid direct confrontation. While they shadow-box in Pacific waters and airspace, they take as much care to avoid war as they do in Europe—recognizing that, as Mao Zedong once said, it only takes a spark to light a prairie fire.

Yet unlike in the Atlantic world, this superpower mutual respect and caution has not prevented numerous small wars from flaring and burning with great intensity. The first of these wars, in Korea, occurred in the most important of the sub-regional balances of power: North-east Asia. It is most vital because it is here that the Soviet and Chinese frontiers meet and that key cities and industries are based. This is also where Japan feels at its most vulnerable. The United States is also more concerned with this region— because of the security of Japan and the possibility of Sino-Soviet war—than anywhere else in the Pacific. And of course the United States is also a north Pacific power more than a south Pacific one. It is barely an exaggeration to say that most discussions of Pacific security really refer only to North-east Asia.

In this area there are four major powers, several cooling or dormant conflicts, and the dangerous instability of Korea. It has the greatest concen-

---

26 Gerhard Hielscher, 'Nobody Asks: "What Did You Do in the War, Daddy?" ' in *Far Eastern Economic Review* (19 February 1987).

tration of military forces outside of Europe and a wide array of types of force in an area about the distance from Paris to Moscow. It is a region riddled with 'fences', on the principle evident in Europe that good fences make good neighbours. Some of the 'fences' rely on the sea and sea-based military power, as in the case of the defence of Japan.

The only other sub-region that can be said to have a pattern of security is South-east Asia. Taking the pattern only since 1975, because the previous one was so different, there is a less important, but more unstable, situation than further up the Eurasian coast. In South-east Asia there are three and a half powers (China, the superpowers, and Vietnam), an anxious uncoordinated ASEAN, and two wars. It is a bewildering maze of conflict, with an active but mostly opportunist Soviet Union, a deeply concerned but frustrated China, a sullen and inactive United States, a haughty but troubled Vietnam, and a deeply divided ASEAN. More people have died in wars in Indo-China than anywhere else in the post-war world, but still there is much insecurity and instability.

No other part of the Pacific has a major international security problem. Many states have unresolved problems of nationalism and territorial claims, such as China and Taiwan or the various Latin American conflicts. Some states suffer domestic unrest that draws in a foreign interest, such as the Philippines or in Central America. Some states, like Australia, have alliances but no serious security problems. To the extent that these issues are ones of international security, they are mostly dominated by the United States and its bilateral relations. They hardly constitute Pacific-wide security issues.

The trends in Pacific security can be summarized as 'more of the same'. No clear balances of power, fewer wars, fewer multilateral alliances, and more tacit arms control. The region will continue to be focused on its north-west corner, less concerned with nuclear weapons than conventional ones, and less likely in future to turn to war as an instrument of policy. If these trends are correct, then the enhancement of national and international security in the Pacific will not follow the same patterns as in Europe—not a surprising conclusion, but a no less vital one for a region that has been so different from the Atlantic world in the past.

IV

THE ECONOMIC DIMENSION

The most persistent motive for people to 'think Pacific' has been an economic calculation of the region's importance. Until recently, most dreams of Pacific prosperity have proven illusory—witness the empty dreams of the China market in the past three centuries or talk of the Pacific Century at the start of the twentieth century. Even Karl Marx believed that 'the Pacific Ocean will have the same role as the Atlantic has now and the Mediterranean had in antiquity and in the Middle Ages—that of the great waterway of world commerce'.[1]

European empires came to the region to colonize, seek raw materials, and find markets for their own products. But they saw the colonies as part of a bilateral, imperial pattern of international relations. They did not try to weld the Pacific, or even East Asia, into a coherent trading system. Although individual empires, such as those run from Britain, Spain, Russia, or the United States, did have trade ties spanning the Pacific, the relationships were rarely vital for more than a handful of countries. The Japanese empire was more ambitious in its attempts to integrate East Asian economies, but the effort led to, and was cut short by, the Second World War.

With the major reorganization of international politics after the war, states were slow to think about trying another form of multilateral economic integration in the Pacific. Most attention was given to the integration across the north Atlantic and within Europe. As the developed economies of the north Atlantic prospered, a more important and clear-cut pattern of international economic relations began to emerge.

The Pacific economies took longer to prosper and therefore observers were slower to think about patterns of economic relations in the region. But even when more people began thinking Pacific, they found the pattern was very different from that in the Atlantic, and above all far more complex. Much as in the case of military and security relations in the Pacific, it is still difficult to see much utility in conceiving of the Pacific as a single economic region. Although there are some possibilities for growing Pacific-wide economic interactions, it seems more likely that at least certain parts of the Pacific economy will become more intertwined in the global economy.

The international economic relations of the Pacific have diverging tendencies. At the regional level, most trade takes place along a few bilateral lines, mostly involving the United States and Japan. Few countries trade with a wide range of Pacific states. To the extent that there are new, developing trade patterns, they are just as often outside the Pacific region. Certainly the developed and rapidly developing states see the Europeans as growing trading partners and a vital part of the global rather than regional-Pacific economy.

[1] Cited in B. Klyuchnikov, 'The Soviet Far East in the Pacific Century' in *Far Eastern Affairs*, 4 (1988).

Of course, despite the obsolescence of the idea of thinking Pacific in terms of regional co-operation, there are certainly important reasons to pay close attention to what is taking place in the Pacific. If only because of the evident success of many economies in the area, and their new ideas on how to achieve economic prosperity, there is a pressing need to understand the Pacific. In addition, the rise of the NICs challenges basic assumptions about the North–South divide, the best path to modernization, and the shifting balance of power in the international economy. The creation of innovative socialist economics, most notably in China, also draws our attention to the Pacific.

17

Pacific Prosperity

If the Pacific had not prospered in recent years, there would be no grounds for discussing a 'Pacific shift'. Indeed, for most of the first two decades after the Second World War, there was little common ground for discussion of the region in economic terms. The United States accounted for well over half the region's GDP and in any case was strongly oriented towards the economic recovery of its most vital allies in Europe. East Asia was seen as a place where wars were fought and selected allies were supported with aid. Australia and New Zealand were more oriented to European trade, and the vast majority of the states of the region were poor and in only the earliest stages of development. Japan was the only East Asian state that could be seen as developed and it was tied to the United States, as were the economies of western Europe.

Two of the largest economies in the Pacific, China and the Soviet Union, were Communist, and the Soviet Union was even more Europe-oriented than the United States. China, the traditional engine of East Asian economic relations, was dragging itself out of the mire of a civil war and then through the rolling catastrophes of a series of failed development strategies. The Soviet model of the 1950s in China was replaced by the disastrous Great Leap Forward and the famine of the early 1960s that led to the death of 20–30 million people. The economy grew in spurts in the early 1960s, but the Cultural Revolution soon threw China back into reverse. Mongolia, North Korea, and North Vietnam were all absorbed in building socialism and often waging war. Their orientation was to their Communist neighbours and certainly not towards the mixed economies elsewhere in the region.

But nor were the other, non-Communist, states of the Pacific following a common road of development. By far the largest number of states in the region could be classed as developing states, and some in South-east Asia, such as Malaysia and Singapore, did not even obtain independence until the 1960s. By then, most developing states were nominally independent, but far from agreed on methods of modernization. Latin American Pacific states remained mostly dictatorships governed by corrupt regimes with mixed economies. In the first two decades of the post-war period they were mostly more prosperous than their counterparts in East Asia. But their economies

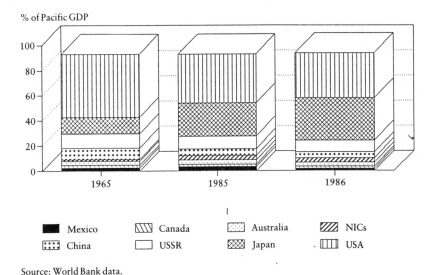

% of Pacific GDP

FIG. 17.1   *Percentage of Pacific GDP: 1965, 1985, 1986*

Legend:
- Mexico
- China
- Canada
- USSR
- Australia
- Japan
- NICs
- USA

Source: World Bank data.

were heavily penetrated by the United States and West Europeans, and had barely any connections to the states of the western Pacific.

PACIFIC ECONOMIES IN 1965

The picture of Pacific economies in 1965 was one of huge disparities. The United States alone accounted for 50 per cent of the region's total GDP (see Figure 17.1).[1] Japan was rising fast with 13 per cent of Pacific GDP. More controversially, the Soviet Union was the region's third-largest economy, accounting for 11.4 per cent of Pacific GDP. No other country accounted for more than 10 per cent of Pacific GDP. The United States and Japan

[1] Figures are calculated from *World Development Report* (World Bank) and count the superpowers and Canada as having half their GDP in the Pacific. It includes all Pacific littoral states as well as Mongolia and Laos. This common, if arbitary, calculation can be seen only as rough and ready, and is intended to be used more for illustrative than precise purposes. The data are used to suggest trends and the specific numbers are often subject to dispute. GDP figures are not reliable. For example, they count some of the inefficiences of economies as part of GDP. When Soviet GDP figures include the cost of abortions necessary because the economy is inefficient in providing basic health care, it is clear that GDP figures are not necessarily reliable guides to prosperity. Indeed, it is far more useful to base such assessments on purchasing-power parities , but reliable figures are available for only a handful of countries.

dominated the non-Communist Pacific economies, while the Soviet Union led and assisted the Communist ones.

The five industrial market economies of the Pacific (the United States, Japan, Canada, Australia, and New Zealand) constituted 69 per cent of the region's GDP. The pattern of United States and Japanese domination of the region was already emerging. The contrast to Europe, where economic power was more evenly distributed, was striking. But counting the Soviet Union as an industrial economy, the Pacific already constituted almost 35 per cent of GDP of the world's industrialized states. The Pacific had not yet caught up with the Atlantic world, but it was coming up quickly.

All other economies were dwarfed in importance. Only China, which constituted 9.2 per cent of Pacific GDP in 1965, was of any consequence. The four low-income economies[2] of the Pacific (China and Indo-China) accounted for barely 10 per cent of Pacific GDP, although, thanks to China, they made up 47 per cent of the GDP of all the world's low-income states.

The middle- and low-middle-income states (Indonesia, the Philippines, Papua New Guinea. Honduras, Nicaragua, Thailand, El Salvador, Peru, Ecuador, Costa Rica, Colombia, and Chile) constituted together some 8 per cent of Pacific GDP. The Latin American states accounted for 5 per cent of Pacific GDP. As a whole, the GDP of these middle-income states represented 23 per cent of the total GDP of the world's middle-and low-middle-income states. The upper-middle-income states of the Pacific (Malaysia, Mexico, Panama, Korea, Hong Kong, and Singapore) contributed 4.5 per cent to Pacific GDP, with only Mexico making it above 1 per cent. They accounted for 22 per cent of the GDP of all upper-middle-income states.

Thus in 1965 the economies of the Pacific were dominated by the United States, while Japan was rapidly developing. The area was also significantly affected by the fact that over 20 per cent of the region's economy was made up of Communist states. The vast majority of states were middle income, mostly in South-east Asia and Latin America. The Pacific was dominated by its North–North dimension of developed market economies. North–South relations existed within both Communist and non-Communist worlds. But the developing states accounted for about 20 per cent of total Pacific GDP and half of that figure was China.

PACIFIC ECONOMIES BY 1986

In 1965 the economies of the Pacific constituted just under 35 per cent of total world GDP. Twenty years later in 1986 it was just under 50 per cent of

---

[2] These categories are those used by the World Bank.

world GDP. More conservative figures for 1982, excluding all Communist states and counting only the North American states and provinces directly bordering on the Pacific, show a rise of Pacific basin GDP form 16.2 per cent of world totals of 23 per cent in 1982. They also show that Pacific basin GDP was 38.5 per cent of that of the Atlantic in 1960 and 57.3 per cent in 1982. Asian Pacific GDP, according to similar calculations, was 18 per cent of United States GDP in 1960 and 53.2 per cent in 1982. The rise of the Pacific as compared to Europe was far less striking, up from 27.5 per cent of West European GDP to 54 per cent, as West European economies also grew quickly.[3] But the Europeans had begun their growth earlier and recovered more quickly than the Pacific states. Nevertheless, the Asian Pacific states contributed 20 per cent of the increase in world GDP in the 22-year period to 1982. In the United States alone, the personal income of its five Pacific states rose to 42 per cent of that of the 18 Atlantic states, up from 28 per cent in 1950.

Whichever figures are used, the states of the Pacific are clearly playing a growing role in the international economy. But the shift to the Pacific states and Europe, both of which took shares from the United States,[4] cannot mask the fact that the Pacific remained as diverse and unequal as it had been two decades before.

Once again taking the more complete GDP figures for 1986, the United States and Japan accounted for some 70 per cent of total Pacific GDP, up from 63 per cent in 1965. But the Japanese proportion had more than doubled to nearly 34 per cent, moving up fast on the United States' 36 per cent. Using the more conservative figures for 1982, Japan is responsible for 46.8 per cent of Pacific GDP and the five Pacific states of the United States for only 17.9 per cent. The Japanese power-house alone constituted 11 per cent of non-Communist world GDP (but counting China) in 1982, compared to 4.2 per cent for the United States' five Pacific states. The total of 23.4 per cent for the Pacific basin still leaves it behind the United States' own 31 per cent or the 30.6 per cent for OECD Europe.

But it is not only the United States that has seen its percentage of Pacific and world GDP decline. While the Soviet Union's share of Pacific GDP declined gently to 9.4 per cent in 1986, China's was halved to 4.6 per cent. Until recently, growing Pacific economic strength clearly owed nothing to its Communist members.

---

[3] Figures from Staffan Linder, *The Pacific Century* (Stanford, Calif: Stanford University Press, 1986), ch. 1.

[4] The percentage of world GDP held by Japan, Europe, and the United States in 1986 may have shown a relative decline for the United States, but they were only back to pre-1940 percentages if Japanese colonies such as Taiwan and South Korea are considered as part of the Japanese 'sphere of economic influence'.

The only other states with more than 1 per cent of Pacific GDP in 1986 were Australia (3.1 per cent), Mexico (2.1 per cent), Canada (1.7 per cent), South Korea (1.6 per cent), Indonesia (1.2 per cent), and Taiwan (1 per cent). With the exception of Mexico, every Pacific Latin American state saw its percentage drop sharply. Pacific Latin America accounted for some 5 per cent of Pacific GDP in 1965 but by 1986 this was down to about 4 per cent Australia and New Zealand saw their combined share drop from 4 per cent to 3.5 per cent and ASEAN states rose from 2.5 per cent to 3.3 per cent of Pacific GDP. The main states to increase their share of Pacific GDP apart from Japan were the NICs and Indonesia. Thus the Japanese miracle was not entirely responsible for Pacific dynamism, but it certainly played by far the largest part, especially in the decade from 1960. Since then the NICs have held their own, and in the past decade even China shows signs of recovering its share.

By 1986, therefore, the Pacific remained deeply divided between rich and poor, but there were important changes among middle-income states. China and Indo-China accounted for about 5 per cent of Pacific GDP and still 48 per cent of world low-income economies. The low-middle- and middle-income states had slipped to about 4.5 per cent of Pacific GDP and to 13 per cent of total low-middle- and middle-income economies. The major change was in the upper-middle-income states who had moved up to roughly 7 per cent of Pacific GDP and grown to constitute 25 per cent of total upper-middle-income GDP. The five industrial economies led by the surge of Japan, had increased their share of Pacific GDP to about 75 per cent. Clearly any discussion of the dynamism and importance of the Pacific economy must concentrate on this latter category of most developed states.

The extent of change in Pacific economies has been vast in some sections and minimal in many others. The obvious change is the growth of Japan as an economic power. The creation of a genuine trilateral balance between Japan, the United States, and western Europe must rank as the most important shift in the international economy since 1945. But this trilateralism is not a complete gain for the Pacific, as the relative decline of the United States 'in the middle' has been of nearly equal benefit to both Europe and Japan.

The second change has been the emergence of NICs in East Asia. Although NICs were first seen in southern Europe, Israel, and then Latin America, the Israeli and Latin American varieties ran into serious problems in the 1970s and 1980s. Some of the Latin American NICs were Pacific states, but only Mexico held a place of importance. The most sustained and dynamic NICs outside of Europe have been in East Asia, but at least in GDP terms they have not had nearly the impact of a fast-growing Japanese economy. Two of the NICs, Hong Kong and Singapore, still have tiny populations and territory. Only Taiwan and South Korea are of a substantial size and the increase in their GDP has had an appreciable impact on the region.

Third, the nature of the Communist regimes has undergone major changes. The Sino-Soviet split in the 1960s was first and foremost a difference of opinion on the question of domestic models of development. China wrecked its economy in the search for 'socialism with Chinese characteristics', and it was not until the 1980s that it stumbled into a new form of reform Communism. The resulting decade of growth and new ideas for reforming poor, peasant socialist economies has had a major impact on the Communist world. By 1986 the Soviet Union had followed with its own version of reform, and was pushing its East Asian allies from Mongolia to Kampuchea to try it out.[5] As in the case of East European reforms, changes in these countries' domestic political economies were leading to new directions in foreign policy.

Of course, a related aspect of economic change in the Pacific has been the changes of types of regime, for example when previously largely non-Communist Indo-China went Communist in 1975. South Vietnam, Laos, and Cambodia were among the poorest states in the region before the coming of Communism, and little has changed since 1975. In terms of Pacific growth, this is a change with no change, although the nature of the political economy has been radically transformed.

Apart from these important trends, most other features of the domestic economies of the Pacific have been remarkably constant. The revolutions in Indo-China did not spread to ASEAN states and the orientation of these and the Latin American developing states remained towards the market economies of the developed world. The dominance by two north Pacific economies remained, and the contrasts between the different socialist and market economic models were blurred, but only at the margins.

The contrast between economic power and military power in the Pacific did, however, increase in the past 20 years. In the immediate post-war period the United States, China, and the Soviet Union were the major military powers, but in economic terms it was only the United States that was an economic superpower. The emergence of competing Communist and market economic systems was similar to developments in Europe, but only in its initial stages. The Soviet Union and China soon disagreed about models and neither was particularly successful in developing its economy.

In the 1960s Japan emerged as an economic great power, and by the 1980s it was clearly the most powerful economy in the Pacific. The balance

[5] Michael Kaser, 'One Economy, Two Systems' in *International Affairs*, 63/3 (summer 1987) and 'Soviet and Chinese Reforms' in *Pacific Review*, 1/1 (1988).

of economic power was best understood in Japanese–American terms. No other state was nearly as important. The steady development of Australia and New Zealand and the rise of NICs and some ASEAN economies meant that there was a bevy of smaller market economies living off and around the Japanese and American superpowers. In order to understand the impact of these changes in the economic balances of power, it is essential to assess the changing pattern of trade and investment in the Pacific.

THE FLOW OF TRADE

It is not surprising that the increased size of the Pacific GDP should lead to changes in patterns o trade (see Figures 17.2 and 17.3). Japan and then the NICs pursued an export-led strategy of growth and thus the impact of their new prosperity was closely tied up with international trade patterns. But what is most striking, considering the rapid development of the region, is the relatively small number of changes in the pattern of trade.

Asian Pacific exports in 1960 were only 9 per cent of total world exports, but by 1983 they had more than doubled to 18.9 percent.[6] In 1960 total Asian Pacific trade was 69.7 per cent of the United States' total, but by 1983 it was 130.8 per cent. When compared to European OECD states, Asian Pacific trade was not up as dramatically, from 23.1 per cent in 1960 to 42.6 per cent in 1983, largely because of the strong intra-European trade. Once again, however, it is clear that the Pacific region has seen a sharp increase in the volume of its trade, and therefore an increase in the absolute value of interaction among its states. Curiously, most states have not shown a significant increase in the percentage of their trade done within the Pacific. Indeed, when looking at the types of trading pattern it is far more difficult to find many changes, despite the vastly increased volume.

In 1960 the United States and OECD Europe provided roughly the same 22 per cent of imports for the Asian Pacific states. Non-Asian Pacific less-developed countries (LDCs) provided another 13 per cent and the Asian Pacific states themselves provided 28.4 per cent. By 1983 there had been some changes but few radical shifts. Both the United States and OECD Europe were less able to export to the Asian Pacific region, with the United States' exports falling 4 per cent and European exports falling 10 per cent. While China nearly doubled its share from 2.8 per cent to 4.4 per cent in the period, the non-Asian Pacific LDCs and Asian Pacific LDCs each saw their shares rise by roughly 10 per cent. In 1983 the Asian Pacific states imported

---

[6] Details from Linder, *Pacific Century*, 15. His figures do not include the Soviet Union.

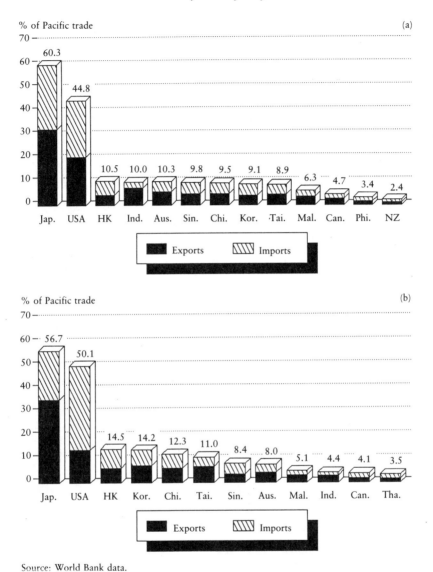

% of Pacific trade (a)

% of Pacific trade (b)

Source: World Bank data.

FIG. 17.2 *Pacific trade: percentage by country (a) 1980, (b) 1987*

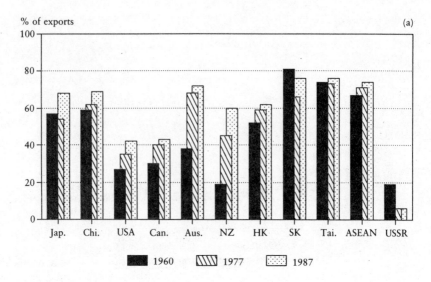

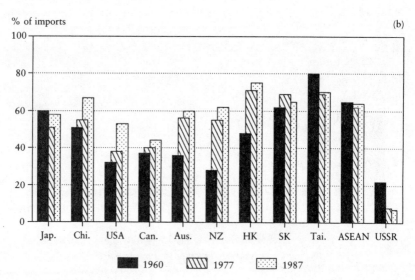

Source: World Bank data.

FIG. 17.3 *Percentage of (a) exports to, (b) imports from the Pacific: 1960, 1977, 1987*

just over 60 per cent of their products from within the Pacific, a rise of merely 7 per cent in just over 20 years. These trends represent to some extent the reliance of the region on fuel and minerals from outside regions, and the rise of Japanese exports to the Asian Pacific.

There are more dramatic changes in patterns of Asian Pacific exports, for it is in this field that their economic success was built. In 1960 both OECD Europe and Asian Pacific countries imported about a quarter of Asian Pacific exports. The United States and non-Asian Pacific LDCs took about 18 per cent each. By 1983 both the United States and the Asian Pacific states saw their percentages rise, to 27 per cent and 34.5 per cent respectively. OECD Europe dropped 10 per cent and non-Asian Pacific LDCs remained about constant. China tripled its share of imports from the region from 0.8 per cent to 2.7 per cent. The basic pattern was a replacement of Europe by the United States as a main export market and the rise in interregional trade, primarily with Japan. For Asian Pacific states, nearly 70 per cent of their trade was within the Pacific, a rise of more than 20 per cent in just over 20 years, but this was distributed unevenly among Pacific states.

These basic, and to an extent loaded, statistics hide some huge variations and inequalities in the trading relationships. While they broadly compare with the extent of trade within the Atlantic world, shares are far less evenly distributed and are therefore more subject to fluctuations and trade problems.

In 1987 Japan and the United States together accounted for 58 per cent of total exports of Pacific states to other Pacific states, but Japan alone took up over 35 per cent of the total.[7] Since 1980 Japan had increased its share by 4 per cent while the United States' share had continued to fall, by 6 per cent in

---

[7] *Direction of Trade* statistics (IMF) are used for all trade statistics in this section. Additional figures, mainly for the Communist world, come from official Soviet statistics and the United Nations Yearbooks on trade. The states covered for these figures are the same as noted in n. 2 above, i.e. all Pacific littoral states plus Laos and Mongolia. Trade figures, unlike GDP figures, are not divided in half for the USSR and the North Americans. Therefore the figures do not distinguish between trade with other Pacific states that is undertaken from Atlantic ports. Inter-Pacific trade is made somewhat larger by counting Soviet–North American trade as Pacific, but it is small in any case. Much more importantly, trade between Pacific states in the Americas is not counted as Pacific trade. Strictly speaking this is unfair, for China–Japan trade is no different from the United States–Canada trade that takes place between its Pacific parts. Thus it is far more accurate to distinguish between Asian Pacific trade and inter-American trade, and both should be distinguished from trade across the Pacific. A more general qualification should also be made about the use of trade statistics. They are used here merely to illustrate that trends are not as accurate as the decimal points may suggest. For example, Japan and China count their trade in different ways, with the Japanese including indirect trade via Hong Kong. The service-sector trade is also notoriously difficult to count and, according to some estimates, up to half the trade between developed economies is really intercompany trade, which is also difficult to count accurately. For some of these issues see *The Economist* (20 August 1988).

that period. Hong Kong, Taiwan, South Korea, and Singapore together accounted for 25 per cent of exports to other Pacific states, up more than 7 per cent since 1980. China accounted for more than 6 per cent, Australia and New Zealand together provided more than 5 per cent, and ASEAN states, led by Singapore with 3.9 per cent and Malaysia with 3.4 per cent, accounted for 13 per cent of total inter-Pacific exports. China had clearly risen from 4.8 per cent in 1980, while Australia and New Zealand had fallen back from 6.8 per cent. But the biggest losers were Indonesia, down from 7.2 per cent as its oil was less desired and less expensive, and its ASEAN partners, whose total was down from 18.8 per cent. In both periods total exports by Pacific Latin American states did not even reach 1 per cent of inter-Pacific exports.

The domination of exports by the most developed states and the hard-driving NICs is plain to see. The decline of the United States was a striking feature as the sweeping tide of Japanese and NIC exports grew. Interestingly enough, the big four West European economies had even managed to increase their share of exports to the Pacific since 1980, suggesting that the problems faced by the Americans and ASEAN in exporting to the Pacific were special cases and that it was not impossible to buck the Japanese and NIC trend.

The rise of the Japanese economic superpower and the decline of the United States also had a similar impact on inter-Pacific imports in this period. In 1980 Japan took 29.6 per cent of inter-Pacific imports while the United States absorbed 25.6 per cent. Seven years later the United States soared to the top of the league with 35.9 per cent while Japan fell back to 21 per cent. This process follows closely the changes in export patterns, and suggests that most of the change in trade can be accounted for by changes in the United States–Japanese relationship. As the two economic superpowers, their bilateral relationship had a domineering effect on overall Pacific trade figures.

The four East Asian NICs took some 23 per cent of total inter-Pacific imports in 1987, marginally up on the figure in 1980. Their ability to withstand the Japanese export drive was testament to their new-found economic strength. Only China matched the United States as a major new importer, lifting its share of imports from the region from 4.8 per cent to 5.9 per cent in the period. China's climb into fifth place as a Pacific importer also lifted it into fifth place overall with roughly 6.2 of total inter-Pacific trade, behind Hong Kong, Korea, Japan, and the United States. The sharp fall in Australian and New Zealand imports from Pacific states meant that by 1987 these two countries were taking only 4.4 per cent of Pacific imports. ASEAN states saw a similar fall, from 14.8 per cent of Pacific imports in 1980 to just under 11 per cent in 1987. Once again, Pacific Latin America accounted for less than 1 per cent of Pacific imports and could be largely ignored as a Pacific trader.

The total imports from Asia Pacific by the big four west European states also fell marginally, so that if they were a Pacific state it would have ranked as the third-largest importer with 13 per cent, and even higher if imports from Pacific North America were counted. Overall, the growing import appetite of the United States and China meant that nearly every other Pacific state saw its share of Pacific imports drop. The dominant role of Japan, the United States, and the NICs was the same as for inter-Pacific exports, although the positions were sometimes changed. But in imports as with exports, Japan and the United States still accounted for more than 50 per cent of the trade and their market share was growing. It seems that assessments of Pacific economic relations need to focus most directly on Japan and the United States, and only then, well down the agenda, on the NICs, ASEAN, China, and Australia/New Zealand.

18

The United States and Japan

In military affairs the main relationship in the Pacific, and indeed elsewhere, is the potential for the so-called mutual assured destruction (MAD) of the superpowers. Each has the ability to inflict unacceptable levels of damage with nuclear weapons on the other, so each is deterred from undertaking action affecting the vital interests of the other. In economic relations, the level of damage cannot be as high, or the catastrophe as irreparable, as nuclear war. But there are three major MAD relationships in the world economy—between western Europe and the United States, Canada and the United States, and the United States and Japan. In the context of international economic politics in the Pacific, the latter relationship constitutes the main feature of the system.

In 1980 United States–Japan trade was 10 per cent of total Pacific trade, making this by far the largest trading relationship. By 1986 the tripling of Japanese exports to the United States meant that their bilateral trade jumped to 14 per cent of all Pacific trade. The evolution of this dominating relationship is one of the main features of international relations in the Pacific, and arguably the single most important relationship in the region.

Japan was the only non-white Pacific state to have fully modernized before the Second World War, and like that other defeated power, Germany, it was always likely to regain its great-power status. Like Germany, Japan was occupied by the United States, but unlike the German state, which was split after the war, Japan was put back on its economic feet as a unified state because the United States feared the rise of Asian Communism. Although American occupation policies no doubt helped Japan revive more quickly, the greatest credit must go to the Japanese people themselves. The American determination to prevent the rearming of Japan, unlike the eventual rearmament of West Germany, allowed Japan to concentrate on economic growth.

Economic recovery began in earnest in 1950 and the Korean War brought added American spending and a further push to growth. By the mid-1950s national production and per-capita national income were zipping past the pre-war heights of the 1930s. Instead of having to pay heavy reparations, Japan was allowed to invest in other friendly East Asian states, Taiwan, the Philippines, and Indonesia. By 1955, under American guidance, Japan was admitted into the General Agreement on Tariffs and Trade and was assuming a normal place in international economic affairs.[1] As a state in the American security system, Japan was offered access to American and allies' markets in Europe. The Americans also provided massive loans and access to technology so as to reduce the burden of supporting allies as soon as possible. Japan insisted that the flow of capital was mostly in the form of loans, thereby maintaining control of its own industries.

Japanese economic recovery was aided by the creation of new industries in specially chosen coastal sites and run by a highly interventionist central planning authority. This was the so-called 'developmental economy', operated on the basis of 'flexible rigidities'.[2] The first export successes were in textiles and light industrial goods, and only later in cameras, shipbuilding, and electronics. The United States was by far the largest market, taking 27 per cent of Japanese exports in 1960, while 30 per cent of Japanese imports came from the United States. Only the South-east Asian states and the white-Commonwealth states of the Pacific—Canada, Australia, and New Zealand—accounted for more than 10 per cent of Japanese trade at the time.

From the United States' point of view, Japan had just become the second most important trading partner, passing Britain (see Figure 18.1). But Japan accounted for only some 7 per cent of United States trade, well down on the 20 per cent of Canada or the combined 19 per cent of the big four West Europeans.

The 1960s saw a rapid transformation of Japan's international trading role and its relationship with the United States. With relatively low wages and advanced industrial skills, Japan became known as a producer of quality goods instead of shoddy ones. Hitachi, Honda, Yamaha, and Datsun became dominant in their markets. De Gaulle spoke of the Japanese Prime Minister as a 'transistor salesman', but the truth was that Japan had already successfully carved out a role as an economic superpower. Japanese business achieved global success where its military had failed in pre-war times. The Japanese government spoke of the 'separation of politics and economics', a feasible strategy so long as other states in the western trading system were bearing the military burden.

The United States remained Japan's patron in the international economy, for example pushing through its membership of the IMF and the OECD in the mid-1960s—thus making Japan the first non-Atlantic member of the

[1] Gary Saxonhouse, 'The World Economy and Japanese Foreign Policy' in Robert Scalapino (ed.), *The Foreign Policy of Modern Japan* (Berkeley, Calif.: University of California Press, 1977).

[2] See Ronald Dore, *Flexible Rigidities* (London: Athlone, 1986) and of course the classic by Chalmers Johnson, *MITI and the Japanese Miracle* (Stanford, Calif.: Stanford University Press, 1982). See also the more contentious Karel Van Wolferen, *The Enigma of Japanese Power* (London: Macmillan, 1989).

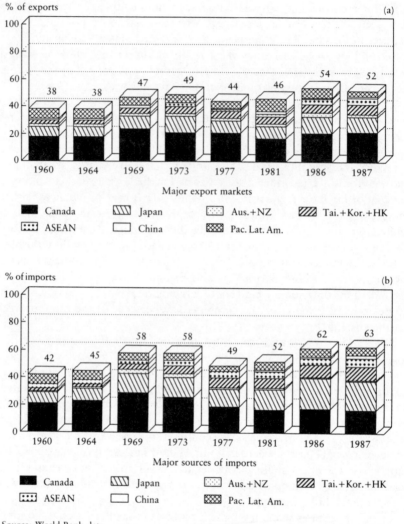

Source: World Bank data.

FIG. 18.1. *USA trade, 1960–87: percentage by (a) major export markets, (b) major sources of imports*

OECD.[3] The Japanese economy continued to hurtle forward at growth rates upward of 10 per cent a year so that by the end of the decade it had displaced West Germany as the world's second-largest market economy. Trade was moving into surplus and Japanese living standards were fast closing the gap on those in western Europe and North America. Most industrial growth was now in heavy industry and electronics, while more labour-intensive light industry such as textiles was lost to the fast-growing NICs in East Asia.[4]

By 1969 the United States was still taking nearly a third of Japanese trade, but now Japanese exports were larger than its imports (see Figure 18.2). The share of Japanese trade held by South-east Asia and the white Commonwealth declined, while imports from western Europe rose. For the United States, the price of its close relationship with Japan was also beginning to rise. By 1969 Japan was clearly the second-largest trading partner (after Canada), with imports from Japan at 14 per cent of total United States imports, opening up a 5 per cent trade gap. The big four West Europeans remained ahead with 18 per cent of United States trade, and theirs was also a more balanced trade than that of Japan.

However, a big shock to the Japanese economy lay just around the corner. With 80 per cent of its energy supplies coming from abroad, the Japanese economic miracle was built on a very fragile base. Oil from the Middle East and coal from Australia and the United States were imported, along with many basic minerals from around the globe.[5] Most of its food and protein came from United States. Without military clout of its own, Japan was heavily dependent on the United States, just at a time when Japan was taking American markets and unbalancing America's trade. After years of holding Japan back from trading with China, the Nixon administration stunned Japan by opening a dialogue with Beijing without consulting Japan.

The 1973 oil price rise following the Arab–Israeli War was a body-blow to the Japanese economy and caused recession around the developed world. This contraction of demand inevitably hurt Japanese exports, but Japan was better able to recover than its fellow market economies. While Japan's energy import bill soared, it kept its economy relatively closed to other imports from developed economies and became an even more ruthless competitor with its friends in the international economy. Now that Japan

---

[3] Frank Langdon, 'Japan and North America' in Robert Ozaki and Walter Arnold (eds.), *Japan's Foreign Relations* (Boulder, Colo.: Westview 1985).

[4] I. M. Destler, Haruhiro Fukui and Hideo Sato, *The Textile Wrangle* (Ithaca: Cornell University Press, 1979).

[5] Saburo Okita, 'Japan's High Dependence on Imports of Raw Materials' in Sir John Crawford and Saburo Okita (eds.), *Raw Materials and Pacific Economic Integration* (Vancouver: University of British Columbia Press, 1978).

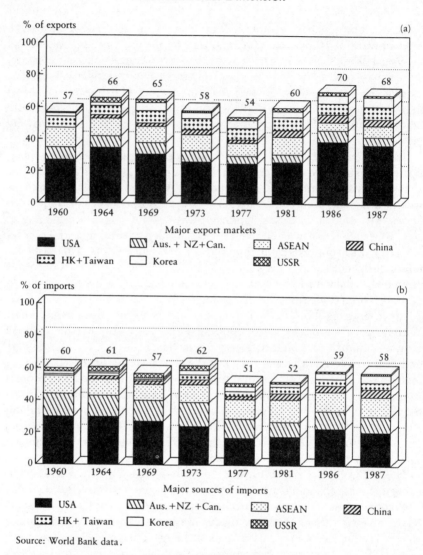

FIG. 18.2. *Japanese trade, 1960–87: percentage by (a) major export markets,
(b) major sources of imports*

was an economic superpower, the United States was far less willing to tolerate Japanese protectionism. The speed of the Japanese penetration of the American market made it a more salient focus for protectionist sentiments in the United States.[6] A potent mix of residual racism, misconceptions about Japanese low wages (no longer true), and snide comments about 'Japan Inc.' made for the first major crisis in Japanese–American relations.

Japan felt that it could muddle through by accepting 'voluntary control' as it had for textiles in 1958, while gradually expanding its market share. But in two devaluations of the dollar in the early 1970s the yen appreciated by 30 per cent and the unilateral limits on United States soya-bean exports to Japan in 1973 made many Japanese wonder about the stability of the economic relationship with the United States.

The result was yet another shift of the Japanese economy, this time out of many heavy industries such as steel and shipbuilding as the NICs closed in on those markets as well. The new direction of high-technology, knowledge-based industries put Japan into direct competition with other developed market economies. But unlike the competition of the 1960s in fading heavy industry, the high-technology sector was a new venture for all developed economies. High-profile exports such as cars to the American market kept the issue of the Japanese economic challenge high on the American agenda. In 1977 the yen was revalued a further 22 per cent as American economic power declined.

Japan had clearly arrived as the third most powerful economy. It took part in the first economic summit of western leaders in France in 1975 and hosted the fifth conference in June 1979. The so-called G-7, a group comprising the United States, Japan, Canada, the United Kingdom, West Germany, France, and Italy, was now routinely described as the 'leading western nations'. But the constant attacks on Japan in the United States for 'unfair trading practices' led many to believe that Japan was not really being accepted as a full member of the G-7. It still felt deeply vulnerable because of its dependence on imported resources and its lack of military reach.[7]

Although the overall volume of Japanese–American trade was booming, the widening of Japanese economic interests meant that the United States played a smaller role in Japanese trade. Exports to the United States stood at 26 per cent in 1981, nearly the same as in 1960. But imports from the United States had dropped to 18 per cent. All of this took place against the background of a rising role for western Europe and ASEAN in Japanese trade.

---

[6] I. M. Destler and Hideo Sato, *Coping With US–Japanese Economic Conflict* (Lexington, Mass.: D. C. Heath, 1982).
[7] Frank Langdon, 'Japan–United States Trade Friction' in *Asian Survey*, 23/5 (May 1983).

While the United States declined as a Japanese trade partner in the 1970s, Japan held its place by taking 9 per cent of American exports and providing 15 per cent of American imports. The big four West Europeans still took 14 per cent of American exports but provided only 13 per cent of American imports. United States–Japanese trade had been more balanced during the 1970s, but by 1981 had fallen back into its 1960s ways of a sharply favourable balance for Japan. The changes in the pattern of United States–Japanese relations were wide-ranging. For example, their civilian air-transport link was the world's fastest growing in the 1980s. Yet it was not only the Japanese that were growing, as the other NICs in particular took advantage of the new transpacific possibilities.[8]

The much-noted shift of American trading patterns to the Pacific was well under way in this period,[9] although it was not until 1984 that the United States traded more with East Asia than it did with Europe. However, the Atlantic still takes more American trade, especially as most trade with the Arab world, Africa, and Latin America travels through or over Atlantic waters. In any case, the shift of trade to Asia was not simply confined to the United States. Britain and West Germany led a similar shift in western Europe, and both countries did more trade with Asia than the United States from 1986.

The globalization of the Japanese economy and the decline of American economic hegemony were crucial components in creating a MAD relationship in Japanese–American trade.[10] Japan began coping with the tension in relations with the outside world by investing heavily in competitors' markets in order to get around economic protectionism. Just as the United States and the West Europeans had penetrated the markets of the developed economies, so Japan was following suit in the 1980s. In some cases, the internationalization was so complex that co-production deals involved more than one country, many of which were European.[11]

Throughout much of the 1980s the United States expanded its economy by means of growing budget deficits that drew in investment from Europe and Japan. The ballooning American trade deficit led America's allies to invest heavily in the United States and buy up parts of the American economy. Further devaluations of the American currency could not stop the relative decline of American competitiveness and the increasing penetration of its market. In 1980 alone, Japan invested $4.2 billion in the United States, just less than the $4.9 billion it invested in all of ASEAN and close to the

---

8 *The Economist* (2 August 1986); *Financial Times* (13 March 1986).
9 For example, Jens Biermeir, 'Atlantic–Pacific' in *Asien Politik*, 38/1 (1987).
10 Edward Lincoln, 'US–Japan Relations: Good Terrible?' in *SAIS Review*, 4/1 (1984).
11 *International Herald Tribune* (15 December 1987).

$5.2 billion the United States invested in all of Asia that year.[12] Japan's net overseas assets increased from $10.9 billion in 1981 to $180.4 billion in 1987. But of the total direct Japanese investment in 1987, western Europe was increasing faster than the United States as a preferred location.[13] The American budget problems in the late 1980s and the lure of the Single European Market in 1992 were leading to a greater balance in Japanese investment strategies. Similar patterns were evident in the foreign-securities market. Out of a total acquisition of foreign securities of $162 billion in 1985/6, $67.3 billion was of American equities and bonds. In the bond market in the late 1980s, the decline in the value of the dollar led Japanese investors to take a greater interest in European currencies.[14]

By 1987, with heavy Japanese and West European investment, the United States had become the world's largest debtor nation. In 1986, Japanese firms invested some $2 billion in new production facilities in the United States. Japan's total direct investment in the United States reached $23 billion, ranking it third after Britain and Holland. But most Japanese investment has been in distribution, finance, and real estate. Manufacturing has been a much smaller proportion of Japanese investment than for other West European investors in the United States.[15] Nevertheless, with 60 per cent of the Japanese trade surplus with the United States coming from car exports, Japanese attempts to invest in production facilities in the United States held the prospect of major reductions in the Japanese trade surplus and even re-exports of American-made Japanese cars to Japan.[16] Although at times it made economic sense for Japan to invest more heavily in lower-labour-cost Asia, for political reasons it was seen as more sensible to choose sites in the United States and western Europe.[17]

But in an age of increasingly global markets and an increasing percentage of trade between international corporations, Japan's changing trade practices were of global rather than merely Pacific-wide concern. As Japan increased its percentage of production in the United States, a significant proportion was headed for the European market. For example, some 50 000 of the 70 000 cars to be exported from Honda's United States operations by 1991 were likely to go to Europe.[18] This was both a way around European objections about Japanese exports and a way of making the United States the ally of Japan on at least some international trade issues.

---

[12] 'Direct Investment in the Pacific Basin' (Tokyo: Japan Center for International Exchange, 15 April 1983).

[13] *The Economist* (13 August 1988).

[14] *Far Eastern Economic Review* (3 December 1987); *The Economist* (5 November 1988).

[15] *Financial Times* (7 December 1987).

[16] *The Economist* (12 December 1987).

[17] *Financial Times* (4 December 1987).

[18] *Business Week* (14 November 1988).

Nevertheless, there was still a major effort by Japan to diversify production, including major investments in Asia. In car production, some have
suggested that the Japanese sun may be setting as fast as it rose.[19] This
much-observed 'hollowing out' of Japan was yet another gloss on the 1986
buzzword of 'internationalization' of Japan. But the changes still had a long
way to go. In 1987, 4 per cent of Japanese companies' production came from
their operations abroad, compared to 17 per cent for the United States and
20 per cent for West Germany.[20] Japan's foreign direct investment by was
worth some $58 billion in January 1987, less than half that of Britain, West
Germany, or Holland, and less than a quarter that of the United States' $260
billion.[21] Over 380 000 of the Japanese-created jobs were in Asia, 100 000
in North America, and only 40 000 in the EEC. Japan had long been driven
from low-cost, labour-intensive jobs to the advantages of economic innova-
tion in high technology. By the late 1980s it was leading many of its NIC
imitators down a similar road—posing an even more serious challenge to the
competitiveness of American industry.[22] Yet in the decade from 1975, the
percentage of total Japanese investment that was in Asia fell by 22 per cent to
11 per cent while that in North America rose from 27 per cent to 45 per cent.
Latin America was up from 11 per cent to 21 per cent and Europe was the
home of 16 per cent instead of 10 per cent. Japanese investment everywhere
else fell.[23] The shift to the United States and western Europe seems directly
related to the concerns of other developed market economies that they will
need additional protectionism against Japanese exports.

The interdependence of Japan and the United States was clearly growing
more equal. A withdrawal of Japanese funds from investments in the United
States in the 1980s could have wrecked the American financial system and
its economic prosperity.[24] But that was hardly in Japan's best interests.
Japan was also increasingly aware that it could no longer drive its foreign
economic policy with the engine of exports. It was no longer an island
isolated from the powerful winds of change in the international economy.
The need to turn to stimulating domestic demand had become clear in the
late 1980s. In 1987 Japan's import bill was still only 40 per cent manufactured goods, as compared to twice that figure in the United States, 70 per
cent in West Germany, and 75 per cent in the UK. Japanese imports were
still worth only the equivalent of 6.5 per cent of GNP, compared to 9.2 per
cent for the United States and an average of 23.2 per cent in the EC.[25].

[19] *The Economist* (24 May 1986, 23 January 1988).
[20] *The Economist* (7 February 1987).
[21] *The Economist* (20 February 1988); DeAnne Julius and Stephen Thomson, *Investment and Foreign-Owned in the G-S* (London: RIIA Discussion Paper No. 12, 1989).
[22] *International Herald Tribune* (4 February 1987, 14 November 1987).
[23] *The Economist* (6 June 1987).
[24] *The Economist* (2 May 1987).
[25] *The Economist* (5 December 1987).

Japan also remained deeply aware of its need to import vital resources from abroad and to pay for them with the earnings from trade with the developed world. The falling price of most commodities in the 1980s made the Japanese system more able to bear the burden of dependency, but it was still aware that it had only a breathing space. When it asked to import Alaskan oil instead of Gulf oil, and thereby reduce the trade deficit with the United States, Washington refused, preferring to keep its own import bill low. The cost was increasing tension with a vital economic ally in the Pacific. To a large extent the rifts were natural and inevitable, with Japan finding it absolutely necessary to export to survive, and to export to the leading economies of the developed world.[26] The United States found it difficult to accept that it could no longer afford to let the Japanese economy collapse, and yet Japan remains a formidable competitor. Nor is the United States able any more to dictate policy to a weak Japan.

By 1986 Japanese trade with the United States had reached its all-time high. With 39 per cent of Japanese exports going to the United States and 23 per cent of imports coming from there (37 per cent and 21 per cent respectively in 1987), Japan could not ignore the increasingly shrill calls in the United States for changes in the relationship. Slogans prevalent in the angry mood of Japan-bashing included 'Zap the Jap' and 'Pearl Harbour in a different guise'. The imposition of trade sanctions in 1987 for the first time since the Second World War marked a new low in over two decades of almost-incessant trade friction.[27]

The American public was clearly ambiguous about the impact of Japanese trade and investment policy, with an element of racism apparently making the Japanese less welcome than the Europeans.[28] The United States itself still had fewer firms doing business with Japan than with the West Europeans, and far fewer Americans living in Japan than in the more culturally familiar Europe.[29]

Thus the pattern of problems in United States–Japan trade relations was more a feature of the global economy than merely a special bilateral problem. Both Japanese and West German currencies were sharply revalued in 1985, as was the British pound in 1987/8, in an attempt to help solve the American deficit. Readjustments in the Japanese–American relationship were worked out primarily at the G-7 level.

In addition, West Europeans were increasing their share of Japanese trade by similar percentages to that of the United States. But in the European case,

---

[26] See 'Introduction' in Crawford and Okita (eds.), *Raw Materials*.

[27] *Far Eastern Economic Review* (5 November 1987).

[28] *The Economist* (19 March 1988).

[29] In 1982 there were about as many American citizens employed in American firms in Japan as there were in Holland: Bernard Gordon, *Political Protectionism in the Pacific* (London: IISS, Adelphi Paper, 228, spring 1988), 34–5.

the greatest increase came in exports to Japan, something the United States was still finding much more difficult to achieve. Of course, to some extent the trade figures tell only part of the story. United States firms, such as Coca-Cola or IBM, have been able to produce and sell in Japan—something that does not show up in trade figures—and in 1986 such operations accounted for sales equal to three times the Japanese trade surplus with the United States. Japanese consumers each spent three times as much on foreign-made goods as American consumers did on the goods of Japanese firms.[30] When the yen rose sharply in 1987, it was the NICs who were the main beneficiaries by virtue of their greater ability to crack the Japanese market. Thus the inability of the United States to export to Japan had more to do with basic problems in the American economy.[31]

Japan's export success, as to some extent the West Europeans had already shown, was more than just an ability to penetrate the American market; it was also part of its more global trading success. But increasingly it was achieved by targeting specific 'market niches' in the developed world rather than mounting an across-the-board challenge.[32] In financial services as well, the growth of Japanese influence was part of a more genuine globalization of international economic relations. Pressures for change in the Japanese financial market came as much from London as New York with the evolution of '24-hour trading' in the late 1980s. The roller-coaster fluctuations in the global markets in the autumn of 1987 were further evidence of the trend to global financial interdependence.[33] Even in the field of science and techno-logy, Japan was increasing its market share and becoming a more powerful actor in the global trade in science and ideas. 'Techno-nationalism', as with trade protectionism, involved Japan in complex global economic rivalries.[34]

From the American point of view, in 1987 Japan had become its largest source of imports, taking 21 per cent of the American market. The relative importance of Japan for the United States was becoming increasingly similar to the United States' long-standing importance for the Japanese economy. Canada remained the United States' largest trade partner, but with Japanese imports from the United States at only 11 per cent the American–Japanese trade was more badly out of balance than ever before. Western Europe also increased its share of the American market, to 16 per cent of imports and exports, but not at the same rate as the Japanese.

The trend for both Japan and the United States was towards a greater

[30] *The Economist* (11 April 1987).
[31] *Financial Times* (4 December 1987).
[32] *Financial Times* (27 October 1987).
[33] *Far Eastern Economic Review* (17 July 1987); The *Economist* (23 August 1986, 4 July 1987, 5 March 1988); *Business Week* (13 July 1987).
[34] *Far Eastern Economic Review* (31 March 1988, 21 May 1988).

concentration on the global economy of the developed market economies and, within that, a stronger role for both the United States and western Europe in the Pacific. But Japan remained a highly vulnerable economy, and therefore equally dependent on a free market in the developing world. Japan was acutely aware of its limits as an economic superpower. And as Japanese–American economic relations settled into what seemed like permanent crisis, there was an increasing need to change the rules of the vital economic game.

19

The Newly Industrialized Countries

A major feature of the international economy is the division between developed and less developed economies. But a crucial underpinning of the north Atlantic community has been the commonality of economic systems and level of development, while most of the rest of the world remained either Communist or less developed. Some of the most important exceptions to the concentration of wealth in the north Atlantic world are to be found in the Pacific, where Japan and white-settled former British colonies attained similar levels of prosperity. As islands, these states can be seen as helping provide economic bridges across the waters.

Japan has been the only non-white state to leap into the category of developed economy. No other state has managed to duplicate the Japanese success, but one category of states, the Newly Industrialized Countries (NICs), have come closest. The phenomenon was first seen in Latin America, Israel, and to some extent southern Europe. Peru, Ecuador, and Colombia can be only barely classified as NICs, whereas Mexico and Chile can be more properly considered Pacific Latin American NICs. But in the 1980s, as their growth rates stagnated and they became less active in the international economy, the Latin Americans had yet to develop as important actors in Pacific international economic relations.

The trading patterns of these Latin American states were overwhelmingly dominated by their powerful North American neighbours and to some extent by the states of western Europe. By far the largest economy, Mexico, saw 65 per cent of its trade go to the United States, with imports from its northern neighbour even reaching 81 per cent in 1981. This pattern had changed little in the 25 years from 1960. Only two Pacific states did any significant trade with Mexico—Australia and Japan. The latter provided a market for a steady 6 per cent of Mexican exports over the 25-year period, but imports from Japan rose from 1 per cent to 6 per cent in that time.

Beginning in the 1970s with the boom in Mexican oil exports, Japan became involved as a purchaser of oil, but also with an interest in establishing a production base for the United States market. Japan became the second-largest creditor of Mexico, holding 20 per cent of the $100 billion debt in 1987. Although the Mexican debt was Japan's largest stake in a developing state, direct Japanese investment was still less than 15 per cent of the Mexican total. In fact, Japanese investment in Brazil, an Atlantic state, was twice as large.[1] Although there are 10 000 Mexicans of Japanese descent in Mexico (there are more than a million in Brazil), the Japanese motive for investment was more a need for resources and for access to the North American market. The big four West Europeans still provided nearly twice the Japanese level of imports. Mexico, with both a Pacific and Atlantic aspect, thus remained an inter-American trader and only a marginal participant in the more distant global economy. It certainly was not a significant Pacific trader.

Unusually enough, Chile, the other Pacific Latin American NIC, did almost as much trade with the big four West Europeans as it did with the United States. In 1960 37 per cent of export and 46 per cent of import trade was with the United States, while the Europeans took 38 per cent and 24 per cent. By 1973 the figures were (9 per cent and 22 per cent for the United States and 34 per cent and 19 per cent for the Europeans. In 1986 the United States climbed back to 22 per cent of Chilean exports and a leading 22 per cent of imports. The big four West Europeans were still the leading export market with 24 per cent, and took 17 per cent of the import market. Japan had increased its proportion from 2 per cent of trade to 10 per cent in 1986, but its share had slipped a bit from the late-1970s high. Chile, like Mexico, was not a Pacific trader, and remained strongly oriented to the Americas and Europe. In 1900 Chile was the third most important destination for ships from Australia, but the decline in trade was sharp after the Panama Canal was opened in 1914.[2]

Of course, to some extent Chilean trade with the United States could as much be considered Pacific trade as, say, that between Australia and China. It is clearly improper to exclude inter-American trade from inter-Pacific trade when trade up the coast of East Asia is counted. Nearly all analysts make this error, including in the calculation of inter-Pacific trade above, even though it should now be clear that so much of what is called Pacific trade is really sub-regional trade. With the exception of certain powerful bilateral relationships such as that between Japan and the United States, the dominant trade relationships are usually between neighbours. Canadian dominance of American trade, like United States trade with its southern neighbours, is a case in point of such sub-regionalism.

On the other side of the Pacific, there are four other states—Hong Kong, Singapore, South Korea, and Taiwan—that have become NICs more recently than those on the eastern Pacific. But their growth has been much more export-oriented and therefore has played a wider and more important role in the international political economy.

[1] *The Economist* (6 June 1987).
[2] *Financial Times* (15 April 1988).

In total in 1987 they accounted for 25 per cent of inter-Pacific exports and 23 per cent of imports. While imports had gradually risen, it was the leap of exports, as evident in the gain of 7 per cent from 1980, that made them such important actors. Hong Kong led the way, accounting for 8.1 per cent of imports and 6.4 per cent of exports in the Pacific, although a large percentage of that trade was part of the hidden, third-party trade in the region: China and Taiwan, and China and South Korea both used Hong Kong for such purposes.

Thus South Korea, with its 7.6 per cent of Pacific exports and 6.6 per cent of imports, was the largest real trader among the NICs. Taiwan with 7.1 per cent of exports and 3.9 per cent of imports was the next most important, with a rising share of Pacific exports. Singapore held 3.9 per cent of exports and 4.5 per cent of imports, but its share had slumped some 0.5 per cent since 1980 as its economy readjusted to trade in higher technology.

Yet apart from this international role, orientation towards the market economies, paucity of resources, and high investment in education, it is difficult to see much that links these four so-called 'East Asian tigers'. Both Hong Kong and Singapore are city states with small populations. They were both created as artificial entrepôt traders, for the China and South-east Asia markets respectively. They both survived their colonial inventors to prosper in similar roles in the post-war and especially post-1960s economy. Not surprisingly the patterns of their trade remained very different.

Singapore's success is built on a firmly directed state capitalism that intervenes in many levels of the life of the individual. The government initially selected labour-intensive manufactures such as textiles, garments, and electrical goods as the instruments of export promotion. After enjoying benefits from the United States' involvement in Vietnam and the resulting investments, the economy was moved into heavier industry such as shipbuilding, industrial machinery, and oil refining.[3] Like Hong Kong, Singapore was to take advantage of its position as a hub for regional communication and services required by those taking part in local economies but wanting a sophisticated base. By the early 1980s some two-thirds of GDP was generated in services such as banking, shipping transport, and tourism. Foreign investment played a crucial role, accounting for 13 per cent of Singapore's manufacturing output in 1980.[4]

In 1960 some 72 per cent of Singapore's imports came from within the Pacific basin, of which 50 per cent came from its immediate neighbours in South-east Asia (see Figure 19.1) Western Europe, led by Britain, sent 13 per

    3 Susumu Awanohara, 'Look East: The Japan Model' in *Asian-Pacific Economic Literature*, 1, 1987.
    4 Nigel Harris, *The End of the Third World* (London: Penguin, 1986), ch. 2; Harry Oshima, *Economic Growth in Monsoon Asia* (Tokyo: University of Tokyo Press, 1987).

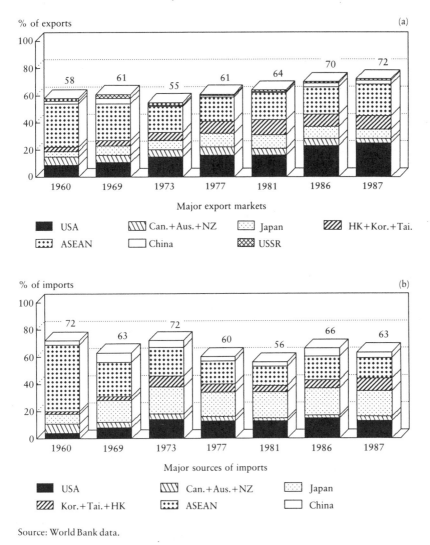

% of exports (a)

Major export markets

| ■ USA | ⧄ Can.+Aus.+NZ | ▦ Japan | ▨ HK+Kor.+Tai. |
| ▦ ASEAN | ☐ China | ▩ USSR | |

% of imports (b)

Major sources of imports

| ■ USA | ⧄ Can.+Aus.+NZ | ▦ Japan |
| ▨ Kor.+Tai.+HK | ▦ ASEAN | ☐ China |

Source: World Bank data.

FIG. 19.1. *Singapore trade, 1960–87: percentage by (a) major export markets, (b) major sources of imports*

cent of imports while the United States sent 4 per cent and Japan 7 per cent. Yet only 58 per cent of Singapore's exports were within the basin, around 34 per cent went to South-east Asian neighbours, 7 per cent to the United States, and 4 per cent to Japan.

The most striking feature of the changing pattern of trade was the decline of Singapore's fellow ASEAN members as partners and the diversification of trade. By 1977, ASEAN states took roughly 18 per cent of Singapore exports and provided a similar share of imports. The West Europeans also slipped a bit, taking only 10 per cent of trade. But other NICs now took over 10 per cent of exports and 4 per cent of imports, the United States took 16 per cent of exports and 13 per cent of imports, and Japan took 10 per cent of exports and led the way in imports with 19 per cent. Some 61 per cent of exports and 57 per cent of imports were within the basin—a drop in imports, indicating the extent to which Singapore had entered the global economy. The more developed states could take its increasingly sophisticated exports as Singapore moved from textiles to heavier industry. With this more developed society, Singaporeans themselves demanded the more sophisticated goods that few of their poorer ASEAN neighbours could provide. The move into financial services was part of this growing sophistication in the Singapore market.[5]

In the earlier period of 1969–75, Japan and the big four West Europeans were the major sources of investment in Singapore, providing a total of $364 million and $255 million respectively, while all other major industrialized states, including the United States, provided less than $100 million. In the early 1980s the percentages of investment remained the same, with Singapore, like many other export-oriented economies, investing in the United States in order to beat import restrictions.[6] But Singapore, like all the other NICs, was benefiting from sharply increased Japanese investment as Japan hollowed out at least parts of its industrial base.[7]

By 1987 little of the pattern of trade had changed with the exception that the United States had become an increasingly lucrative export market, taking 25 per cent of Singapore's total exports. Exports to Australia and to some extent the NICs contracted as trade shifted among developed economies. Exports to the Pacific were less, 72 per cent of the Singapore total. Imports from the region climbed to 63 per cent as trade with the Middle East fell back a bit. But compared to 1960 Singapore took fewer imports from the Pacific in 1987. Yet Singapore remained a strong Pacific trader, dominated by distant Japan and the United States. ASEAN trade was still the largest single block, with Malaysia taking roughly 14 per cent of total trade, but Singapore had clearly oriented itself more to the attractive trade with developed market economies. Trade with the main Europeans was also increasing since the 1970s, suggesting that the main focus was on trade with developed, market economies.

Hong Kong stands in striking contrast to the rigidly planned pattern of

[5] *The Economist* (19 July 1986).

[6] All data from annual volumes of *Geographical Distribution of Financial Flows to Developing Countries* (Paris: OECD, various years).

[7] *Far Eastern Economic Review* (12 June 1986).

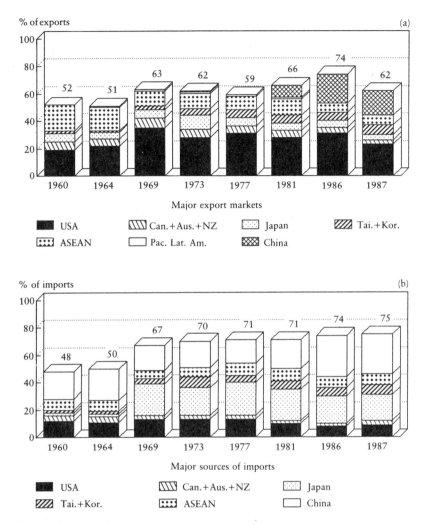

Source: World Bank data.

FIG. 19.2. *Hong Kong trade, 1960–87: percentage by (a) major export markets,*
(b) major sources of imports

economic development in Singapore (see Figure 19.2). Its free-ranging
economy is only barely nudged into planned growth by central government,
and foreign financial policy is virtually unrestricted. The island colony has
prospered as a processing zone and provider of services to China and the
China trade.

To a large extent because of its more exposed role in the international economy, Hong Kong's fortunes have fluctuated to a remarkable extent with the general western global economy. In the 1970s there was a major change in the type of Hong Kong exports, moving into higher-value and more skilled inputs. Almost all exports were in light industry, and concentrated on textiles and electrical machinery. The textile industry accounted for nearly half of manufacturing output in the mid-1970s, taking advantage of the skills of those who fled Communist China, especially in the first instance those from Shanghai.[8]

In 1960, Hong Kong trade was dominated by the United States and the big four West Europeans. The Americans took 19 per cent of exports and 12 per cent of imports while the Europeans took 19 per cent and 16 per cent. With 52 per cent of its exports going to the basin and 48 per cent of its imports coming from there, Hong Kong was already a major Pacific trader. By 1973 its trade with the United States had increased to 28 per cent of exports and 13 per cent of imports, while the European four had slid back to 21 per cent and 12 per cent. But Japan had clearly jumped into third place, taking 10 per cent of exports and providing the largest share of imports at 20 per cent. Trade with Hong Kong's local market, China, provided 19 per cent of imports, just about the same as in 1960. But unlike Singapore's local market, China held its share of trade. Then as China opened its door to the West, Hong Kong became increasingly important as a source of services.

Hong Kong also faced increasing protectionism in developed economies. With the Multifibre Agreement limiting its textile exports, Hong Kong began diversifying. It also began investing in other East Asian states to take advantage of cheaper labour and unused textile export quotas. Hong Kong Chinese entrepreneurs made use of their ethnic contacts in the region and just inland in China itself to maintain a competitive edge in light industrial products.

By far the most important change in Hong Kong's position came with the opening of China to foreign investment and trade. In 1987 China accounted for 18 per cent of Hong Kong exports and 29 per cent of its imports, down from slightly higher peaks in the previous year. Large parts of that trade were simply re-export trade and the provision of services for the China trade. Hong Kong's port became the world's fifteenth largest and its airport the eleventh largest in terms of passenger movements. The service industries such as tourism played a growing role in the economy.

The United States' share of the Hong Kong market remained second to China's, but sliding to levels last reached in 1960. Japan's share declined less sharply after the opening of the China market and in 1987 it was down to

---

[8] See note 6.

levels last reached in the late 1960s. Western Europe's share of Hong Kong trade was in steady decline until the 1980s when it began to level off as Hong Kong's third most important trade partner.

However, with the sharp appreciation of the yen in the late 1980s, Hong Kong, like the other NICs, was able to step into the Japanese market, emphasizing the quality of its products and sound local knowledge.[9] This concentration on local trade raised the level of Hong Kong's trade within the Pacific to account for 63 per cent of its imports and 58 per cent of its exports—a genuine Pacific trader. But Hong Kong exports to the Pacific were lower than at any point since 1977 and imports were lower than at any time since the mid-1960s. Unlike Singapore, Hong Kong was more dependent on its local market and had an uncertain political future.

One of the most distinctive aspects of the Hong Kong experience was the extent to which it was forced to become an investor in other states in order to beat export restrictions. It was a large investor in ASEAN states as well as the United States, all the while continuing to receive aid and investment, primarily from Japan and western Europe. By 1987 Japan was still investing more than twice as much in Hong Kong as in any of the other NICs, and nearly twice as much as in Indonesia.[10] By the 1980s Hong Kong investment in the United States was booming, in part as people moved assets out of Hong Kong in preparation for the 1997 transition to Chinese rule (see below). In 1986 direct investment from Hong Kong into the United States was $145 million, mainly in California where the 'ready-made infrastructure' of the local Chinese community was a great attraction.[11]

But West Europeans and above all Japanese still poured money in. In 1982–5 Japan invested half as much in Hong Kong as it did in all of China and five times as much as in Taiwan. In 1986 the United States still provided 41 per cent of investment in Hong Kong, with Japan holding 21 per cent, China 15 per cent, and Britain 6 per cent. The Americanization of Hong Kong is said to be evident in the fact that by 1986 the Americans were the single largest expatriate community in the colony.[12]

The Anglo-Chinese agreement on Hong Kong in 1984 provided for the incorporation of the colony into China in 1997, albeit with special status for 50 years. The question mark over the ability of the world's second-largest Communist state to incorporate and run perhaps the world's most free-wheeling market economy has meant a steady drain of funds and skills from Hong Kong. But to some extent Hong Kong has already moved well down the road of close co-operation with the Chinese economic system as it fulfils

[9] *Financial Times* (28 August 1987).
[10] *The Economist* (23 January 1988).
[11] *Far Eastern Economic Review* (3 February 1987).
[12] *The Economist* (29 November 1986).

the role of entrepôt for the China trade. As China builds up its special economic zone on the Hong Kong frontier, the dividing line between ideologies is blurred. But none the less there is far greater uncertainty hanging over the future of this most remarkable of NICs than there is over that of Singapore. And with the growing ease of contacts between hostile states, for example between China and Korea, and China and Taiwan, there is any case a declining need for Hong Kong's skills in serving as a secret rendezvous for entrepôt trade.

The last two of the East Asians NICs are in many ways more impressive, for with their larger populations they constitute more normal states. Both are also locked in a civil war that drains resources for the armed forces and both have followed the state-capitalist path to directed, export-oriented growth.[13]

South Korea, savaged by a civil war in which open hostilities ended only in 1953, then had 47 per cent of its GNP provided by agriculture and 9 per cent by manufacturing. By 1980 the figures were 16 per cent and 30 per cent. Within a generation, South Korea had yanked itself up from one of the poorest nations on earth to one of the fastest growing and a candidate for the status of 'the new Japan'.[14]

Japan had dominated Korea's pre-war economy but it had also established a rudimentary infrastructure for a modern economy. After the civil war, however, only the memories of skills remained. Under firm guidance from the United States, and heavy investment from America and later Japan, the economy was revitalized and land reform undertaken. A military coup in 1960 imposed a dictatorship that also brought astounding economic growth. In 1960 Japan took 61 per cent of South Korean exports and 17 per cent of its imports, while the United States accounted for 11 per cent of exports and 34 per cent of imports (see Figure 19.3). This was an economy obviously distorted by war and the presence of a wealthy neighbour.

Under a strict regime of import control and export promotion, the South Korean miracle took off in the late 1960s. Heavy industry such as shipbuilding, vehicles, and heavy machinery was so successful that Japan was edged out of many of these markets by lower-priced South Korean equivalents.[15] By 1977 the pattern of trade was still dominated by the United States and Japan. The United States took 31 per cent of exports and 23 per cent of imports while Japan took 21 per cent of exports and 36 per cent of imports. Some 63 per cent of exports and 68 per cent of imports were within the

13 See generally Gordon White and Robert Wade (eds.), *Developmental States in East Asia* (Brighton: IDS Research Report, 16, 1985).

14 *The Economist* (20 February 1988).

15 Richard Luedde-Neurath, 'State Intervention and Export-oriented Development in South Korea' in White and Wade, *Development States*.

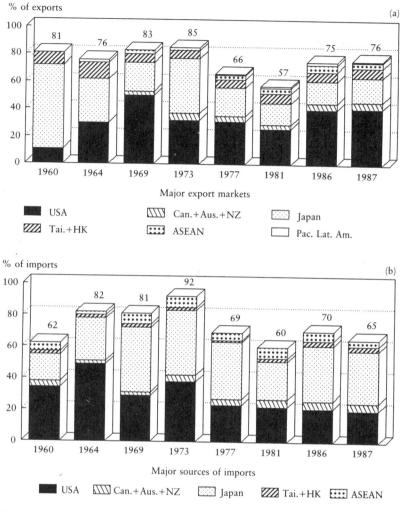

FIG. 19.3. *South Korean trade, 1960–87: percentage by (a) major export markets, (b) major sources of imports*

Source: World Bank data.

basin, but the trade was still dominated by the two economic giants. This remained the most distorted of all of the NICs' trading patterns, but it was still a recipe for success.

In the early 1980s South Korea loosened up some aspects of its state control in an attempt to stimulate more private enterprise. The level of debt was by some accounts even higher than that of Brazil in 1985, and in 1986

South Korea was still Asia's largest debtor. Yet South Korea had a far more effective export sector, a far better ability to meet its obligations, and a declining need for imported energy.[16] Foreign investment played a part in the Korean economic expansion, but it was less than 20 per cent of Mexican levels in 1970–6 and as a ratio of GNP it was half that of Brazil. It seems that foreign investment, mostly Japanese, followed growth as South Korea was seen as a cheaper production base than that available at home. As the Japanese trade surplus with the United States grew and production costs in Japan increased, South Korea took an increasing share of Japanese investment as a way to solve the trade gap problem. By 1988 a good chunk of Korea's $10 billion surplus with the United States was really Japanese exports, and in any case Japan ran a $5 billion surplus with South Korea.[17]

In the first half of the 1970s the United States and Japan provided the vast majority of aid and investment in South Korea and, apart from Indonesia, South Korea received more investment than any other Pacific state. Even in the first half of the 1980s this pattern remained virtually unchanged. But with growing American complaints in the 1980s about the unfair trading practices of South Korea, Seoul, like Tokyo, began trimming a bit to keep the Americans happy. South Korea was the second-biggest Asian investor in the United States in 1986 with a total of $325 million. A major steel project in 1986 was an attempt to beat American import restrictions.[18] But South Korea remained an export-led economy, the world's twelfth largest in 1987, in a time of growing protectionism in the United States. It was also heavily dependent on Japan at a time when many South Koreans were calling for a reassessment of the closeness of the ties with Japan.[19] Much like the transformation of Japan's economy in the 1970s, South Korean strategy was due for an overhaul. Its heavy dependence on several large corporations, which in turn were heavily dependent on foreign trade, made the South Korean economy vulnerable in an age of a rapidly changing international economy.

In general, despite the rapid change in the economy and the new trends in the types of goods produced, by 1987 there had been little significant change in South Korea's pattern of trade. The United States took 41 per cent of exports and 20 per cent of imports while Japan accounted for 18 per cent of exports and 33 per cent of imports.

A potentially significant exception to this relatively stable pattern of trade was the growth in South Korea's hidden trade with China. Some estimates

---

16 Chalmers Johnson, 'South Korean Democratization: The Role of Economic Development', *Pacific Review*, 1, 1989.
17 *The Economist* (20 February 1988).
18 *Far Eastern Economic Review* (3 December 1987).
19 *The Economist* (12 December 1987); *Financial Times* (4 September 1987).

put it at $2 billion annually in the late 1980s, roughly equal to total trade with Canada or Australia and possibly even ranking fourth among South Korean trade partners.[20] Considering the closeness of China and the complementarity of their economies, such trade made obvious sense, as it would for the Soviet Union and South Korea.

Somewhat surprisingly, the percentage of trade within the Pacific was down from the peaks of the early 1970s so that by 1987 some 73 per cent of exports and 62 per cent of imports were within the Pacific. But as in the past, South Korean trade was still dominated by two trading partners. The South Korean miracle was not a Pacific process—to all intents and purposes the country could have been an island in between Japan and the United States. But the dangers of such an isolated position were leading South Korea to develop new ties with China and indeed to broaden its participation in the global market economy.

Taiwan, which *is* an island, has had perhaps the most remarkable development of all the NICs. The lessons of land reform and much else that Chiang Kai-shek failed to implement on the mainland of China when he had the chance were imposed on the people of Taiwan in a ruthless, but stunningly successful way. By the 1980s Taiwan was the most advanced of the NICs, and the one most likely properly to emulate Japan's path to development.[21] By 1988 its 20 million people had an official per-capita GDP of $5000, but one estimate put the real figure, including the underground economy, nearer to $8000.[22] It had had no negative rates of growth for 34 years and had reduced agriculture to under 10 per cent of GDP. Exports had increased their share from 11 per cent to 50 per cent of GDP, with textiles and clothing leading the way. By the 1980s the main export products were machinery and above all electrical goods. By 1982 Taiwan was the largest exporter of electronic products among the less developed countries, with Mexico second and South Korea fourth.[23]

While both Taiwan and South Korea had the advantages of heavy United States support, balanced by the problems of heavy defence spending, Taiwan had the 'advantage' of a longer period under Japanese colonial rule when more infrastructure was developed. Taiwan also has less than half the population of South Korea and is 15 per cent of its size. Taiwan developed its industrial capacity only after agricultural reform was undertaken and the government allowed the domestic market to expand well before that in

20 *The Economist* (20 August 1988).
21 I. M. D. Little, 'An Economic Reconnaissance' in Walter Galenson (ed.), *Economic Growth and Structural Change in Taiwan* (Ithaca: Cornell University Press, 1979).
22 *The Economist* (19 March 1988).
23 Harris, *Third World*, 47; *The Economist* (12 March 1988).

South Korea.[24] Taiwan still had a centrally directed economy, but was more dominated by light industry and a larger number of smaller, labour-intensive operations. State intervention was less direct and comprehensive than in Korea, but by virtue of government control of the financial sector it was still effective and important.[25]

In the early 1960s the level of aid declined and the government expanded exports and encouraged foreign investment. The pattern of trade was nearly as heavily distorted as that of South Korea, with Japan taking 36 per cent of exports and 35 per cent of imports (see Figure 19.4). The United States took 11 per cent of exports and 36 per cent of imports. Other nascent NICs took 18 per cent of exports but only 2 per cent of imports, and South-east Asian states took only 8 per cent of Taiwan exports and 3 per cent of imports.

Taiwan clearly depended on Japan for a push-start into the international trading economy, but it was the United States that soon took the leading role. Much like South Korea, Taiwan's trade remained dominated by these two developed economies. In 1977 the United States took 39 per cent of Taiwan's exports and 25 per cent of imports, while Japan took a further 19 per cent of exports and 38 per cent of imports. The share of the big four West Europeans rose to about 10 per cent of Taiwan's total trade, a little more than the ASEAN states and greater than the 10 per cent of exports and 5 per cent of imports taken by other NICs. With 77 per cent of its exports and 75 per cent of its imports within the Pacific basin, Taiwan was one of the most Pacific-oriented trading states, but close to three-quarters of those figures was accounted for by just two states.

The unreality of Taiwan's international position as 'China' was exposed in the 1970s when the United States opened a dialogue with the Communists on the mainland. Since the early 1970s Taiwan has increasingly lost diplomatic recognition but continued to prosper as a trading state. By 1987 it had diplomatic relations with only 23 states, but trading relations with well over 100, including the mainland (mostly via Hong Kong). Taiwan showed the extent to which business speaks louder than politics in a globally interdependent economy. Even without formal diplomatic relations Taiwan's total trade of over $19 billion with the United States in 1985 was more than twice the $8.3 billion achieved by mainland China. (Japan, on the other hand, did $19 billion trade in that year with China and only half that with Taiwan).

Both Japan and the United States had also been the main sources of

[24] Mick Moore, 'Economic Growth and the Rise of Civil Society' in White and Wade (eds.), *Developmental States*.

[25] Robert Wade, 'State Intervention in "Outward-Looking" Development' in White and Wade (eds.), *Developmental States*; Oshima, *Economic Growth*.

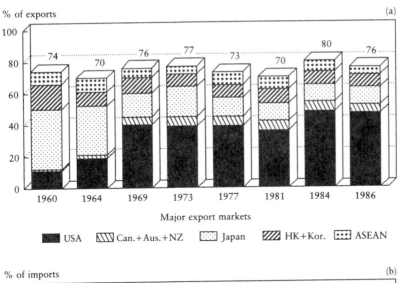

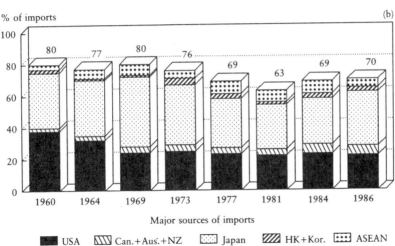

Source: World Bank data.

FIG. 19.4. *Taiwan trade, 1960–86: percentage by (a) major export markets, (b) major sources of imports*

financial flows to Taiwan. Between 1969 and 1975 the United States was the source of $720 million, nearly twice the Japanese figure, and in 1980 the pattern was roughly the same. But in the 1982–5 period Taiwan began investing more heavily in the United States in order to beat export restrictions, while Japan was still a net investor in Taiwan, as was western Europe.

By 1986 the percentage of Taiwan's trade within the basin had crept up even further, but only because trade with the United States had risen even more sharply. While Japan took only 11 per cent of exports and accounted for 27 per cent of Taiwan's imports, the United States took 48 per cent of exports and provided 23 per cent of imports. Only the NICs could withstand this swing, taking 12 per cent of exports and 4 per cent of imports. The ASEAN states and the big four West European economies stood about equal, taking 7 per cent of Taiwanese trade. Taiwan, like South Korea, was an undoubted economic success story, but it was in effect a trading island dominated by dealings with only the United States and Japan. With the trade disputes of the 1980s leading to the ballooning United States trade deficit, Taiwan, like South Korea, faced the immediate need to diversify beyond the Pacific, and closer ties with western Europe were seen as the next new strategy to pursue.[26] The narrower the economic base of success, the more likely it was to tip over into serious trade problems.

In sum, the NICs are a remarkable success story. Each has carved out an important share of the global economy and of Pacific trade. Each has made striking progress to the status of a developed economy and has thereby reduced the number of developing states in the region. The NICs have also forced reassessments in traditional thinking about North–South relations and theories of dependence.

But to some extent the NICs' very success is forcing important changes in their international position. In early 1988 the United States announced that, effective from 2 January 1989, the four East Asian NICs would lose their concessional trade status under the generalized system of preferences, with Taiwan suffering the most.[27] Along with pressing demands by the developed economies for the NICs to abide by such rules of trade as international copyright, there was also strong pressure for the revaluation of currencies. More positively, by 1988 the call for the NICs to join the OECD indicated their new acceptability as industrial states, albeit at a price of greater international economic co-operation.

Although some of the NICs felt a regional, Pacific-wide type of OECD made more sense, the main trend suggested a broadening of the more Atlantic-centred existing institutions. The Europeans were increasingly seen as key partners in the NICs' efforts to diversify away from undue dependence on the United States and Japan. Especially at a time of ever more shrill American demands for changes in the NICs' policies, diversification and internationalization were increasingly attractive.[28] Also feeling the hot

---

[26] *Financial Times* (19 February 1988).
[27] *Far Eastern Economic Review* (11 February 1988).
[28] Bernard Gordon, *Political Protectionism in the Pacific* (London: IISS, Adelphi Paper, 228, spring 1988), 5–12.

breath of the 'four dragons', even in the more modern industries, Japan too was learning to live with a more complex regional dimension to the global economy.

But despite their obvious success, and apart from their reliance on export-led growth, the NICs offer no simple model of development or participation in the international economy. The city states have somewhat more diverse patterns of trade, but each is heavily dependent on its own region as well as on Japan and the United States. The more normal states, South Korea and Taiwan, have trade patterns dominated just by Japan and the United States. All trade heavily with the Pacific, but only Singapore does a significant amount of trade with a large number of Pacific states. The NICs are less involved in a web of Pacific interdependence than hanging by a few broad cables.

20

South-east Asia

Non-Communist South-east Asia has taken its contemporary form of six states—Brunei, Singapore, Malaysia, Thailand, the Philippines and Indonesia—only since the mid-1960s. The exit of the last colonial power, Britain, left these traditional trading peoples to reorganize their affairs in a new pattern that suited their new condition, the new environment in the Pacific, and the global economy. The backdrop of a very hot war in nearby Indo-China was hardly likely to produce coherent and consistent foreign economic policies. The natural disparity in the size, ethnic composition, and political orientation of the states concerned also made co-ordination difficult.

The economic range of regimes was even greater than for the NICs, with Singapore doing nicely as a wealthy NIC and the Philippines struggling along as a very poor developing state. Brunei, of course, has a higher per-capita GDP than Singapore, but its population is tiny and its economy is heavily dependent on the oil sector. It is thus far more akin to the Gulf states. Yet as will be discussed below, ASEAN states have shared some important similarities in the international economy, if only in terms of their local trade and growing commerce with the developed economies of the Pacific.

But the South-east Asians have not had the kind of economic success associated with the NICs. With Singapore in a class by itself and Brunei too tiny to count, only Malaysia and Thailand look likely to break out of the developing states category. Indonesia and the Philippines seem much less promising.[1] In part because they have larger populations than most NICs, the developing South-east Asian states have pursued a less export-oriented strategy. Thus despite their far larger populations, they are less important than the NICs for the Pacific and global economy, and their part in both fluctuates more wildly. In 1980, on the tail end of higher commodity prices, they accounted for 19.4 per cent of inter-Pacific exports and 13.6 per cent of imports. Seven years later the region took only 13 per cent of their exports and provided 10.7 per cent of imports, with the decline in Indonesia's role the main factor.

---

[1] Harry Oshima, *Economic Growth in Monsoon Asia* (Tokyo: University of Tokyo Press, 1987).

INDONESIA

Indonesia's pattern of trade, like that of much of the rest of ASEAN, did not fully readjust to its post-colonial role until the late 1960s. By 1969 it had settled into a pattern dominated by Japan, which took 29 per cent of exports and provided an equal share of imports (see Figure 20.1). The United States

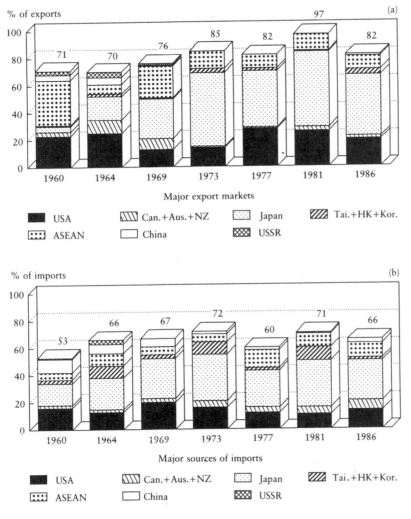

Source: World Bank data.

FIG. 20.1. *Indonesian trade, 1960–86: percentage by (a) major export markets, (b) major sources of imports*

accounted for 13 per cent of Indonesia's export and 20 per cent of imports, while fellow ASEAN states accounted for 23 per cent of exports and only 6 per cent of imports. Australia took 8 per cent of exports while China sent 6 per cent of imports. The big four West Europeans retained a strong trade surplus, providing 13 per cent of imports and taking only 6 per cent of exports. This still left 76 per cent of Indonesia's exports and 67 per cent of its imports within the Pacific—one of the highest figures for a Pacific state.

Indonesia also benefited from remarkably large financial flows from the developed world. In 1969–75 it received 27 per cent of all Japanese disbursements to the developing states of the Pacific, nearly twice the American percentage although only $400 million more in cash terms. The big four West Europeans gave half the American total, yet this sum accounted for 22 per cent of their total disbursements to the region. But by the 1982–5 period all three major donors were giving roughly the same amount. For Japan and the United States it was only 10 per cent of their flows to the region, while for the Europeans it was 19 per cent. Despite all these funds, Indonesia remained one of the weaker economies of the region, although by virtue of its size, much like China, still an important Pacific trader.

As for most states in the region, the rise of OPEC along with the surge in oil prices brought major changes for Indonesia. As a major oil exporter, and the only member of OPEC in the region, Indonesia saw its trade balance and share of Pacific trade gain sharply as neighbours sought its oil. In 1981 energy-starved Japan was taking 55 per cent of Indonesian exports and the United States 26 per cent. Nearly 100 per cent of exports went to Pacific basin states—a record for the region.

But by 1986 the oil price had slipped and the economies of developed states had adjusted to the oil shock. Japan still took 45 per cent of Indonesian exports and 29 per cent of imports and the United States took 20 per cent and 14 per cent respectively. But the ASEAN share of exports slipped to 10 per cent, almost all of which went to Singapore. The West Europeans held their share while the white-Commonwealth states provided 7 per cent of imports. Total trade with Pacific states was still high at 82 per cent of exports and 64 per cent of imports. But the dependence on Japan and the United States had increased sharply. Like most of the NICs, Indonesia was really tied to only two states for trade, and its immediate neighbours in ASEAN and the south Pacific accounted for less than 15 per cent, a figure well down on the situation 25 years previously.

With the decline in the value of oil and the setback to the economy, the so-called Berkeley Mafia of American-trained economists began urging Indonesia to develop an NIC-style, export-oriented economy. But the dominant strain of autarky seemed set in place and, combined with an industrial sector run largely along family and faction lines, the inefficiency and austerity that had marked Indonesia's economy seemed set to remain.[2]

MALAYSIA

Malaysia has been described as a monsoon economy in transition from plantations to industry.[3] By the 1980s half of its workforce was employed in industry as the agricultural sector declined. By then it was even importing workers from Indonesia as the economy expanded. The change had taken place in the 1960s with the decision to open up to foreign investment and to promote exports. With a system of free-trade zones and industrial estates, it was possible to attract foreign investors and many came. However, critics pointed to the fact that the zones provided only partial benefits to the country as a whole.[4]

However, the Malaysian economy was clearly more successful, with a more diversified trade pattern, than Indonesia. In 1969 the largest proportion of trade was with South-east Asia, mainly Singapore, with 25 per cent of exports and 18 per cent of imports in the region (see Figure 20.2). Japan accounted for 18 per cent of exports and 16 per cent of imports, roughly the same proportion as the 13 per cent of exports and 19 per cent of imports from the big four West Europeans. The United States accounted for 15 per cent of exports but only 6 per cent of imports. With 64 per cent of exports and 52 per cent of imports within the Pacific, Malaysia was nevertheless closely tied to global trade with developed economies mainly because of the still-important ties to Britain.

In keeping with the more developed state of its economy, Malaysia received smaller financial flows, taking only 5 per cent of the Japanese and 8 per cent of the big four West European funds in 1969–75. In the 1982–5 period, there followed a sharp increase in Japanese investment as Japan sought lower labour rates in ASEAN. With the decline of the European voice in Malaysia's economic affairs, Japan was left to provide the bulk of the funds, 12 per cent of its total to the Pacific.

With growing economic success and an export profile moving more into light industrial and especially electrical goods, by 1987 Malaysia had moved closer to Japan and the United States. In 1986 it was the world's largest exporter of semiconductors.[5] The West European share declined to 8 per

[2] *The Economist* (15 August 1987).

[3] Oshima, *Economic Growth*, ch. 8.

[4] J. Meerman, *Public Expenditure in Malaysia* (Oxford: Oxford University Press, 1979); J. Snodgrass, *Inequality and Development in Malaysia* (Oxford: Oxford University Press, 1980).

[5] *The Economist* (31 January 1987).

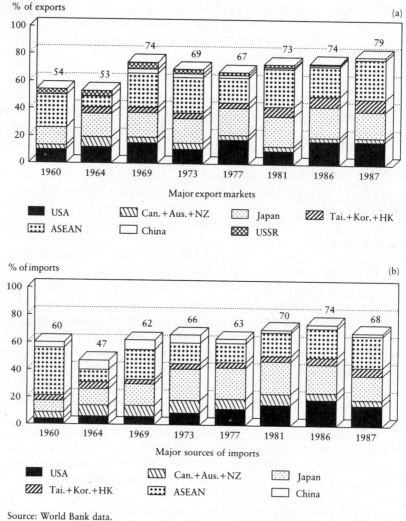

% of exports   (a)

Major export markets

USA   Can.+Aus.+NZ   Japan   Tai.+Kor.+HK
ASEAN   China   USSR

% of imports   (b)

Major sources of imports

USA   Can.+Aus.+NZ   Japan
Tai.+Kor.+HK   ASEAN   China

Source: World Bank data.
Note: 1960 statistics for Malaya only.

FIG. 20.2. *Malaysian trade, 1960–87: percentage by (a) major export markets,*
         (b) major sources of imports

cent of Malaysia exports and 12 per cent of imports, and trade with
ASEAN remained relatively stable at 24 per cent of exports and 25 per cent
of imports. Japan led the way by taking 36 per cent of exports and 18 per
cent of imports, and the United States took second place with 17 per cent of
exports and a large increase in imports to 15 per cent.

Almost unique among Pacific states, Malaysia saw its trade within the Pacific grow, although a sharp rise in exports was in contrast to a relatively steady level of imports. By 1987 some 79 per cent of exports were within the Pacific while some 69 per cent of imports came from the same region. In 1981 some 70 per cent of imports were from within the Pacific while 73 per cent of exports were to the region.

Although Malaysian trade remained more focused on local ASEAN trade, it too had developed an increasing stake in trade with the United States and Japan. Yet there still remained a basic balance between the four major trading partners, almost all of which, counting Singapore as the main part of ASEAN trade, were developed economies. As with the NICs, modernization brought greater integration into the global economy and especially its main Pacific components. But most observers remain skeptical that Malaysia is another NIC in the making. As one put it, the Malaysian tiger, once fed, is quite happy to roll over and have its tummy tickled.[6]

THAILAND

Thailand must rank as one of the quietest success stories of South-east Asia.[7] With steady, if less spectacular, growth rates than some of its neighbours, it overtook Indonesia and the Philippines on the road to industrialization.[8] With a more enlightened leadership and a complex political system, Thailand managed to waste less in corruption and to rely more on technocratic skills. Management styles and political culture clearly had a great deal to do with the failure of the Philippines to keep up with the Thai pace.

The Thais had moved in the 1960s to a policy of import substitution using mostly private enterprise and only some larger state-directed enterprises. But with only short-lived gains they moved in the 1970s to a more clear-cut export-promotion plan using an undervalued currency. By 1987 over 50 per cent of exports were manufactured goods, whereas in the 1970s over 80 per cent of exports were in such primary commodities as rice, rubber, and tin.[9] Foreign investment, and especially American-run enterprises, were kept under stricter control than in the Philippines. And of course, in non-Catholic Thailand, a faster decline in the birth rate meant that more of the gains of modernization could be shared by fewer people.

---

[6] *The Economist* (31 January 1987).
[7] William Overholt, 'Thailand: The Moving Equilibrium' in *Pacific Review*, 1/1 (1988).
[8] Oshima, *Economic Growth*, ch. 7.
[9] *Financial Times* (2 December 1987).

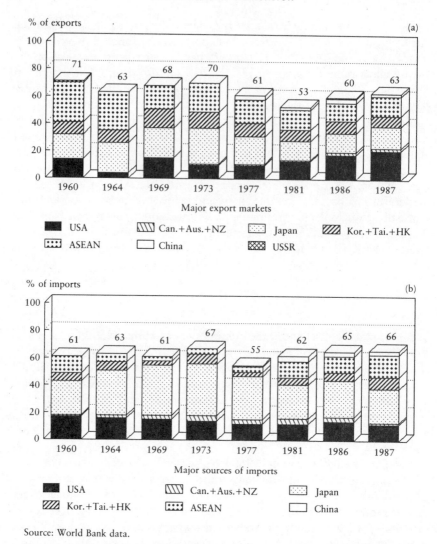

Source: World Bank data.

FIG. 20.3. *Thailand trade, 1960–87: percentage by (a) major export markets,*
(b) major sources of imports

The profile of Thai trade in the 26 years from 1960 is remarkably
constant (see Figure 20.3). Apart from the decline of ASEAN trade and to
some extent that with western Europe, there has been remarkably little
change in the direction of trade. Japan remains the main trade partner with
18 per cent of exports falling to 16 per cent by 1987 and imports remaining
steady at 25 per cent. The United States accounted for 14 per cent of exports

in 1960 and 21 per cent in 1987, while the 17 per cent of imports declined to 12 per cent in the same period. The West European big four accounted for 9 per cent of exports in 1960 and 12 per cent in 1987, while their 21 per cent of imports dropped sharply to 12 per cent. The sharpest falls came in ASEAN trade, with exports dropping from 29 per cent to 13 per cent and imports starting at 12 per cent declining, and then rising back to 16 per cent. The trade with South Korea, Taiwan, and Hong Kong remained largely unchanged at 9 per cent of exports and 5 per cent of imports by 1987.

Thailand received only a tiny percentage of financial assistance from the developed economies until its economy began to take off in the early 1980s. Then, in the period 1982–5, Japan led the way, sending 8 per cent of its financial assistance to Thailand in search of lower labour costs for Japanese manufacturers. As with nearly all other ASEAN states, this dominant role for Japanese finance in the region was part of the Japanese assumption of the leading role in the regional economy. By the late 1980s Japan saw Thailand as the leading candidate of the 'proto-NICs' to be raised to full NIC status. Japan sought relief from revalued currencies in the NICs and from rising wage costs, and shifted production to South-east Asia, and to Thailand in particular.[10]

By 1987, 63 per cent of exports and 66 per cent of imports were within the Pacific, figures lower than the average for ASEAN states and roughly the same as in the 1960s. But the most striking pattern was the relatively equal balance in trade partners. Although in imports dependence on Japan was high, it was down from a peak of 38 per cent in 1973. Like the city state NICs, Thailand had one of the more complex patterns of trade, and also one with nearly the largest role for the Europeans.

THE PHILIPPINES

By contrast, the trade pattern of the Philippines was the most skewed of the ASEAN states and perhaps worse than that of South Korea (see Figure 20.4). In 1960 the United States alone accounted for 48 per cent of exports and 42 per cent of imports, with Japan taking 23 per cent and 22 per cent. The United States' role declined somewhat so that by 1987 it accounted for 'merely' 36 per cent of exports and 22 per cent of imports. Japan's role also faded to 18 per cent of exports and 17 per cent of imports. The NICs and ASEAN states were each taking about 8 per cent of trade by 1987 and the big four Europeans were holding their share steady at 11 per cent of exports

---

10 *The Economist* (5 November 1988).

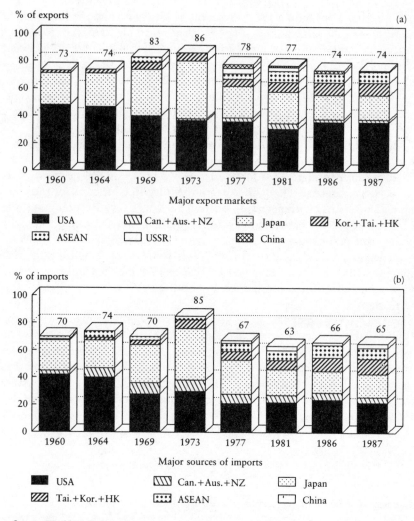

FIG. 20.4. *Philippines trade, 1960–87: percentage by (a) major export markets, (b) major sources of imports*

and 8 per cent of imports. Some 70 per cent of Philippines exports and 61 per cent of imports went to Pacific states, but the United States and Japan dominated this trade. Unlike Thailand or the city-state NICs, this trade pattern did not mark a genuine involvement in a web of Pacific trade.

Also in contrast to Thailand, the Philippines received a shrinking percentage of the financial flows from the economies of the developed Pacific. In the 1969–75 period Japan had sent 9 per cent of its funds to the Philippines, while the United States and the big four West Europeans each provided about 4 per cent. By 1982–5 the Europeans had dropped to 2 per cent. Japan still led the way in absolute terms with $992 million, but like the United States gave only 4 per cent of its financial flows to the faltering and corrupt Filipino economy.

In sum, the ASEAN states, taken together, constitute a major presence in the Pacific economy. But they are in fact rarely seen as a single unit by their main trading partners. They only trade with each after they trade first with Japan and the United States. Singapore, Thailand, and Malaysia have more balanced patterns of trade, but the poorer states of Indonesia and the Philippines remain more skewed to the powerful duo of Japan and the United States. The picture of Pacific trade is still more one of heavy lines connecting the richer states to the poorer, but with growing differences among ASEAN states depending on their own level of development and political culture.

21

The Communist Pacific

It is a difference much remarked upon between East Asia and Europe that in the Pacific there is no simple division between East and West in ideological terms. Yet East Asia does have nearly as many Communist states as does Europe. Certainly the largest percentage of the population and territory of the Communist world is in East Asia. The latest addition to the 'comradeship' of the Communist world, such as it is, is to be found in Indo-China. Yet the important differences between the types of Communist system in East Asia, and the much lower level of development there, have meant that East Asian Communists are more divided amongst themselves and less important for Asian Pacific commerce.

With the exception of China in the past decade, the Communist states of East Asia have barely registered a presence in Pacific trade. China's role has climbed steadily so that by 1987 it provided 6.4 per cent of Pacific exports and took 5.9 per cent of the region's imports, the fifth-largest player in the Pacific trade game. Only one other Communist state was above 1 per cent of Pacific trade: the USSR had 1.7 per cent of exports and imports. The Soviet figure is comparable to that of France and Canada, and somewhere between Malaysia and Thailand. None of the five other East Asian Communist states—Mongolia, North Korea, Vietnam, Laos, and Kampuchea—accounts for even 1 per cent of Pacific trade. With the exception of China and the Soviet Union, Pacific Communists were a world apart.

Yet by comparison, the Communist states of eastern Europe are not much more integrated into European and Atlantic trade. The Soviet Union takes barely 2 per cent of West European trade, although the averages for all Soviet and East European trade with their capitalist neighbours does approach the 10 per cent figure achieved in the Pacific when Chinese trade is included. Thus the Communist states of Europe are not actually any closer in trade terms to their non-Communist neighbours than their comrades in the Pacific.

The difference lies in the extent of inter-Communist trade. Trade volumes between Communist states in general are lower than in the more trade-oriented capitalist world. But even so, within eastern Europe (but not all of CMEA, which includes Mongolia and Vietnam), the inter-Communist trade accounts for 40–50 per cent of total trade. In the Pacific or, more properly, East Asia, trade among Communist states is at best peripheral for most.

SINO-SOVIET RELATIONS

In terms of trade volume, the most important relationship is that between China and the Soviet Union. After the signing of the February 1950 Treaty of Friendship, Alliance, and Mutual Assistance, the Soviet Union became heavily involved in assisting the growth of the new Communist regime in China. While the Soviet Union itself was hardly in a position to offer vast sums given its own post-war recovery tasks, it did make an effort to help China. The extent of this assistance was the focus of much recrimination when Sino-Soviet relations later deteriorated.[1]

It is undoubtedly true that China hoped for more aid, was disappointed with the low level of credit, and was upset that much of the aid had to be paid back when relations deteriorated.[2] But it is also true that only the Soviet Union was willing to assist China and that, given the nature of Chinese ideology and policy at the time, Beijing cut itself off from western assistance and trade. Western academics were later to regret this turn of events, but the largest portion of the responsibility for that policy lies with the Chinese themselves.[3]

Sino-Soviet relations under Khrushchev initially showed improvement over the Stalin period. In 1954 Khrushchev visited China and the scale of aid and trade was sharply increased. Between 1950 and 1957 the Soviet Union provided 8.1 billion roubles of assistance for the construction of 211 projects. By 1967 the total number of projects completed was 291, worth 20 billion roubles. Khrushchev ordered Soviet advisers to return home in the summer of 1960 in an apparent attempt to show China just how much it needed Soviet assistance. The Soviets claim that 198 projects were completed by them, whereas some western estimates put the number as low as 130. According to the Soviet Union, total credits to China were $2 billion, but some western estimates put the figure at closer to $3 billion. All credit had been repaid by 1965.[4]

The period of Soviet assistance to China in the 1950s is generally known

[1] John Gittings, *Survey of the Sino-Soviet Dispute* (Oxford: Oxford University Press, 1969).
[2] Mineo Nakajima, 'Foreign Relations from the Korean War to the Bandung Line' in *The Cambridge History of China* (Cambridge: Cambridge University Press, 1987), xiv.
[3] John Garver, *Chinese-Soviet Relations, 1937–45* (Oxford: Oxford University Press, 1988).
[4] Nakajima, 'Foreign Relations', 282–3.

as the 'Soviet-model period' and so it was. It has also been described as the 'honeymoon'. In most spheres of Chinese life, the Soviet Union provided guidance for establishing a new Communist regime, from industry to education, from the arts to the armed forces. The only parallel in Pacific economic relations was the American assistance to Japan.

The course of the split in Sino-Soviet relations is well known.[5] Its basic cause was the Chinese dissatisfaction with the Soviet model and the search for a more Sinified version of Communism. The Soviet emphasis on heavy industry rather than light industry or agriculture was unsuited to China. The Chinese revolution had been made by proud people with a vast heritage of statecraft and, unlike many of the East European regimes then being shaped by Moscow, the Chinese Communists had their own revolutionary experience.

When Mao Zedong led his Communist comrades down the road to the Great Leap Forward and the abandonment of the Soviet model, Sino-Soviet relations tumbled towards open polemics.[6] Sino-Soviet trade collapsed along with political relations. The combination of the absurdly optimistic policies of the Great Leap, natural disasters, and the withdrawal of Soviet advisers in 1960 led to the famines of 1960–1. Some 20–30 million Chinese died, by far the largest single human catastrophe of the post-war world. As the Chinese drifted into the Cultural Revolution in 1965–9, a main target of the campaign was Soviet-style 'revisionism'. Party-to-Party ties between China and the Soviet Union were severed in March 1966, marking the most serious step open to comrades.

The recovery of Sino-Soviet economic relations was one of the earliest products of their *détente* in the 1980s.[7] In the intervening 20 years, India and to some extent Vietnam had taken China's place in the Soviet pattern of trade with developing states. China meanwhile had opened its door to western aid and trade. But for a potent mix of political and economic reasons, both Communist great powers eventually saw reasons to improve their economic relations again.

From the Soviet point of view, trade with China could help provide consumer goods and food for its isolated Pacific territory. Soviet development of the region had failed to materialize to the extent planned, and even attempts to involve Japanese investment had not been successful.[8] The vast

[5] Donald Zagoria, *The Sino-Soviet Conflict* (Princeton: Princeton University Press, 1962); William Griffiths, *Sino-Soviet Rift* (London: Allen & Unwin, 1964).

[6] Roderick MacFarquhar, *The Origins of the Cultural Revolution* (Oxford: Oxford University Press, 1983), ii.

[7] Gerald Segal, *Sino-Soviet Relations After Mao* (London: IISS, Adelphi Paper, 202, 1985.

[8] Donald Zagoria (ed.), *The Soviet Union in East Asia* (London: Yale University Press, 1982); Gerald Segal (ed.), *The Soviet Union in East Asia* (London: Heinemann, 1983); Rodger Swearingen, *Siberia and the Soviet Far East* (Stanford, Calif.: Hoover Institution, 1987).

potential locked up in Soviet Asia is clear to see, but the traditional Soviet problem has been how to exploit that potential given the obviously inhospitable conditions in much of the region.[9]

In August 1986 Mikhail Gorbachev toured the Soviet far east and in 1987 a major new investment plan was announced. By 1988 it was clear that the plan was inadequate and it was sent back to Moscow for reform. The late 1980s was a time of major debate about the Soviet Union's overall economic strategy, let alone its specific approach to its far east and the Pacific region.

As Sino-Soviet relations improved, the Soviet Union began to learn about the Chinese reforms of socialism, which included special economic zones for foreign production and the widespread use of joint ventures to acquire foreign technology and boost exports. While the Soviet Union has been discussing the possibility of establishing some special economic zones of its own, the entire process of reform of the Soviet economy is taking longer than many first expected. What looks likes emerging is a strategy stressing the more 'independent' development of the Soviet far east. It has become clear that there was simply not a large amount of funds from within the Soviet Union available to develop the region. The success of the plans to entice foreign investment depended on the wider reforms in the Soviet economy, few of which were expected to be in operation until the early 1990s.

The Soviet reform process looked like involving the Soviet Union, eventually, in more exploitation of local possibilities for economic co-operation and trade.[10] The greater Soviet interest in Pacific co-operation was apparent in 1988 when a national committee on Pacific co-operation was established. China, as the only other Communist state involved in the co-operation schemes, was seen as a tacit ally in the Soviet campaign to gain wider regional recognition as part of the attempt to develop the Soviet far east.

From China's point of view, there was a need for a different 'open door' from those ajar to western countries. Western technology was superb but expensive, and difficult to use in a developing country with insufficient infrastructure support. Western aid came with loans that could be difficult to finance. Western trade required foreign currency and brought the problem of finding suitable goods to export to highly developed western markets. Hence the attraction of barter and balanced trade with a neighbour which could also provide some sophisticated technology. The Soviet Union, too, preferred to trade in accordance with plans and therefore to keep a modicum of stability in foreign economic relations.

The door to the Soviet Union swung open and in 1985 a major five-year

<hr>

9 Swearingen, *The Soviet Far East*; Allen Whiting, *Siberian Development and East Asia* (Stanford, Calif.: Stanford University Press, 1981).
10 Gerald Segal, 'The USSR in Asia' in *Asian Survey* (January 1988, January 1989). See also Michael Kaser, 'Reforms in the Soviet Union and China' in *Pacific Review*, 1/2 (summer 1988).

trade agreement provided for the return of Soviet advisers to help refurbish 17 old Soviet plants and to build seven new ones. Cross-border trade increased and overall trade boomed.[11] In 1987 the trade growth stagnated as the reform process in both countries caused major disruptions and ossified bureaucracies were slow to adapt, mainly on the Soviet side. In 1988 some of these problems were sorted out and trade, especially cross-border trade, began to boom again.

As the two great Communist states were struggling with the problem of how to reform a massive, centrally planned socialist economy, they at least recognized the extent to which there were important ties that bound the two economies and societies. Chinese reforms had already been studied and in part incorporated into the Gorbachev reforms. Each Communist state, to some extent, held up the other as a 'mirror to socialism' and each was clearly fascinated with the other's experience in reform.[12] The struggles between rapid and slow reformers, central planners and decentralizers, were common to both. By the mid-1980s Sino-Soviet economic relations had clearly become closer than at any point since the economic split in 1960.[13]

The value of Sino-Soviet trade climbed steadily in the 1980s. By 1986 it totalled $2.7 billion, constituting some 4 per cent of Chinese exports and 3 per cent of imports (see Figure 21.1). The Soviet Union was China's fifth-largest trading partner and by far its largest in the Communist world. Although trade with China was still only about 1 per cent of Soviet foreign trade, China had become the Soviet Union's second-largest trading partner in the Pacific after Japan, if the USA and Canada are treated as Atlantic partners. It was also the Soviet Union's second-largest partner in the developing Communist world after Cuba, having surpassed Vietnam in 1983. Although trade stagnated in 1987 and China slipped back in the Soviet league table, the longer-term trend still suggested that China had regained its place as the key to Soviet economic relations in the Pacific.[14]

OTHER INTER-COMMUNIST TRADE

Of the five other Communist states in East Asia, only North Korea and Vietnam have had any international economic relations of note apart from close bilateral relations with aid donors. Mongolia is heavily tied to the Soviet economy and has been so even since it was formed in 1921[15] Over half

11 *The Economist* (12 September 1987).
12 Gilbert Rozman, *The Mirror for Socialism* (London: I. B. Taurus, 1985) and *Chinese Debates about Soviet Socialism* (London: I. B. Taurus, 1987).
13 Gerald Segal, 'Sino-Soviet Detente' in *World Today* (May 1987).
14 Socialist Industry in BBC, SWB, SU, W0026, A1.
15 Alan Sanders, *Mongolia* (London: Frances Pinter, 1986).

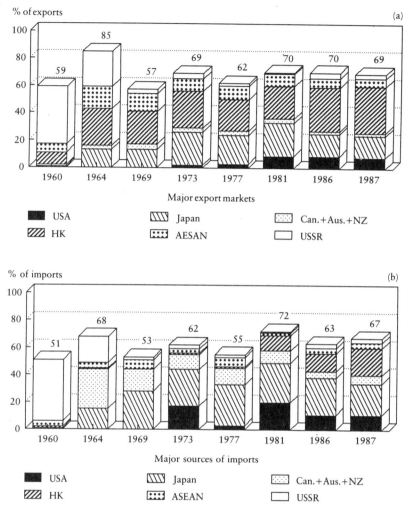

% of exports (a)

Major export markets

USA   Japan   Can.+Aus.+NZ
HK   AESAN   USSR

% of imports (b)

Major sources of imports

USA   Japan   Can.+Aus.+NZ
HK   ASEAN   USSR

Source: World Bank data.

FIG. 21.1. *Chinese trade, 1960–87: percentage by (a) major export markets, (b) major sources of imports*

of Mongolian industry was established with Soviet aid and some 80 per cent of its trade is with the Soviet Union. Mongolia ranks top among CMEA beneficiaries of aid from the Soviet Union.[16] From the Soviet point of view, Mongolia takes about 1 per cent of Soviet trade.

Mongolia, with its sparse population, remains on paper the richest of the Pacific socialist states with a per-capita GDP approaching half of Taiwan's $5000. Next in line is the far east of the Soviet Union. By virtue of its tiny population of 8 million, this region would rank just ahead of Malaysia as a developing state. Of course, both Mongolia and the Soviet Union are the exceptions that prove the rule of relative poverty of Pacific Communist states.

Vietnam once had a trade relationship more balanced between China and the Soviet Union, but with the deterioration of relations with China in the late 1970s Vietnam also shifted to a Mongolia-type model. Some trade with China continued to be done through Hong Kong and Singapore, as much as a fifth of Vietnamese trade with these two entrepôts, but the vast majority was now with the Soviet Union and its allies in CMEA. In 1986 some 70 per cent of the $800 million of Vietnamese exports were agricultural products and raw materials sent to the Soviet Union. Japan was the only significant non-Communist trade partner, with $280 million total trade in 1986, but under ASEAN pressure the limits to trade growth were clear. As a CMEA member since 1978, Vietnam benefited from aid, which by 1987 reached $5 million per day from the Soviet Union alone. But it was also in 1987 that the Soviet Union began exerting sharper pressure on Vietnam to engage in its own economic reforms so as to perk up the economy and lighten the burden on its allies.[17]

North Korea still retains its more balanced trading pattern with its Communist neighbours, but by 1986 trade with the Soviet Union was worth twice Sino-Korean trade. In the decades before the 1970s the trade had regularly been more balanced, but China's opening to the West meant a lower priority for trade with North Korea. Clandestine Chinese trade with South Korea, value by some at $2 billion in 1986, was well over three times the total with the Communist North.

The Soviet presence in North Korea was far less pervasive than in Mongolia, but economic ties still operated in the time-honoured fashion of co-ordinated central plans, project aid, and close integration of specialists and technicians. At times, for example in the early 1970s, North Korea had been encouraged by the Soviet Union to open up to the rest of the Pacific.

---

[16] Kazayuki Kinbara, 'The Economic Dimension of Soviet Policy' in Gerald Segal (ed.), *The Soviet Union in East Asia* (London: Heinemann, 1984).

[17] *Far Eastern Economic Review* (23 July 1987).

But the huge problems in arranging investment, especially by Japanese, kept North Korea out of the Pacific pattern of trade.

With the new reforms in its two Communist neighbours, North Korea has been pushed to open up once again. With booming growth and success in the South, the Communist North is clearly falling behind its neighbours and the region, both materially and in terms of new ideas. North Korea remains the Communist state in the Pacific most able, after China and the Soviet Union, to join the ranks of the modernizers in the Pacific, but like its Communist neighbours it can do so only when domestic reform is begun.

The two remaining states, Kampuchea and Laos, are the poorest in the Pacific, and the most cut off from its growth and international relations. Trade with all states except Vietnam is negligible. To all intents and purposes of Pacific economic relations, these two states might as well not exist.

RELATIONS OUTSIDE THE COMMUNIST PACIFIC

Unlike the Communist states of Europe, the two largest ones in the Pacific, China and the Soviet Union, trade most heavily with the non-Communist world. In the Soviet case, the trade is heavily skewed to Japan, which took twice as much Soviet trade as China did in 1986 and 1987 ($5.5 billion). Although this trade with Japan constitutes some 50 per cent of total Soviet trade in the Pacific, the percentage is falling. i. reached its height at over 80 per cent in the 1970s when trade with Japan was growing and trade with China was stuck in the doldrums.

Japan is of course a neighbour of the Soviet Union, and the only one in the Pacific that is a developed society, potentially hungry for Soviet resources and able to provide modern technology. Japan also sits off the Soviet Pacific coast with a large population and a dynamic economy that threatens Soviet ideology. The Japanese challenge to the Soviet Union has rarely been seen from Moscow as an opportunity.

The 1957 Soviet-Japanese trade agreement led to a rapid increase in trade in the late 1950s and early 1960s.[18] The Japanese interest was to exploit the natural resources of Siberia in order to help spread the risks of Japanese vulnerability to blockade. Even though the Soviet Union espoused a hostile ideology, Japan has always shown itself pragmatic in its trade dealings, in keeping with its priority for an economics-led foreign policy.

From the Soviet point of view, the idea, as in western Europe, was to take

[18] Kinbara, 'Economic Dimension'.

advantage of western technology and to some extent to build political ties that would help undermine American alliances on either side of the Soviet Union. In periods of superpower *détente*, trade with Japan increased and the prospects for greater Japanese investment in Siberia improved. Grandiose plans for the exploitation of Siberian resources with Japanese technology were formulated and then abandoned when the economic and political problems mounted.

While Japan was bound by COCOM regulations, the Soviet Union regularly found Japan to be the best conduit for such sensitive technology as could be had. With the rise of Japan as a leader rather than a skilled copier of western technology, the attractions of dealing with Japan naturally grew. By by 1977 the rise in trade had slowed sharply and it stagnated until 1988. The problems are at their root more economic than political. An unreformed Soviet Union lacked the skills and capital to exploit its resources. The conditions in the Soviet far east are harsh and the decline in fuel prices in the 1980s reduced the competitiveness of Soviet resources. The absence of local initiative made it difficult to strike deals.[19]

The Gorbachev initiatives in the late 1980s and the prospects for reform and development in the Soviet far east have increased speculation that Soviet–Japanese co-operation can be expanded. Japan's need for resources in the long run is not diminished and tensions in the Gulf War suggest just how fragile the Japanese economy might be without resources closer to home. The Soviet Union has also revised its assessment of the Japanese economy, and begun lavishing praise on Japan's new ideas in economics and its increased international role.[20] The Soviet Union understood that if it was to become accepted into schemes for Pacific co-operation it would have to prove its good intentions to Japan above all. By the late 1980s it looked as if the Soviet Union was finding a more sympathetic Japanese ear to the Soviet case. Conditions for Soviet–Japanese co-operation have changed in important ways since the 1970s. The fall in oil prices and the rise of the yen have both made the Soviet Union and Japan less attractive to each other.[21]

No doubt a part of the Soviet desire is to encourage Japanese independence and divisions with the United States, although it must recognize that the Soviet Union cannot serve as an alternative for the United States in Japanese foreign economic relations. But some important changes on the margins are possible.

Ever since the late 1960s Japan has also been China's main trading

---

19 Whiting, *Siberian Development*.
20 Gerald Segal, 'The Soviet Union and the Pacific Century' in *Journal of Communist Studies* (December 1987).
21 *Far Eastern Economic Review* (12 June 1986).

partner. Although Hong Kong has consistently been a better export market for China, by the 1970s Japan was taking a roughly similar 20–5 per cent of Chinese exports. But far more importantly, Japan has provided 27–30 per cent of Chinese imports, easily the largest swathe of Chinese imports for close to 20 years.[22]

As China's doors to foreign trade opened in the late 1970s, and it became a more important part of Pacific trade, Japan was the first to step through the door and exploit the China market.[23] Japan took remarkably quick advantage of the Chinese desire for technology, even for entire factories, and consumer goods. In the 1980s Sino-Japanese economic relations were so much to Japan's advantage that by 1986 China had forced Japan to allow more balanced trade. But even then, in 1987 Japan took only 16 per cent of Chinese exports (only half the 34 per cent going to Hong Kong) while providing 23 per cent of Chinese imports (a bit more than the 20 per cent coming from Hong Kong).

From the Japanese point of view, in 1987 China took 4 per cent of its exports and provided 5 per cent of its imports, a figure just under that of trade with South Korea. China ranked third among Japan's Pacific trade partners and Sino-Japanese trade was the fifth-largest bilateral trade flow in the Pacific. Of course, the two countries are close neighbours (like the United States and its American neighbours, whose trade flow is not counted as Pacific), but they are divided by ideology. Clearly there is much scope in Pacific trade for trade across or around ideological barriers, a lesson not lost on observers in the nearby Soviet Union.

Yet ideology can get in the way, as the question of COCOM regulations has repeatedly shown. In 1987, when Japan and its Toshiba Corporation were forced by the United States to impose stricter controls on the leaking of sensitive technology to the Soviet Union, Sino-Japanese trade also suffered as Japan restricted access to Chinese Communists.[24] This was a clear example of the kinds of problem faced when mixing politics, economics, and military affairs.

The overall decline in Sino-Soviet trade and the emergence of Sino-Japanese trade relations are the only major new developments in Pacific trading patterns since the 1950s. Although trade volumes have increased dramatically among the market economies, there has clearly been remarkable stability in the pattern of economic relations in the region. Apart from the decline in Sino-Soviet trade, China's trade pattern with other states has not been nearly as dramatically different. To be sure, trade with the United

22 Wolf Mendl, *Issues in Japan's China Policy* (London: Macmillan, 1978); Laura Newby, *Sino-Japanese Relations* (London: Routledge, 1988).
23 Robert Taylor, *The Sino-Japanese Axis* (London: Athlone, 1985).
24 *The Economist* (3 October 1987); *International Herald Tribune* (5 January 1988).

States rose from nothing in the 1960s to some 10 per cent of Chinese trade by 1987. But the change reflected the fact that the United States was now providing products that Canada and Australia once did. Both these white-Commonwealth states now accounted for only 5 per cent of Chinese imports and 2 per cent of its exports, whereas in the late 1960s they provided 16 per cent of imports and took 4 per cent of exports.

China's trade with western Europe has remained remarkably constant even through the Soviet-model period, the 1960s, and the new open-door strategy. By 1987 the big four West Europeans provided 14 per cent of imports and took 7 per cent of exports, well up on the American figures. China's overall trade with Pacific states crept up from 57 per cent of exports and 53 per cent of imports in 1969 to 70 per cent of exports and 67 per cent of imports by 1987. These were figures in line with most other East Asian states, but unprecedented for other Pacific Communist states.

China's high degree of involvement in Pacific trade has developed in only a slightly more balanced way than for many other Pacific states. Japan and Hong Kong remain main partners with China and both are in a real sense 'local' and represent a form of 'border trade'. The percentage of trade going further afield has not changed much, if anything it has shrunk since China opened its door. Curiously enough, as China has concentrated on its own backyard, its trade with ASEAN states has declined as a percentage of overall trade. In 1969 the ASEAN states took 11 per cent of exports and provided 7 per cent of imports, but by 1987 the figures were down to 6 per cent and 4 per cent. The magnet of Japan and the hidden trade with Taiwan and South Korea via Hong Kong are the major reasons for the decline.[25] China is thus a more important power in Pacific economic relations, but it remains more local than genuinely region-wide like Japan.

Of course, China's approach to foreign trade has been vastly reformed in the past decade.[26] Foreign trade now accounts for some 12 per cent of Chinese GDP, double the figure in the pre-1978 period. There are now hundreds of joint ventures with foreign firms, and a string of special economic zones have been established along the coast in a Chinese-style emulation of the export-led success of the NICs. As part of a more general policy of decentralization, foreign trade has begun to take on different regional orientations.[27] In addition, with provinces the size of European countries, so much of what smaller countries call foreign trade the Chinese have to call domestic trade. Western-style T-shirts, slit skirts, and Japanese

[25] *Far Eastern Economic Review* (10 December 1987).
[26] Harry Harding, *China's Second Revolution* (Washington DC: Brookings, 1987).
[27] Martin Lockett, 'The Regional Foundations of Foreign Trade' in David Goodman (ed.), *China's Regional Development* (London: Routledge, 1989).

advertising in China are superficial indicators of the complexity and breadth of the change.[28]

To be sure, this opening to the outside world is more reform than revolution. China's reform in the 1950s had an equally strong influence from the Communist models and trade patterns were dominated by the Soviet Union. In both the past and present cases, domestic and foreign policy reform were closely linked. What is most interesting about the more modern strategy is the extent to which China is determined to hold open a number of doors rather than rely on one major partner.

Of course, China remains a continental, and so to some extent closed, economy where the local market takes priority.[29] Unlike Japan, and to some extent the United States, China is like the Soviet Union in focusing on domestic affairs. But in comparison to the Soviet Union, China is far more integrated into the Pacific trading world.

As low as Chinese trade with ASEAN might be, Soviet trade is even lower. In the 1970s it was half the Soviet Union's total trade with North Korea; by 1980 it had increased to a level 20 per cent higher than North Korean trade, but by 1986 it was down to one-quarter. In 1986 total Soviet–ASEAN trade (minus Indonesia) was less than Sino-Indonesian trade that year. The two largest trading partners for the Soviet Union were Malaysia for its commodity exports and Singapore for its commercial services. But there was clearly a vast potential for growth in this relationship, beyond the traditional commodity imports, such as, rubber and machinery exports.[30]

Australia and New Zealand have accounted for more than twice the entire ASEAN–Soviet trade totals, largely because of grain exports. But trade with the Soviet Union has declined to half the total trade between Australia / New Zealand and China. For both Communist states, the main dimension of trade with Australia remains raw materials rather than processed goods.[31]

If there is an obvious area for growth in Soviet trade with the Pacific apart from China and Japan, it is with the NICs, and especially South Korea and Taiwan. The new pragmatism in Soviet policy in the region, and the lesson of China's pioneering pragmatism, makes it more possible to exploit the 'structural compatibilities' between the Soviet economy and those of the NICs. While the Japanese economy may have moved too far into higher-value production, the NICs still need Soviet raw materials and can provide

---

[28] Martin Lockett, 'Economic Growth and Development' (London: RIIA, Chatham House Paper, 32, 1986).

[29] Doak Barnett, *China's Economy in Global Perspective* (Washington DC: Brookings, 1981); Bruce Reynolds, 'China in the International Economy' in Harry Harding (ed.), 'China's Foreign Relations in the 1980s (London: Yale University Press, 1985).

[30] Leszek Buszynski, *Soviet Foreign Policy in Southeast Asia* (London: Croom Helm, 1986).

[31] *Financial Times* (1 July 1987); *Far Eastern Economic Review* (16 July 1987).

the more practical technology and investment that the Soviet Union requires. Soviet trade with South Korea in 1988 was still barely $300 million, but it was increasingly travelling directly between the two states. The Soviet Union and South Korea opened official trade offices in each other's country in 1989. Trade with Taiwan was minuscule. But trade delegations had been exchanged and the Soviet Union had encouraged Hungary to establish formal relations with South Korea in 1988. There were clearly some prospects of the Soviet Union emulating Chinese involvement in the Pacific, although the Soviet Union has a much smaller population in the Pacific and its potential will remain limited. Nevertheless, a more pragmatic and economically intertwined Soviet Union can only be good for the stability of the Pacific.

In sum, while China has become a more important trader in the Pacific, the Soviet Union has barely changed its role despite some short-lived fluctuations. To the extent that Soviet trade in the Pacific has increased, it has been mostly with other Communist states and especially China. Under the Gorbachev administration, there has clearly been a rapidly growing Soviet interest in the potential for expanding Soviet trade with the Pacific. Only 20 per cent of the already-meagre Soviet exports to Pacific basin states are actually produced in the Soviet far east and most of the rest is raw materials or forest products.[32] To date, the major initiatives have come in relations with the Communist part of the Pacific. But the increasingly regular dispatch of high-level delegations to the NICs ASEAN states and Japan indicates that new initiatives are being considered.[33] If the entry of China into the Pacific economic pattern is anything to go by, the Soviet Union has a great deal of potential as a Pacific trader. Of course, it may yet choose to remain stuck within the limits of the Communist world.

[32] N. L. Shlyk, 'The Soviet Far East and the International Economy' in John Stephan and V. P. Chichkanov (eds.), *Soviet–American Horizons on the Pacific* (Honolulu: University of Hawaii Press, 1986).

[33] *International Herald Tribune* (31 March 1986); Gerald Segal, 'Pacific Century' and 'Soviet Union in Asia' in *Asian Survey* (January 1988, January 1989).

22

The White Commonwealth

There is no such thing as the 'white Commonwealth' as an organization, but there is a distinctive quality to the three Pacific economies in white-settler states created by Britain. In 1986 Canada was the third-wealthiest Pacific country, Australia the fourth and New Zealand the sixth. Despite their small populations—each has well under 1 per cent of the Pacific population, half of Canada included—they accounted for 7.3 per cent of Pacific exports and 6.5 per cent of imports in 1987. That is somewhat more than China, but achieved with only 3 per cent of China's population. Only Japan has a greater percentage of Pacific trade on a per-capita basis, and the figure for these white-Commonwealth states is similar to that for the United States.

Yet there are important differences between the three white-Commonwealth states. Canada's trade figures have consistently been some of the most unbalanced in the world. Between 65 per cent and 70 per cent of its exports have gone to the United States achieving the latter figure in 1987. Imports from the United States have hovered around the upper 60s as a percentage of the Canadian total. Some 30 per cent of the Canadian GNP was derived from exports to the United States. By 1987 Canada had invested $18 billion in the United States while Americans had invested $50 billion in Canada.[1] Thus it is even more remarkable that none of this massive trade, the largest bilateral trade totals in the world, is counted as Pacific trade. At least a portion of the Canada–United States trade is between the Pacific parts of both countries, and is in theory no different from Sino-Japanese trade.

Given the dominance of the United States, there are few Pacific states that can claim more than 1 per cent of Canadian trade. Of course, Japan had 5 per cent of exports and 6 per cent of imports in 1987, up from the 3 per cent and 2 per cent in 1960, but these figures were not very different from the 7 per cent of exports and 4 per cent of imports achieved in 1973.[2] Australia retains 1 per cent of Canadian trade; South Korea has won slightly more as its export drive gains speed. Hong Kong and China are the only other significant Pacific traders with Canada. Thus, although Canadian Pacific trade had risen to 8 per cent of exports and 10 per cent of imports by 1987, as a

---

[1] *The Economist* (19 December 1987).
[2] Klaus Pringsheim, *Neighbours Across the Pacific* (London: Greenwood, 1983).

percentage that is tiny by the standards of all but the Latin American members of the Pacific basin or the Soviet Union.

The still-small growth of Canadian trade in the Pacific is masked by the dominating presence of the United States. Most exports are of raw materials and food, while imports are mostly manufactured goods and textiles from the NICs and Japan. The centrality of the United States has been the main reason for the negotiation in 1987 of a free-trade agreement between Canada and the United States.[3] Unlike in the EC, this agreement did not provide for a common external tariff barrier and only a quarter of the trade by value between the two was affected by tariffs. Unusually, the deal did set rules for free trade in services.

But just as the formation of the EC led to concerns about protectionism and limits on the globalization of trade, so the possible formation of a North American free-trade grouping upset exporters in the Asian part of the Pacific, who feared they would now find it harder to sell to their single most important market. Car manufacturers in Japan and South Korea in particular were concerned about their ability to establish plants in North America in order to beat the restrictions on trade that were explicitly targeted by the formulators of the new agreement.[4]

Yet the Canadian market remained less penetrated than did the United States by the Asian Pacific exporters. It was, of course, a smaller market, but from the point of view of Japan and the NICs, looking around for new growth areas in an age of a more protection-sensitive United States, Canada was the last of the developed states of the Pacific to be fully opened up. The Canadians, for their part, were equally interested in diversifying away from their undue dependence on the United States.[5]

The other white-Commonwealth state with a significant population, Australia, had long been oriented to the Pacific for its trade. In fact, it can be argued that Australia and Japan have led the way in establishing a pattern of trade in the Pacific. If only by virtue of its geographical location, Australia is forced to trade at longer distances, and across Pacific waters.

With 4 per cent of Pacific trade in 1987. Australia has clearly lost some ground from the 5 per cent it held in 1980 (see Figure 22.1). As its economy has faltered and Japan and the NICs have stepped into the Pacific market, Australia, unlike Canada, has faded as a Pacific trader. Singapore, with its even tinier population, has moved ahead of Australia in the league table as the seventh largest Pacific trader.

Like Canada, Australia has played a part in Pacific trade as an importer of

3 *The Economist* (23 May 1987).
4 *Financial Times* (11 December 1987).
5 *Far Eastern Economic Review* (18 September 1986).

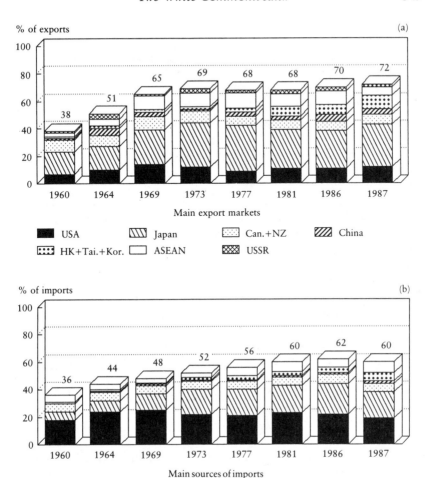

FIG. 22.1. *Australian trade, 1960–87: percentage by (a) major export markets,*
(b) major sources of imports

a wide range of goods from some developing states, but in recent years
mostly from Japan and the NICs. Australia's main exports have been such
items as grain and natural resources. But unlike Canada, Australia has
always had a far greater percentage of its trade in the Pacific. Although
exports to the region have ranged between 60 and 65 per cent of Australian

exports since the 1960s, imports have climbed steadily from around 50 per cent in the 1960s to 62 per cent in 1987.

The share of trade held by the West European big four dropped from 31 per cent of Australia's exports and 36 per cent of its imports in 1964, dominated by Britain, to 9 per cent and 17 per cent in 1981. Since then, the Europeans have clawed their way back into the market, taking 12 per cent of exports and 21 per cent of imports. As Australian firms become more integrated into the global economy, the European market increases in importance. For example, Australian food companies operate at home, in the NICs, and in ASEAN, but are tied into complex take-overs in Europe.[6]

Apart from the decline in the European share before the 1980s, the only other significant change in Australian trade has been the rise of Japan. In 1960 Japan took 16 per cent of Australian exports and 6 per cent of imports, but by 1973 it had shot up to 32 per cent and 18 per cent, surpassing the United States as Australia's major trade partner. Since the late 1970s Japan has reduced its purchases of raw materials, but by 1987 the trade advantage held by Australia had reappeared after having slipped in the interim. In 1987 Japan took 31 per cent of exports and 19 per cent of imports. By that year Australia was said to be importing more per capita from Japan than any other OECD country. With the appreciation of the yen, Japan's economy moved more up-market, and out of the areas that had previously been fed by imports of Australian raw materials.[7]

Yet Australia was in the nearly unique position among Pacific traders of having a consistent and significant trade surplus with Japan (this applies to some extent also to Indonesia). Although the volume of Australian exports to Japan was dwarfed by that of the United States, this was still a remarkable achievement in an age of complaints about Japanese trade policies. Some observers have suggested that this trend must change as Australian protectionism is ruining its economy,[8] but it also seems clear that, as a storehouse of food and resources, Australia has a solid exporting place in Pacific trade.

Australia had similar relationships with the NICs, although the trade surplus was less obvious except with South Korea. In 1973 the NICs accounted for 5 per cent of Australia's exports and 4 per cent of its imports, but by 1987 their share was over 12 per cent of exports and 8 per cent of imports. That 1987 figure was roughly comparable to Australian trade with the much closer ASEAN states, although the ASEAN share had barely changed in two decades.

[6] *The Economist* (29 August 1987).
[7] *Far Eastern Economic Review* (12 June 1986).
[8] *The Economist* (7 March 1987).

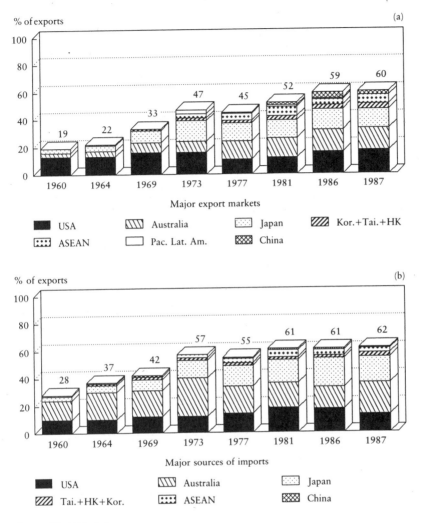

Source: World Bank data.

FIG. 22.2. *New Zealand trade, 1960–87: percentage by (a) major export markets, (b) major sources of imports*

The pattern of Australian trade is therefore unusual in the Pacific. Australia runs surpluses with Japan and the NICs and imports heavily from the United States and Europe. What is more, its trade is more evenly balanced than any other Pacific state. In economic terms Australia, more than Japan, can be described as the first and only truly Pacific state.

Australia's neighbour, New Zealand, has always held a special place in the Australian trade pattern (see Figure 22.2). As New Zealand's stepping-stone to Asia and as a more powerful, wealthy, and populous neighbour, Australia has always loomed largest in the New Zealand world-view. But in terms of trade, New Zealand has gone from a distant link with Britain half-way around the world to a remarkably balanced position in the 1980s.

As late as the 1960s the big four West Europeans, led by Britain, took well over half New Zealand's trade. In the 1970s that percentage tumbled, so that by 1981 the Europeans accounted for 18 per cent of exports and 14 per cent of imports, New Zealand mostly exports primary products and imports manufactured goods. The percentage of trade within the Pacific has grown accordingly, and by the 1980s reached Australia-like levels. In 1987 New Zealand sent 62 per cent of its exports to the Pacific states and took 65 per cent of its imports from the region.

What is most striking about New Zealand trade in the 1980s is the even balance, in 1987, between the United States with 17 per cent of exports and 13 per cent of imports, Japan with 14 per cent and 19 per cent, Australia with 16 per cent and 23 per cent, and the big four West Europeans with 16 per cent and 21 per cent. ASEAN, the NICs, China, and Canada were the other significant traders. This remarkable balance was achieved by the rise of Japan, the much smaller rise of the United States, and the shift of Australia from being mainly an exporter to New Zealand to become its largest importer. The West Europeans, after a decline in the late 1970s, have returned as more important Pacific traders in the 1980s.

There has long been free trade in labour between Australia and New Zealand, but with the new mood of protectionism in the 1980s the two began to move seriously towards a so-called 'Closer Economic Relationship'—a milder version of the North American free trade pact. But politicians on both sides of the Tasman Sea, like the North Americans, have rejected the idea of a common market because of their opposition to common tariffs and currency.[9] But once again, the tendency in the Pacific, as in Europe, seems to be to look to closer economic relations as part of an effort to hold their own in the tougher Pacific-wide and global economic competition. New Zealand, with a much smaller domestic market, needs such ties more than most. But New Zealand remains, like Australia, one of the few genuine Pacific traders. Also, like the other two white-Commonwealth states in the Pacific, New Zealand's importance extends far beyond the size of its minuscule population.

[9] *Far Eastern Economic Review* (3 December 1987; 7 July 1988).

23

The Fringes of Pacific Trade

There are a number of states whose shores are lapped by Pacific waters, but who are not significantly involved in Pacific economic relations. All the Latin American states apart from Mexico, Chile, and Panama have a Pacific trade which is worth less than half of 1 per cent of their total exports and imports. Panama is an exception only because it is a trans-shipment point and therefore a statistical anomaly, like part of Hong Kong's and Singapore's trade.

All these Latin American states are dominated by trade with the United States, other Latin Americans, and Europeans. Of all East Asian states, only Japan figures with trade worth more than 1 per cent of some Latin American states' imports and/or exports. Peru has also had significant exports to China and South Korea in the mid-1970s, and Chile may be developing a link with China based on its copper resources.[1]

In terms of trade volume, Mexico is by far the most important Latin American state in Pacific trade. By virtue of its geography, and specifically its border with the United States, Mexico is a suitable 'platform' for low-wage-based exports to the developed economies of the United States and Canada. The maquilas—low-wage, labour-intensive assembly plants nestled against the United States–Mexico border—employed some 300 000 Mexican workers in 1988. Their wage rates look increasingly attractive with the rise in such costs in the NICs. Japan accounts for 10 per cent of the maquilas' operations and Taiwan and South Korea have followed soon after. Japan has now become Mexico's second-largest trade partner, lender, and foreign investor after the United States.[2] Nevertheless, Japan's trade with Mexico remains roughly equal to that of France and Germany combined.

But it should be reiterated that in most cases trade between other Pacific Latin American states approaches levels found in ASEAN trade or between the NICs. It is difficult to argue in principle that this trade on the eastern shores of the Pacific is any less 'Pacific' than that on the western shores. It is perhaps most useful to conceive of the former as inter-American and the

---

[1] *Financial Times* (3 April 1987).
[2] *Far Eastern Economic Review* (27 October 1988).

latter as inter-Asian, much like French–Portugese trade is seen as European rather than Atlantic.

The Pacific islands are far too tiny to figure in patterns of trade. The only important exception is Papua New Guinea. Although it is Melanesian, its location and growing relationship with ASEAN makes it better understood in the ASEAN context. Its proportion of Pacific trade, like that of Chile, is about 0.1 per cent. But the importance of Pacific trade to Papua New Guinea is obviously much higher. In 1969 45 per cent of its exports went to the Pacific while a whopping 80 per cent of its imports came from the region. By 1986 there had been only a slight drift to the Pacific with 56 per cent of exports and 86 per cent of imports in the region.

A near-constant factor that accounts for Papua New Guinea's gap between Pacific exports and imports is the 32 per cent of exports to the big four West Europeans in 1969, rising to 37 per cent in 1986. But like many ASEAN states, Japan holds a major place among Pacific traders with Papua New Guinea, taking 27 per cent of exports and 15 per cent of imports in 1986, down from the highs of 37 per cent and 17 per cent in 1973. Australia is Papua New Guinea's main trade partner, accounting for 13 per cent of exports and 45 per cent of imports in 1986, down from 33 per cent and 53 per cent in 1969. The NICs take about 12 per cent of trade, a rise from virtually nothing in the early 1970s. The United States accounts for about 5 per cent of trade.

Papua New Guinea may live on the fringes of ASEAN and the Pacific trading system, but it looms larger over even smaller neighbours in the scattered islands. These, some of last people to be decolonized, are more Pacific in geographic terms than anywhere else, but adrift and isolated when it comes to Pacific trade flows.

It is this very marginality that introduces some economic uncertainties. The 10 independent island states are highly dependent on their larger neighbours in Papua New Guinea, Australia and New Zealand, and the more distant, but still powerful, United States. Their precarious circumstances make them extremely reliant on foreign aid and revenue from fishing. As many of these states obtained independence in the 1980s, they sought to increase their revenue and freedom of action by raising the prices charged for fishing rights in their waters.

The United States, led by its Tunamen Association, was opposed to paying more for fishing. The Soviet Union took advantage of this short-sightedness and reached an agreement with Kiribati in 1985 for a $1.7 million fishing deal. The near-exhaustion of phosphate deposits had made the economy even more dependent on fishing. In June 1986 the Soviet Union established diplomatic relations with Vanuatu. This diplomatic fishing in troubled waters was inexpensive, but had the potential seriously to disrupt the American security network in the region.[3] Other Soviet offers to the Solomon Islands, Tuvalu, and Western Samoa were rejected.

There are some prospects for the diversification of the economies of the islands, but the dependence on natural resources and commodity exports seems likely to continue. Whether or not a gold boom follows the phosphate production as some suggest, the close involvement of multinational corporations from Australia, Japan, the United States, and Europe is likely to continue.[4]

The island economies have little ability to withstand outside pressures. Islands such as Tonga or Vanuatu are losing people as islanders go in search of greener pastures elsewhere in the Pacific, where the dynamism of the region is more evident. Unlike even African states, it is unlikely that most of these Pacific islands will ever be able to create and sustain a viable economy for themselves.[5]

Some islands, such as Tahiti, at least have the benefits from French investment in its nuclear-weapons programme. This creates an artificial economy, but at least a more prosperous one.[6] France is also able to improve its position by buying influence in such states as Fiji, which was ostracized by many Commonwealth states for its declaration of martial law in 1987.[7] Many of the American-dominated islands which serve useful military roles also suffer from the same mix of economic blessing and curse that comes with military interest.

In 1987 the United States reached agreement with the Forum Fisheries Agency, which represents the islands' fishing interests, that $60 million would be paid over five years. Although this agreement will go a great deal of the way to undercutting Soviet influence, it opened up a rift with Japan which was driving an even harder bargain with the islands by keeping the negotiations bilateral.[8] The Japanese concern to get the best economic deal was running into conflict with American concern with political and military calculations. The Pacific islands may be weak and marginal to Pacific economic relations, but they do have options and the potential to disrupt stability.

[3] *The Times* (7 August 1986); *Radio Free Europe*, RL 284/86 (21 July 1986).
[4] *Financial Times* (3 April 1987) on the gold boom.
[5] *International Herald Tribune* (30 June 1987).
[6] *Far Eastern Economic Review* (25 December 1986).
[7] *International Herald Tribune* (16 November 1987).
[8] *Far Eastern Economic Review* (23 July 1987).

24

Economic Integration

If trade is co-operation, and modern trade is increasingly intertwining the states of the world, then most of the discussion above has already been about a form of economic integration. But of course, trade is also a way of furthering the interests of the state and its inhabitants, and therefore is often as much about competition as co-operation.[1] In fact, trade is for what the Chinese call 'mutual benefit'. The rise of the so-called 'trading states' may represent a more peaceful pattern of international relations than a world of 'warring states'[2] but, as we have seen, trade itself does not reduce the amount of international tension. Indeed, it can be argued that the Pacific portion of the Second World War had important roots in Japan's dissatisfaction with its international economic position.

Given the obvious role that economic development has played in the transformation of the Pacific, states have struggled to find the most advantageous position in the regional international political economy. We have noted that there have been relatively few dramatic changes in the patterns of trading relationships, only in their volume. We have also observed an increasing tendency for the more developed economies to dominate trade in the region, while at the same time these states in fact fit into a global, rather than Pacific, economy.

In the global economy, there have been several attempts at multilateral economic integration. The most common type is global organizations such as the IMF or the World Bank. There are more specialized groupings on a world-wide basis, including the OECD for developed capitalist economies or the so-called Group of 77, the poorer side of what is described as the North–South conflict between developed and developing states. There are also regional organizations like the EC, alliances of states with no internal trade barriers but with protection against the outside world. A number of these attempts at multilateral integration of international economic interests have had their counterparts in the Pacific, but with very different results.

---

[1] Nathan Rosenberg and L. E. Birdzell, *How the West Grew Rich* (New York: Basic Books, 1986), ch. 3; Robert Gilpin, *The Political Economy of International Relations* (Princeton: Princeton University Press, 1987).

[2] Richard Rosencrance, *The Rise of the Trading State* (New York: Basic Books, 1986).

THE ASSOCIATION OF SOUTH EAST ASIAN NATIONS

It is easy to be cynical about ASEAN, especially by comparing it to the far more organized, but still far from wholly successful, enterprise in Europe—the European Community. But given the lower level of development of the states involved, the less evident reasons for their co-operation, and the less clear-cut definition of an external 'threat', ASEAN can be said to have done reasonably well.

As the states of South-east Asia obtained independence, they grew increasingly aware of their common problems instead of just their uncommon struggles against different colonial powers. The distinctive heritage of the peoples of South-east Asia has already been outlined. Rivalries between these people have long roots in the past. It is this tension between traditional competition and the new pressures for co-operation that slowed ASEAN integration.

In July 1961 the Philippines, Thailand, and Malaysia formed the Association of Southeast Asia (ASA) in order to promote economic and social co-operation. But even among these non-Communist states there were deep differences. The Philippines and Malaysia fell out over North Borneo, which joined the Malaysian Federation in September 1963. Also in 1963, oil-rich Brunei joined the Federation. Malaysia and Singapore fell out over communal and economic policies, which led to the formation of an independent Singapore in 1965.

The idea of ASA was rocked by political disputes, but it was revitalized by Thai mediation between Indonesia and Malaysia and by the fall of the radical Indonesian leader, Sukarno, in 1967. On 8 August 1967 Indonesia, Malaysia, Singapore, the Philippines, and Thailand met in Bangkok to form ASEAN. Brunei joined in 1984 and Papua New Guinea now sits in as an observer.

This organization was little more than a name until the triumph of Communism in Indo-China in 1975. With its 280 million people, ASEAN is the second-largest grouping of market economies and has a population equal to all of Latin America.[3] But until the mid-1970s this collection of non-Communist states was deeply divided over what attitude to adopt to events in Indo-China. Plans for economic co-operation and the promotion of social growth never got beyond discussion. The first ASEAN summit was not held until February 1976, in Bali. The first serious attempts at inter-regional economic co-operation were not begun until the 1976 Declaration of ASEAN Concord.

---

[3] A. Broinowski, *Understanding ASEAN* (London: Macmillan, 1982).

In these first ten years, ASEAN managed to issue a proposal for a Zone of Peace in the region, but it remained deeply divided on the nature of the external threat. Indonesia and Malaysia, in particular, feared China more than the Soviet Union. With the onset of Sino-American *détente*, the closer allies of the United States, Thailand, and the Philippines began to reassess their own view of China. If alliances and integration depend on a commonality of national interests, in such a time of fluid interests integration was a pious hope.

The possibilities for economic co-operation were also in flux because of major changes in the region.[4] The rise of Japan had helped feed economic prosperity in some ASEAN states, but the benefits were unevenly spread. Singapore and to some extent Malaysia were the main beneficiaries. By contrast, the sharp rise in the price of oil benefited the region's oil producers, mainly Indonesia and Brunei. Also the rise of the EC led some in ASEAN to work towards specific trade negotiations with the major trading blocks of the developed world—the EC, the United States, and Japan.[5]

In 1975 only 12.9 per cent of ASEAN states' trade was conducted within the grouping. Japan took 24.6 per cent, the United States 17 per cent, and the EC 14.3 per cent. By 1980 inter-ASEAN trade had crept up to 15.1 per cent; Japan had slipped to 22.3 per cent, the United States to 15.4 per cent, and the EC to 12.1 per cent.[6] But the progress was painfully slow and the level of inter-ASEAN trade was still only about a quarter of the percentage attained in the EC. A trade accord with Japan was reached in order to pump development aid and investment into ASEAN, but the funds were never deemed adequate by the South-east Asians.

A series of agreements was reached by the early 1980s among ASEAN states in an effort to boost trade between members. There was common recognition of driving licences, and co-operation on nature conservation was agreed in 1985. Trade agreements eliminated tariffs on chillies, which all the ASEAN states grow, and snowploughs, which none need. Of course the main problem was that their economies were remarkably similar both in their production of basic commodities and in their need to create export-oriented industry for the developed market economies. Only Singapore, with its NIC status, stood to gain clearly from further integration and it was therefore the main supporter of more effective integration.

By the mid-1980s inter-ASEAN trade had crept up to 20 per cent of the group's total, but by 1985 it had fallen back to 18.7 per cent. Japan held its

---

[4] D. Crow, *The ASEAN States* (New York: Praeger, 1983).

[5] A. Jorgensen-Dahl, *Regional Organisation and Order in Southeast Asia* (London: Macmillan, 1982); Gavin Boyd, 'ASEAN Regional Policies' in Gavin Boyd (ed.), *Region Building in the Pacific* (Oxford: Pergamon, 1982).

[6] *Far Eastern Economic Review* (3 December 1987).

share at 22 per cent, as did the United States at 17 per cent and the EEC at 12 per cent. After a decade of more serious attention to economic integration, little had changed in trade patterns. Most of the fluctuation, such as it was, in inter-ASEAN trade could be explained by Singapore's import of crude oil and its export of refined-oil products. No real progress had been made in creating a free-trade zone and in agreeing tariffs against the outside world. Consider just the case of the free port of Singapore, for whom a raising of the tariff wall would be suicidal.

Although the number of items traded within ASEAN at preferential rates did increase, the number of items excluded as 'sensitive' accounted for 25 per cent of the trade of the Philippines 39 per cent of Malaysia, 54 per cent of Indonesia, and 63 per cent of Thailand. Singapore excluded only 2 per cent, and with its diversifying economy in 1987 Thailand began to cut the size of its exclusion list.[7] The attempts to create ASEAN industrial projects have also had meagre results despite high-level fanfare. The idea was to create companies owned 60 per cent at home and 10 per cent by other ASEAN members. Few of the projects have been completed.

By the time of the December 1987 ASEAN summit in Manila, the first for a decade, the hope of revived investment from Japan was the latest idea for encouraging ASEAN integration.[8] In 1987 the Japanese Prime Minister promised $2 billion of such aid and ASEAN members generally sought greater Japanese investment, taking advantage of the rise of Japanese overseas investment in search of lower labour costs. Yet it was equally clear that manipulating the spending of other people's money was no substitute for serious thinking about internal ASEAN co-operation. In any case, the Japanese were only too well aware that there were limits to how far and how fast they could become involved in the ASEAN economies. When their profile in ASEAN rises too high, many people begin Japan-bashing and recalling past 'Japanese invasions'.[9] What is more, apart from Indonesia with its massive oil exports to Japan, ASEAN runs a chronic deficit in trade with Japan. Short of huge Japanese investment, the deficit is unlikely to be cut.[10] ASEAN is worried that Japan is far more interested in China, and that Japanese investment in, and imports from, China should be coming to ASEAN.

The increasing turn to Japan was encouraged by gruffer noises from Washington, upset at the ability of some ASEAN states to penetrate the American market.[11] This was part of a related American demand that Japan

7 *Far Eastern Economic Review* (3 December 1987); *Financial Times* (10 July 1987).
8 *International Herald Tribune* (12 December 1987).
9 *Far Eastern Economic Review* (26 June 1986).
10 *Far Eastern Economic Review* (12 June 1986).
11 Secretary of State Shultz to ASEAN, reported in *International Herald Tribune* (20 June 1987).

open its market to the exports of developing states. Of course, the United States was not pleased to see the NICs increasing their share of Japanese imports when the United States itself was unable to do so. ASEAN states, looking at the success of the NICs, seemed more interested in selling outside ASEAN and to the developed world than in enhancing local co-operation. To the extent that they faced common problems in exporting to the developed world, there was reason for co-operation. But then this argument applied only to the more developed, export-oriented economies, and was one shared with the NICs who were not members of ASEAN.

Yet, for all these problems in ASEAN integration, states still want to join. Papua New Guinea, already an observer, and Fiji have explored the possibilities of extending ASEAN into the wider Pacific. Their main motives have more to do with seeking a political place in the changing Pacific than any expectation of large economic benefits.[12] To some extent, this south Pacific shift to ASEAN is part of a dissatisfaction with Australia and New Zealand, and a result of improving relations with Indonesia. The decline in the number and ferocity of territorial disputes by the late 1980s also helped open up this new ASEAN opportunity.

Although ASEAN has become less divided over territorial disputes, politics is still far from an easy subject at summits. Indonesia and Malaysia take a more co-operative attitude to Vietnam and its problem of getting out of Kampuchea than do Thailand and the Philippines. Of course these states also differ over the extent to which either China or the Soviet Union and Vietnam are perceived as a greater threat.

It is difficult to imagine that if ASEAN had not existed its members would have been forced to create it. It is true that it is probably the most successful organization of developing states, and it has achieved marginal political and economic success. But its main problem seems to be that it is stuck in a region of rapid change, while at the same time its members lack sufficiently strong reasons to co-operate, let alone agree on a common sense of threat. As the states become more differentiated, with the move of Singapore, Malaysia, and possibly Thailand into the NIC category, then the possibilities for more complementary than competitive economic relations are increased. But the success of a number of the economies of the Pacific has led people to entertain even more grandiose ideas. Some have suggested that the real future of ASEAN lies with an even wider co-operative scheme—a Pacific Economic Community (PEC).

---

[12] *Far Eastern Economic Review* (2 April 1987).

A PACIFIC COMMUNITY

If it is easy to be cynical about ASEAN, the most successful of regional economic organizations in the developing world, it is even easier to be dismissive of a 'Pacific Economic Community'. The proliferation of papers, articles, study groups, quasi-official working parties, and intergovernmental organizations on the subject has often led to easy disdai of the idea of economic co-operation in the Pacific as little more than hot air. While co-operation in a closely integrated form such as the European Community is unlikely to develop, some useful ideas about easing the economic strains between states have emerged. By focusing on the essentials of such regional economic co-operation, it becomes evident that the Pacific Economic Community is an idea whose time has passed, and the most sensible route seems to lie in closer collaboration with the broader global economy.

As the history of the EC, by far the most successful of these integrative organizations, makes clear, the institution-building-first approach to integration provides jobs for the bureaucrats, but precious little genuine integration. Real integration is based on political, military, and economic interest, and only latterly can be supported by building institutions. Real common economic interest is difficult to find and is complicated by the addition of more members, and especially those of differing levels of development and with widely different ideologies and cultures.

It is true that the EC and many states of the Pacific have shared the experience of rapid economic growth. But they are not comparable in terms of common economic interest, political system, level of development, or relative absence of distracting political/military differences. If anything, the idea of a PEC is akin to that of a common European security spanning East and West. It is fine as an aspiration, but nearly devoid of political reality.

The concept of a PEC can be traced even as far back as 1917, when the Pan-Pacific Union was formed to sponsor conferences.[13] One would have little problem in finding positive statements about the idea from nearly every state in the Pacific. In the post-war period, Japan has been the leading advocate: for example Foreign Minister Takeo Miki suggested a Pacific Association in the mid-1960s and Japanese academics proposed a Pacific Free Trade Association in 1965. Proposals then followed for an Asian Development Fund on the model of the Marshall Plan.[14] Trade and Development Conferences were begun in Japan in 1968 and still continue.

---

[13] Palitha Kohona, 'The Evolving Concept of a Pacific Basin Community' in *Asian Survey*, 26/4 (April 1986); Richard Holbrooke and Maria Zammit, 'Toward a Pacific Basin Community—Slowly', *SAIS Review*, 4/1 (1984).

[14] Michael Oborne and Nicholas Fourt, *Pacific Basin Economic Cooperation* (Paris: OECD, 1983).

More than 400 major companies from the wealthier states and some developing members of the Pacific formed the Pacific Basin Economic Council to promote the study of trade and investment issues. The Pacific Trade and Development Conference (PAFTAD) grew out of the Japanese proposals for a Pacific Free Trade Area, and with government sponsorship this series has met 16 times between 1968 and 1987. By 1988 the non-governmental Pacific Economic Co-operation Conference (PECC) had met six times since its first assembly in Canberra in September 1980. In recent years it has become the organization most discussed as the basis of a full-blown PEC. But even its strongest supporters remain doubtful that it can keep up with the rapidly changing Pacific and global economy.[15] Its strengths are mainly to be found in its ability to focus on narrow, technical issues, as is done in some of the PECC's specialized groups.

In the late 1970s the United States became much more interested in the idea and a major report was presented to Congress.[16] The result was a new organization to promote trade and development. The Organization for Pacific Trade and Development (OPTAD) was a forum for discussion intended to lead to a community of nations with economic ties in the region. The membership would include the five OECD members in the Pacific, six members of ASEAN, and South Korea, with special status for the Pacific islands, Taiwan, and Hong Kong.

The growth in interest in a PEC in the United States has begun to rival that in Japan.[17] The main focus is along the American Pacific coast, and especially California, through which more than half the American trade with the Pacific passes. But for all the words and papers on the 'Pacific Century', as one analyst pointed out 'The Pacific rim is sexy, but it is not simple.'[18] The proliferation of acronyms of Pacific co-operation may even be approaching the number in the strategic-studies field. One study in 1983 counted over 800 titles of publications on the subject.[19]

The logic of a PEC is based on the growing development of the region, and the risks that conflict in a number of realms might threaten future growth. Schemes for co-operation in all the areas of conflict have been proposed. Inasmuch as the basis of this 'thinking Pacific' is economic, most schemes have focused on economic issues such as protectionism, co-operation on technology, and exploitation of resources.[20]

---

[15] David Arase, 'Pacific Economic Cooperation' in *Pacific Review*, 1/2 (1988).

[16] *An Asian-Pacific Regional Economic Organisation* (Washington DC: Committee on Foreign Relations, United States Senate, 1979); *Pacific Basin Interdependencies* (Washington DC: Joint Economic Committee, United States Congress, June 1981).

[17] W. W. Rostow, *The United States and the Regional Organisations of Asia and the Pacific, 1965–85* (Austin: University of Texas Press, 1986).

[18] *Los Angeles Times* (9 November 1987).

[19] Oborne and Fourt, *Pacific Basin Economic Cooperation*.

[20] Peter Drysdale and H. Patrick, 'An Asian-Pacific Regional Economic Organisation' in

The search for an effective multilateral institution to enhance integration in the Pacific, and the slowness with which Atlantic-focused bodies have adapted to the growth of Pacific economies, has also led its proponents to reject already-existing international organizations as unsuitable. The Economic and Social Commission for Asia and the Pacific (ESCAP), a UN body based in Bangkok, was supposed to facilitate economic and social development in the region. It was successful in setting up the Asian Development Bank (ADB), but like ESCAP the Bank focuses on Asia as the unit of organization rather than the Pacific. Established in 1965 and led by Japan and the United States, the Bank is especially useful in providing loans to Asian developing states. But it has notably failed to adapt to the new conditions of the Pacific, where many developing states make less demands on it while China and India make more. Nor has the Bank adjusted to the fact that Japan now provides a third of its funds and yet remains equal with the United States in holding only 12.5 per cent of the votes.[21] In any case, the ADB has an important part of its capital structure supported by its European members and thus, like most of the international capitalist economy, is concerned with global issues as well.

Various Latin American groupings also exist, as do global economic bodies such as the IMF, the World Bank, and GATT. In fact, it seems that the focus of economic co-operation may be shifting increasingly to these global levels rather than concerning merely the Pacific. Most of the issues relating to the Pacific economy are really global issues. For example, China and the Soviet Union wish to take part not only in the PECC but also in GATT. Some of the NICs are increasingly interested in joining the OECD rather than setting up a Pacific-wide equivalent. It seems quaint and anachronistic to think of a booming international economy and imagine that there will be much appeal in Pacific-wide co-operation. Increasingly, issues in the Pacific, for example the coal industry, are actually discussed as global matters, with a vital part played by the Europeans and other developed, industrialized states.[22] With so much more of international trade turning out to be intra-company trade, and foreign direct investment complicating calculations of national economic policy, it is too late to think of Pacific prosperity being possible without more global integration.

There are some groupings within the Pacific that do not encompass all states, but still undertake serious work. The most notable among them, ASEAN, has already been discussed. Others cover such detailed issues as

John Crawford and G. Seow (eds.), *Pacific Economic Cooperation* (Singapore: Heinemann, 1981); Staffan Linder, *The Pacific Century* (Stanford, Calif.: Stanford University Press, 1986).

[21] *The Economist* (2 May 1987, 7 May 1988); *International Herald Tribune* (25 April 1988).

[22] *Far Eastern Economic Review* (10 March 1988); BBC, SWB, FE, 0090, Al, 1 (3 March 1988).

mineral prospecting or protecting the environment.[23] Perhaps the most promising is the South Pacific Bureau of Economic Co-operation, established in Suva in 1973. Its permanent Secretariat became the official Secretariat of the South Pacific Forum (SPF) formed in 1974, which gathers the heads of government of independent and self-governing states in the region.

The SPF is not an organization conspicuous by its success. Despite general agreement on French nuclear testing or fishing disputes, it has failed to take effective, co-ordinated positions on any issue that brings any of its members into conflict.[24] The richer, white-Commonwealth members dominate and yet fail to open their doors wide enough to the exports of the smaller SPF members.[25] The formation of the South Pacific Regional Trade and Economic Co-operation Agreement (SPARTECA) by Australia and New Zealand was intended to help solve this trade problem.

These efforts to integrate the region founder on the basic problems of regional diversity, including on such vital matters as fishing resources. They provide little grounds for optimism that an even wider Pacific organization could be formed. Indeed, the problems facing such region-builders are readily admitted by their supporters.[26]

The first problem is of course membership.[27] None of the groupings established so far includes any of the Communist states of the Pacific except China. There seems to be a willingness to include Canada and the Latin American states with their tiny Pacific trade, but not the Communist states with their higher percentages of commerce within the region. As has already been pointed out, there are huge variations in the percentage of trade undertaken by states in the Pacific and in how far afield that trade travels.

The potential to wreck arrangements by fomenting international tension has already been demonstrated in the region, and a PEC would really thrive only in a peaceful environment where the threats of war are under control. It would also make far more sense for the region to integrate the resource-rich economy of the Soviet Union, along with that of North Korea bordering the booming South Korea, and the low-labour-cost economies of Indo-China.

Second, there is the problem of leadership and inequality among partners in a PEC. As we have already seen, Japan and the United States, and a few very close neighbours, dominate trade flows to an extent unknown in other

---

[23] *International Herald Tribune* (28 November 1986) on the environmental pact.

[24] *Financial Times* (18 November 1987).

[25] Kohona, 'Basin Community'.

[26] Lawrence Krause, *Economic Integration in the Pacific Basin* (Washington DC: Brookings, 1980); Linder, *The Pacific Century*.

[27] Stephen Whalley, 'The Membership Dilemma and What to do About It' in Robert Downen and Bruce Dickson (eds.), *The Emerging Pacific Community* (Boulder, Colo.: Westview, 1984).

integrating economic organizations. There is very little existing, and almost as little developing, genuine multilateral Pacific trade.

The age of American hegemony in international economics is passing, but it is not being replaced by Japanese hegemony.[28] Japan may be anxious to take a more assertive role in such regional organizations as the ADB, but it has refused to do so in the World Bank. Japan has provided increasing proportions of the World Bank's funds, but has kept its staffing presence at the level of Sri Lanka and in 1987 refused a position of leadership.[29]

Even if Japan were willing to take a more important role, there are a number of states who would be very upset to see a new version of Japan's 'Co-prosperity Sphere'. Many are only too well aware that Japan stands to gain most by organizing the region in its own image, and by being able to do so without recourse to military power.[30]

If anything, the Pacific is dividing up between its developed states and the fast-growing NICs on one hand and the poorer states of the region on the other. Only a few states, such as China with its huge market and Indonesia with its oil, can make a significant contribution across this dividing line. The old category of North–South conflict in the Pacific has been replaced by a far more complex interaction between NICs and developed states, all of which are increasingly tied into an international economy rather than a Pacific-wide one. The continuing, and by the 1980s increasing, importance of Europeans in these states' trade suggests that, even if there was once a window for the development of a PEC, it has probably now passed.

Of course, the North–South divide has not entirely been erased from the Pacific. The developing states, including the NICs, still wish to see greater access to the markets of the developed states. But the NICs are now less opposed to the free-trade arguments. Nor are they as concerned as they once were about the problems of debt and high interest rates. Many of the economies of developing states are now more diversified and thus less subject to the debilitating effects of depressed commodity prices. To a large extent, integrating the economies even of only the non-Communist states of the Pacific would be just as complex as doing it on a global basis. It seems far more fruitful to seek either bilateral or possibly multilateral arrangements on an *ad hoc* basis between a smaller number of states on a narrower range of subjects, or else deal with the basic problem of the global economy. Thinking Pacific in economic terms has little obvious logic.

There are deep differences between heavily indebted NICs, such as Mexico, and most of the East Asian NICs, who have coped with the debt

---

[28] Hideo Sato, 'Japan and the International Economy' in *Pacific Review*, 1, 2 (1988).
[29] *Far Eastern Economic Review* (23 July 1987).
[30] Sueo Sekiguchi, 'Japan's Regional Policies' in Boyd (ed.), *Region Building*.

problem more successfully. Yet debt is still a major problem for some East
Asians, such as the Philippines. The problems of commodity economies also
affect Pacific states in different ways. Mexico and Indonesia are oil exporters
and Indonesia and Malaysia are also dependent on other raw-material
prices. But the NICs want lower commodity prices both for raw materials
and to keep the developed economies buoyant as markets. Of course, these
differences are some of the reasons why the North–South agenda has not
been taken up, but it is instructive that the earliest stages of the decline of the
idea of 'the South' took place in the Pacific.

The third problem for region-builders is conceiving an agenda for co-
operation that would form the basis of a PEC. Trade friction cannot even be
resolved on a bilateral basis, as more than two decades of Japanese–
American trade problems shows. With the emergence of the NICs and a
strong European trading bloc, the complications are now even greater. The
United States may be successful in forcing open the Japanese economy but
the NICs and Europeans are the ones to benefit most. The entry of China
threatens the interests of other developing states, especially when they see
deals being done with China more in recognition of its political and military
standing than because of an appreciation of its economic prowess or
profitability. And of course, as the ASEAN example shows, few states in
the region want genuine integration when they can do better by striking
individual deals in the global economy.

Perhaps the most important problem is that many of the types of integration sought for a PEC are already taking place, but as part of the natural
evolution of a global economy. The region has managed to develop quite
nicely so far without resort to another bunch of international bureaucrats.[31]
Individual multinational corporations, many of which come from the NICs,
have forged their own international linkages.[32] The complex requirements
of beating trade barriers have led to much cross-Pacific, and actually global,
investment in order to produce, for example, a Japan–Germany joint
venture in Europe and the United States for export to Taiwan and Australia.
Trade in technology has been equally complex and is already highly
interdependent.

In the late 1980s the most effective of the ineffective PEC-type bodies has
been the PECC, which has developed into a low-tension talking-shop for
Pacific issues. The high hopes for more effective organizations have been
replaced by an assessment that there already exist enough global bodies such
as GATT or the IMF to deal with what were essentially global issues. Even

[31] *Far Eastern Economic Review* (21 December 1979).
[32] Peter Buckley and Hafiz Mizra, 'Asian-Pacific Multinationals', in *Pacific Review*, 1/1
(1988).

the Japanese, who led the charge for a PEC, are having second thoughts, with many in MITI arguing the case for thinking global instead of Pacific.[33]

Of course, the emergence of the NICs, the success of the region as a whole, and the increasingly positive role of its Communist members have meant that the nature of economic discussions in the Pacific will always be different from that in the global economy. A good case can be made that the real value in thinking Pacific concerns greater participation in trade with Pacific states and learning from the experience of their economic success. The lessons for both North and South are complicated, but important. What is more, much of the strident North–South rhetoric, well known from the Group of 77, is moderated in the Pacific by the recognition of growing common interests in free trade and complex linkages of multinationals, investment, and technology flows.

Perhaps a more useful model, but also one with little chance of organizational success, is trilateralism—the idea that the United States, Japan and its allied NICs, and the West Europeans have a common interest in managing the international economy. As the Pacific trends suggest, however, the growing role not only of proto-NICs but also of China and the Soviet Union makes such grandiose theorizing difficult to sustain.[34] It is one of the basic realities of the new international economy that few states can have near-complete control over their own economies and some can have only a marginal effect. Especially with the decline of the Bretton Woods system and American hegemony, the reality of economic interdependence has hit the Pacific as it did Europe a decade or so earlier.[35] Just as there is little that most individual states can do to shift the international system to their advantage, so there is little that a grouping of states can do to control events.

To be sure, the larger economic powers, such as Japan and the United States, can have an important impact when they act in concert with their G-7 partners, for example in setting currency rates. Changes in commodity prices or the American withdrawal from active wars in Asia can affect the economies of the region. There are different rates of adjustment to these changes as a result of national economic policies, or the failure to formulate such policies, as with the United States' energy resources and budget deficit. But in general the pattern of international economics has been set by events within a complex interaction of states and corporations beyond the control of individual or groups of states. As compared to military affairs, the economic pattern is more complex, and beyond national control.

To some extent in economic affairs, as in military affairs, the pattern

---

33 *Far Eastern Economic Review* (12 June 1986).
34 Gavin Boyd, 'Introduction' in Boyd (ed.), *Region Building*.
35 Lawrence Krause and Sueo Sekiguchi (eds.), *Economic Interactions in the Pacific Basin* (Washington DC: Brookings, 1980).

seems to be a fluid mix of nationalisms in a complex international environment. This very complexity provides a useful degree of independence of action, but it also sets strict limits on its possible scope—much like, in many of the Confucian societies of the region, the individual acts within a constraining, even if often informal, framework. The term 'flexible rigidities' is as apt for international politics in the Pacific as it is for Japanese domestic economic policy. Look, for example, at the airline business in the Pacific, now 25 per cent of the world passenger traffic, where impressive growth rates were achieved, but by the efforts of individual national carriers. Now that more carriers want to break into the market the often state-owned airlines are using all their skills at informal pressure to keep the system closed. Limited regional co-operation is possible, but far more genuine co-operation is carried out on the global level.[36] Thus the pattern in the Pacific is a complex mix of the successful economics of some local states becoming tied up with global pressures for change. Of course it is useful to think Pacific when it means peering into a laboratory of economic change. But the region is likely to be a poor example of regional economic co-operation.

Not surprisingly, there have been remarkably few formal Pacific multilateral economic negotiations that affect the interests of Pacific states. The most important arrangements are global, for example through the IMF or GATT. Even the Multifibre Agreement, restricting the amount of textile exports from the NICs and developing states to the developed world, was not a specifically Pacific enterprise. Thus, to the extent that there is *de facto* economic integration of parts of the Pacific, it is merely a portion of a global pattern. Even if there was once a chance for a Pacific Economic Community, the time has now certainly past. It is striking that not until recently has the vast 'Pacific shift' in economic terms been assessed or detailed statistics collected.[37] Those wishing to 'manage' the process have apparently missed the Pacific boat.

[36] *International Herald Tribune* (18 December 1987).
[37] *The Economist* (3 May 1986).

Conclusions: Patterns In The Pacific

The central conclusions of this book should, by now, be clear. While it is vital to 'think Pacific', it is a different type of thought than is usually undertaken by those who believe in the possibility of a coherent Pacific region. The importance of the Pacific is in the economic success of some of its parts and the new ideas it offers about North–South relations and the role of the superpowers. The new ideas and experiences in the Pacific help shape a new pattern of international relations. But the importance of the Pacific is best understood in the context of global trends in international ideology, security, and economic affairs. For West Europeans who are experimenting with different aspects of the same trend towards the decline of state sovereignty and greater international interdependence, it is vital to understand the Pacific for its successes and the way in which both the European and East Asian experiences contribute to the new pattern of international politics.

In fact, the Europeans have a long tradition of understanding the changing importance of the Pacific. Before the coming of the Europeans in the fifteenth century, there was not even a sense that 'the Pacific' existed. The very name was given by Magellan and it was the Spanish in the sixteenth century who first traded across its waters. What is more, it was not until the twentieth century that military strategists began thinking Pacific. The first arms-control pact in the Pacific was not reached until the 1920s. The first Pacific-wide war was not fought until the 1940s.

Yet even with the growing sophistication of Pacific politics since, it is hard to argue that the foreign policies of the states of the region are dominated by a Pacific-consciousness. Certainly in comparison to the consciousness of being West European or a part of an Atlantic community, the Pacific is far from a coherent region. In the case of Europe, the key to a genuine sense of regional belonging was the awareness of a common culture and strong similarities of ideology. Some scholars may date the origins of these shared values in Europe to the eleventh century and some would place them later in the sixteenth century.[1] But nearly all would agree that ideology and culture lie at the roots of the West European political system. With massive emigration, especially since the seventeenth century, much of those cultures and their values was transmitted across the Atlantic to the Americas. Trade and military strategy accompanied the people, and helped create what is now called the Atlantic community.

The most striking ingredient that is absent from a putative Pacific

---

[1] Philippe Wolff, *The Awakening of Europe* (London: Penguin, 1968).

community is precisely that sense of shared cultures and ideologies. The reason for this fragmentation of Pacific politics can be traced in large measure to the politics of East Asia, and more especially to China's failure to diffuse its culture and ideology. For milleniums, China's was the world's most sophisticated civilization. It spread through the vast region we now call China, a territory much larger than western Europe. Culture and ideology within China was far more coherent, and lasted longer, than the equivalent in western Europe. It influenced neighbouring cultures in Japan, Korea, and South-east Asia. The differences in these variations on Chinese-style Confucianism are apparent, but not much greater than the differences between, for example, Italian and English cultures and ideologies.

Unlike the European experience, however, the Chinese-dominated East Asian culture did not spread beyond its homeland. Nor did it enhance its coherence when faced with challenges from the outside. In fact, East Asian culture and ideology has, if anything, become more fragmented, unlike that of Europe and the Atlantic.

The key differences seems to lie with the absence of political systems to rival China. To be sure, Chinese empires waxed and waned and independent dynasties were able to develop in Korea, Japan, and South-east Asia. But none of these dynasties was ever a serious rival to China for any length of time. In Europe the rivalry of empires bred a 'thriving' international system and fed the appetite for foreign conquest and ideological imperialism. By contrast China's monopoly bred self-satisfaction and was accompanied by only a passing interest in international commerce and even less interest in exploration and emigration.

When this self-satisfaction was eventually smashed by European, American, and then Japanese imperialism, the result was great disorder in East Asian international politics. As the Chinese empire shrank, independent states emerged that were shaped by different ideologies and cultures from those in Europe, the United States, and Japan. In contrast to Europe, where most of the invasions were carried out by fellow Europeans, East Asians had their political culture reshaped by visitors from further afield and with very different ideas and values. In many senses, the strength of China in the past and its eventual collapse made East Asia especially vulnerable to invasion, colonialism, and fragmentation.

By the time the Chinese revolutions in the twentieth century had reconstituted most of the Chinese empire, the region around China had changed out of all recognition. Some rival empires, like Russia, had come by land and were determined to hold on to what they had grabbed from China. The British held Chinese territory, retained colonies in South-east Asia and the south Pacific, exercised naval power in Pacific waters, and had planted vigorous white-settler states in Canada, Australia, and New Zealand. Other

Europeans, including France and Holland, held their own colonies and, like Britain, oriented large parts of the region's international trade and politics to Europe and away from Asia.

The largest of the white-settler states of the Pacific, the United States, had begun to create its own empire. With its own growing Pacific population and an equally rapidly expanding naval presence in the Pacific, the United States, like the Europeans before it, was beginning to think and act 'Pacific'. Unlike all the 'European' powers except Russia, the United States was a Pacific power with home territory lapped by Pacific waters. Like Russia, the United States was a rival empire likely to stay in the Pacific.

But all these rival empires were white, or at least non-Asian. The major exception, and thus perhaps the main rival to China, was Japan. As the only non-white state to make the leap to great-power status and modernization, Japan was better placed than anyone to seize territory and influence in the Pacific. Japan was also notable for its development of a new version of Confucianism—one better suited to modern industrial and technological revolutions, and also a major rival to Chinese-dominated Confucianism. Therefore Chinese ideology and culture not only failed to spread in the Pacific, but it also came under serious challenge from European and now rival East Asian ideologies.

There might have been some chance for a coherent East Asian, if not Pacific, community if Japan's attempt at imperialism had not run foul of the coalition of European, Russian, and United States power. Japan's attempt to forge an East Asian Co-prosperity Sphere was never likely to succeed, but it did achieve fleeting unity when its rivals were distracted by European conflict. The Pacific War was part of the first genuinely global war, but by 1945 Japan was left alone to take on the alliance of European, Russian, and American power. When this coalition concentrated its strength on Japan, the fundamental limits of Japanese power were made apparent.

POST-WAR RECOVERY

In the immediate aftermath of the war, the Pacific saw its most sudden realignment of international politics. For some 15 years from 1945 the region developed an overlay of superpower bipolarity on top of the existing pluralisms of differing political systems and cultures. For some observers and participants at the time, the Pacific had been reshaped into something that was not very different from, if less important than, the Atlantic.

The war had brought the United States across the Pacific in force. Although its only colony, the Philippines, was granted independence, American influence remained, and was vastly increased by its support for the Chiang Kai-shek regime on Taiwan, its defence of South Korea, and of course its occupation of Japan. By the mid-1950s a regional security scheme in South-east Asia was added, bringing American power more on-shore in Asia. United States economic influence in these states was powerful, providing most of the capital and dominating trade patterns. For some people, the analogy to American support for a 'fringe' of democracies in Europe was striking. The Soviet Union, with its support for Communism in Mongolia, North Korea, North Vietnam, and above all China, was seen to be attempting to expand its influence in the Pacific in just the way it had done in eastern Europe.

The fundamental flaw in the bipolar reasoning, apart from the fact that few American allies were continental Asian states, was that beneath the thin superpower overlay there were deep differences among states. Communism was not monolithic, European colonialism had not yet fully retreated, and American allies from the Philippines to Korea were deeply suspicious of each other and separated by vast gulfs of culture and ideology. There were a number of bilateral patterns linking the United States to its allies, but there was little of the genuine multilateralism evident in Europe and across the Atlantic.

The wars of the 1950s encouraged some to believe that the Pacific region was becoming increasingly coherent. In the Korean War, the United States and other like-minded Pacific states sent troops to defend their 'common values'. But troops were also sent from Europe and the cause was seen as part of a global, rather than a Pacific, struggle against Communism. In any case, the regime in South Korea could hardly be described as sharing the political values of the pluralist democracies. When West Berlin was being defended against the Soviet blockade in 1948-9, the commonality of values between the western powers and the West German people was far more obvious.

The United States' defence of Taiwan in its conflict with China in the 1950s was also cast in terms of the struggle between East and West, although the regime in Taiwan was hardly democratic. The United States was defending a military and putative economic ally, and the cry of shared anti-Communism merely masked deep differences among allies.

The other major conflicts in the region took place in South-east Asia, where European colonialism was in retreat. While Britain successfully beat back Communist rebels in Malaya, France failed in its attempt to hold the line against Communism in Vietnam. The Geneva settlement provided for French retreat, the temporary partition of Vietnam, and the second round of fighting which added a cold-war veneer to the decolonization conflict. The formation of SEATO suggested parallels to Europe and NATO, but the

East Asian variety was barely a shadow of the European success story. The rhetoric of the 1950s in the Pacific was not very different from that in Europe, but the reality was worlds away.

MOVING TO MULTIPOLARITY

If there was a time in the period since 1945 to shape a Pacific community it was before the early 1960s. It would have required much more massive direct American intervention in East Asia and an impossibly difficult fundamental reshaping of political cultures in the 'allied' regimes. But the United States remained a reluctant imperial power, feeling a need to get more involved, but increasingly aware of its limitations and the natural fault lines of the region. The next 15 years from 1960 saw the failure of pax Americana and the clear emergence of different levels of Pacific politics. The Pacific became more important as an arena of international power but, despite musings to the contrary, less and less likely to be shaped into a Pacific community. A pattern was set at this time, but it was a pattern of diversity.

The veneer of unity in both the Communist and the capitalist worlds came unstuck in the 15 years from 1960. In the Communist camp it was China that challenged Soviet authority and split the ideological unity of so-called scientific Communism. The Chinese revolution always had strong national characteristics, but it was the failure of the Soviet model in the 1950s that led to the Chinese search for alternative, more Sinified, models.

The coming of Communism to East Asia after 1945 might have provided the opportunity for an alternative kind of international system in Asia, much as Soviet-dominated Communism in Europe was an alternative to the Atlantic community of capitalist states. But unlike eastern Europe, where at least some elements of Byzantine and Slavic culture held the uneasy allies of the Warsaw Pact and CMEA together, East Asian Communists were separated by deep fissures of culture. Marxism-Leninism was in its origins a European system of beliefs. It was unsuited to East Asia unless it could be given new components consistent with the development needs of poor, peasant states.

Chinese Communists believed they found such a formula, adding 'Mao Zedong thought' to Marxism-Leninism. The ensuing differences in basic tenets of ideology, coupled with already-evident differences in culture and national rivalries, led to the Sino-Soviet split. While China may have felt in the 1960s that it was well placed to lead other East Asian Communists, the Chinese, like the Russians before them, suffered from revolutionary and cultural hubris. Neither North Korea nor Vietnam was happy to be subservient to either Communist great power and both played their patrons off against each other. Although both North Korea and Vietnam could be described as inheritors of the Confucian tradition, both were anxious to preserve their independence. Unlike the East Europeans, who were held too closely under the Soviet thumb and could not take advantage of the split in Communism to enhance independence, East Asian Communists could tread their own paths.

Of course, in both economic and military terms, the designation of part of East Asia as a single entity called 'Communism' still made sense. For all their differences, the five East Asian Communist countries were all one-party states led by a Communist Party pursuing socialism through the mechanism of a command economy. All opposed capitalist states and North Korea and Vietnam sought support from both Communist great powers for unification of their divided countries. Both Communist powers provided such support, although in the case of North Korea neither wanted to see a return to open warfare.

In the case of Vietnam, both China and the Soviet Union supported the North Vietnamese with military and economic power. There was no formal 'United Action', but in fact North Vietnam received the support it needed. The ties binding Communist states in East Asia were every bit as tight as in Europe, except, and it is a major exception, that there were two Communist great powers holding them, not one. Thus there was no monolithic Communism in the Pacific, even though it sometimes worked out that they all pushed and pulled in the same direction.

Elsewhere in the Pacific, the American umbrella was extended and folded in response to local events. With the retreat of European empires apart from Russia, the United States became the main great-power defender of, and trader with, South-east Asia, Australia, and New Zealand. If anything, the American security umbrella now covered more territory. The United States' vision of the Pacific as an 'American lake' was more true than ever before. In fact, not only was American influence dominant in Pacific waters, but it was also tried in strength on the East Asian continent.

The successful defence of South Korea in the 1950s, and the successful deterrence of the Soviet Union in Europe and Latin America, led many Americans to believe that East Asians could be defended against Communism through an American security network. When Vietnamese Communists took on the American challenge, the United States defended its perception of regional and global order by sending more troops to South Vietnam than it deployed in Europe.

South Vietnam, like South Korea, was hardly a pluralist democracy. The United States' defence of a principle, when to many people it came to be seen as the wrong war in the wrong place and above all for the wrong cause, merely highlighted the power of nationalism in the Pacific. North Vietnam's determination to win what it perceived to be a civil war was the first major defeat inflicted on the United States since 1942. That the defeat was inflicted in the Pacific was a symbol of both the fallacy of thinking Pacific with cold-war perspectives and the limits of American power. The holes in the American security umbrella were visible to all in the region and that umbrella barely covered the fringes of East Asia.

But it was on the level of economics that the most serious challenge to American hegemony and a Pacific community was to develop. If the emergence of China was a blow to Soviet political power, the emergence of Japan was a nearly equally massive knock to the United States. A major difference was that Japanese power was in economics—a field where the principle of 'mutual benefit' is supposed to govern. Thus to some extent the rise of Japan as an economic superpower, like the recovery of western European economic power a few years before it, was seen as a benefit to the United States.

Inside the edifice of Pacific politics the American-dominated space on the economic floor shrank as Japan took markets away. Japan also became a larger market for United States goods. But above all Japanese firms made American workers unemployed as they took an increasing chunk of the United States' domestic markets. Unlike the Atlantic community, where the pattern of trade was more balanced, in the Pacific the United States lost far more than it gained in the supposed 'mutual benefit' of trade. Thus whereas in the Atlantic the expansion of European influence was a cause of greater Atlantic unity, in the Pacific the expansion of Japanese influence was a cause of friction. For much of the 1960s, however, the United States remained basically pleased that it had put its ally back on its feet and, given that in military terms all the other news out of Asia was bad news, Japan was a success story.

But the Japanese miracle was above all a Japanese success. What is more, it was a solo miracle without the benefit of like-minded neighbours that the West Europeans enjoyed. Japan's isolation in Asia fed its sense of uniqueness, distance from Asia, and suspicion of other industrialized powers, including the United States. Japan remained bound to the United States in security terms, and tension in the relationship was eased by the return of territory to Japanese sovereignty. But unlike the West Europeans, Japan continued to free-load on the American defence effort. It also managed the trick of becoming an economic superpower without almost any trappings of great-power status in other dimensions. The description of Japan as pursuing the 'foreign policy of the trader' rather than that of the diplomat was apt. It also meant that the floors of the Pacific edifice looked very different as the region's second-largest economy was a military and political broom-cupboard. It is true that West Germany also used to be criticized for having only an economic policy. But the presence of EC and NATO allies, and Germany's leading role in both, soon made such arguments obsolete.

The cultural and ideological floors of the building in this period were under renovation. Behind the walls of Communism, there was the seething turmoil of China's Cultural Revolution. This was also the period of personality cults—Mao's in China, Kim Il Sung's in North Korea and Ho Chi Minh's in North Vietnam. Nationalism mixed with ideology was a potent, and mostly radical, brew.

The picture in the non-Communist Pacific, as in the non-Communist world as a whole, was even more confused. The initial signs of an emerging global culture among certain élites were misunderstood as an American culture. It was true that the United States to some extent replaced waning European cultural influence. But the European influence in the Americas in the 1960s remained powerful, which in turn helped reshape American culture.

For most people outside the white-settler states of the Pacific, this global culture barely touched their lives. Many states were recently decolonized and experimenting with their own national ideals and modernized culture. For those that experienced growing economic success and the trials of industrialization and urbanization, the changes in political culture were often part of a global process of modernization. The resulting tensions owed more to the 'narrowcasting' influence of modernized national styles than to the 'broadcasting' of an American or global culture. Certainly in comparison to western Europe and the Atlantic community, where values and levels of development were already much more alike, the Pacific remained deeply fragmented and was, if anything, becoming more so.

THE PACIFIC AND INTERNATIONAL POLITICS

I have always heard politicians use the word Europe when they were making requests to other powers that they did not dare formulate in the name of their own country.[2]

While Bismarck's cynical assessment of Europe was no doubt valid for his age, in the latter half of the twentieth century it is far less so. The use of the name 'Pacific', however, does seem to conform far more to Bismarck's cynicism. In the years since 1975 there have been repeated assertions that a Pacific community is being created or needs to be created. These assertions and predictions are often accompanied by comparisons to the European Community and/or disparaging remarks about the decline of the far less

---

2 Quoted in Luigi Barzini, *The Impossible Europeans* (London: Weidenfeld, 1983), 104.

formal Atlantic community and the onset of 'Eurosclerosis'. The reality is very different, and above all far more complex.

The undoubted, if laborious, success of the E C is, as has been pointed out, based on shared values and close cultural ties. It feeds off similar economic systems and is supported by generally agreed principles of foreign policy. It is not a Europe-wide unity, for the cold-war lines still run through the heart of the continent and the middle of the German people. But there has never been a Europe-wide unity. Within the geographic entity of Europe, different cultures have shaped different political systems and international relationships. The existence of the matching organizations of NATO and the Warsaw Pact and the EC and COMECON may not always follows 'natural' political boundaries, but they are more than mere children of the post-1945 cold war.

By contrast, the Pacific is different in almost every single important dimension. These differences have perhaps grown even wider since 1975, although it is undoubtedly true that in economic terms some of the states of the Pacific are more important than they once were. It is incorrect, however, to speak of 'the Pacific' itself as more important, except in the sense that some states in the geographic region are more economically successful and some international political trends in the area are novel. There is no important cultural, ideological, political, economic, or even military sense in which it is particularly useful to talk of 'the Pacific'.

What is more, for all the talk of great changes in the Pacific, there have actually been remarkably few changes in the pattern of international power and influence in the region since the early 1960s, with the notable exception of Sino-American *détente*. To the extent that new trends have emerged, they have been more revelations of underlying realities than startling new developments. It is possible that this very stability is the necessary prerequisite for the emergence, after many false dawns, of a genuine Pacific community. But it seems unlikely. Most of the changes, and indeed the international importance of the region, lie in the increasing role of specific states in the pattern of global international politics, the new models of modernization for developing states, and the relative decline of the superpowers and the use of force.

The enduring gap in building the Pacific community remains the absence of cultural and ideological unity. The vast distances of the Pacific are increasingly 'reduced' by new technology, but those technologies seem to serve narrowcasting of cultural and other values as much as region-wide broadcasting. In both the immeasurable dimensions of culture, such as religion, food, and the arts, and the more measurable patterns of tourism and books published, there is every sign that potential regional patterns are being dominated by the twin pressures of globalization and local national styles.

On some levels, the influence of international styles primarily affects the wealthy and business classes. These styles are not especially American or even Japanese, and in many senses when it comes to 'high' culture European influences are often more prevalent in the Pacific. The decline of American hegemony is felt in culture as well as at military and economic levels. The Europeans may have departed in the 1950s, but they are increasingly returning to the Pacific with new ideas.

Mass cultures in non-Communist states of the Pacific remain rooted in local traditions. Even though modernization has meant changes in these traditions, it has rarely meant wholesale adoption of American or even international trends. Japan is perhaps an extreme example of how a strong culture can adapt to modernization and end up enhancing a sense of uniqueness and cultural identity. The contrasts to modern western Europe, where the sense of national uniqueness has faded, could not be more striking.

In the Communist world there is a similar mix of global trends and emphasis on national styles. Because of the Leninist nature of international Communism, the tendency towards a single orthodoxy has always been greater than in the non-Communist world. Thus it is still true that to an important extent Communist Parties are very sensitive to change in other 'fraternal' (or even not-so-fraternal) Parties. Witness the different ways in which the reform Communism of the 1980s has been dealt with in the Communist Pacific.

Chinese reforms since late 1978 were in part learned from the experience in East Europe. But they took a great deal of time before setting the pace elsewhere in the Communist Pacific. Despite Beijing's proddings, the reforms were not taken up anywhere else in the region until the Soviet Union under Mikhail Gorbachev took its own, sometimes strikingly parallel, road to reform. Chinese and Soviet socialisms have served as sorts of mirror of each other and, while the opposite is also true, nothing succeeds like success.

The differences between Chinese and Soviet reforms are as clear as the similarities. So are the pressures that both have imposed on friends and rivals in the Communist Pacific. Vietnam, Mongolia, and North Korea are the primary targets, although all have implemented reforms in their distinctive fashions. Coherence in the Communist Pacific remains far less than in eastern Europe.

The growing incoherence of the Pacific is most evident in military terms. For one thing, where have all the alliances gone? China and the Soviet Union have come to blows and, despite their *détente* of the 1980s, they still deploy the largest concentration of hostile troops outside the European theatre. The Chinese alliance with Vietnam collapsed in a bloody war in 1979. The two Communist powers' ties to North Korea are now tethers that restrain

Pyongyang's aggressiveness, but cause more friction than fraternal feeling. Soviet ties to Vietnam were strengthened for a time in the late 1970s but have now loosened while Moscow pursues *détente* with China and a more pacific Pacific policy.

The general trend towards less military conflict in the Pacific has shown the military alliances to have been composed largely for short-term convenience. Unlike the European and Atlantic arenas, where alliance ties have hardly deteriorated, although they have been strained,[3] there are no significant multilateral military alliances left in the Pacific.

The United States has watched the collapse of SEATO and ANZUS, and the failure of other grandiose plans like the mooted North-East Asian Treaty Organization. The main cause for the collapse of these alliances, and indeed the main difference with NATO, is the absence in the Pacific of a shared definition of threat. With a fragmented 'enemy' in Communism, one that kills more of the citizens of its supposed comrade-states than it does the citizens of non-Communist countries, it is hard to feel actively threatened in the same way that the states of western Europe have done.

It remains true that the United States retains a number of key bilateral military alliances. Japanese–American ties are undoubtedly the most important bilateral alliance in the Pacific. But even they have been strained by the obvious reluctance of Japan to take on an increased defence burden commensurate with its economic superpower status. The near-farce of the 1980s when the United States and western Europe were protecting primarily Japanese oil supplies in the Persian Gulf was a vivid symbol of the differences between the United States' security relations with Europeans and with East Asians. The United States and its NATO allies squabble about levels of defence spending, the deployment of nuclear weapons, and the best strategies for dealing with the Soviet Union. But at least the NATO allies spend much more on defence, deploy American nuclear weapons on their soil, and can reach formal agreement on arms-control and confidence-building measures in the Helsinki and CSCE process.

The United States manages to cope with the diversity of threat perceptions in the Pacific only by keeping a series of flexible military alliances. Thus the alliance with Japan allows that Japan is not going to increase defence spending to any considerable degree and that both parties must fudge the presence of American nuclear weapons in Japan. Both sides accept that there is relatively little peacetime preparation and co-ordination of defence efforts—a primary feature of NATO.

Other American bilateral alliances reflect the degree to which the

[3] Gregory Treverton, *Making the Alliance Work* (New York: Cornell University Press, 1985).

assessment of threat is shared. South Korea, with its obsession about its Communist neighbour, finds it easier to fit in with the threat perspectives of the United States. Australia shares more of an ideology and culture with the United States and the UK, but remains ambivalent about the extent of the Soviet threat. The Philippines is fixated on its domestic Communist threat and finds its agreement permitting American bases on its territory to be a useful bargaining card for increased American aid. Nearly all other vital American security relations are with tiny islands that are effectively ruled from Washington. Few of these bilateral alliances have similarities to the American alliance with the West Europeans. None of the European alliances have collapsed, while multilateral and even bilateral military alliances in the Pacific, for example with Taiwan, have been wrecked by the shifts in Pacific alignments.

A vivid symbol of European, or even Atlantic, security has been the pattern of arms control. No such formal pattern exists in the Pacific, except for treaties that are global and so cover the Pacific as well. Some limited, sub-regional efforts such as in the south Pacific have been attempted. But there are no parallels to the 1975 Helsinki accord, the 1986 Stockholm agreement on confidence-building measures, or the 1987 INF agreement. The INF agreement in fact ended up as a global accord covering inter-mediate-range weapons in Asia too, but in essence it began as, and remained, a European arms-control measure. Then there are the so far less successful, but still continuing, European/Atlantic negotiations on conventional force reductions.

Arms control in the Pacific is informal, most often bilateral, and emphasizes local confidence-building measures. It may be that the conflicts in the Pacific merely have to remain dormant for a longer period, as they have in Europe since the 1940s, before formal arms control can become more likely. But the conditions and perceptions of security in the Pacific remain far more complex than in Europe. Without common perceptions of security there can be no formal, multilateral arms control. Of course, without such a sense of common security, there is little chance either of people 'thinking Pacific'.

But when most people think about the Pacific they think first about trade and economics. Most schemes for a Pacific community have been dominated by economic issues and the perceived need for an organization to help mediate trade problems. It is undoubtedly true that on the economic level the Pacific has been the most successful. But it is hard to see the basis on which a grander, specifically Pacific-wide, co-operation can be built. The rise and rise of the NICs may have transformed traditional North–South relations and models of economic development, but it has not created much new unity among developed or developing states. It is clearly important to think Pacific in terms of understanding the new ideas in the region and in order to take advantage of trading opportunities. But this is not the same as seeing the Pacific as a coherent region.

The analogy that is made to the EC is deeply flawed. The European economies share an ideology, a cultural heritage, and a perception of security. They are at roughly the same level of development and no single economy predominates. They also have much experience of trading with each other in a relatively small area. None of this is true of the states of the Pacific.

The economies of the Pacific range from poor, peasant Indonesia to wealthy Japan. Their trade patterns are dominated by the United States and Japan. The more developed the states become, the more they usually trade with other developed economies, rather than with the poorer states of the Pacific or even their competitors in the region. This often means trade with Europe. The trade within the Pacific that is not with Japan or the United States or a handful of other developed economies is with close neighbours. Far too many analyses of the volume of Pacific trade make too much of such essentially bilateral patterns as that between China and Japan—a relationship akin to that between Canada and the United States. This is local trade.

Much has also been made of the growing trade between North America and East Asia. Far less has been made, except of course in Europe, of West European trade with East Asia. Although the Europeans are a few years behind the North Americans, the pattern is the same: as East Asians develop, they trade more with the developed world. European trade is seeing a Pacific shift that is remarkably similar to the American pattern. Japan and the NICs are vital actors in the international political economy. The age of epithets about 'the retreat of Europe' and 'Eurosclerosis' has clearly passed. The creation of a single European market after 1992 is likely to be even more attractive to East Asian traders looking for new markets and eager to benefit from the Europe-wide standardization imposed by the EC. After 1992 the largest single market economy will be Western Europe.

What is more, genuine links around the Pacific are confined to a remarkably small number of states. Japan dominates the so-called Pacific trade. Most of the Pacific boom is really mostly bilateral trade with Japan. The NICs are often cited as proto-Japans, but they are only lumped together for reasons of convenience. The differences between them in ideology, culture, and economic systems are far greater than anything in western Europe. The NICs, like ASEAN, really do little trade among themselves. They are natural competitors and not co-operators as in Europe. The pattern of a string of uneven bilateral relationships is very different from the complex interlinkages of European corporations and joint government-sponsored enterprises. To some extent these are differences in level of development that might moderate with the passage of time. But they are mostly the result of deep and natural differences in type of regime and level of development, and therefore the gaps are unlikely to be closed noticeably except in the odd case.

The Communist states of the Pacific are strikingly different from their European counterparts. China and the Soviet Union are the largest Communist trading partners. Yet both do far more trade with the non-Communist Pacific and both are dominated by a concern with Japanese technology. Both Communist powers trade with smaller Communist states in the region, but in no case does such trade constitute more than 2 per cent of trade. Of course, the smaller states do rely more heavily on trade and aid from China and especially the Soviet Union, but even taken together they constitute a tiny fraction of Pacific trade.

China's shift to an open-door strategy in the 1980s has been the only major change in Pacific trading patterns since the 1950s. While volumes of regional trade in the Pacific are up sharply, the direction of trade is little changed.[4] But trading with Communist states holds special problems. It is not done on a large scale in Europe and the attempt to do so in the Pacific is another major difference from the European/Atlantic economic pattern.

China used to dominate regional trade, but for well over a century had not been an active Pacific trader. Even now, as its trade with the Pacific increases, its trade with Europe (Eurasian trade) is vastly higher and is growing faster than its trade across the Pacific. China, like the NICs and Japan, is entering the world of global trade. Thinking Pacific is an anachronism when compared with the reality of growing global interdependence and the complex multinational deals worked out around the world. Japanese investment in Europe is expanding and the spread of even the NICs' multinationals around the globe makes the thought of a specific Pacific grouping seem far too limiting.

The main motive for a Pacific Economic Community—to limit the impact of economic disputes—is certainly not what the EC is primarily about. The EC is about building protection and greater economies of scale in the global competition with the United States and Japan. The EC's recurrent squabbles over the Common Agricultural Policy are sufficient witness to the problems of close co-ordination of policy.

But the interests of Pacific economies are even more dissimilar and even less likely to be tied so closely together. Especially given the rapid development of the NICs and the need for 'extraordinary measures' to protect local

---

[4] Japan took market share from the United States in the 1950s, but since the 1960s there has been little increase in the Japanese percentage of most Pacific states' trade. The major exception, of course, is that Japanese trade with the United States has risen sharply, as indeed it has with most developed economies.

markets and industries, the notion of a common market is all but irrelevant. Japan would dominate any East Asian grouping, and Japan and the United States would dominate a specifically Pacific body.

Most problems of rapidly changing economies are now handled by the market and by global negotiations or organizations such as the World Bank, the IMF, or GATT. To the extent that the Pacific shift is really based on integration in the global economy, then it is to revitalized and more powerful international bodies that the states of the Pacific will increasingly turn. The experience of ASEAN suggests that Pacific states are not yet ready to co-operate genuinely with each other in economics and are much happier taking their chances in the world market-place. After all, most non-Communist East Asian economies are already success stories without having to contend with the nuisance of extra bureaucracy and regulation.

NEW PACIFIC THINKING

It was Ivan Turgenev who said in 1856:

The people who bind themselves to systems are those who are unable to encompass the whole truth and try to catch it by the tail. A system is like the tail of truth, but truth like a lizard, leaves its tail in your fingers and runs away knowing full well that it will grow a new one in a twinkling.[5]

The kind of Pacific thinking that conceives of the region as a coherent, or imminently coherent, zone is thinking that, like the tail of Turgenev's lizard, has been left behind.

Yet for all the outdated images of the Pacific Century, there is still some point in thinking Pacific. Some important new ideas have developed in the region since 1945. First, to adapt the phrase used by Ronald Dore with reference to the Japanese economy, it is best to see the Pacific edifice as a 'flexible rigidity'. It is one building in a zone of high-rises, but a building quite unlike any other. Its floors have very different-sized rooms, with for example Japan dominating the space on the economic floor but little in evidence on the military level. The lower floors of ideology and culture are mostly divided up into small national rooms with little real communication between them. Ideas do flow between them but these often have their origins in Europe rather than from within the Pacific.

Since 1975 the pattern of states in the Pacific has probably settled down into a more stable structure. Divisions between political systems, cultures,

---

[5] Quoted in Daniel Boorstin, *The Discoverers* (London: Penguin, 1986).

and types of economy now seem relatively fixed after years of uncertainty. Patterns of trade are also remarkably constant. However, the system is still flexible in that there is little need for military alliances or formal arms control. There is little chance or need or rigid economic organizations as trade and contacts have boomed within the region's present confines. Indeed, there is need for even more flexibility because the opportunities for future growth lie both within and outside the Pacific. Visitors from Europe come increasingly frequently to the region and the inhabitants of the Pacific states will be travelling more in the outside world too. Some Pacific dwellers, such as the Latin Americans, have never been transfixed by Pacific perspectives and are likely to want to do most of their business with the Europeans and the Americans.

Of course, the Pacific remains an area of vital growth and stimulating new ideas. But these are rarely 'Pacific' thoughts so much as products of bright, innovative ideas and systems in a increasingly complex and interdependent world. It will be increasingly important to understand the policies of Pacific states, if only because Japan is the world's second-largest economy and the East Asian NICs are the world's most consistent, fast-growing developing states. They are the only states, apart from some poor southern European states, which have real prospects of joining the club of developed countries. Japan is the only other state to have made the transition. According to one American assessment, by the year 2020 China will have overtaken all but the United States in total GDP but, like the Soviet Union, will be a less developed superpower. It will also be vital to understand how these modernizing states adapt their cultures and ideologies to the methods and conventions of the western-dominated international system. Is Confucianism in its various national guises adaptable as a new model of development? Can East Asian states remain 'unique' in an increasingly interdependent world?

Thus the second major characteristic of the region is the introduction of new ideas about political development. It would be incorrect to see Confucianism or the semi-authoritarian capitalism of the NICs as a single coherent ideology. But it is distinct from the European/American system of pluralist market economies and certainly different from the command socialism of the traditional Soviet model. A number of East Asian states, from China through to Japan, will force a reassessment of political ideology.

The need to evolve a new vocabulary for these new ideas is related to the third and fourth characteristics of the Pacific. Not only has the Manichean view of an East–West conflict faded in the Pacific, but so has the matching Manicheanism of North–South conflict. Certainly in terms of the ideological foundation of the organization of states, the European and Atlantic divisions have little relevance. The NICs have pulled away from their fellow developing states in the South and have led many to forecast 'the end of the Third World' as a concept in thinking about international politics.

The decline in the utility of thinking purely in East–West terms is closely linked to the fifth characteristic, the relative decline in the power of the superpowers. In virtually all categories, they are less important than they were in 1945. While these trends have often been mused about in Europe, they are already evident in the Pacific. With the rise of Japan as an economic superpower and China's switch to the fast lane to development, there is a new pattern of international politics. To some extent it begins to approximate the nineteenth-century European multipolar balance of power,[6] but it has close similarities to the Pacific's own tradition of multipolarity. A major difference from the past is that only one Pacific power, the United States, is now a major player at all levels, while Japan is a force only in terms of economic power and the Soviet Union primarily a military power. Multipolarity of this sort looks inherently unstable.

To some extent, the pattern of military affairs has already changed to take into account these new Pacific realities. In recent years the superpower balance in the Pacific has become increasingly irrelevant and as a result the importance of economic power has risen in its place. With a marked decline in the number of wars, calculations of power are less concerned with the military balance sheet. International security is now maintained primarily through the informal means of a complex balance of power and a concentration on economic relations. Arms control does take place, but it is usually informal. Nuclear weapons are a far less salient feature of the pattern of international security.

THINKING ABOUT THE 'PACIFIC CENTURY'

There has already been far too much speculation about the twenty-first century being the Pacific Century. If the comparison is with the coherence of the North Atlantic community, the Pacific will not fulfil its supposed promise. While there are likely to be a number of dynamic individual economies in the Pacific, these will produce little that can be called regional coherence. Patterns of culture, ideology, security, and trade will continue to be characterized by a changing mixture of local conditions and global trends.

The Pacific is likely to be dominated by two great trading states, Japan and the United States, both of which are also dependent on trade with western Europe. The region will also be dominated by four great military

---

6 Paul Kennedy, *The Rise and the Fall of Great Powers* (New York: Random House, 1987).

powers, the two superpowers, China, and Japan, although threats to the military security of the Pacific states is likely to decline. In cultural and ideological terms, the Pacific looks like remaining very fragmented, with a superficial overlay of the global 'cultural' of modernization.

It is notable that different aspects of politics in the Pacific change at different paces. Except at times of revolution, ideology and culture change most slowly. Only in times of war or high tension does international security and the balance of military power rapidly change. But in times of relative peace, as evident now in the Pacific, the most swiftly changing sphere of international relations is economics. At a time of trade wars or fierce economic competition, failure to adapt fast enough forces a withdrawal from the fray. Therefore it is to the realm of economic affairs that one must turn first for signposts to the future of the Pacific in the twenty-first century.

Economics

The most significant ties of interdependence are likely to be global rather than Pacific-wide, and even then they will vary considerable according to the very uneven spread of wealth and modernization. Economic interdependence is likely to grow among the more developed economies. The links between the United States, Japan, the NICs, the white Commonwealth, and to a lesser extent ASEAN are part of the pattern of global trade. The West Europeans, like the North Americans, are increasingly important trading partners.

It is fairly obvious to argue that there will be ups and downs in the economies of some of the rapidly prospering parts of the Pacific. Nevertheless, there is a clear trend that the more developed Pacific economies will continue to take an increasing part in the international economy. For that reason alone, we will need to think Pacific in the twenty-first century.

Equally, it will become clear that the idea of a Pacific Economic Community is an opportunity that, though it might have once existed, is now long past. Interdependence is likely to be a major trend for the future, but it will be global not Pacific-wide interdependence. Resolution of the undoubtedly pressing problems of trade protectionism, variable rates of growth in domestic economies, and the impact of new technologies will best be tackled at a global level, or else they will be 'resolved' by that volatile mixture of market forces driven by politics.

It seems apparent that the twin pillars of Pacific economic prosperity, the United States and Japan, will shift and change in size. The decline of the relative position of the United States is both clear and much commented upon. The rise of Japan, as with western Europe in the Atlantic world before it, is likely to lead to changes in the broader pattern of international relations. Yet Japan of all the Pacific powers has done the least positively to shape its future international position. There can be no greater uncertainty in the Pacific than the question of what Japan really means by 'internationalization'. It certainly seems unwilling to assume the American or British roles of the past as 'balancers' of international power. Japan's previous rise to power led to a destructive imperialism and defeat, but in the next century it will be less likely or able to follow such a path. Perhaps the fate of Britain and Europe really does tell us something about the future of Japan—a rich country, but one basically dependent on a co-operative international environment and reliable allies. As Japan is driven to greater interdependence with a wider range of developed states, it will become less unusual or worrisome to its partners.

The second great uncertainty must be the fate of China—the largest Pacific market and possibly even the region's largest economy in the twenty-first century. Predictions about the fate of China have been notoriously unreliable. But if the reasonable assumption of the continuation of reforms in one form or another is made, then China is likely to develop into an important Pacific economy. As a mostly closed continental economy, it has been far less important for international economic relations than even the much smaller Taiwan. But if China's doors remain open to foreign trade and commerce, it is likely to play a vital role as a low-wage challenger of the NICs and ASEAN, as a market for the specialized exports of the developed economies, and as a major trade partner for the socialist economies.

It will be quite some time, if ever, before tomorrow's China begins to approach the kind of market domination that ancient China demonstrated. So much depends on the success of the domestic reforms. A similar caveat can be made for the Soviet Union, which also harbours a great deal of untapped economic potential for the Pacific. Soviet reforms lag behind those of China, and its smaller population on the Pacific rim offers a far smaller market to the developed Pacific economies. But given successful reforms, the Soviet role as a Pacific trader is bound to grow and help shape the Pacific economy.

If the Soviet Union is to succeed in the Pacific, it will have to resolve its dilemma of whether to emphasize trade with the socialist economies or with the more booming capitalist ones. It seems increasingly clear that the Soviet Union, like China before it, is opting for closer integration of the socialist economies with those of the capitalist world. Given such a trend, coupled with successful domestic reforms in the other socialist economies of the region, it is possible to foresee new markets and challenges for the NICs and ASEAN, especially from a more determined North Korea or a reconstructed, low-wage Vietnam. The example of the eastern European economies, lagging as they do far behind those of western Europe, is hardly encouraging. But in an age of reform-socialism, the twenty-first century in the Pacific might well include some dynamic new actors with still basically planned, socialist economies.

Of course, in the twenty-first century one of the NICs, Hong Kong, will be formally absorbed into China. Whether or not we then adopt the IMF's term of 'Newly Industrialized Economies' (NIEs) instead of NICs, it looks likely that these entities will continue to be very special features of inter-national politics. Most NICs are already moving up-market into higher-value products and are therefore likely to follow Japan into greater global inter-dependence. Their transformation into developed states, along perhaps with Malaysia and Thailand, will reshape some basic features of the international economy. The gap between rich and poor may well increase, but the membership of each group will change and patterns of co-operation and conflict will vary. For example, wealthy Canada, Australia, or even the Soviet Union will prosper primarily as providers of raw materials, while developing states such as resource-poor Taiwan or South Korea will buy the raw materials to fuel their economic success from the already rich. The traditional North–South disputes, wherein the poor have demanded aid from the rich in the last half of the twentieth century, will decline in importance, at least in the Pacific.

Military Affairs

For much of the post-war era, military affairs have figured most prominently in discussions of Pacific-wide issues. But with a scaling down of superpower influence, the decline in the number of hot wars, and even the beginning of tacit arms control, the Pacific has begun to live up more properly to its name. It is unlikely that the region will see the sorts of major change of regime that have occurred repeatedly in the past 40 years. Decolonization is nearly complete and there are few revolutionary wars that do much more than smoulder. What is more, these days the great powers are anxious to control crises, such as those in Korea, rather than exacerbate them.

Territory tends to change hands when there is a roving imperialist power in the region or serious domestic unrest that leads to a change of regime. With the two superpowers increasingly recognizing the limits to their power, the only great power with unsatisfied territorial demands is China. The transfer of Hong Kong's 5 million people to Chinese control in 1997 will be the single largest handover of people and sovereignty since the early 1950s. China also claims control of Taiwan as well as various islands in the South China Sea. As China grows strong, it may also grow more able and willing to take what it claims. If the Chinese gunboat diplomacy of 1974 (seizing the Paracels) and 1988 (taking part of the Spratly Islands) is anything to go by, China will use its military force when it sees the opportunity. This irredentism must rank as the largest challenge to the status quo, either in the Pacific or anywhere else.

Naturally, however, China has not been, and will not be, unopposed in its efforts to reshape the borders around it. Moreover, most of China's territorial disputes, for example with the Soviet Union, look like being controlled. As it becomes increasingly emeshed in economic interdependence, China may also find it more difficult to use force in the Pacific.

Similarly, the only other potentially active great power, Japan, is also likely to eschew the use of force. The experience of the Second World War has taught Japan that it is essentially vulnerable, especially in the modern era, with its economy so dependent on trade. In an age of active Russian and Chinese power in the Pacific, Japan can have few illusions that it might become again a military power with offensive military force. The age of low defence budgets has begun to dawn on most Pacific states, and indeed, as those with high military budgets successfully modernize, the defence burden will ease. Much as the West Europeans have shown, minimum defence, even while constantly agonizing about 'how much is enough', is likely to be the policy of the future.

Of course, just because we appear to be pleasantly trapped in a virtuous rather than vicious circle does not mean that wars are unlikely to take place in the Pacific. One can imagine that Chinese pursuit of territorial claims in the South China Sea might lead to a Sino-Japanese arms race and ASEAN anxiety. War may become a less useful instrument of policy in the Pacific, but peace will not be complete.

Naturally, a minimum role for weapons and warfare depends on the continuing stability of the nuclear balance. Although balances of power in the Pacific are more complicated than in Europe, there is no sign that nuclear weapons are seen as a useful instrument of policy except for deterrence. Yet by its nature nuclear deterrence will remain an element of uncertainty in Pacific security, as it has done in European security, and will mean that the link to European and global security is maintained.

Arms-control issues, for example the 1987 INF Treaty, will also illustrate the linkages that make up global security. But the more novel forms of tacit arms control that have developed in the Pacific are also likely to be maintained. As military power continues to decline relatively in importance, unilateral arms control will also have its place. Then, in a reasonably stable military environment, as it is in Europe, formal arms control might well become a forum for ritualized combat. However, the basic complexity of

alignments in the Pacific will prevent the creation of anything as comprehensive as a Pacific-wide security regime.

As the number of hot wars declines and old conflicts turn cold, so the
military purpose of alliances will also fade. Unlike in Europe, where the
alliances were part of the framework that controlled the conflicts and are
therefore crucial to keeping the peace, in the Pacific there was never any need
for anything more than pragmatic bilateral alliances. Such pragmatism in
military affairs will produce a different pattern of security from that in
Europe, but one that could still be nearly every bit as peaceful.

Ideology and Culture

Unlike the North Atlantic world, divided between its two ideologies of
capitalism and Communism, the Pacific remains far more deeply fragmented. Communism and capitalism have taken on much more varied
forms, overlaid as they are on equally varied cultural heritages. The twenty-
first century is unlikely to reduce the number of such fragments. Indeed, it
may well create more as developing states experiment with models of
modernization and state-building in divided societies.

Of course, on one level, the developed states of the Pacific will continue to
acquire elements of the so-called global culture of modernization. To that
extent, the Pacific, like the Atlantic, will partake of global culture. But as the
experience of Japan and Korea makes plain, modernization in the Pacific can
strength local culture and ideology, even while borrowing elements of a
global culture. Japan's sense of its uniqueness is unlikely to fade for some
time, if at all. Nor is ASEAN shaping a common regional culture and
ideology among its member states. Compare the ASEAN experience to that
of the European Community, where new regulations are creating a common
internal labour market with the expectation of a nearly free movement of
goods and people within the community. To the extent that such communication is taking place in the Pacific, it is again part of global, not regional,
trends.

Yet many states of the Pacific have been so successful in their experi-
mentation with new ideas developed at home that these have been picked up
by others looking for new ideas. Thinking Pacific involves other capitalist
economies learning from the success of Japan and the NICs, just as other
state socialists are already learning from Chinese reforms. As different paths
to modernization are discovered and refined, it is likely that the world
beyond the Pacific will continue to learn from the success of some states in
the region. If, as seems increasingly likely, the differences between the
socialist and capitalist worlds are blurred, at least in economic terms, then

the diverse experiences and ideologies to be found around the Pacific rim may not seem so polarized. Already it is clear that the successful state capitalism of Japan and some of the NICs offers a bridge of sorts between the two ideals of 'East and West'. Yet, even if the antagonisms between the two basic systems diminish, there will still be a distinct diversity of cultures and ideas. The trend is towards more, and identifiably different, national models, with little inclination to form firm ideological blocs. The Pacific will continue to be ideologically and culturally fragmented, and those alliances that do emerge will still reach well beyond the confines of the basin.

In general, the Pacific pattern of diversity is one with a long tradition. It is a pattern that increasingly lives up to its name by achieving greater integration of individual states into the world economy. The ring of states around the Pacific is testimony to the enduring importance of culture and ideology as the roots of international conduct. With all the attention that is paid to economics and military affairs, especially in the Pacific, political culture cannot be neglected. It is precisely these two elements of culture and ideology which remind us that if thinking Pacific means thinking only in regional terms then this is not the thought of the twenty-first century so much as the outdated longings of the 1960s. We are far better advised to look forward to what the states of the Pacific can teach us about their experience in economic modernization, controlling military conflict, and developing new variations on traditional culture. This is a challenge to the United States, Europe, and indeed the people of the Pacific. But perhaps the single most important conclusion is that the success of the Pacific states is owed less to their place in the region than to their ability to play the global game.

Index

Kanagawa, Treaty of (1854) 55
Khmer empire 24
Khmer Rouge 188, 195, 196, 198,
  200, 202
Khrushchev, Nikita 210, 235
Kim Il Sung 265, 376
Kiribati 109, 226, 354
Kissinger, Henry 191, 211
Korea 10, 31, 32, 56, 67, 71, 72, 73,
  82, 95, 96, 115, 118, 120,
  130–1, 149, 213, 267, 273, 316
  see also North Korea, South Korea
Korean War 94, 101, 144, 186,
  203–8, 209, 215, 219, 220, 236,
  243, 246, 265, 269, 278, 296,
  372
Krusenstern, A. J. van 49
Kurile Is. 58, 82, 232

Ladurie, E. Le Roy 1
Laos 88, 106–7, 115, 187, 188, 191,
  238, 277, 289, 341
Latin America 12–13, 37–9, 82, 92,
  97–8, 112, 122, 124–5, 149,
  162–3, 228–9
  economy and trade 284, 286, 288,
    294, 308–9, 353, 363
  relations with USA 61, 139, 235,
    263, 279, 374, 384
  revolt against Spain 51–2
League of Nations 67, 70
Lewis and Clark expedition 50
Liaodong 56, 57, 58, 71
LDCs 290–3
Lombok–Makassar Strait 224
London Naval Limitation Agreement
  (1930) 69
Lon Nol 88
Los Angeles 60
Lu Xun 131–2

Macao 37, 109, 172
MacArthur, General Douglas 81, 100
MacBride Report (1980) 156–61
Mackenzie, Alexander 50
Mackinder, Sir H. 82
Magellan, Ferdinand 36, 87, 369
Mahan, Alfred 60, 82
Malacca, city and Strait 23, 32, 33,
  39, 48, 224, 227, 231

Malaya 45–6, 63, 64, 77, 81, 104–5,
  253, 372
Malaysia 91, 93, 95, 99, 112, 113,
  118, 122, 123, 135–6, 142, 191,
  254
  economy and trade 284, 294, 327–9
Manchuria (Manchukuo) 58, 70, 71,
  82, 83, 209, 235
Manila 82
Manila Treaty and Pact (1954) 237–9,
  253
Mao Zedong 102, 115, 164, 209,
  214, 336, 373, 376
Marco Polo Bridge incident 78
Marcos, Ferdinand 97, 122, 249
Marianas Is. 75, 109
Marquesas Is. 47
Marshall Is. 27, 109
Marx, Karl 282
Marxism–Leninism 102, 114, 373
Mayans 22, 26
MBFR 269
'media imperialism' 155–61
Melanesia 8, 22, 24, 25, 47
Mexico 12, 37, 52, 124–5, 139
Micronesia 8, 25, 71, 109
Midway I. 60, 80
Moluccas Is. 35
'moneytheism' 97
Mongolia 115, 256, 266, 284, 338,
  340
Monroe Doctrine 52
Multifibre Agreement 314
Murdoch, Rupert 156
Mutual Defence Pact (1954) 243

Nakasone, Prime Minister 244
Nanking, Treaty of 53
NATO 112, 205, 211, 223, 235, 237,
  238, 241 ff., 246, 249, 259, 273,
  372, 377, 379
Nauru 107–8
'neo-Europes' 88, 97, 99, 126, 141,
  162, 180
Nerchinsk, Treaty of (1689) 41
New Caledonia 47, 62, 75, 109
New Guinea 76
  see also Papua New Guinea
New Zealand 44, 46–7, 62, 73, 75,
  92, 93, 135, 146, 149, 251, 253,
  254